The Digital Transformation of Professions

Globally and across industries, professions are being reshaped by rapid advancements in digital technologies. From AI-powered diagnostic tools in healthcare to automated legal research systems and predictive financial platforms, the very foundations of professional expertise, value, and trust are evolving. Amid this change, one truth remains: professions that fail to adapt risk irrelevance.

The Digital Transformation of Professions offers a timely and essential roadmap for understanding and navigating the profound shifts underway in how professional work is organized, delivered, and governed. While digital disruption has challenged long-standing roles and business models, digital transformation represents a deeper opportunity: to reimagine how professionals create value, maintain public trust, and build new futures. This book explores how digital transformation manifests across every layer of professional life, from day-to-day professional roles, workflows and career pathways to governance structures, public confidence, and inter-professional boundaries. The book:

- Explains how advancements in digital technologies drive digital disruption of the professions and how digital transformation offers a deeper opportunity to reimagine professional roles, services, and value.
- Unpacks how digital profession transformation manifests across all levels of a profession, from individual roles and workflows to governance structures, public trust, and institutional identity.
- Discusses the new digital and/or digitally enhanced professional services, roles, workflows, and competencies that professionals must adopt to remain relevant and impactful.
- Examines how professional bodies, educators, firms, and policymakers can support professionals in co-creating digitally capable and ethically grounded professions.
- Identifies strategies and real-world examples of how professionals are adapting their identities, practices, and relationships in response to accelerating technological change.

- Showcases case studies from key professions, including teaching, accounting, engineering, medicine, law, nursing, and human resource management, to illustrate how digital transformation is unfolding in practice.
- Provides a comprehensive and accessible framework for understanding digital transformation in the professions, making it essential reading for students, educators, practitioners, and leaders across professions.

Drawing on cutting-edge research and global examples, the book unpacks how professionals, firms, professional bodies, educators, and policymakers can co-create digitally capable, ethically grounded, and future-ready professions. Whether an educator, student, practitioner, professional leader, or policy adviser, any professional benefits from this book's in-depth look at what's changing, what's at stake, what must be done, and viable strategies that can be and are being used to ensure professions continue to serve society in a digitally transformed world.

The Digital Transformation of Professions

A Roadmap for Remaining Trusted, Relevant, and Future-Ready

Richard Busulwa, Wahed Waheduzzaman,
and Nandana Wasantha Pathiranage

Routledge
Taylor & Francis Group
NEW YORK AND LONDON

Designed cover image: Web Large Image (Public)

First published 2026
by Routledge
605 Third Avenue, New York, NY 10158

and by Routledge
4 Park Square, Milton Park, Abingdon, Oxon, OX14 4RN

Routledge is an imprint of the Taylor & Francis Group, an informa business

ISBN: 9781032997803 (hbk)
ISBN: 9781032998930 (pbk)
ISBN: 9781003606604 (ebk)

DOI: 10.1201/9781003606604

Typeset in Times
by KnowledgeWorks Global Ltd.

Contents

PART III The Digital Transformation of Professions

List of Tables

Disclaimer

Declaration of generative AI and AI-assisted technologies in the writing process: During the preparation of this work the authors used ChatGPT 4.0, Gemini 2.5 Flash, Claude Sonnet 4.5, and Copilot's GPT4 Turbo in order to check the authors' analyses for any oversights or misleading statements, for any potential use cases or references that could have been missed, to test and enhance reliability of our literature search and arguments, and to rephrase our written paragraphs for improved logical flow and readability. After using these tools/services, the authors reviewed and edited the content as needed and take full responsibility for the content of the publication.

About the Authors

Richard Busulwa (PhD, MBA, B.Info.Sys) is a senior lecturer and researcher in the Business School at Swinburne University of Technology, home to Australia's first fully immersed Industry 4.0 facility. His digital transformation research explores different digital technology advancements, how they drive disruption, and their implications for particular industries, business functions, and professions. He is the author of *Strategy Execution and Complexity: Thriving in the Era of Disruption* (Routledge), *Start-up Accelerators: A Field Guide* (Wiley), *Digital Transformation and Hospitality Management* (Routledge), and *Digital Transformation in Accounting* (Routledge). Before entering academia, Richard worked as a managing director, COO, CFO, middle manager, and frontline manager. He is the co-founder of Digital Keys, the world's first NBIoT smart lock platform.

Wahed Waheduzzaman (PhD, MBA) researches and teaches in HRM and organization studies. His major research interests include human resource management, public service management, local government, sustainable development goals, corporate governance, and stakeholders engagement. He has published several books, peer-reviewed articles in various journals and international conferences. He has been a guest editor with Administrative Sciences and recently published book: "MGMT5: Introduction to Management," 5th Asia-Pacific Edition (Cengage Publishers).

Nandana Wasantha Pathiranage (PhD, MBA, CA) researches and teaches accounting and finance at Swinburne University of Technology. Nandana primarily uses quantitative and case study research methods. His research has been published in several grant-funded research reports as well as highly ranked international accounting, finance, and management journals. Further, he has published a research method case study (2023) with SAGE publishers.

Part I

The Evolution of the Professions

1 Introduction and Need for This Book

NEED FOR THIS BOOK

Professions such as medicine, law, accounting, teaching, engineering, and nursing are deeply embedded in the fabric of modern society. These professions have long been associated with trust, legitimacy, public service, and specialized knowledge. They uphold rigorous standards of education, ethics, and practice. Yet, in the early 21st century, professions around the world are confronting a new, complex challenge: the accelerating digital disruption of professional work and resultant digital transformation imperative. This transformation imperative is not simply about adopting new technologies. It involves the reconfiguration of professional roles, processes, competences, governance systems, public trust, and even professional identity for the digital business era. Unfortunately, the discourse around digital transformation of the professions is often unclear, jargon-laden, and fragmented. Terms such as "*digital disruption*," "*digital transformation*," "*platform professional services*," "*algorithmic judgment*," "*AI-driven diagnostics*," and "*digital ethics*" are used inconsistently across academic, policy, and practitioner contexts. This conceptual ambiguity can make it difficult for stakeholders to build a shared understanding of what needs to change, why, how, when, and who is responsible for what. Perhaps related to this ambiguity, many professionals are also understandably skeptical about digital disruption and digital transformation, especially when they are argued to threaten traditional pathways to expertise, human-centered service, or the autonomy of professional judgment. These uncertainties are compounded by the fact that digital transformation operates at multiple levels. It manifests in the redesign of individual workflows and client interactions; the emergence of new digital professional roles; the transformation of service delivery models within professional services firms; and the evolution of professional governance, accreditation, and ethical standards. It even challenges the broader social compact between the professions and the public. Without a clear, integrated account of how digital transformation occurs across these levels, professions' digital transformation initiatives risk being reactive, piecemeal, or misaligned.

While there are many books discussing digital disruption and the digital transformation imperative for the profession, books providing guidance on how to undertake digital transformation of the professions and the roles different stakeholders need to play are rare. This book seeks to fill this critical gap. It provides a structured, research-informed, and accessible guide to understanding how to digital transform professions. It cuts through the noise and hype to offer clarity about what digital transformation really means for professional practice, education, and governance.

DOI: 10.1201/9781003606604-2

It explains how it manifests at different levels, outlines its key aims, identifies key strategies and how to execute them, and identifies how different actors in the professional ecosystem—including individual professionals, educators, professional bodies, regulators, and technology providers—can best engage with the transformation strategically and ethically.

RESEARCH FOR THIS BOOK

The development of this book involved five key research stages. These stages were designed to gather insights from both academic and practitioner sources, as well as from real-world case studies. Together, they ensure that the book is grounded in rigorous evidence and theory, while also being deeply connected to professional practice. Stage 1 involved a comprehensive review of interdisciplinary academic literature, including sociology of the professions, information systems, business and management studies, organizational change, and digital innovation. The objective was to understand the evolving definition and functions of professions, the drivers and dynamics of digital disruption, and the conceptual models explaining how professions respond to technological change. This review clarified the historical foundations of professions and identified how digital disruption and transformation challenge established structures, values, and work practices. In stage 2, we examined professional reports, white papers, policy documents, and credible web pages from professional bodies, professional service firms, think tanks, government, international organizations, and other entities playing key roles in the governance and advocacy of professions. The aim was to understand how they were interpreting and responding to digital disruption and the digital transformation imperative. This included analysis of strategies adopted by professional bodies and professional service firms, digital skills frameworks promoted by professional associations, position statements on digital transformation or digital technologies, and the types of digital services gaining traction across different professional sectors.

In stage 3, a range of profession-specific case studies were reviewed. These included examples from medicine, law, education, accounting, engineering, nursing, and human resource management. The goal was to examine the discussed current state of the digital disruption of these professions, their responses to the digital transformation imperative, the specific digital transformation strategies being pursued, how digital transformation was manifesting across different levels of the profession, the roles of different stakeholder groups in the profession's digital transformation, the challenges being faced, and more. In stage 4, we broadened the scope of reviewed literature to include literature on curriculum transformation, competency-based education, workforce digital upskilling, and continuing professional development. This literature provided important insights into how professional education providers and professional development programs are responding to the demand for new digital competencies, including both technical know-how and broader digital mindsets. Finally, in stage 5, we synthesized our findings from the previous stages into a coherent framework for understanding the digital transformation of professions. This framework was translated into the structure of this book and the structure

TABLE 1.1
Key Literature Reviewed and Focus Areas

Stage	Focus Area
Stage 1	Review of interdisciplinary academic literature on the digital disruption and digital transformation, including sociology, information systems, business and management studies, organizational change, and digital innovation literatures on digital transformation of the professions specifically or digital transformation generally
Stage 2	Review of practitioner literature on the digital disruption and digital transformation of professions. Including: professional reports, white papers, policy documents, and credible web pages from professional bodies, professional service firms, think tanks, government, international organizations, and other entities playing key roles in the governance and advocacy of professions
Stage 3	Review of case studies on the digital disruption and digital transformation of specific professions, including medicine, law, education, accounting, engineering, nursing, and human resource management
Stage 4	Review of curriculum, capability, and workforce development literatures informing professional education responses
Stage 5	Integration of concepts into a comprehensive framework for understanding the digital transformation of professions

of each of the case study professions. The result is a practical, conceptually grounded roadmap for navigating and shaping the future of professional work.

STRUCTURE OF THIS BOOK

The book is organized into four parts, each addressing a key dimension of the digital transformation of professions. Part 1 includes Chapters 1 to 3. It introduces the rationale for the book, explores what makes a profession a profession, and outlines the historical and societal evolution of professions. This part provides the context for understanding why the digital transformation of professions matters. Part 2, encompassing chapters 4 and 5 analyze the broader phenomenon of digital disruption across organizations, industries, institutions, and society, before focusing specifically on how this disruption is reshaping the professions. It identifies the external pressures and internal tensions that are driving the need for transformation. Part 3, encompassing chapters 6 and 7 focus on what digital transformation of the professions means and unpacks specific profession digital transformation strategies. Part 4, encompassing chapters 8 and 9 focuses on how to adapt and thrive during the digital transformation of professions. It first focuses on how individual professionals can thrive and future proof their careers, and then turns to how education curricula can adapt and thrive. Finally, part 5, encompassing chapters 10 to 16, offers detailed explorations of the digital disruption and digital transformation of seven very different professions: teaching, accounting, engineering, medicine, law, nursing, and HRM—with important lessons from the implementation of real-world digital profession transformation strategies.

HOW TO USE THIS BOOK

This book is aimed at professionals and professional bodies, educators and curricula designers, students and early career professionals, as well as researchers and policy makers. For professionals, it offers a structured lens to understand how their roles are changing and how to develop the competencies required to thrive in digitally transformation professions. For professional bodies, it helps them assess the adequacy of current professional standards, codes of ethics, and certification models in light of the digital transformation imperative, in light of the aims of digital transformation, and in light of the digital transformation strategies being pursued by other professions. It also supports the development of future-focused professional learning frameworks. For educators and students, this book can be an important supplementary text to help students understand the digital disruption and digital transformation of their professions, to understand how they can future proof their careers, to understand what their professions key strategic leadership and advocacy bodies should be doing, and to understand the roles current and future professionals can play to optimize their contribution to their professions' digital transformation. For this reason, we have incorporated discussion questions at the end of each chapter that educators and students can use in formal and informal assessment activities. If educators do not set these as assessment activities, students can answer them on their own and then use them as LLM (Large Language Model) prompts to contrast theirs and the LLM's answers.

Finally, for researchers, the book provides a foundation for further scholarly inquiry into effective strategies for the digital transformation of professions, the adequacy of profession digital transformation efforts, and whether or how different profession stakeholders can better support the profession's digital transformation efforts. And for policymakers, the book offers insights into how professional regulation, funding, and workforce strategies may need to evolve to support digitally transformed professions. In short, this book is designed as a comprehensive yet accessible guide for anyone with a stake in the future of professional work. Whether you are a seasoned practitioner, a student, an educator, or a policymaker, the insights within these pages will help you navigate, contribute to, and lead in the digital transformation of professions.

2 What Makes a Profession a Profession?

INTRODUCTION

The concept of a profession is fundamental to understanding modern occupational structures, societal organization, and individual identity (Saks, 2012). As work and technologies continue to evolve, it becomes increasingly important to contextualize what constitutes a profession and to develop a deeper understanding of its characteristics and functions. This chapter explores the definition of a profession, the key elements that distinguish it, various types of professions, and the critical roles they play in society. It concludes by examining contemporary issues and debates surrounding the nature and future of professional work.

DEFINITION OF A PROFESSION

A profession is best understood as an occupation requiring specialized knowledge, extensive formal education, and adherence to codified ethical standards, often overseen by professional bodies that regulate entry, competence, and behavior (Buhai, 2012). Recognized professions, such as medicine, law, and engineering, are characterized by a high degree of autonomy, the possession of formal credentials, and an explicit orientation toward public service (Brint, 2020). These features distinguish professions from other forms of employment by legitimizing their authority and grounding their social value in the pursuit of collective well-being.

Professions vs Trades

Although professions and trades both involve skilled labor, their differences are significant and multidimensional. Professions are grounded in abstract, theoretical knowledge acquired through prolonged, higher-level education (Olgiati, 2010). For example, the path to becoming a physician typically involves years of formal study and rigorous credentialing. In contrast, trades such as plumbing or carpentry emphasize practical, hands-on expertise, often transmitted through apprenticeships and vocational training (Picciotto, 2011). Moreover, professionals exercise a high level of autonomy and are self-regulated by formal organizations, such as bar associations or medical boards, that enforce ethical norms and protect public interest (Becker, 2017). In contrast, tradespeople, while highly competent, generally operate under more direct supervision and lack the same institutional mechanisms for self-governance (Olgiati, 2010).

DOI: 10.1201/9781003606604-3

Societal Role of Professions

The societal role of professions further distinguishes them from trades. Professions are inherently oriented toward addressing broad societal needs, such as health, justice, or education, often placing public welfare above economic self-interest (Brint, 2020). On the other hand, trades typically engage in market-driven service delivery, with a focus on tangible outcomes (Den Boer, 2014). Consequently, professions tend to enjoy higher social prestige and economic reward, reflecting both the complexity of their responsibilities and their perceived contribution to the public good (Becker, 2017). For instance, while an electrician ensures the safe installation of wiring, a doctor operates within a framework of ethical codes and clinical judgment to safeguard human life – underscoring the broader societal mission of professional practice.

Historical and Ethical Dimensions

The etymology of the term "profession" illuminates its historical and ethical dimensions. Derived from the Latin *professio*, meaning a public declaration or vow, the term originally referred to religious or monastic commitments (Faitini, 2017). In medieval Europe, the so-called "learned professions," divinity, law, and medicine, were distinguished by their intellectual rigor and moral responsibility, symbolized through formal oaths to uphold communal values (Wilson, 2017). Over time, this conception evolved to include secular occupations that retained similar characteristics: advanced knowledge, formal training, ethical codes, and a duty to serve (Picciotto, 2011). This evolution underscores the continuing importance of public trust and accountability as foundational to professional identity.

Social Exchange and the Concept of Calling

Professions also operate within a framework of social exchange, in which society grants practitioners' autonomy, prestige, and material compensation in return for their expertise and ethical service (Faitini, 2020). This reciprocal relationship is sustained through mechanisms such as credentialing, licensure, and professional codes of conduct, which collectively ensure that the public interest remains prioritized (Pareto, 2017). The normative dimension of this exchange is often reinforced by the concept of the "calling," which lends moral and existential significance to professional work (Wilson, 2017). Max Weber and Stephen Kalberg (2013), in The Protestant Ethic and the Spirit of Capitalism, conceptualized a "calling" (*Beruf*) as work imbued with moral purpose and social value, rooted in Protestant theology. From this perspective, professions are not simply occupations, but vocations marked by a disciplined commitment to the common good (Berkelaar & Buzzanell, 2020). Professions such as law and medicine as exemplary callings because they require individuals to prioritize ethical obligations and public service over personal gain (Pareto, 2017). This outlines that a profession not just for material gain, but because one believes the work is inherently meaningful or serves a greater good.

Vocation and Personal Fulfillment

Closely related to calling is the idea of "vocation," derived from the Latin *vocatio*, meaning a summons (Dawson, 2005). Whereas a calling emphasizes duty and moral responsibility, a vocation is more aligned with personal fulfillment and individual passion (Dik & Duffy, 2009). In practice, the two often intersect. A teacher may pursue education as a vocation due to intrinsic interest yet also view it as a calling in service of social development (Faitini, 2020). In professional contexts, the interplay between vocation and calling reinforces the alignment of individual values with collective needs.

While professional identity is frequently associated with altruism, economic exchange remains essential (Olgiati, 2010). The costs of professional development, such as formal education, licensure, and continuous training, necessitate financial investments (Saks, 2012). For example, medical practitioners invest heavily in their education and ongoing learning to maintain clinical competence, which must be compensated to ensure sustainability (Becker, 2017). However, ethical codes are designed to ensure that financial incentives do not eclipse the public service mission. Researchers noted that professional ethics serve as a moderating force, aligning economic reward with moral obligation (Black et al., 2022). A physician's duty to patient care, for example, must supersede concerns about billing or profit, preserving the integrity of the calling while recognizing the necessity of material support.

Economic Considerations and Ethics

In line with long standing definition of profession, the rise of digital technologies introduces new complexities to the professional landscape. Digital transformation has expanded access to information, thereby challenging the exclusivity of professional knowledge (Bues & Matthaei, 2016). While online platforms and open-access scholarly articles empower professionals to remain current, they also allow clients and the general public to access similar resources by eroding traditional knowledge asymmetries (Susskind & Susskind, 2015). Moreover, the automation of routine tasks through artificial intelligence and machine learning is reshaping the scope of professional work, prompting a shift toward human-centric skills such as empathy, judgment, and critical thinking (Brynjolfsson & McAfee, 2014).

IMPACT OF DIGITAL TECHNOLOGIES

Digital innovation has also given rise to new professional domains, such as data science and cybersecurity, which blend traditional attributes of professionalism, such as expertise and ethical accountability, with novel technological competencies (Susskind & Susskind, 2022). However, these emergent professions often lack the regulatory frameworks that govern traditional professions, raising questions about legitimacy, credentialing, and oversight (Bues & Matthaei, 2016). Additionally, digital tools introduce new ethical dilemmas, such as algorithmic bias or data privacy, requiring updated codes of conduct to preserve public trust in digital-era professions (Larson, 2017).

This discussion thus highlights, a profession is far more than a form of employment; it is a socially legitimized role grounded in specialized knowledge, ethical standards, and a service-oriented mission. Distinguished from trades by their theoretical foundations, institutional autonomy, and societal purpose, professions operate within a complex web of social and economic exchanges. The concepts of calling and vocation underscore their moral and personal dimensions, while economic remuneration enables their sustainability without undermining their public mission. In the digital age, professions are being reshaped by technological advances, but their core identity, anchored in the pursuit of societal good, remains vital to their enduring relevance.

KEY ELEMENTS OF A PROFESSION

Scholarly literature identifies several key elements that distinguish a profession from other occupations, often highlighting a combination of technical, normative, and institutional characteristics (see Table 2.1). Central to the concept of a profession is the possession and control of a specialized body of knowledge that is both abstract and esoteric, typically acquired through prolonged formal education and rigorous training (Saks, 2012). This knowledge base grants professionals a form of epistemic authority and jurisdiction over specific domains of practice (Dawson, 2005). Closely linked to this is the credentialing process, which acts as a gatekeeping mechanism to ensure competence, standardize entry, and maintain the quality and consistency of professional services (Abbott, 2014). Professions also exhibit a high degree of autonomy, both at the individual and collective levels, allowing

TABLE 2.1
Comparison of Professions and Trades

Criteria	Profession	Trade
Knowledge Base	Theoretical, abstract, scientific or academic	Practical, technical, and skill-based
Education & Training	University-level education; long and formalized	Apprenticeship or vocational training
Credentialing & Licensing	Mandatory licenses, certifications, and professional exams	Certifications may be required but are usually skill- or tool-specific
Regulatory Bodies	Self-regulated through professional associations (e.g., medical boards, bar associations)	Often regulated through trade unions or industry standards
Autonomy	High level of autonomy in judgment and decision-making	Supervised or directed within operational limits
Ethics & Public Service	Strong ethical obligations, public trust is central	Focus on quality and efficiency of service delivery
Social Status	High prestige and social recognition	Respectable, but typically lower in social hierarchy
Examples	Medicine, Law, Engineering, Architecture, Academia	Plumbing, Electrician, Carpentry, Welding

practitioners discretion in their judgment and decision-making without direct supervision (Suddaby & Viale, 2011). This autonomy is legitimized by societal trust and the expectation that professionals will act in the public interest.

Another defining element is the adherence to a formalized ethical code, which governs professional conduct and reflects a normative commitment to client welfare, integrity, and accountability (Evans, 2010). Such ethical codes are enforced by professional bodies that not only regulate behavior but also serve to protect the profession's collective identity, reputation, and standards (Tapper & Millett, 2015). Institutionalization further reinforces the profession's status through legal recognition, self-regulatory mechanisms, and the establishment of exclusive jurisdictions (Becker, 2017).

Additionally, professions are often characterized by a service ideal, an ethos that frames professional work as a vocation or calling, that transcends mere economic transactions and embeds it within broader societal roles and responsibilities (Weber & Kalberg, 2013). As a result, the professional is seen not merely as a technical expert, but also as a moral agent entrusted with public goods, such as health, justice, or knowledge (Brint, 2020). Collectively, these elements construct a profession as a distinct social institution with both functional utility and symbolic capital, contributing to its enduring authority and prestige within society.

TYPES OF PROFESSIONS

The classification of professions has evolved in tandem with societal development, reflecting shifts in knowledge production, labor organization, and institutionalization (Pareto, 2017). Broadly, professions can be categorized into traditional, emergent, and hybrid types, each characterized by distinct historical trajectories, knowledge domains, and regulatory structures. Traditional professions such as medicine, law, theology, and academia, are typically rooted in long-standing institutional frameworks and are defined by well-established bodies of knowledge, formalized education pathways, licensing requirements, and strong professional associations (Faitini, 2023). These professions have historically enjoyed high status, autonomy, and public trust, grounded in their service to essential societal functions and their normative commitment to ethical standards (Faitini, 2023).

In contrast, emergent professions have arisen in response to technological, economic, and social changes, particularly in the late 20th and early 21st centuries. Examples include data science, information security, digital marketing, and sustainability consultancy (Susskind & Susskind, 2022). These fields often blend interdisciplinary knowledge and are shaped more by practical competencies and industry certifications than by long-standing academic traditions (Brint, 2020). While they may lack the historical legitimacy and formal regulatory structures of traditional professions, they are increasingly formalizing through associations, standards, and credentialing mechanisms (Barker, 2010). These emergent professions reflect a shift towards knowledge work that is agile, innovation-driven, and embedded in globalized, digital economies.

Further, hybrid professions have developed at the intersection of traditional and emergent domains, combining elements of both. For instance, healthcare informatics fuses medical expertise with information technology, while legal technologists bridge the gap between jurisprudence and digital systems (Becker, 2017). These hybrid roles often emerge as solutions to complex, cross-disciplinary challenges and are emblematic of a broader transformation in professional boundaries and identities (Susskind & Susskind, 2015). Such transformations also highlight the fluidity of professional status in contemporary society, as traditional hierarchies are challenged by new forms of expertise, platform-mediated labor, and global knowledge networks (Brint, 2020).

Overall, the typology of professions is not fixed but continually reconstructed through institutional legitimation, technological innovation, and evolving societal needs. Understanding these types allows scholars to critically assess how professions adapt to changing environments and how professional identity, autonomy, and authority are renegotiated in the digital and post-industrial age.

ROLE OF PROFESSIONS IN SOCIETY

Professions occupy an important role in modern society as both agents of social order and contributors to the distribution of knowledge, authority, and services. At their core, professions are trusted intermediaries between complex bodies of knowledge and the public, translating expertise into practical interventions that enhance individual and collective well-being (Faitini, 2020). Whether diagnosing illness, adjudicating legal disputes, or designing infrastructure, professionals are relied upon to exercise judgment and discretion in contexts of uncertainty (Pareto, 2017). This trust is institutionalized through licensure, ethical codes, and disciplinary mechanisms that provide public assurance of competence and accountability (Susskind & Susskind, 2018). Yet this reliance also grants professionals significant social influence, positioning them as gatekeepers to essential resources and arbiters of legitimate knowledge.

Critically, the role of professions extends beyond technical expertise; they shape the moral and cultural frameworks of the societies they serve (Suddaby & Viale, 2011). Through the enactment of professional norms and ethical standards, professions help to define what is considered right, just, or appropriate in specific domains (Brint, 2020). For instance, medical ethics shape societal understandings of life, death, and dignity, while legal ethics influence concepts of fairness, justice, and procedural integrity. This normative role reinforces professions as custodians of public interest but also raises concerns about their capacity for self-regulation (Ayala & Ayala, 2020). The power to define problems, prescribe solutions, and exclude alternative viewpoints can entrench particular ideologies or serve narrow institutional interests, especially when professional bodies are closely aligned with state or corporate power. Consequently, the professional claim to moral authority must be subject to ongoing public scrutiny and democratic oversight.

In the digital and globalized era, professions also mediate the interface between local practices and global standards. As knowledge becomes increasingly transnational and technologies disrupt traditional service models, professionals are called to navigate cultural pluralism, jurisdictional diversity, and the ethical implications of innovation (Susskind & Susskind, 2018). For example, engineers working on artificial intelligence systems must balance technical precision with concerns about surveillance, bias, and inequality, while healthcare professionals using global telemedicine platforms must reconcile local patient needs with international data regulations (Ayala & Ayala, 2020). These developments reconfigure the role of professions as not only national stewards of knowledge but also as adaptive actors in global governance. Accordingly, the future of professional work hinges on an expanded vision, one that integrates technical competence with ethical reflexivity, cultural competence, and responsiveness to societal transformation.

KEY TOPICS AND ISSUES RELATING TO THE PROFESSIONS

Autonomy vs Accountability

The professions have long served as cornerstones of modern society, marked by their unique blend of expertise, ethics, and social responsibility (Faitini, 2020). Yet, as institutional forms, they are deeply entangled in tensions and contradictions that reflect broader socio-economic transformations. One enduring tension lies in the ambiguous relationship between autonomy and accountability. Historically, professionals have claimed a high degree of independence, underpinned by mastery of specialized knowledge and a normative commitment to client welfare (Brint, 2020). However, this professional autonomy is increasingly curtailed by regimes of audit, standardization, and managerial control. In fields such as education, medicine, and social work, metrics-driven oversight often displaces judgment-based practice, reshaping the very nature of professional discretion (Susskind & Susskind, 2018). While accountability mechanisms may protect against malpractice or inefficiency, they also risk undermining the intrinsic motivations and values that define professional life (Pareto, 2017).

Calling vs Vocation

Closely related is the conflict between the notion of profession as a "calling" versus a "vocation," a tension first articulated by Max Weber (1978). The idea of a profession as a calling (*Beruf*) evokes a moral or spiritual obligation to serve society, emphasizing intrinsic motivation, duty, and ethical commitment (Weber & Kalberg, 2013). In contrast, viewing a profession as a vocation places emphasis on formal occupation, economic reward, and personal advancement (Faitini, 2020). In contemporary professional discourse, these two orientations frequently collide. For example, in healthcare or education, practitioners often find themselves torn between their ethical commitment to serve and the institutional pressures to meet performance targets or increase efficiency. This dualism complicates professional identity and raises critical questions about what it means to "be professional" in an era where market and managerial logic increasingly dominate professional practice.

Digital Disruption of Professional Knowledge

Another significant issue concerns the changing nature of professional knowledge and its destabilization in the digital era. Professional authority has traditionally rested on control over esoteric knowledge, legitimized by credentialing and lengthy formal training (Susskind & Susskind, 2018). Yet, digital platforms and AI-driven tools are eroding this monopoly by making information more accessible and enabling laypersons to perform tasks once reserved for credentialed experts (Susskind & Susskind, 2022). From AI-assisted legal research to automated diagnostic tools in healthcare, the digital turn has both democratized and destabilized professional domains (Armour & Sako, 2020). These developments force a rethinking of what constitutes expertise, as well as who qualifies as a legitimate professional. Professions must now engage in ongoing learning and adaptation, which challenges static notions of credentialed authority and calls for new ethical and regulatory frameworks that can accommodate rapidly evolving competencies.

Social vs Economic Exchange

The tension between social exchange and economic exchange offers a foundational lens for understanding the professional project. In the social exchange view, professions are institutionalized responses to societal needs; they exist to serve the public good through trust-based relationships, ethical standards, and accountability to collective norms (Brint, 2020). This perspective emphasizes the reciprocal obligation between professionals and the communities they serve (Berkelaar & Buzzanell, 2020). In contrast, the economic exchange view frames professional services as commodities to be traded in the labor market. Here, professionals are sellers of specialized labor, competing for clients, income, and prestige (Abbott, 2014). The proliferation of fee-for-service models, commercial branding of professional firms, and strategic positioning of credentialing bodies exemplify this market logic (Ferguson et al., 2021). While both logics coexist, their uneasy reconciliation often produces contradictions in practice. For example, when ethical obligations clash with client demands or when regulatory decisions prioritize market competitiveness over public interest.

Commodification and Market Logic

Further complicating the professional landscape is the commodification of services and the encroachment of market logic into professional ethics. The increasing resemblance of professional-client interactions to consumer transactions risks transforming the professional role into that of a service provider whose primary loyalty is to paying customers rather than the broader public (Ferguson et al., 2021). This is particularly evident in privatized sectors such as law, healthcare, and education, where professionals must navigate pressures to deliver client satisfaction while also maintaining integrity, confidentiality, and adherence to ethical codes. The commodification process not only challenges the normative foundations of professionalism but may also erode public trust, especially when economic incentives override considerations of equity, access, and justice.

Diversity and Inclusion

The professions also face growing scrutiny over their internal hierarchies and social exclusivity, particularly concerning diversity, equity, and inclusion. Many traditional professions emerged from elite, male-dominated institutions and have historically been gatekept through costly education, exclusive networks, and cultural capital (McEwen & Trede, 2014). Despite progressive rhetoric, these structural barriers remain entrenched, limiting access and upward mobility for women, racial minorities, and those from lower socio-economic backgrounds (Susskind & Susskind, 2015). Moreover, credentialism and professional socialization often reinforce dominant norms and marginalize alternative epistemologies or ways of knowing. Addressing these issues requires more than inclusive recruitment strategies; it demands a critical interrogation of how professions reproduce privilege and how power circulates within professional institutions (Faitini, 2023).

Globalization and Transnationalization

Finally, the globalization and trans-nationalization of professions further complicate their regulation and identity. As professional practices and standards circulate across borders, new tensions emerge around credential portability, cultural relevance, and jurisdictional authority. While globalization offers opportunities for knowledge exchange and collaboration, it can also result in the imposition of dominant models, often Western, onto local contexts, thereby erasing indigenous practices and knowledge systems (Kroon et al., 2021). For instance, transnational healthcare workers may face challenges aligning their home-country training with host-country regulations, or they may encounter ethical dilemmas when global protocols conflict with local values. These developments call for a more pluralistic and reflexive approach to professionalization, one that recognizes the interplay of global structures and local contingencies.

This literature outlines, professions are not static institutions but dynamic, contested, and often contradictory formations. They are simultaneously called to serve the public good, generate economic value, uphold ethical integrity, and adapt to technological and global changes (see Table 2.2). Understanding the professions today requires a critical lens that accounts for these tensions, between autonomy and regulation, calling and vocation, social and market exchange, stability and transformation. Only by engaging these complexities can scholars and practitioners begin to reimagine the role of professions in a rapidly evolving world.

TABLE 2.2
Key Tensions in Professional Practice

Tension	Description
Autonomy vs Accountability	Professionals seek independence in decision-making, but are increasingly subject to oversight, audits, and standardization that may constrain their discretion.
Calling vs Vocation	A calling emphasizes moral duty and public service, while vocation focuses on personal fulfillment and economic reward, creating identity conflicts.
Social vs Economic Exchange	Professions are expected to serve societal needs ethically, yet they also operate in market-driven environments that prioritize financial gain.
Commodification vs Ethics	Market logic transforms professional services into commodities, potentially undermining ethical standards and public trust.

CONCLUSION

Professions remain foundational to the fabric of modern society, embodying a unique synthesis of technical expertise, ethical obligation, and social trust. As this chapter has shown, the professional ideal is historically rooted in specialized knowledge, public service, and normative commitments, distinguishing professions from other occupations through their institutional autonomy and symbolic authority. However, this ideal is increasingly challenged by shifting technological, economic, and social dynamics. The rise of digital platforms, performance metrics, and globalized labor markets is reshaping professional boundaries, practices, and values. Tensions between vocation and calling, social exchange and market logic, and autonomy and accountability now define the contemporary professional landscape. At the same time, growing demands for diversity, inclusivity, and ethical reflexivity are prompting critical reassessments of who becomes a professional and under what conditions. In this context, understanding the evolving nature of professions requires a nuanced and critical perspective – one that balances tradition with innovation, and ethical purpose with adaptive practice.

DISCUSSION QUESTIONS

1. How do professions differ from trades in terms of education, autonomy, and societal roles?
2. What is the significance of the concepts of 'calling' and 'vocation' in shaping professional identity?
3. How has digital transformation impacted the traditional characteristics of professions?
4. What are the key tensions between autonomy and accountability in professional practice?
5. How do social and economic exchanges influence the ethical obligations of professionals?
6. What challenges do professions face in promoting diversity, equity, and inclusion?
7. How can professionals navigate the complexities of globalization and transnational standards?

REFERENCES

Abbott, A. (2014). *The system of professions: An essay on the division of expert labor.* University of Chicago press.

Armour, J., & Sako, M. (2020). AI-enabled business models in legal services: from traditional law firms to next-generation law companies? *Journal of Professions and Organization, 7*(1), 27–46.

Ayala, R. A., & Ayala, R. A. (2020). Nursing as a Profession: Old tensions, new insights. Towards a Sociology of Nursing, 9–29.

Barker, R. (2010). No, management is not a profession. *Harvard business review, 88*(7–8), 52–60.

Becker, H. S. (2017). The nature of a profession. In: *Sociological work* (pp. 87–104). Routledge.

Berkelaar, B. L., & Buzzanell, P. M. (2020). Calling, profession, and work. In: *The routledge handbook of economic theology* (pp. 185–194). Routledge.

Black, E. L., Burton, F. G., & Cieslewicz, J. K. (2022). Improving ethics: extending the theory of planned behavior to include moral disengagement. *Journal of Business Ethics, 181*(4), 945–978.

Brint, S., 2020, The changing role of professionals in politics and public life. Princeton, New Jersey: Princeton University Press

Brynjolfsson, E., & McAfee, A. (2014). *The second machine age: Work, progress, and prosperity in a time of brilliant technologies.* W.W. Norton & Company.

Bues, M. M., & Matthaei, E. (2016). Legaltech on the rise: Technology changes legal work behaviours, but does not replace its profession. In Liquid legal: Transforming legal into a business savvy, information enabled and performance driven industry (pp. 89–109). Cham: Springer International Publishing.

Buhai, S. L. (2012). Profession: A definition. *Fordham Urban Law Journal, 40,* 241–253.

Dawson, J. (2005). A history of vocation: Tracing a keyword of work, meaning, and moral purpose. *Adult Education Quarterly, 55*(3), 220–231.

Den Boer, P. (2014). *History as a profession: The study of history in France, 1818–1914.* Princeton University Press.

Dik, B. J., & Duffy, R. D. (2009). Calling and vocation at work: Definitions and prospects for research and practice. *The counseling psychologist, 37*(3), 424–450.

Evans, T. (2010). Professionals, managers and discretion: Critiquing street-level bureaucracy. *The British journal of social work, 41*(2), 368–386.

Faitini, T. (2017). The Latin roots of the 'Profession': Metamorphoses of the concept in law and theology from ancient Rome to the Middle Ages. *History of Political Thought, 38*(4), 603–622.

Faitini, T. (2020). Shaping the profession: some thoughts on office, duty, and the moral problematisation of professional activities in the Counter-Reformation. *Journal of Early Modern Christianity, 7*(1), 177–200.

Faitini, T. (2023). Shaping the Profession–And Reshaping Socio-Political Inclusion. *Soft Power, 10*(20), 1–6.

Ferguson, S. L., Smith, C., & Kietzmann, J. (2021). Hands-off? Lessons from high-touch professionals about going virtual. *Business Horizons, 65*(3), 303.

Kroon, N., do Céu Alves, M., & Martins, I. (2021). The impacts of emerging technologies on accountants' role and skills: Connecting to open innovation—a systematic literature review. *Journal of Open Innovation: Technology, Market, and Complexity, 7*(3), 163.

Larson, M. S. (2017). The rise of professionalism: A sociological analysis. Class: The anthology (eds Stanley Aronowitz and Michael J. Roberts), 263–286. https://doi.org/10.1002/9781119395485. Hoboken, NJ: Wiley-Blackwell

McEwen, C., & Trede, F. (2014). The academisation of emerging professions: Implications for universities, academics and students. *Power and Education, 6*(2), 145–154.

Olgiati, V. (2010). The concept of profession today: A disquieting misnomer? *Comparative Sociology, 9*(6), 804–842.

Pareto, V. (2017). *The rise of professionalism: Monopolies of competence and sheltered markets.* Routledge.

Picciotto, R. (2011). The logic of evaluation professionalism. *Evaluation, 17*(2), 165–180.

Saks, M. (2012). Defining a profession: The role of knowledge and expertise. *Professions and professionalism, 2*(1), 1–10.

Suddaby, R., & Viale, T. (2011). Professionals and field-level change: Institutional work and the professional project. *Current Sociology, 59*(4), 423–442.

Susskind, D., & Susskind, R. (2018). The future of the professions. *Proceedings of the American Philosophical Society, 162*(2), 125–138.

Susskind, R., & Susskind, D. (2015). *The future of the professions: How technology will transform the work of human experts.* Oxford University Press.
Susskind, R., & Susskind, D. (2022). *The future of the professions: How technology will transform the work of human experts.* Oxford University Press.
Tapper, A., & Millett, S. (2015). Revisiting the concept of a profession. In: *Conscience, leadership and the problem of 'dirty hands* (pp. 1–18). Emerald Group Publishing Limited.
Weber, M. (1978). The protestant ethic and the spirit of capitalism (T. Parsons, trans.). Scribner.
Weber, M., & Kalberg, S. (2013). *The protestant ethic and the spirit of capitalism.* Routledge.
Wilson, L. (2017). *The academic man: A study in the sociology of a profession.* Routledge.

3 The Evolution of the Professions

INTRODUCTION

The concept of a profession, as a distinct occupational category characterized by specialized knowledge, ethical standards, and societal trust, has undergone profound transformations over time (Susskind & Susskind, 2022). This chapter explores the historical roots, pivotal developments, drivers of change, responses to transformation, and contemporary challenges facing professions. By examining these dimensions, we gain insight into how professions have shaped, and been shaped by, the broader social, economic, and technological contexts in which they operate.

HISTORICAL CONTEXT OF THE PROFESSIONS

Early Occupational Roles in Ancient Civilizations

The evolution of the professions is deeply intertwined with broader social, economic, and institutional transformations across history. Although specialized occupational roles existed in ancient civilizations, such as the priest-scribes of Egypt or the physicians and jurists of classical Greece and Rome, these roles were primarily tied to religious, aristocratic, or state authority (Brante, 2013). What distinguished them was not only their exclusive access to specialized knowledge but also their alignment with elite power structures (Johnson, 2016). However, these early forms lacked the systematic codification, formal training pathways, and self-regulatory institutions that define the modern concept of a profession.

Guilds and Universities in the Medieval Period

The foundations of the modern profession were laid during the Middle Ages in Europe, with the emergence of guilds and the establishment of the first universities (Brown & Luzmore, 2021). Guilds, such as those for physicians, lawyers, and apothecaries, established standards of practice, training, and ethical conduct, laying the groundwork for professional identity (Evetts, 2013). The establishment of universities in the 11th and 12th centuries, such as those in Bologna and Paris, formalized education for clergy, lawyers, and physicians, marking a shift toward codified knowledge as a hallmark of professional status (Bhattacharya, 2012). These institutions transformed access to expertise from hereditary privilege or religious ordination into a matter of formal education and scholarly attainment, thereby advancing the secularization and rationalization of knowledge.

DOI: 10.1201/9781003606604-4

The Rise of the Learned Professions in the Early Modern Era

By the early modern period, the term "profession," originating from the Latin "to profess," initially signified public declarations, often religious, but expanded to include callings requiring intensive preparation and high standards. (Berkelaar & Buzzanell, 2020). By the sixteenth century, the "learned professions" of divinity, law, and medicine gained distinct social standing, often attracting younger generations of the nobility who sought prestige outside the commercial marketplace (O'Day, 2023). This period also saw the emergence of professional self-consciousness, as these fields increasingly emphasized autonomy, codes of conduct, and service to the common good.

Professions in the Modern Era

The industrial and urban revolutions of the nineteenth century served as a crucible for the expansion and institutionalization of professions. Rapid societal change, technological innovation, and the complexity of emerging social problems created demand for expert knowledge that could not be met by traditional apprenticeship systems alone (Pelling, 2023). In response, professional associations, such as the Royal College of Physicians in Britain or the American Medical Association in the United States, were established to formalize entry standards, regulate practice, and protect public welfare (Brint, 2020; McClelland, 2014). This institutional consolidation was not merely administrative but ideological, which framed professionals as custodians of specialized knowledge who, in exchange for social trust and autonomy, pledged to act in the public interest (Brint, 2020).

This period also marked a shift in the basis of professional legitimacy, from a top-down imposition to one rooted in social recognition. The case of dentistry in the United States exemplifies this transition. In the wake of the 1837 financial panic, dental practitioners mobilized to professionalize their field by founding the American Journal of Dental Science (founded in 1839), the Baltimore College of Dental Surgery (established in 1840), and the American Society of Dental Surgeons (established in 1840) (Fejerskov et al., 2018). Although formal licensing remained delayed due to prevailing ideals of individualism (Fejerskov et al., 2018), these early efforts were pivotal in asserting moral and epistemic authority. Such developments reveal that professional identity was not only imposed from top-down by institutions but actively constructed by practitioners themselves, who sought collective recognition, ethical coherence, and legitimacy in the eyes of society.

Professions, then, emerged not solely as technical occupations but as social institutions embedded in cultural norms and regulatory frameworks. Their historical development has been shaped by the interplay of knowledge production, social status, economic forces, and public accountability (Brint, 2020). As such, understanding the historical context of the professions reveals not only how they acquired their authority, but also how that authority has been continuously negotiated in response to changing societal expectations.

EVOLUTION OF THE PROFESSIONS AND DEFINING MOMENTS IN HISTORY

The history of the professions is deeply intertwined with broader economic, social, and political transformations. While occupations based on specialized knowledge have long existed, the modern conception of a "profession" as a distinct and institutionalized domain emerged gradually, shaped by key moments that redefined their structure, legitimacy, and societal function (Faitini, 2017). These pivotal junctures often coincided with periods of industrialization, scientific advancement, and state intervention, each altering the trajectory of professional development (Becker, 2017).

One of the earliest catalysts for the modern professions was the Industrial Revolution, beginning in the late 18th century (Susskind & Susskind, 2018). As mechanized production and market economies expanded, so too did the demand for technical expertise and formal knowledge systems (Abbott, 2014). This period saw the emergence of professions such as engineering, accounting, and architecture, which were no longer confined to artisanal or guild-based traditions. The creation of professional associations such as the Royal College of Surgeons (chartered in 1800), the Institution of Civil Engineers (founded in 1818), the Law Society (founded in1825, chartered 1831), the Pharmaceutical Society (established in 1844), and the Royal College of Veterinary Surgeons (established in 1844), and the Royal Institute of British Architects (founded in 1834) marked a turning point for the evolution of professions (Holland, 2009; Pelling, 2023). These institutions introduced standardized qualifications, ethical codes, and exclusive jurisdictions over practice, laying the groundwork for modern professional authority.

In the way to grow, the 19th century witnessed the formalization of medical and legal professions, both of which became emblematic of the broader process of professionalization (Den Boer, 2014). In medicine, developments such as the establishment of the Royal College of Surgeons and the Apothecaries Act of 1815 in Britain reflected growing state interest in regulating medical practice (Pelling, 2023). In North America, the Flexner Report of 1910 was especially influential, exposing inadequacies in medical education and prompting the closure of substandard schools (Holland, 2009). This ushered in a more rigorous and science-based model of training, elevating the prestige and social status of medical professionals. Law followed a parallel trajectory with the emergence of bar associations, formal education standards, and codified ethical practices that aimed to ensure competence and social trust (Buhai, 2012).

The professional landscape expanded further in the late 19th and early 20th centuries. A broader array of occupations, including nursing, psychology, librarianship, and social work, gained recognition as professions (Johnson, 2016). This was accompanied by a philosophical shift: rather than deriving authority from aristocratic lineage or patronage, legitimacy increasingly stemmed from intellectual merit, specialized training, and public accountability (Faitini, 2023). Governments played an active role in this transformation, supporting the institutionalization of training programs and professional oversight (Brint, 2020).

However, the second half of the 20th century challenged this heroic image. Critics questioned the neutrality and beneficence of professional power, pointing to how professions can serve monopolistic interests and maintain social hierarchies under the guise of public service (Johnson, 2016). The term "post-professionalism" came into use to describe the era's complex occupational landscape, marked by the proliferation of white-collar roles, managerialism, and the blurring of boundaries between expert and lay knowledge (Burns, 2019). Technological advancements, such as the rise of information systems, also transformed professional practice and IT emerged as entirely new professional domains.

The global dimension of professional evolution became increasingly prominent in the 21st century. Countries began reshaping higher education systems to better align with labour market demands, as evidenced by the conversion of general universities into polytechnic institutions in emerging economies and the imposition of deliberate restrictions on entry into certain professional fields (Brown & Luzmore, 2021). These reforms reflect growing tensions between national policy priorities, global mobility, and the governance of professional education. The COVID-19 pandemic (2020–2023) served as a contemporary inflection point, laying bare the critical dependence on professional expertise, particularly in healthcare and logistics, while also exposing systemic vulnerabilities and inequities (Sayilan & Kulakac, 2023). Such crises prompted re-evaluation of training regimes, ethical standards, and the resilience of professional institutions.

Recent innovations in digital technologies, particularly AI platforms, are further reshaping the nature and structure of professional work (Trincado-Munoz et al., 2025). On the one hand, these technologies democratize access to knowledge, enabling clients and the public to access information and perform tasks once reserved for credentialed professionals. On the other hand, they challenge traditional jurisdictional boundaries and raise fundamental questions about accountability, expertise, and the role of human judgment (Susskind & Susskind, 2022). As AI continues to augment or automate core professional tasks, the distinction between expert and non-expert is being renegotiated, compelling professions to adapt not only their practices but also their ethical frameworks and value propositions in an increasingly digitized society (Trincado-Munoz et al., 2025).

In sum, the evolution of the professions has been shaped by moments of disruption and renewal (see Table 3.1). From the early institutionalization of technical and

TABLE 3.1
Historical Milestones in Professionalization

Period	Milestone	Impact
Ancient Civilizations	Priest-scribes, physicians, jurists	Exclusive knowledge tied to elite power
Middle Ages	Guilds and universities	Standardized training and ethical codes
Early Modern Period	Learned professions (law, medicine)	Social prestige and autonomy
19th Century	Professional associations	Formal regulation and public trust
20th Century	Flexner Report, expansion of professions	Scientific rigor and institutional legitimacy
21st Century	Digital transformation and globalization	Redefinition of expertise and ethics

medical expertise during the Industrial Revolution to the critical scrutiny of professional power in the late 20th century and the global realignments of the 21st, the history of professions reflects broader societal transformations. Understanding these defining moments not only illuminates how professions have adapted to changing conditions but also raises enduring questions about their social purpose, authority, and accountability in an increasingly complex world.

DRIVERS OF CHANGE

The evolution of professions has been propelled by a constellation of interrelated forces that continue to reshape professional roles, structures, and values. Among the most significant of these are technological innovations, which have radically transformed how professionals operate across a broad range of fields (Susskind & Susskind, 2022). The progression from industrial mechanization to digitalization and, more recently, to artificial intelligence and automation, has redefined professional competencies. In domains such as accounting and law, routine and procedural tasks are increasingly delegated to intelligent systems, freeing professionals to focus on interpretive, advisory, or strategic dimensions of their work (Armour & Sako, 2020; Kroon et al., 2021). In healthcare, telemedicine and digital diagnostics have expanded access and reoriented the geography of service delivery, challenging traditional models of in-person interaction and centralized institutions (Ferguson et al., 2021).

Economic and market dynamics have also exerted considerable influence. The Industrial Revolution established the foundations for professional services by intensifying the demand for specialized expertise (Pareto, 2017). However, it was the late twentieth-century shift toward neoliberal economic policies that introduced unprecedented market rationality into previously protected professions (Crompton, 2019). Deregulation, privatization, and the commodification of professional services have pressured practitioners to adopt client-centred and efficiency-driven models, often in tension with foundational ethical principles (Trincado-Munoz et al., 2025). The expansion of global markets has added another layer of complexity. Professionals today must navigate varied legal and regulatory landscapes, where norms differ not only between nations but even within regional jurisdictions (Faitini, 2023). For example, while countries like Canada and the United States uphold strict licensure requirements for certain professions, others, such as the UK, maintain more flexible arrangements, privileging title over practice regulation (Leslie et al., 2023).

Societal expectations have also become a catalyst for change. As the public becomes more informed and engaged, trust in professional authority is no longer taken for granted (Brint, 2020). High-profile instances of malpractice, corruption, or ethical lapses have prompted calls for greater transparency and accountability (Burns, 2019). The push for diversity, equity, and inclusion has further disrupted the traditional composition of many professions, historically dominated by white, male elites (Susskind & Susskind, 2022). The increasing representation of women and historically marginalized groups has prompted structural adaptations and new discourses around inclusion and professional identity (Susskind & Susskind, 2018). However, these developments have also exposed persistent disparities, highlighting the need for ongoing cultural and institutional reforms (Burns, 2019).

TABLE 3.2
Drivers of Change in Professions

Driver	Description
Technological Innovation	AI, automation, telemedicine, digital diagnostics
Economic Forces	Neoliberal policies, market rationality, global competition
Societal Expectations	Demand for transparency, diversity, and inclusion
Regulatory Frameworks	New standards for data privacy, sustainability, ethics
Educational Reforms	Access to credentials, lifelong learning pathways

Regulatory and legal frameworks continue to evolve in response to both internal and external pressures. Emerging fields such as data privacy, environmental sustainability, and digital ethics have required the creation or adaptation of regulatory standards, often resulting in the formalization of new professional domains (Trincado-Munoz et al., 2025). These shifts underscore the importance of reflexivity within professions, which must continually adjust to remain legitimate and socially responsive (Faitini, 2020). Moreover, changes in education have played a vital role in professional evolution. The democratization of higher education, alongside the development of specialized credentials and lifelong learning pathways, has allowed a broader segment of society to access professional careers, while also ensuring that practitioners are better equipped to meet contemporary challenges (Brown & Luzmore, 2021).

Taken together, these drivers of change illustrate that professions are not static entities but dynamic institutions, constantly shaped by technological, economic, social, legal, and educational forces (see Table 3.2). Their continued legitimacy and relevance depend on their capacity to adapt to these evolving conditions while maintaining public trust and upholding the values that justify their privileged status in society.

HOW PROFESSIONS HAVE GENERALLY RESPONDED TO CHANGE

Professions, by their very nature, occupy a complex space between tradition and transformation. Over time, they have responded to technological, regulatory, and societal changes through a combination of adaptation, resistance, and innovation (Faulconbridge et al., 2025). These responses reflect the tension between preserving core professional values and embracing the evolving demands of modern society.

Adaptation has been one of the most visible strategies in professional response to change (Petrakaki et al., 2025). As digital technologies have reshaped the landscape of work, many professions have gradually integrated these tools into their practice (Kroon et al., 2021). The widespread adoption of computer-aided design in architecture, electronic health records in medicine, and virtual learning environments in education illustrates how technology has become embedded in professional routines

(Petrakaki et al., 2025). To remain relevant and competent, professional associations have revised accreditation standards and training curricula to include emergent skill sets such as data analytics in finance, artificial intelligence in engineering, and cybersecurity in law (Ferguson et al., 2021). Moreover, the introduction of mandatory continuing professional development requirements ensures that practitioners stay attuned to the shifting technical and ethical dimensions of their work (Leslie et al., 2023). Such institutionalized learning frameworks indicate that professional communities are not passive recipients of change but active participants in shaping its course.

Nonetheless, not all change has been welcomed. Resistance remains a characteristic feature of how professions navigate reform, particularly when external pressures threaten established norms or challenge traditional autonomy (Petrakaki et al., 2025). Historical and contemporary cases reveal that reforms perceived as undermining professional self-regulation or altering service delivery models often generate opposition (Faulconbridge et al., 2025). The initial reluctance of medical professionals to embrace telemedicine, despite its potential to expand access and efficiency, exemplifies concerns about depersonalization and quality (Petrakaki et al., 2025). Medical professionals initially resisted telemedicine, citing concerns about quality of care, though its adoption surged during the COVID-19 pandemic. Similarly, debates within the UK psychological community over statutory regulation in 2008 highlighted fears that externally imposed rules might restrict professional discretion or dilute disciplinary identity (Kwiatkowski & Jackson, 2021). Resistance, therefore, often reflects a deeper negotiation over legitimacy, values, and control within the professional domain.

In parallel, innovation has emerged as a proactive avenue through which professions reimagine their relevance and societal contribution (Berkelaar & Buzzanell, 2020). One notable trend is the growth of interdisciplinary collaboration, whereby traditional boundaries between fields are softened to address complex, multidimensional problems (Becker, 2017). Healthcare has led the way in this regard, with teams comprising clinicians, data scientists, and behavioural experts working jointly to manage chronic disease or respond to public health crises (Petrakaki et al., 2025). Likewise, the legal profession has begun to integrate design thinking and digital tools to enhance client engagement and service delivery (Armour & Sako, 2020). In such contexts, innovation is not merely about adopting tools but about reconfiguring professional logic and purpose.

Professional associations and regulatory bodies serve as vital mediators in this landscape of change (Ayala & Ayala, 2020). Their role extends beyond standard-setting to include advocacy, public trust building, and ethical stewardship. Institutions such as the Law Society and the American Bar Association have historically revised their codes of conduct, credentialing procedures, and equity policies to reflect the evolving expectations of stakeholders (Bues & Matthaei, 2016). Initiatives aimed at fostering diversity and inclusion, once peripheral, are now central to professional legitimacy (Faitini, 2023). This shift signals a broader redefinition of professional success, one that encompasses not only competence and expertise but also social responsiveness and representational justice.

In sum, the professional response to change is neither monolithic nor unidirectional. It is a contested and negotiated process involving adaptation to external stimuli, resistance to perceived encroachments, and innovation aimed at maintaining relevance. The future of the professions will likely depend on their continued ability to reconcile tradition with transformation in ways that are ethically grounded, socially inclusive, and technologically forward-looking.

CURRENT ISSUES AND CHALLENGES

The contemporary landscape of professional work is marked by unprecedented complexity, shaped by converging technological, economic, ethical, and societal forces (Ferguson et al., 2021). At the forefront is the accelerating pace of technological disruption. Automation, artificial intelligence, and data-driven systems are transforming the core competencies of traditional professions, displacing routine tasks and altering the labour market's expectations (Faulconbridge et al., 2025). Diagnostic tools powered by machine learning are redefining clinical decision-making, while automated legal analytics are reducing the demand for entry-level legal professionals (Bues & Matthaei, 2016). According to the World Economic Forum, by 2030 nearly 40% of core job skills will have changed, compelling professionals to embrace not only technical upskilling in domains such as cybersecurity, big data, and artificial intelligence, but also to develop distinctly human capabilities, critical thinking, adaptability, creativity, and ethical judgment, that resist automation (WEF, 2023).

Simultaneously, the professions face a crisis of engagement and well-being. In 2025, employee engagement has reached an 11-year low, with overall satisfaction at a record low, and employees seeking new opportunities at the highest level since 2015 (Wigert & Tatel, 2024). This phenomenon, termed "The Great Detachment," reflects a workforce that feels disconnected but remains in their roles due to economic concerns, with professions needing to bridge this gap (Wigert & Tatel, 2024). Hybrid work models add another layer of complexity, requiring professions to create effective charters for collaboration, maximize in-office interactions, and continuously refine practices to support both remote and in-person work (Burns, 2019).

Another pressing challenge is the erosion of public trust in professional authority (Brint, 2020). High-profile scandals in finance, medicine, and media, ranging from ethical lapses in corporate governance to the spread of misinformation during the COVID-19 pandemic, have undermined the perceived legitimacy of professional expertise (Leslie et al., 2023). Professions are increasingly scrutinized not just for their technical competence but for their accountability, transparency, and alignment with the public good (Berkelaar & Buzzanell, 2020). Rebuilding trust necessitates an explicit reaffirmation of the social contract, whereby professionals serve not only their clients or organizations, but also the broader public interest.

Issues of equity, diversity, and inclusion (EDI) remain persistent and structural. Despite decades of advocacy, many professions continue to reproduce patterns of exclusion, particularly at leadership levels (Burns, 2019). Gender, race, and socioeconomic status continue to influence access, mobility, and recognition within professional hierarchies (Fitzgerald, 2020). While numerous initiatives exist to address these gaps, the pace of change remains uneven (Neumeier & Brown, 2021). Moreover, the rise of precarious and gig-based employment, especially among early-career professionals in fields such as academia, journalism, and creative industries, compounds existing inequities and calls into question the sustainability of professional pathways (Faitini, 2020).

Finally, the moral terrain of professional practice is being reshaped by globalization and environmental imperatives (Nuttman-Shwartz, 2017). In an interconnected world, professionals frequently encounter ethical tensions between local norms and global standards, especially in transnational legal, health, and engineering contexts (Susskind & Susskind, 2022). Climate change adds another layer of urgency, compelling professionals to reconcile the demands of economic growth with ecological sustainability (Nicholas & Breakey, 2017). For instance, engineers, architects, and financial analysts must now integrate environmental criteria into decision-making, often in the face of conflicting stakeholder interests (Wade et al., 2018). These challenges necessitate a re-articulation of professional ethics that accounts for collective responsibility, intergenerational equity, and planetary stewardship.

This discussion thus reveals that the contemporary professions operate within a fluid and contested terrain. Navigating these challenges requires a re-examination of foundational values, a commitment to lifelong learning, and institutional support structures that foster inclusivity, integrity, and resilience. The capacity of the professions to evolve in response to these pressures will determine their legitimacy and relevance in the decades to come.

CONCLUSION

The evolution of professions reflects a dynamic interplay between historical context, societal needs, and external pressures. From their roots in ancient, specialized roles to their modern incarnations as regulated, knowledge-based occupations, professions have continually adapted to changing environments. Pivotal moments, such as the Industrial Revolution and technological advancements, have reshaped their practices, while drivers like technology, globalization, and societal expectations continue to challenge their traditional models. Professions have responded with a blend of adaptation, resistance, and innovation, but current issues, such as eroding trust, technological disruption, and inequities, demand ongoing reflection and reform. As professions navigate these challenges, their ability to uphold their social contract while embracing change will determine their relevance and impact in an increasingly complex world. While the core characteristics of professions, specialized knowledge, ethical standards, and public service, remain consistent, the ways in which professionals operate have shifted dramatically. The 21st century presents both challenges and opportunities for the continued evolution of established professions, as well as the emergence of new ones.

DISCUSSION QUESTIONS

1. How have historical developments shaped the legitimacy and structure of modern professions?
2. What role did professional associations play in the institutionalization of professions?

3. How are technological innovations like AI and automation transforming professional roles?
4. In what ways have professions adapted or resisted societal and regulatory changes?
5. What are the implications of declining public trust for professional accountability?
6. How can professions address persistent issues of equity, diversity, and inclusion?
7. What ethical challenges do professionals face in a globalized and environmentally conscious world?

REFERENCES

Abbott, A. (2014). *The system of professions: An essay on the division of expert labor.* University of Chicago press.

Armour, J., & Sako, M. (2020). AI-enabled business models in legal services: From traditional law firms to next-generation law companies? *Journal of Professions and Organization, 7*(1), 27–46.

Ayala, R. A., & Ayala, R. A. (2020). Nursing as a Profession: Old tensions, new insights. Towards a Sociology of Nursing, 9–29.

Becker, H. S. (2017). The nature of a profession. In: *Sociological work* (pp. 87–104). Routledge.

Berkelaar, B. L., & Buzzanell, P. M. (2020). Calling, profession, and work. In The routledge handbook of economic theology (pp. 185–194). London: Routledge.

Bhattacharya, N. (2012). The evolution of knowledge in the university. *The Information Society, 28*(4), 208–227.

Brante, T. (2013). The professional landscape: The historical development of professions in Sweden. *Professions and Professionalism, 3*(2), 1–18. https://doi.org/10.7577/pp.558

Brint, S., 2020, The changing role of professionals in politics and public life. Princeton, New Jersey: Princeton University Press

Brown, C., & Luzmore, R. (2021), "A brief history of education – From ancient Greece to the enlightenment," Educating tomorrow (Society now), Emerald Publishing Limited, Leeds, pp. 39–55. https://doi.org/10.1108/978-1-80043-660-220211003

Bues, M. M., & Matthaei, E. (2016). Legal tech on the rise: Technology changes legal work behaviours, but does not replace its profession. In *Liquid legal: Transforming legal into a business savvy, information enabled and performance driven industry* (pp. 89–109). Cham: Springer International Publishing.

Buhai, S. L. (2012). Profession: A definition. *Fordham Urban Law Journal, 40*, 241–253.

Burns, E. A. (2019). The post-professional transition. In: Theorising professions: A sociological introduction (pp 187–222). Palgrave Macmillan, Cham. https://doi.org/10.1007/978-3-030-27935-6_6

Crompton, R. (2019). Professions in the current context. In: *Management of healthcare* (pp. 325–344). Routledge.

Den Boer, P. (2014). *History as a profession: The study of history in France, 1818–1914.* Princeton University Press.

Evetts, J. (2013). Professionalism: Value and ideology. *Current Sociology, 61*(5–6), 778–796.

Faitini, T. (2017). The Latin roots of the 'Profession': Metamorphoses of the concept in law and theology from ancient Rome to the middle ages. *History of Political Thought, 38*(4), 603–622.

Faitini, T. (2020). Shaping the profession: Some thoughts on office, duty, and the moral problematisation of professional activities in the counter-reformation. *Journal of Early Modern Christianity, 7*(1), 177–200.

Faitini, T. (2023). Shaping the Profession–And reshaping socio-political inclusion. *Soft Power, 10*(20), 1–6.

Faulconbridge, J., Sarwar, A., & Spring, M. (2025). How professionals adapt to artificial intelligence: The role of intertwined boundary work. *Journal of Management Studies, 62*(5), 1991–2024.

Fejerskov, O., Uribe, S., & Mariño, R. J. (2018). Dentistry in a historical perspective and a likely future of the profession. In: Mariño, R., Morgan, M., Walmsley, A. (eds) Career paths in Oral health. pp. 3–19, Springer, Cham. https://doi.org/10.1007/978-3-319-89731-8_1

Ferguson, S. L., Smith, C., & Kietzmann, J. (2021). Hands-off? Lessons from high-touch professionals about going virtual. *Business Horizons, 65*(3), 303.

Fitzgerald, A. (2020). Professional identity: A concept analysis. *Nursing Forum, 55*(3), 447–472.

Holland, L. M. (2009). *The development of professional services in nineteenth century county towns: a case study of the county towns of Stafford* (Doctoral dissertation, University of Leicester).

Johnson, T. J. (2016). *Professions and power (Routledge revivals).* London: Routledge. https://doi.org/10.4324/9781315471372

Kroon, N., do Céu Alves, M., & Martins, I. (2021). The impacts of emerging technologies on accountants' role and skills: Connecting to open innovation—a systematic literature review. *Journal of Open Innovation: Technology, Market, and Complexity, 7*(3), 163.

Kwiatkowski, R., & Jackson, C. (2021). Professional identity, behaviour and values: A partial and provocative history of the code of ethics of the British psychological society. In: *Handbook of international psychology ethics* (pp. 143–173). Routledge.

Leslie, K., Myles, S., Schiller, C. J., Alraja, A. A., Nelson, S., & Adams, T. L. (2023). Protecting the public interest while regulating health professionals providing virtual care: A scoping review. *PLOS Digital Health, 2*(4), e0000163.

McClelland, C. E. (2014). *Queen of the professions: The rise and decline of medical prestige and power in America.* Rowman & Littlefield: Lanham, Maryland.

Neumeier, S. A., & Brown, L. X. (2021). Beyond diversity and inclusion: Understanding and addressing ableism, heterosexism, and transmisia in the legal profession: Comment on Blanck, Hyseni, and Altunkol Wise's national study of the legal profession. *American Journal of Law & Medicine, 47*(1), 76–87.

Nicholas, P. K., & Breakey, S. (2017). Climate change, climate justice, and environmental health: Implications for the nursing profession. *Journal of Nursing Scholarship, 49*(6), 606–616.

Nuttman-Shwartz, O. (2017). Rethinking professional identity in a globalized world. *Clinical Social Work Journal, 45*(1), 1–9.

O'Day, R., 2023, The anatomy of a profession: The clergy of The church of England, in *The professions in early modern England*, Prest, W. (Ed.). (pp. 39–92). London: Routledge.

Pareto, V. (2017). *The rise of professionalism: Monopolies of competence and sheltered markets.* Routledge.

Pelling, M. (2023). Medical practice in early modern England: Trade or profession? In *The professions in early modern England*, Prest, W. (Ed.). (pp. 90–128). London: Routledge.

Petrakaki, D., Chamakiotis, P., Russell, E., & Charlwood, A. (2025). Resistance, tensions and consent to digital working in healthcare. *Social Science & Medicine, 368*, 117691.

Sayilan, A. A., & Kulakac, N. (2023). The effect of the COVID-19 pandemic on the professional perception and image of nursing among nurses working in surgical units: An online study. *Work, 74*(2), 407–414.

Susskind, D., & Susskind, R. (2018). The future of the professions. *Proceedings of the American Philosophical Society, 162*(2), 125–138.

Susskind, R., & Susskind, D. (2022). *The future of the professions: How technology will transform the work of human experts.* Oxford University Press.

Trincado-Munoz, F. J., Cordasco, C., & Vorley, T. (2025). The dark side of AI in professional services. *The Service Industries Journal, 45*(5-6), 455–474.

Wade, F., Murtagh, N., & Hitchings, R. (2018). Managing professional jurisdiction and domestic energy use. *Building Research & Information, 46*(1), 42–53.

WEF, (2023). *Future of Jobs Report*, Insight Report, May 2023, World Economic Forum, Geneva, https://www.weforum.org/reports/the-future-of-jobs-report-2023/

Wigert, B., & Tatel, C. (2024), The Great Detachment: Why Employees Feel Stuck, GALLUP, https://www.gallup.com/workplace/653711/great-detachment-why-employees-feel-stuck.aspx

Part II

The Digital Disruption of Professions

4 The Digital Disruption of Organizations, Industries, Institutions, and Society

INTRODUCTION

Digital disruption is fundamentally altering the way organizations, industries, institutions, and societies operate. Driven by advancements in digital technologies, digital disruption interrupts established routines, processes, and competitive dynamics, forcing organizations, institutions, and societies to adapt or face loss of relevance. From Uber's disruption of the taxi industry to social media's redefinition of human connections, digital disruption reshapes expectations, market structures, and operational practices. This chapter explores the concept of digital disruption, focusing on its causes, dynamics, and effects. We examine how advancements in technologies such as artificial intelligence, blockchain, and cloud computing enable new entrants to challenge established players and create entirely new competitive landscapes. We also unpack how digital disruption influences customer expectations, reshapes data use and value, and redefines the bases of competition. The chapter sets the stage for the proceeding chapter investigating the digital disruption and digital transformation of professions.

DIGITAL DISRUPTION

Disruption is the process or effect of interrupting normal routines, preventing events from proceeding as expected, and introducing disorder into established professional practices, procedures, or activities. Digital disruption, then, refers to digital technology induced disruption. Or disruption driven or caused by the introduction of new digital technologies or enhancements in existing ones. While commonly examined at the organizational level (e.g., the digital disruption of Blockbuster video—see Downes & Nunes, 2013), it can also disrupt entire industries (e.g. Uber's digital disruption of the taxi industry—see Berger et al., 2018), professional institutions (e.g., digital disruption of the accounting profession—see Busulwa & Evans, 2021), or societies (e.g. social media disrupting how people connect and keep in touch—see Berghel, 2024). See Table 4.1 for definitions and examples of key concepts that are often used when discussing digital disruption. understanding differences in the boundaries between these terms is essential for more specific understanding of digital disruption.

DOI: 10.1201/9781003606604-6

TABLE 4.1
Key Digital Disruption Concepts

Concept	Definition	Example
Digital Disruption	The technology-induced interruption of established practices, processes, or value systems at organizational, industry, institutional, or societal levels.	Uber disrupting the taxi industry using mobile platforms and GPS technologies.
Digital Technology Advancements	Significant improvements or innovations in computing, connectivity, or data processing that enable new possibilities or performance breakthroughs.	AI, cloud computing, 5G, IoT, blockchain, and neuromorphic computing.
Organizational Disruption	When internal processes, structures, or business models of a firm are undermined or must be reinvented due to digital advancements.	Traditional banks adopting online platforms to compete with fintechs.
Industry-Level Disruption	When entire industry structures, competitive dynamics, or value chains are transformed by digital entrants or new business models.	Streaming services disrupting the entertainment industry's distribution model.
Societal-Level Disruption	When societal norms, expectations, or behaviors are altered due to widespread adoption of digital technologies.	Social media disrupting communication norms and public discourse.

DIGITAL TECHNOLOGY ADVANCEMENTS AND DIGITAL DISRUPTION

Digital technologies are tools that bring together information (data), computing (problem-solving with computers), communication (sharing information), and connectivity (linking devices or systems)—see Vial (2019). Examples of these technologies include social media, mobile devices, data analysis (analytics), cloud computing, the Internet, the Internet of Things (IoT), software, platforms, artificial intelligence (AI), robotics, drones, satellites, blockchain, and others (see Busulwa, 2022). These technologies are rapidly evolving and improving at an incredible pace (e.g. see Bonnet & Westerman, 2020). For example, there have been remarkable improvements in how fast computers can process information, how much data they can store, the clarity of digital camera images, the power of software, and the speed and capacity of networks (see Busulwa, 2022). New technologies like blockchain, edge computing, advanced wireless networks (5G and 6G), brain-computer interfaces, 4D printing, hardware inspired by the human brain (neuromorphic hardware), wearable exoskeletons, and quantum computing are being developed and adopted (e.g. see Vincent & Igou, 2023).

When we talk about advancements in digital technologies, we mean either entirely new tools, like 3D printing and 5G, or significant improvements in existing ones, such as better computing power, more capable cloud storage, or smarter artificial intelligence (e.g. see Vial, 2019). These advancements are the underlying drivers of digital disruption (Vial, 2019). That is, whenever an advancement occurs, it enables startup firms or other competitive organizations to leverage the advancement to offer new and better products/services or the same products in more efficient/effective ways. When these startups or competitors offer new and better products/services or the same products more efficiently/effectively, all other competitors are forced to adopt these new products/services or efficient/effective ways of working. If they don't, they risk going out of business as the value they offer to customers will likely be inferior or unsustainable (Christensen, 2015; Christensen et al., 2015; Henderson, 2006). For example, Uber, as a startup, leveraged advancements in cloud computing, mobile computing, and GPS to offer a new and better taxi product (Baron, 2018). Existing taxi companies either had to adapt to offer a similar product to Uber or they went out of business or they shifted their business to aspects of taxi services that are much more difficult to digitally disrupt (e.g. government mandated traditional taxi services that aren't dependent on an internet/cellular connection)—see Goldstein (2018).

ORGANIZATION, INSTITUTION AND SOCIETY LEVEL DIGITAL DISRUPTION

Digital disruption is often discussed at an organization level—that is, with discussion often focusing on how digital technology advancements are preventing business processes and value creation from occurring as they have been occurring (e.g. see Bonnet & Westerman, 2020; Vial, 2019). But digital disruption can also be discussed at industry level, at an institutional level (e.g. the digital disruption of profession), and societal level (e.g. digital disruption of how society functions, or how people communicate and relate)—see Vial (2019) and Table 4.2. At an industry level,

TABLE 4.2
Levels of Digital Disruption and Their Core Characteristics

Level of Disruption	Primary Impact Area	Typical Disruptions	Examples
Organizational Level	Internal operations, roles, business models, service delivery	Need for automation of workflows, new roles, customer self-service platforms	Banks, hospitals, retail stores needing to adopt AI chatbots and workflow tools
Industry Level	Competitive dynamics, market entry barriers, value chains	Entry of digital-first competitors, need to shift to digital platforms, need for new revenue models	Streaming services disrupting music and film industries
Institutional Level	Shared norms, governance, legitimacy of entire systems	Need for changes in professional standards, accreditation norms, or governance structures	Online legal platforms challenging traditional law firms
Societal Level	Cultural norms, social interactions, public expectations	Redefinition of trust, identity, communication, or employment relationships	Social media platforms reshaping political discourse and social norms

digital disruption involves the introduction of disruptive new or enhanced products/services, new or enhanced business models, new or restrengthened competitors, and a change in market dynamics. For example digital disruption of the taxi industry saw the introduction of disruptive new products/services, disruptive new business models, and new competitors—all exemplified by UBER and Didi offerings. At an institutional level, digital disruption often involves DTs advancements driving the disruption of institutional structures, processes, culture, and other aspects. Whether occurring at the level of organizations, institutions, or societies, advancements in digital technology typically drive three critical disruptions. These are the disruption of customer and other stakeholder expectations, which are reshaped by new digital capabilities; the disruption of the competitive landscape and the bases of competition, as organizations adopt innovative technologies to gain an edge; and the disruption of data availability, characterized by the proliferation of accessible, high-volume, and real-time data streams that influence decision-making processes (Busulwa, 2022; Vial, 2019). We will discuss each of these from a business or organization level for easier understandability.

Disruption of Customer and Other Stakeholder Expectations

Businesses generate revenue and maintain their operations by continuing to offer products or services that people want and choose to buy (Busulwa, 2022). Customers typically prefer options that provide the best value for their money, often considering factors such as quality, brand reputation, ease of use, and suitability for their specific needs, all within a reasonable price range (Kotler et al., 2016). Digital technologies, such as search engines, social media, data analytics, and artificial intelligence, have significantly empowered consumers by giving them unprecedented access to information about products and services. With a few clicks, consumers can compare options, evaluate the benefits and costs, and explore alternatives. For example, in the banking sector, customers can quickly check whether a bank offers modern services such as online banking, mobile payments, blockchain transactions, and cardless cash withdrawals. This access to information shapes consumer expectations and behaviors, making it crucial for businesses to meet or exceed these expectations to remain competitive (Chaffey et al., 2009).

If a business, such as a bank, fails to offer competitive pricing or modern services, it risks losing customers to competitors who can better meet these demands. For instance, a bank without mobile or blockchain payment options may struggle to attract new customers and to retain existing ones, as these features are increasingly seen as standard expectations. Beyond changing expectations, technological advancements often alter consumer habits (Vial, 2019). The rise of driverless cars, for example, is expected to reduce driving, car ownership, and demand for related products such as car parts, thereby disrupting industries dependent on these consumer routines. This disruption of customer and other stakeholder expectations of businesses can lead to various challenges for businesses, including losing customers, facing price drops, struggling to secure suppliers, losing talented employees, and encountering difficulties in accessing funding. Companies that fail to adapt to these challenges risk diminishing business performance and, ultimately, their survival (Christensen et al., 2015).

Disruption of the Competitive Field and Bases of Competition

Digital technology advancements have made it easier for new companies to enter existing industries and for companies in other fields to join as competitors (Vial, 2019). In the music industry, for example, new companies like Spotify emerged and grew to dominate streaming, while other new companies like SoundCloud and Tidal found smaller but loyal audiences (e.g. see Towse, 2020). Similarly, tech giants like Apple, Google, and Amazon, who were in different fields, used their existing strengths, like large customer bases, well-known brands, and technology expertise to also enter the music industry and succeed with services like Apple Music, YouTube Music, and Amazon Music (e.g. See Meier & Manzerolle, 2019). New digital technology tools reduced the cost of creating, sharing, and selling music (e.g. see Towse, 2020). Instead of making and delivering physical CDs, companies could stream music instantly to anyone with internet access, saving time and money (Moreau, 2013). This allowed new businesses to offer music at lower prices and to reach more people. These changes also weakened the advantages older music companies once relied on, like exclusive partnerships, big budgets, and control over how music was sold (Meier & Manzerolle, 2019; Moreau, 2013). New companies didn't need traditional methods like big marketing campaigns or physical stores. They used tools like social media and apps to reach fans directly. Today, music platforms compete by offering better apps, attracting more users, and making it easy for musicians to share their work Meier & Manzerolle, 2019). This shift has transformed how people create, discover, and listen to music. Thus, digital technology advancements disrupt the competitive field by enabling new, more, and better competitors to enter the industry (Busulwa, 2022; Vial, 2019). And digital technology advancements disrupt the bases of competition by weakening the competitive advantages or bases of competition of existing or older companies (e.g. control over how music CDs are made and sold), and by introducing new competitive advantages or bases of competition (e.g. highly engaging apps, instantaneous access)—see Busulwa, 2022.

Disruption of Data Availability

When organizations use new or improved digital technologies, they are often able to collect and access much more information (Busulwa, 2022). This includes data about their customers, how their products or services are made and delivered, and the overall trends in their industries. This data gives them new advantages (Vial, 2019). For example, they can sell it to other companies, as Facebook and Google do by offering targeted ads based on user behavior. Or they can use it to improve their own product offerings, for example Amazon uses its data to adjust prices for products in real time (Busulwa, 2022). Beyond selling data, companies can use it to improve customer experiences, run their operations more efficiently, and spot trends in their markets (Warner & Wäger, 2019). They can also combine this data with advanced artificial intelligence to create automated tools, like ChatGPT or other large language model (LLM) based AI agents. In the hotel industry, for instance, Hilton has trialed using robots like Connie to assist guests. Organizations can also use data collected by others—such as governments, suppliers, or online platforms—to gain better insights into their industry and into consumer preferences/behaviors (Busulwa, 2022).To stay competitive, companies must adjust how they collect, store, and use data (Vial, 2019). By doing this well, they can improve their decision-making and performance. Ignoring these changes puts businesses at risk of falling behind competitors who use data effectively.

CONCLUSION

This chapter unpacked digital disruption, defining it as the interruption of established routines and practices caused by advancements in digital technologies. Digital disruption disrupts how organizations, industries, institutions, and societies operate, mandating that they adapt to new ways of operating and acting or risk loss of relevance. An example of industry level digital disruption included Uber's disruption of the taxi industry by leveraging advancements in mobile computing, cloud computing, and GPS. An example of society level disruption included Facebook and other social media companies' disruption of traditional social interactions. Rapid advancements in digital technologies—such as artificial intelligence, blockchain, cloud computing, and 5G have been a key driver of digital disruption. These advancements lower barriers for new entrants, enable innovative new business models, and alter competitive dynamics. For instance, in the music industry, platforms like Spotify have revolutionized how consumers access content, bypassing traditional models of production and distribution. Digital disruption forces organizations and industries to respond to shifting customer expectations, new competitive landscapes, and the increasing proliferation and importance of data as a base for competitive advantage.

DISCUSSION QUESTIONS

1. How would you describe the key differences between digital disruption at the organizational level versus the societal level? Provide examples from the chapter and ask ChatGPT, Gemini, or another LLM platform of your choice, to identify other industries experiencing similar disruptions.
2. What role do advancements in digital technologies, such as AI and blockchain, play in accelerating digital disruption? Use ChatGPT, Gemini, or another LLM platform of your choice to explore recent examples of these technologies disrupting industries not covered in the chapter.
3. How does digital disruption influence consumer behavior and expectations? After discussing the examples in the chapter, ask ChatGPT, Gemini, or another LLM platform of your choice to predict how emerging technologies like quantum computing might reshape customer expectations in the future.
4. The chapter mentions that digital disruption lowers barriers for new entrants into industries. How might this phenomenon reshape traditional professions? Use ChatGPT, Gemini, or another LLM platform of your choice to explore how startups have recently challenged long-established professions like law or medicine.

5. In what ways do digital technologies enable companies to weaken the traditional advantages of established competitors? Use ChatGPT, Gemini, or another LLM platform of your choice to suggest strategies traditional firms can adopt to defend against such disruptions.
6. The chapter discusses the disruption of customer and stakeholder expectations. How might these disruptions force professions to redefine their value propositions? Use ChatGPT, Gemini, or another LLM platform of your choice to suggest ways professions can stay relevant in an era of rapid digital change.
7. What similarities and differences exist between the examples of industry-level and institution-level disruptions provided in the chapter? Ask ChatGPT, Gemini, or another LLM platform of your choice to analyze these differences and propose how professions might proactively prepare for institutional disruption.

REFERENCES

Baron, D. P. (2018). Disruptive entrepreneurship and dual purpose strategies: The case of Uber. *Strategy Science*, *3*(2), 439–462.

Berger, T., Chen, C., & Frey, C. B. (2018). Drivers of disruption? Estimating the Uber effect. *European Economic Review*, *110*, 197–210.

Berghel, H. (2024). social media, cognitive dysfunction, and social disruption. *Computer*, *57*(05), 118–124.

Bonnet, D., & Westerman, G. (2020). The new elements of digital transformation. *MIT Sloan Management Review*, 62(2), 82–89.

Busulwa, R. (2022). *Navigating digital transformation in management*. Routledge.

Busulwa, R., & Evans, N. (2021). *Digital transformation in accounting*. Routledge.

Chaffey, D., Ellis-Chadwick, F., & Mayer, R. (2009). *Internet marketing: Strategy, implementation and practice*. Pearson education.

Christensen, C. M., Raynor, M. E., & McDonald, R. (2015). What is disruptive innovation? *Harvard Business Review*, 93(12), 44–53

Christensen, C. M. (2015). *The innovator's dilemma: When new technologies cause great firms to fail*. Harvard Business Review Press.

Downes, L., & Nunes, P. (2013). Blockbuster Becomes a Casualty of Big Bang Disruption. Retrieved April 26, 2020, from Harvard Business Review website: https://hbr.org/2013/11/blockbuster-becomes-a-casualty-of-big-bang-disruption

Goldstein, M. (2018). *Dislocation and its discontents: Ride-sharing's impact on the taxi industry*. Forbes. Retrieved from https://www.forbes.com/sites/michaelgoldstein/2018/06/08/uber-lyft-taxi-drivers/#6a5415559f0d

Henderson, R. (2006). The Innovator's dilemma as a problem of organizational competence. Journal of Product Innovation Management, 23(1), 5–11.

Kotler, P., Keller, K. L., Brady, M., Goodman, M., & Hansen, T. (2016). *Marketing management* (*3rd* ed.). Pearson.

Meier, L. M., & Manzerolle, V. R. (2019). Rising tides? Data capture, platform accumulation, and new monopolies in the digital music economy. *New Media & Society*, *21*(3), 543–561.

Moreau, F. (2013). The disruptive nature of digitization: The case of the recorded music industry. *International Journal of Arts Management*, *15*(2), 18–31.

Towse, R. (2020). Dealing with digital: The economic organisation of streamed music. *Media, Culture & Society*, *42*(7–8), 1461–1478.

Vial, G. (2019). Understanding digital transformation: A review and a research agenda. *The Journal of Strategic Information Systems*, *28*(2), 118–144.

Vincent, N., & Igou, A. (2023). Emerging Technologies for Business Professionals: A Nontechnical Guide to the Governance and Management of Disruptive Technologies.

Warner, K. S., & Wäger, M. (2019). Building dynamic capabilities for digital transformation: An ongoing process of strategic renewal. *Long Range Planning*, *52*(3), 326–349.

5 The Digital Disruption of Professions

INTRODUCTION

The digital disruption of professions represents a transformative shift in how professional work is structured, governed, and performed. Digital technology advancements are reshaping institutions by altering established norms, rules, and governance structures, with professions being no exception. As digital tools and platforms redefine professional roles, they challenge traditional practices, ethical standards, and the very foundation of professional authority. This chapter explores how digital disruption impacts professions both directly—by transforming job roles, processes, and competencies - and indirectly, through broader organizational and societal changes. Key disruptions include shifting client and public expectations, evolving business models, increased data availability, and new tools that augment or replace human expertise. Additionally, digital technologies are redefining professional value, altering best practices, and expanding cybersecurity and ethical challenges. The chapter also examines the growing reliance on AI and automation, the erosion of professional boundaries, and the reconfiguration of education and skill development pathways. As professions navigate this technological upheaval, adaptation is critical. Those who successfully integrate digital skills while maintaining human-centric expertise will continue to thrive, while those resistant to change risk obsolescence. This chapter provides a comprehensive discussion of these trends, offering insights into the future of professional work in an increasingly digital tech-rich economy.

THE DIGITAL DISRUPTION OF PROFESSIONS AS A SUBSET OF INSTITUTION LEVEL DIGITAL DISRUPTION

Institutions are enduring systems of rules, norms, and structures that govern behavior within society (North, 1990). Examples of institutions include governments, the family, education institutions, religions, and the economy (Scott, 2013). And examples of their enduring systems of rules, norms, and structures governing behavior within society include the family institution establishing norms for relationships, child-rearing, and care of others (Parsons, 2013). Another example is governments providing structures like laws, courts, and public services to enforce order (Ostrom, 1990). Professions can be considered institutions when they establish shared practices, ethical standards, and formal governance to maintain societal trust and to regulate their members' conduct - thereby contributing to societal order and stability (Abbott, 2014). The digital disruption of institutions refers to digital technology (DT)

DOI: 10.1201/9781003606604-7

advancements driving disruptions of institutional structures, processes, rules, and norms that govern behavior within society (Zuboff, 2023). Extending this, the digital disruption of professions, as an institution, refers to DT advancements disrupting the shared practices, ethical expectations and behaviors, and formal governance/regulation of professionals—making it challenging for professionals to maintain societal trust in them to continue contributing to societal order and stability (Susskind & Susskind, 2015).

DIRECT AND INDIRECT DISRUPTION OF PROFESSIONS

The digital disruption of professions occurs both directly and indirectly. Indirectly, disruption stems from the digital disruption of organizations and society (Vial, 2019; Busulwa, 2022). At the organizational level, digital disruption creates new expectations of leaders and managers, requiring them to lead the organization's adaptation to digital disruption and to lead digital business transformation efforts (Westerman et al., 2014; Busulwa & Evans, 2021). These leaders, in turn, expect professionals to support their change initiatives by taking on new digital or digitally enhanced job roles. For example, accountants may expand their roles to incorporate insights from broader data, beyond financial data, into decision-making (Busulwa & Evans, 2021; Vial, 2019; Moll & Yigitbasioglu, 2019). And marketing professionals may expand their roles by leveraging advanced digital platforms to drive greater customer engagement (Lamberton & Stephen, 2016).

At the societal level, digital disruption reshapes people's expectations and behaviors, work cultures, and government regulations (Vial, 2019; Bughin et al., 2018). For instance, in relation to people's expectations, the rise of remote work and anywhere/anytime/any-device/digital-first products and services results in people expecting, and therefore indirectly pressures organizations to prioritize digital product and service offerings (Vial, 2019; Busulwa, 2022). Professionals are increasingly expected to align their practices with these changes—for example, HR specialists may be expected to manage virtual recruitment and performance management processes, while educators may need to design hybrid learning models that leverage the latest digital platforms.

To meet these evolving demands, professionals must adapt their roles, processes, and activities. This includes acquiring new technical skills, such as proficiency in data visualization or cybersecurity, and embracing cross-disciplinary collaboration (e.g. see Vial, 2019). Processes like project management may need to be facilitated by digital workflow management platforms, and to integrate agile methodologies (Busulwa, 2022). And activities like customer acquisition and engagement may increasingly rely on digital tools such as large language models (LLMs) and machine learning platforms.

In contrast to indirect disruption of professions, the direct disruption of professions involves digital technology advancements driving profession specific changes in required professional roles, processes, workflows, and competencies (Busulwa & Evans, 2021). The direct digital disruption of professions manifests itself as 10 specific disruptions (see Table 5.1). We discuss each of these further below.

TABLE 5.1
Examples of Direct Disruptions of the Professions Caused by Digital Technology Advancements

Type of Disruption	Explanation	Example
Disruption of client and public expectations	Clients expect faster, more transparent, and digitally delivered services.	AI-powered legal assistants like Harvey prompt clients to expect faster services.
Disruption of professional services and business models	Shift from traditional, human-centered models to data-driven, automated services.	Need to use real-time financial reporting platforms in accounting.
Disruption of data available to professionals	Increased volume and variety of data accessible for professional use and by clients.	Need for hotels to use Hotels using online travel agencies (OTAs), dynamic pricing engines, and customer analytics platforms to optimize bookings and revenue.
Disruption of tools for professional work	Emergence of AI, cloud, and data tools that enhance or automate professional tasks.	Need to use cloud-based accounting platforms and AI diagnostic tools.
Disruption of the value professionals can create	Professionals can now deliver faster, deeper, or more strategic value.	Need to use drones in mining for real-time stockpile accounting.
Disruption of optimal work practices	New digital approaches redefine what is considered "best practice."	Growing use of full-dataset audit techniques using AI instead of sampling.
Disruption of required competencies	Professionals need new digital, data, and transformation-related skills.	Accountants needing data analytics and AI audit competencies.
Disruption from competing substitutes	Non-professionals or AI systems now perform professional-level tasks.	Need for professionals to compete with chatbots offering basic medical or legal advice.
Disruption of education and development pathways	Accelerated, ongoing, and modular learning models replace "learn once" paradigms.	Competition from micro-credentials and online platforms like Coursera.
Disruption of professional bodies and governance	Need for digitally enhanced member engagement, credentialing, and standards.	Emerging use of blockchain for credential verification; online AGMs.

Disruption of Client and Public Expectations

From a professional perspective, the disruption of customer and other stakeholder expectations can be viewed as digital technology advancements altering clients' and society's expectations of professionals across various fields. Client's awareness of professionals' ability to use digital technologies like artificial intelligence (AI) is leading clients to anticipate more efficient, cost-effective, and personalized solutions from professionals. For instance, in the legal profession, AI tools like

"Relativity" (a legal data and legal process/workflow management platform) and "Harvey" (a specialist AI powered legal assistant) are automating tasks such as document review and contract analysis, prompting clients to expect faster and more accurate services (Glaser & Borna, 2024). Similarly, in wealth management, the adoption of AI enables advisors to offer detailed financial insights and improved efficiencies, aligning with clients' growing expectations for sophisticated advisory services (O'Neill, 2024). Societal expectations are also evolving, with a greater emphasis on transparency, accessibility, and adaptability in professional roles. The COVID-19 pandemic accelerated disruption of client and public expectations, leading to a shift in leading to greater expectations of remote consultations and digital interactions, requiring professionals to adapt to new modes of client engagement (e.g. see Cosa, 2024). In healthcare, for example, telemedicine has become an essential service, reflecting society's expectation for accessible and flexible healthcare delivery (Ortega et al., 2020). Clients and the public also increasingly expect to be much more skilled in the use of DTs to deliver services and also to upgrade their knowledge and skills—we will discuss this more later. Overall, this ongoing disruption of client and public expectations suggests a need for ongoing education and adaptability among professionals to meet the changing demands of clients and society.

Disruption of Professional Services Business Models and product/service Offerings

Digital technology advancements are driving disruptions of the business models and service offerings of professional service firms (PSFs) and professionals. Traditionally, PSFs and professionals relied on human-centered, knowledge-intensive models. But advances in digital technologies like artificial intelligence (AI) and big data analytics are enabling the leveraging of data-driven business models. By leveraging these digital technologies, PSFs and professionals can automate routine tasks, enhance decision-making processes, and deliver more efficient professional services. For instance, in the legal profession, leveraging AI-powered platforms enables automated document review and faster or more comprehensive legal research. It also enables prediction of legal outcomes and analysis of contract completeness/implications/impacts, thereby reducing reliance on manual processes (e.g. see Fielt et al., 2019).

Many PSFs and professionals have adapted by integrating digital technology tools into their existing practices and workflows. This approach allows firms to enhance their service offerings without completely overhauling their traditional models. For example, consulting firms and consulting professionals have incorporated AI to analyze large datasets, providing clients with deeper insights and more strategic advice (e.g., see Pemer & Werr, 2023). Other PSFs and professionals are embracing Digital Service Innovation (DSI), the practice of creating new, digitally-enabled services. DSI transforms how services are designed, delivered, and consumed, often leading to the development of entirely new service offerings. In the accounting profession, for example, some accounting firms have developed digital platforms that offer real-time financial analysis and reporting, providing clients with up-to-date information and more control over their financial data (see Rabetino et al., 2024). And some accounting firms have leveraged AI to automate routine processes, allowing accountants to focus on more technical or strategic advisory roles. Other accounting firms have leveraged AI based automation to scale their service offerings to a much greater level than they were able to under the much more human-centered, knowledge-intensive traditional service delivery model.

Overall, digital technology advancements are driving disruption of professional service firms by mandating a shift from traditional, human-centered models to more automated, data-driven, and technology tool augmented service delivery models. PSFs and professionals embracing digital technologies can enhance their service offerings, improve efficiency, and maintain their professional relevance. PSFs and professionals who do not embrace and leverage digital technologies to enhance or redesign their business models and product offerings risk being replaced by those who do.

Disruption of Data Available to Professionals and Others Within or Outside the Organization

The exponential growth in the volume and variety of data now available is profoundly reshaping professional services and roles, presenting both opportunities and challenges (Busulwa, 2022). On one hand, this explosion of data allows professionals to enhance the breadth, completeness, and reliability of the roles they play and the services they provide, by using the expanded data as a more robust evidence base (Davenport & Patil, 2012). For example, lawyers can analyze structured case law data alongside unstructured client communications and AI-generated opinions (Surden, 2019), while doctors can integrate medical imaging with patient records and AI-driven analysis to deliver more accurate diagnoses (Topol, 2019). However, to fully capitalize on these opportunities, professionals must acquire new competencies. These include understanding diverse data types (e.g., structured, unstructured, machine-generated, video, and image data) and their value for professional services, as well as mastering sophisticated analytics tools to extract the most meaningful insights from the data (Busulwa & Evans, 2021). Additionally, professionals increasingly need to be able to analyze data in real time for predictive and prescriptive purposes and to communicate insights effectively through engaging, interactive, and customizable methods (Busulwa & Evans, 2021).

On the other hand, the availability of vast data and advanced tools poses significant risks to professionals' traditional roles. New competitors—such as artificial intelligence agents and professionals leveraging algorithmic tools—are entering domains historically dominated by human expertise, challenging professionals' relevance and service offerings (Susskind & Susskind, 2015). Further, clients and stakeholders increasingly have access to the same data and tools as professionals, enabling them to perform tasks that were once the exclusive domain of professionals, or allowing them to audit and cross-check the quality of professionals' work (Busulwa, 2022). This dynamic creates intense pressure for professionals to deliver unique value-added services, and to ensure the quality and timeliness of their work can withstand scrutiny in both substance and presentation. Consequently, modern professionals must prioritize rigor, transparency, accelerated learning, and adaptability to thrive in a rapidly evolving, data-driven landscape (Davenport, 2018).

Disruption of the Tools that can Be Used to Perform Professional Work

Digital technology advancements are disrupting the tools needed to effectively perform professional work by introducing new alternative tools (e.g., see Busulwa & Evans, 2021; Brynjolfsson & McAfee, 2014). These new tools typically offer more efficient and effective ways of carrying out professional activities, enabling professionals to deliver higher-quality services (Manyika et al., 2017). For instance, the introduction of cloud computing has led to the development of platforms and tools that allow professionals to provide anywhere, anytime, real-time services (Marston et al., 2011). In accounting, for example, cloud-based software enables remote collaboration and instant financial reporting (Busulwa & Evans, 2021; Richins et al., 2017). Similarly, artificial intelligence (AI) tools can automatically analyze vast and diverse datasets, streamlining tasks like financial audits in accounting (Busulwa & Evans, 2021), legal research in law (Surden, 2019), and diagnostic processes in medicine (Topol, 2019). Meanwhile, data visualization technologies enhance the presentation of insights, enabling professionals to communicate complex information more effectively through engaging and interactive visual formats (e.g., see Busulwa & Evans, 2021).

However, these advancements also disrupt the nature of professional work. They redefine how professional activities are performed, who (or what) can perform them, and how efficiently and effectively these tasks can be accomplished (Susskind & Susskind, 2015). Automation and AI, for example, can now perform routine accounting, legal, or engineering tasks once exclusively carried out by humans (e.g., see Busulwa & Evans, 2021). To remain proficient in such evolving landscapes, professionals must continuously develop their digital competencies (Davenport, 2018). This includes mastering an ever-expanding range of technologies, from AI tools to cloud platforms and data visualization software, to ensure they can adapt to changing professional demands (Westerman et al., 2014).

Disruption of the Type of Value Professionals Are Able to Create

As digital technology advancements disrupt the tools used for professional work, they indirectly redefine the value that professionals can create, and the roles they can play (McAfee & Brynjolfsson, 2017). The new or enhanced tools for professional work enable professionals to perform traditional activities much faster and more accurately, freeing up capacity for higher-value tasks (Manyika et al., 2017; Busulwa & Evans, 2021). For instance, an accountant in a mining organization can use drones, video analytics, and computer vision technologies to automatically count inventory levels, such as mineral stockpiles, in real time and with greater precision—eliminating the need for on-site visits (Busulwa & Evans, 2021). This can save weeks of effort, which can then be redirected to addressing more critical organizational challenges like digital risk management, change facilitation, or digital transformation enablement (Busulwa & Evans, 2021). By leveraging this freed-up value creation capacity, professionals can deliver more innovative and meaningful outcomes for stakeholders. As professionals deliver such outcomes, stakeholder expectations grow, expanding reliance on professionals to provide strategic insights and solutions (Busulwa & Evans, 2021). For example, lawyers who automate routine legal research with AI can spend more time on client engagement and strategic or preventative advice, helping clients navigate regulatory changes or complex legal risks (Surden, 2019). Similarly, doctors who integrate AI with medical imaging can improve diagnostic accuracy and speed, enabling them to spend more time on patient-centered care—such as better tailoring care to patient values and preferences, improving patient communication, and enhancing care coordination (Topol, 2019).

As well as the expanded value creation opportunities, there are also professional risks from this disruption. Professionals who fail to adopt digital technologies to improve efficiency and expand the value they create risk under delivering on stakeholder expectations, potentially losing relevance (Davenport, 2018; Busulwa & Evans, 2021). Ultimately, to remain competitive, professionals increasingly need to not only embrace digital tools, but also redefine their roles by leveraging uniquely human capabilities, such as empathy, ethical decision-making, and creative problem-solving (Wilson & Daugherty, 2018). These shifts require professionals to continuously develop digital competencies, adapt to changing expectations, and focus on providing strategic, innovative, and high-impact services in an increasingly data-driven and technology-driven world (McAfee & Brynjolfsson, 2017).

Disruption of the Optimal Ways to Perform Professional Work

Digital technology advancements are expanding the repertoire of approaches that can be used to perform professional work (Busulwa & Evans, 2021; McAfee & Brynjolfsson, 2017). Many of the new work approaches enable professionals to achieve much greater efficiency, accuracy, and rigor in their work (Busulwa & Evans, 2021; Davenport & Ronanki, 2018). For example, in auditing, digital tools such as machine learning allow auditors to review entire datasets for fraud instead of relying on traditional sampling methods (Busulwa & Evans, 2021). Additionally, natural language processing (NLP) enables the analysis of an organization's contracts, invoices, and emails in their entirety, while advanced technologies like knowledge graphs, neural networks, and deep learning uncover patterns and facts that the human mind could never detect on its own (Busulwa & Evans, 2021).

By expanding the range of possibilities for how professional work can be performed, digital technologies also disrupt what is considered optimal or best-practice methods (Busulwa & Evans, 2021). The definition of "best practice" becomes fluid as professionals adopt new technologies and workflows, challenging long-held norms in fields like accounting, law, engineering, and education. For instance, in education, teachers can now use AI tools to design adaptive learning experiences tailored to individual students, disrupting the traditional one-size-fits-all teaching model (Luckin & Holmes, 2015). To remain competitive and provide high-quality services, professionals increasingly need to stay vigilant to advancements in digital technology and remain proactive in experimenting with these innovations and the improvements in efficiency and effectiveness they enable (Manyika et al., 2017). Continuous learning and testing of these tools are critical to identifying the most effective ways to perform professional processes and workflows (Wilson & Daugherty, 2018). Those who fail to adapt risk falling behind as stakeholders increasingly demand faster, more innovative, and impactful services (Busulwa & Evans, 2021).

Disruption of the Competencies Required to Perform Professional Work

Digital technology advancements are reshaping the competencies required to perform professional work effectively in two key ways. First, they create a demand for skills in new digital tools adopted to enhance traditional workflows. Second, they require professionals to take on new or digitally enhanced roles and processes, necessitating unique digital competencies (Busulwa & Evans, 2021; McAfee & Brynjolfsson, 2017). Professionals are under pressure to first cultivate the skills to use new digital tools and products in their traditional professional workflows. For example, nurses increasingly need proficiency in electronic health record (EHR) systems, telehealth platforms, and wearable health monitoring devices (Topol, 2019). EHRs streamline documentation and improve real-time decision-making (Topol, 2019), telehealth enables virtual patient care in remote areas (Bashshur et al., 2020), and wearable devices provide continuous health data, fostering preventive care (Islam et al., 2015).

Second, professionals are also under pressure to master competencies relating to new digital or digitally expanded roles. Accountants, for instance, increasingly require data analytics, artificial intelligence, and cybersecurity skills to fulfill new digital or digitally expanded roles such as assess cyber risks and auditing AI decision models (Busulwa & Evans, 2021; Richins et al., 2017). To fulfill emerging new digital or digitally enhanced roles for accountants—such as technology adoption and digital transformation enablers, process and control experts, and strategy execution enablers—accountants increasingly require new or expanded digital transformation and digital business-related competencies (Busulwa et al., 2024). Similarly, clinicians increasingly require AI-related skills to interpret machine-generated diagnostic outputs (Yu et al., 2018). And lawyers are increasingly utilizing legal analytics platforms and predictive models to craft case strategies (Surden, 2019). Engineers are increasingly leveraging IoT data and machine learning for predictive maintenance, infrastructure monitoring, and design optimization (Lee et al., 2015). Teachers increasingly need to master adaptive learning tools and digital platforms to deliver personalized education (Luckin et al., 2016).

To thrive, professionals increasingly need to integrate three core competency areas. These include traditional competencies unique to their profession, digital technology and digital business-related competencies (e.g., AI systems, big data tools, and digital ethics), and accelerated transformation methodologies (e.g., Lean, Agile, accelerators, and design thinking) (Busulwa & Evans, 2021). These combined skills enable professionals to improve efficiency in traditional roles, adapt to evolving demands, and lead accelerated change and digital transformation initiatives.

Disruption of Competing Substitute Professional Service Providers

Digital technology advancements are driving disruptions in professions' roles and in professional services by introducing competing substitutes to the roles professionals play and the services they provide (Busulwa & Evans, 2021; Susskind & Susskind, 2015). These substitutes often leverage advanced technologies like artificial intelligence (AI), machine learning, and automation to replicate or enhance roles and services traditionally performed by professionals—often at a lower cost or with greater efficiency (Busulwa & Evans, 2021; Davenport & Ronanki, 2018). For example, in law, platforms like automated contract analysis tools and AI-driven legal research systems allow non-lawyers to access legal insights without requiring professional legal advice (Surden, 2019). This can reduce reliance on lawyers for routine legal tasks like document review and case law research. Similarly, in accounting, robotic process automation (RPA) and AI-powered bookkeeping platforms, such as QuickBooks and Xero, enable businesses to manage their finances, reconcile accounts, and generate financial reports with minimal input from human accountants (Busulwa & Evans, 2021; Richins et al., 2017). In healthcare, wearable devices and telehealth platforms allow patients to monitor their own health, and to receive automated alerts or basic diagnoses, reducing their dependency on doctors and nurses for routine care (Topol, 2019). For instance, AI-driven chatbots can provide preliminary diagnoses and recommendations, serving as a first point of contact for patients (Yu et al., 2018). Meanwhile, in engineering, tools like Building Information Modeling (BIM) software can allow clients to visualize, simulate, and analyze construction projects without relying as heavily on consulting engineers.

These technological substitutes challenge professionals by creating alternatives that can perform tasks faster, cheaper, and, in some cases, more accurately than human expertise alone (Busulwa & Evans, 2021; McAfee & Brynjolfsson, 2017). They also shift client expectations, as stakeholders increasingly demand similar levels of efficiency and convenience from professional services (Busulwa & Evans, 2021; Manyika et al., 2017). To remain competitive, professionals increasingly need to adapt by differentiating themselves through unique value creation. That is, they can focus on tasks that technology cannot fully replicate, such as strategic decision-making, personalized advice, ethical judgment, and complex problem-solving (Wilson & Daugherty, 2018). For example, doctors can complement AI-driven diagnostic tools by offering more empathetic, holistic care that accounts for the psychological and emotional needs of patients in ways that algorithms cannot (Topol, 2019). Accountants can move beyond routine financial tasks to take on strategic advisory roles in digital transformation, risk management, and sustainability initiatives (Busulwa & Evans, 2017).

Disruption of Education Requirements and Professional Development Pathways

Digital technology advancements are driving disruption in education requirements and professional development pathways. They do this by expanding the breadth and depth of digital technology-related competencies professionals need to effectively perform their work (e.g., see Busulwa & Evans, 2021; Suskind & Suskind, 2015), as well as by changing how professionals must learn in order to keep up with evolving competence requirements (McAfee & Brynjolfsson, 2017; Busulwa, 2022). In relation to the cultivation of these digital technology competencies, traditional degree programs are increasingly adapting to include training on critical and emerging technologies such as artificial intelligence (AI), data analytics, and other digital tools tailored to specific fields (Busulwa et al., 2022). For example, nursing curricula are placing greater emphasis on telehealth platforms and wearable health technologies (Bashshur et al., 2020), while accounting degrees are incorporating data management, data analytics, and robotic process automation (RPA) skills (Busulwa & Evans, 2021; Richins et al., 2017). Similarly, legal education is increasingly integrating courses on AI-driven legal research and contract analysis tools (Surden, 2019).

The ongoing and accelerating expansion in the breadth and depth of required digital technology competencies is driving a shift toward accelerated and lifelong learning, as professionals must continuously upskill in a timely manner to remain relevant (Busulwa & Evans, 2021; Manyika et al., 2017). For instance, doctors increasingly need to learn to leverage AI-based diagnostic tools in patient care, while teachers increasingly need expertise in learning management systems and digital teaching tools (Luckin et al., 2016). Certifications and micro-credentials in digital technology areas such as data science, cybersecurity, and digital business are becoming critical for maintaining competence and advancing careers (Busulwa & Evans, 2021; Davenport & Ronanki, 2018). Alternative learning pathways, such as online platforms like Coursera and LinkedIn Learning, are increasingly leveraged by both professionals and educational institutions to provide flexible, accelerated learning options (Kato et al., 2020). For example, engineers can pursue specialized certifications in IoT or machine learning, supplementing traditional academic programs (Lee et al., 2015).

Collaborations between professional organizations, educational institutions, and technology providers are also reshaping competence development pathways. Many accounting firms, for instance, are increasingly partnering with software companies to ensure their professionals and services stay up to date with the latest technologies. Similarly, many educational institutions are partnering with technology vendors to provide students with hands-on experience using digital work tools. In many of these cases, partnerships with technology firms enable professionals to learn directly from digital technology specialists, gain access to technical support when adopting/using specialist digital tools, and provide input into technology strategy-related decisions.

Disruption of the Roles of Professional Bodies and Associations

Digital technologies are disrupting how professional bodies, accreditation organizations, and strategic leadership entities operate and deliver value to their members and society (e.g., see Susskind & Susskind, 2015). For example, cloud-based systems now enable the automation of administrative processes, online platforms facilitate continuous professional development monitoring, and digital collaboration tools allow these entities to shift from hierarchical to networked governance structures (e.g., see Westerman et al., 2014). Additionally, digital tools now provide real-time insights into members' needs, challenges, and career trajectories, replacing traditional surveys and anecdotal evidence with data-driven decision-making to enhance member engagement (e.g., see Manyika et al., 2017). Digital technologies can further improve governance and member engagement by enabling more transparent and participatory decision-making processes, with virtual annual general meetings, online voting systems, and digital consultation platforms becoming standard features (e.g. see Tapscott & Tapscott, 2016; Busulwa & Evans, 2021). Similarly, digital technology advancements are transforming professional advocacy through expanding digital channels. Social media, online campaigns, and digital networking platforms can amplify reach and impact, enabling rapid mobilization on key issues and real-time communication with policymakers (e.g. see Chadwick, 2017). Accreditation processes are also being disrupted. Digital technologies now support continuous assessment, automated verification of professional development activities, blockchain-based credentialing, and dynamic updates to professional standards in response to evolving industry needs (El Koshiry et al., 2023).

Despite these opportunities, professional leadership entities face challenges in maintaining sustainable value propositions and meaningful member offerings. On one hand, membership models now compete with online professional communities that often provide similar benefits with fewer formal structures and compliance requirements. On the other hand, professional leadership entities struggle to adopt and leverage new technologies effectively for efficiency and innovation. The major challenge for professional leadership entities is how to change their internal governance and operations management structures quickly, while simultaneously redesigning and optimizing their member value proposition. At the same time, they must drive changes in the capacity of professionals to thrive and remain relevant in a technology-rich future.

IMPLICATIONS FOR PROFESSIONS

Accelerating Automation and the Need to Re-Evaluate the Role of Human Expertise in Professional Services

Digital technology advancements are accelerating automation across professional services, fundamentally reshaping how work is performed. Many routine and repetitive tasks traditionally carried out by professionals—such as legal research, financial auditing, diagnostic analysis, and architectural modeling—are now being automated using cloud computing, the internet of things (IoT), artificial intelligence (AI), robotic process automation (RPA), and machine learning. These technologies enable faster, more accurate, and scalable execution of tasks, reducing reliance on manual human labor. In law, AI-driven platforms can scan millions of legal cases in seconds, automating tasks once handled by junior lawyers (McGinnis & Pearce, 2019). In accounting, AI systems can perform tax calculations, detect fraud, and conduct audits with greater precision than human accountants (Frey & Osborne, 2017). In medicine, AI-powered diagnostic tools analyze medical images and identify diseases with accuracy matching or surpassing human radiologists (Topol, 2019). In engineering and architecture, generative design software can produce and evaluate thousands of structural models, streamlining the design process (Pena et al., 2021).

As automation advances, it necessitates a re-evaluation of human expertise in professional services. The role of professionals is shifting from executing tasks to interpreting, advising, and making strategic decisions based on AI-generated insights. For instance, doctors are increasingly trialing the integration of AI-generated diagnoses with patient histories and clinical judgment. Accountants and financial advisors are focusing on strategic value creation and risk assessment rather than transaction recording, data visualization, and analysis that stakeholders can draw from AI tools. Lawyers are increasingly specializing in negotiation, legal strategy, and ethical considerations, as more basic activities like contract review and legal analytics become automated. These shifts have significant implications for professionals – for example, see Table 5.2. Success in this evolving landscape may require developing uniquely human capabilities, including critical thinking, problem-solving, ethical reasoning, and emotional intelligence. Professionals likely need to embrace lifelong

TABLE 5.2
How Digital Disruption Is Reshaping Core Aspects of Professional Life

Aspect of Professional Life	Examples of Digital Disruption	Implication for Professionals
Professional identity	Traditional identities eroded as tools like AI and platforms reshape expertise boundaries.	Professionals must redefine their identity and value beyond technical knowledge.
Professional judgment	Algorithmic decision-making challenges human expertise.	Judgment increasingly needs to incorporate or interpret machine outputs.
Client relationships	Clients increasingly engage through digital channels and expect personalized, real-time access.	Professionals must manage hybrid client experiences (human + digital).
Value creation	Shift from task execution to strategic, interpretive, and insight-driven contributions.	Professionals must focus on creativity, empathy, and complex problem-solving.
Professional boundaries	Roles once exclusive to a profession can be performed by non-professionals or AI / quantum computing assisted systems.	Professions must differentiate based on human qualities and high-stakes work.
Knowledge and skill lifespan	Rapid obsolescence of technical knowledge and tools.	Lifelong learning and adaptability become core professional responsibilities.
Global delivery of services	Remote work and platforms enable cross-border delivery of professional services.	Increased global competition; need to specialize and leverage local context.
Dependence on tech providers	Reliance on proprietary platforms, AI systems, and digital infrastructure.	Raises risks of vendor lock-in, data breaches, and loss of autonomy.
Ethical and legal frameworks	New risks from AI errors, data misuse, and digital surveillance.	Professionals must uphold ethical standards in unfamiliar digital contexts.

learning, continuously updating their skills to effectively leverage emerging digital tools. Rather than being replaced, professionals who adapt will redefine their value by working alongside AI, focusing on tasks that require human judgment, creativity, and interpersonal expertise (McAfee & Brynjolfsson, 2017; Susskind, 2020).

Erosion of Professional Boundaries, Challenges to Professional Judgment, and Redefinition of Professional Identity

Digital technology advancements drive erosion of professional boundaries by enabling non-professionals to perform tasks traditionally reserved for experts (Susskind & Susskind, 2015). For example, legal software now allows individuals to create basic contracts and wills without attorneys, while diagnostic AI helps patients conduct preliminary medical assessments before seeing doctors (Joshi & Mooney, 2023). This democratization of professional knowledge challenges the traditional gatekeeping role of professions and disrupts established jurisdictional claims. Professional judgment, a critical remit of professions, faces mounting pressure as algorithmic decision-making systems increasingly match or exceed human expertise in specific domains (Davenport & Kirby, 2015). Radiologists may find themselves increasingly competing with AI in detecting tumors, while financial advisors may find themselves increasingly contending with robo-advisors in the provision of investment advice (McAfee & Brynjolfsson, 2017). This technological encroachment raises questions about when human judgment should prevail over machine recommendations, and how professionals should integrate AI insights into their decision-making processes (Pasquale, 2020).

The redefinition of professional identity is occurring as practitioners grapple with their evolving role in a digitally mediated environment. Architects are increasingly required to master complex modeling software rather than traditional drafting, while teachers may find themselves increasingly transitioning from information providers to learning facilitators in technology-rich classrooms (Brown & Duguid, 2000). These shifts may force professionals to reconceptualize their value proposition and core competencies. The implications for professionals and professional services are profound. Success increasingly requires hybridizing traditional expertise with digital literacy, developing new skills in human-AI collaboration, and focusing on uniquely human capabilities like complex problem-solving, emotional intelligence, and ethical reasoning (Frey & Osborne, 2018). Professional services firms may need to reimagine their service delivery models, emphasizing high-value advisory roles while automating routine tasks to maximize efficiency and effectiveness (Acemoglu & Restrepo, 2021).

Skill Obsolescence/upskilling Imperatives and Shortening of Knowledge Lifespan

Digital technology advancements and the resultant digital disruption are fundamentally altering professional work, consequently creating unprecedented pressure for continuous skill renewal (Frey & Osborne, 2017). Studies indicate that technical skills now have an average half-life of just 2-5 years, with some specialized digital competencies becoming obsolete even faster (World Economic Forum, 2020). This rapid skill decay is particularly evident in fields like software development, where frameworks, tools, and digital products can become outdated within months. The timespan during which professional knowledge remains current has contracted significantly. For instance, legal practitioners face constant updates to regulations around emerging technologies and their uses. This knowledge lifespan contraction and the growing knowledge demands have made traditional "learn-once" professional education models increasingly inadequate. These forces are creating critical implications across professions. Accountants are increasingly transitioning from computation to advisory roles as AI handles routine tasks. Architects increasingly need to master complex modeling software that evolves yearly. Healthcare professionals increasingly need data analysis skills to leverage AI diagnostic tools effectively. For professionals and firms, this presents three key imperatives: First, establishing systematic approaches to continuous learning, including dedicated time for skill updating. Second, developing metacognitive abilities to identify emerging skill gaps proactively. Third, creating organizational structures that support rapid knowledge diffusion and cross-training.

Need for Redefinition of Professional Value and Nature of the Client Relationship

The digital disruption of professional work is forcing changes in how professionals create and demonstrate value to clients (Susskind & Susskind, 2015). Traditional professional expertise, once closely guarded and accessible only through direct consultation, is increasingly being commoditized through widely available, and often free, AI systems and other digital tools (Christensen et al., 2013). As a result, professionals are increasingly finding themselves needing to redefine their core value proposition beyond just technical knowledge. For example, redefining their role from being mere information providers to strategic advisors who interpret complex data, offer nuanced insights, and guide clients through uncertainty in value-added ways that AI systems just cannot (Christensen et al., 2013). The client relationship is similarly being transformed. As digital tools enable clients to have more direct access to professional knowledge and the ability to carry out professional processes and workflows themselves, they increasingly expect on-demand engagement, and faster, more personalized interactions through multi-channel communication, online portals, and mobile apps. Professionals who adapt to these changing expectations and at the same time effectively leverage digital technologies can enhance precision in decision-making and strengthen client trust.

Challenges to Traditional Practices and Introduction of New Best Practices

Digital disruption of the professions forces changes in traditional practices and in what is considered best practice (e.g. see Busulwa & Evans, 2021). This occurs when new digital technologies or advancements in existing ones, enable new and often much more efficient and/or effective ways of performing professional processes by digitizing and/or automating complete processes or aspects of processes (Busulwa & Evans, 2021). For instance, in medicine, aspects of diagnostic processes now routinely use AI-powered diagnostic tools. And in the legal profession, some legal professionals routinely employ machine learning for document review and case research. Once these new practices are introduced that are drastically more efficient and effective, they tend to take over traditional existing practices to become the new best practices (Busulwa & Evans, 2021).

Expanding Cybersecurity Risks, Data Integrity Risks and New ethical/legal Dilemmas

Digital disruption of the professions is driving expanding cybersecurity risks, data integrity concerns, and new ethical and legal dilemmas for professionals and professional services. As professionals increasingly rely on online artificial intelligence (AI), big data, and cloud-based platforms, they must navigate complex risks associated with data security, privacy, and ethical decision-making. Cybersecurity risks are intensifying as professional services increasingly digitize sensitive client data. Lawyers, accountants, and healthcare providers store vast amounts of confidential information on digital platforms, making them prime targets for cyberattacks. Law firms, for example, are vulnerable to breaches that expose privileged legal documents, while hospitals face ransomware attacks that compromise patient records (Topol, 2019). Accounting firms must safeguard financial data against fraud and hacking attempts (Frey & Osborne, 2017). Data integrity risks are also increasing as professionals rely on AI and machine learning models for decision-making. AI-generated insights can be compromised by biased training data, algorithmic errors, or deliberate manipulation, raising concerns about accuracy and reliability. In medicine for example, flawed AI diagnoses could lead to harmful treatment decisions, while AI-driven financial analysis in accounting and finance may misinterpret market trends, impacting investment strategies (McAfee & Brynjolfsson, 2017). Use of new digital technologies like artificial intelligence introduces new ethical and legal dilemmas. AI-driven decision-making raises questions about accountability—who is responsible when an AI system makes an error? Professionals must also navigate conflicts between data privacy regulations and the need for data-driven insights. As digital disruption accelerates, professionals increasingly need to develop strong cybersecurity awareness, data governance practices, and ethical frameworks to ensure trust, compliance, and accountability in an increasingly complex digital landscape (Susskind, 2020).

Dependence on Technology Providers and Need to Cooperate and Compete with Algorithms

Digital disruption of the professions is driving a growing dependence on technology providers when carrying out professional workflows and delivering professional services, while also forcing professionals to navigate a complex dynamic of both cooperating and competing with algorithms (e.g., see Susskind & Susskind, 2022). As professional services become increasingly digitized and automated, professionals depend more and more on cloud computing, artificial intelligence (AI), the internet of things (IoT), and other technologies and platforms developed by third-party providers to execute core tasks (e.g., see Porter & Heppelmann, 2014). Many industries now require professionals to integrate proprietary digital tools into their workflows (Susskind & Susskind, 2022). In healthcare, nursing and medical staff increasingly depend on electronic health record (EHR) systems and AI diagnostic tools to provide patient care (Topol, 2019). In the legal profession, lawyers are increasingly reliant on AI-powered legal research and contract review platforms (e.g. see Susskind, 2019). And in accounting, accountants are increasingly depending on automated tax preparation and fraud detection software (e.g. see Busulwa & Evans, 2021). This growing dependence creates risks, as professionals must trust external providers for cybersecurity, data integrity, system availability and reliability, and timely updates (Porter & Heppelmann, 2014). This increasing dependence can create vendor lock-in, impact service pricing, and impact competitive positioning. At the same time, professionals must learn to lead, cooperate with, and yet differentiate their abilities from those of AI-driven algorithms (Susskind & Susskind, 2022).

Digital disruption of the professions is driving a growing dependence on technology providers when carrying out professional workflows and delivering professional services, while also forcing professionals to navigate a complex dynamic of both cooperating and competing with algorithms (e.g., see Susskind & Susskind, 2015. As professional services become increasingly digitized and automated, professionals depend more and more on cloud computing, artificial intelligence (AI), the internet of things (IoT) and other technologies and platforms developed by third-party providers to execute core tasks (e.g., see Porter & Heppelmann, 2014). Many industries now require professionals to integrate proprietary digital tools into their workflows (Susskind & Susskind, 2022). In healthcare, nursing and medical staff increasingly depend on electronic health record (EHR) systems and AI diagnostic tools to provide patient care (Topol, 2019). In the legal profession, lawyers are increasingly reliant on AI-powered legal research and contract review platforms (e.g. see Susskind, 2019). And in accounting, accountants are increasingly depending on automated tax preparation and fraud detection software (e.g. see Busulwa & Evans, 2021). This growing dependence creates risks, as professionals must trust external providers for cybersecurity, data integrity, system availability and reliability, and timely updates (Porter & Heppelmann, 2014). This increasing dependence can create vendor lock-in, impact service pricing, and impact competitive positioning. At the same time, professionals must learn to lead, cooperate with and yet differentiate their abilities from AI-driven algorithms. In law, AI-powered contract analysis reduces the need for manual review, shifting lawyers toward strategic advisory roles (McGinnis & Pearce, 2013). In finance, robo-advisors provide algorithm-driven investment recommendations, requiring human advisors to focus on complex financial planning and client relationships. As AI expands its capabilities, professionals must redefine their roles, leveraging their uniquely human skills—such as judgment, creativity, and ethics—while integrating AI as a tool for enhanced efficiency and insight (Susskind, 2019; McAfee & Brynjolfsson, 2017).

Democratization of Expertise, Remote Work, and Globalization of Work

The digital disruption of professions is transforming how expertise is created, shared, and accessed (Susskind & Susskind, 2015). Online platforms, artificial intelligence, and sophisticated digital tools have democratized professional knowledge that was previously confined to members of particular professional bodies and particular locations. For instance, legal service platforms like ClearDocs and medical symptom checkers have made basic professional knowledge freely accessible to the public (Christensen et al., 2013). And more pervasive and reliable online connectivity, as well as remote work technologies (like Zoom or Microsoft Teams) have severed the traditional link between expertise and physical location. The COVID-19 pandemic accelerated this trend, with a rapidly growing number of professionals across fields adopting virtual service delivery (Frey & Osborne, 2017). This shift has enabled the globalization of professional work, creating worldwide markets for expertise. Indian radiologists can now analyze X-rays for US hospitals, while Filipino accountants can process tax returns for Australian firms (Baldwin, 2019). These changes have introduced numerous substitute competitors to traditional professional roles and services. Even in areas like healthcare, telemedicine platforms can connect patients to cheaper and or better healthcare practitioners around the world (Acemoglu & Restrepo, 2019). And professional service firms are facing more and more competition from gig economy platforms that match clients directly with independent practitioners.

Generational Shifts and Inequality in Access to Technology

Digital disruption of the professions is driving significant cultural and generational divides (Susskind & Susskind, 2015). For example, younger professionals, particularly those from Generation Z and Millennials, have been shown to adapt more readily to using digital tools and platforms, while older generations have been argued to struggle more with technological transitions (Anderson & Smith, 2022). This "digital native" advantage could create implicit biases in professional advancement and recruitment practices. The technological divide extends beyond age demographics to create socioeconomic disparities. Professionals in developing regions and lower-income areas have been found to face significant barriers in accessing advanced digital tools, high-speed internet, and best practice professional development resources (e.g. see Gebremichael & Jackson, 2006). Professionals and potential professionals in economically disadvantaged locations can face a "professional poverty trap" where limited access to technology restricts career advancement opportunities. For example, in healthcare, older physicians report difficulties adapting to electronic health records and telemedicine platforms, while rural healthcare providers struggle with inadequate digital infrastructure (Scott Kruse et al., 2018). And in education, teachers in underfunded areas lack access to modern educational technology, limiting their ability to prepare students for the digital economy (Warschauer & Matuchniak, 2010).

PROFESSION LEVEL DIGITAL DISRUPTION AND THE FUTURE OF WORK

Given the aforementioned disruption and reshaping professional work, it is easy to conclude that the future of professional work is widespread job displacement (e.g. see Frey & Osborne, 2017). But research is increasingly pointing to a more nuanced future where technology mostly augments human expertise rather than replaces it (Davenport & Kirby, 2015; Autor, 2022). In this future, tasks requiring complex judgment, emotional intelligence, and contextual understanding remain resistant to full automation, leading to the rise of hybrid work models in which professionals leverage sophisticated digital technologies like AI to enhance their productivity and effectiveness (McAfee & Brynjolfsson, 2017). However, automation's impact is uneven across industries and job types. While high-skill professionals benefit from AI-driven augmentation, lower-skilled workers face greater risks of displacement or wage stagnation due to task automation (OECD, 2019). Organizations that effectively integrate human expertise with technology tend to outperform those relying solely on either human labor or automation (Wilson & Daugherty, 2018). This shift necessitates new competencies, particularly depth and breadth of digital competences and human-machine collaboration skills, to ensure workers can adapt to evolving job and professional service demands (Howard & Reeves, 2019).

CONCLUSION

The digital disruption of professions represents a transformative shift in how professional work is structured, governed, and performed. Digital technologies are reshaping professions by altering traditional norms, ethical standards, and governance structures. This disruption occurs both directly—by transforming job roles, processes, and required competencies—and indirectly, through broader organizational and societal changes. Key disruptions include shifting client expectations, evolving business models, increasing data availability, and the introduction of new technology tools that augment or replace human expertise. Automation and artificial intelligence (AI) are redefining professional value, eroding boundaries between professions, and reshaping skill development pathways. Professionals increasingly need to integrate digital competencies alongside traditional expertise to remain relevant. Digital disruption also introduces challenges such as cybersecurity risks, ethical dilemmas, and accelerating knowledge obsolescence, requiring faster ongoing learning and adaptation. Professional bodies and education systems are under pressure to modernize training and governance structures.

Despite fears of job displacement, research suggests a future where technology mostly augments human expertise rather than replacing most of it. Success in this evolving landscape requires professionals to develop strategic, creative, and ethical decision-making skills. It also requires them to develop accelerated learning and change practices. Those who effectively integrate digital tools while maintaining human-centric expertise will continue to thrive, while those resistant to change risk obsolescence.

DISCUSSION QUESTIONS

1. How does digital disruption challenge traditional professional authority and governance structures?
2. In what ways has artificial intelligence changed client expectations across different professions?
3. What are the biggest risks associated with the increasing reliance on digital tools in professional work, and how can professionals mitigate them?
4. How does the erosion of professional boundaries impact the role and identity of professionals in fields such as law, healthcare, and accounting?
5. What strategies can professionals use to differentiate their value in a world where AI and automation can perform many routine tasks?
6. How should education and professional development systems evolve to prepare future professionals for an increasingly digital workplace?
7. To what extent should professionals collaborate with technology providers, and what risks arise from this growing dependence?

REFERENCES

Abbott, A. (2014). *The system of professions: An essay on the division of expert labor.* University of Chicago press.

Acemoglu, D., & Restrepo, P. (2019). Automation and new tasks: How technology displaces and reinstates labor. *Journal of Economic Perspectives, 33*(2), 3–30.

Autor, D. (2022). *The labor market impacts of technological change: From unbridled enthusiasm to qualified optimism to vast uncertainty* (No. w30074). National Bureau of Economic Research.

Baldwin, R. (2019). *The globotics upheaval: Globalization, robotics, and the future of work.* Oxford University Press.

Bashshur, R., Doarn, C. R., Frenk, J. M., Kvedar, J. C., & Woolliscroft, J. O.. (2020). Telemedicine and the COVID-19 pandemic, lessons for the future. *Telemedicine and e-Health, 26*(5), 571–573.

Bughin, J., Seong, J., Manyika, J., Chui, M., & Joshi, R. (2018). Notes from the AI frontier: Modeling the impact of AI on the world economy. McKinsey Global Institute, 4(1).

Busulwa, R., Birt, J., Gepp, A., & Oates, G. (2024). Lost in translation? The required vs. Actual technology skills of accountants. In Digital transformation in accounting and auditing: Navigating technological advances for the future (pp. 121–151). Cham: Springer International Publishing.

Busulwa, R., & Evans, N. (2021). *Digital transformation in accounting.* Routledge.

Busulwa, R., Evans, N., Oh, A., & Kang, M. (2021). Hospitality management and digital transformation. Hospitality management and digital transformation. Routledge, London. https://doi.org/10.4324/9780429325205.

Chadwick, A. (2017). *The hybrid media system: Politics and power.* Oxford University Press.

Christensen, C. M., Wang, D., & Van Bever, D. (2013). Consulting on the cusp of disruption. *Harvard Business Review, 91*(10), 106–114.

Cosa, M. (2024). Business digital transformation: Strategy adaptation, communication and future agenda. *Journal of Strategy and Management, 17*(2), 244–259.

Davenport, T. H. (2018). *The AI advantage: How to put the artificial intelligence revolution to work.* mit Press.

Davenport, T. H., & Kirby, J. (2015). Beyond automation. *Harvard Business Review, 93*(6), 58–65.

Davenport, T. H., & Patil, D. J. (2012). Data scientist. *Harvard Business Review, 90*(5), 70–76.

Davenport, T. H., & Ronanki, R. (2018). Artificial intelligence for the real world. *Harvard Business Review, 96*(1), 108–116.

El Koshiry, A., Eliwa, E., El-Hafeez, A., & Shams, T. (2023). Unlocking the power of blockchain in education: An overview of innovations and outcomes. *Blockchain: Research and Applications, 4*(4), 100165.

Fielt, E., Desouza, K. C., Gable, G., & Westerveld, P. (2019). Data-driven business models and professional services firms: A strategic framework and transitionary pathways. In The ecosystem of e-business: Technologies, stakeholders, and connections: 17th workshop on e-business, WeB 2018, Santa Clara, CA, USA, December 12, 2018, Revised Selected Papers 17 (pp. 26–38). Springer International Publishing.

Frey, C. B., & Osborne, M. A. (2017). The future of employment: How susceptible are jobs to computerisation? *Technological forecasting and social change, 114*, 254–280.

Gebremichael, M. D., & Jackson, J. W. (2006). Bridging the gap in Sub-Saharan Africa: A holistic look at information poverty and the region's digital divide. *Government Information Quarterly, 23*(2), 267–280.

Glaser, J., & Borna, S. (2024, October 24). AI: the new legal powerhouse—why lawyers should befriend the machine to stay ahead. Reuters. https://www.reuters.com/legal/legalindustry/ai-new-legal-powerhouse-why-lawyers-should-befriend-machine-stay-ahead-2024-10-24/

Islam, S. R., Kwak, D., Kabir, M. H., Hossain, M., & Kwak, K. S. (2015). The internet of things for health care: a comprehensive survey. *IEEE access, 3*, 678–708.

Kato, S., Galán-Muros, V., & Weko, T. (2020). The emergence of alternative credentials. OECD Education Working Papers. https://doi.org/10.1787/b741f39e-en

Lamberton, C., & Stephen, A. T. (2016). A thematic exploration of digital, social media, and mobile marketing: Research evolution from 2000 to 2015 and an agenda for future inquiry. *Journal of marketing, 80*(6), 146–172.

Lee, J., Bagheri, B., & Kao, H. A. (2015). A cyber-physical systems architecture for industry 4.0-based manufacturing systems. *Manufacturing letters, 3*, 18–23.

Luckin, R., & Holmes, W. (2016). Intelligence unleashed: An argument for AI in education.

Manyika, J., Chui, M., Miremadi, M., Bughin, J., George, K., Willmott, P., & Dewhurst, M. (2017). A future that works: AI, automation, employment, and productivity. McKinsey Global Institute Research. *Tech. Rep, 60*, 1–135.

Marston, S., Li, Z., Bandyopadhyay, S., Zhang, J., & Ghalsasi, A. (2011). Cloud computing—The business perspective. *Decision support systems, 51*(1), 176–189.

McAfee, A., & Brynjolfsson, E. (2017). *Machine, platform, crowd: Harnessing our digital future*. W. W. Norton & Company.

McGinnis, J. O., & Pearce, R. G. (2013). The great disruption: How machine intelligence will transform the role of lawyers in the delivery of legal services. *Fordham L. Rev, 82*, 3041.

North, D. C. (1990). *Institutions, Institutional change and economic performance*. Cambridge University.

O'Neill, M. (2024, June 28). Wealth managers need to adopt AI—and fast. Financial Times. https://www.ft.com/content/dc4cb53c-dd70-4c51-a4b4-b46b8720bc2e

Organisation for Economic Co-operation and Development. (2019). OECD employment outlook 2019: the future of work. Organisation for Economic Co-operation and Development.

Ortega, G., Rodriguez, J. A., Maurer, L. R., Witt, E. E., Perez, N., Reich, A., & Bates, D. W. (2020). Telemedicine, COVID-19, and disparities: policy implications. *Health policy and Technology, 9*(3), 368–371.

Ostrom, E. (1990). *Governing the commons: The evolution of institutions for collective action*. Cambridge university press.

Parsons, T. (2013). *The social system*. Routledge.

Pasquale, F. (2020). *New laws of robotics*. Harvard University Press.

Pemer, F., & Werr, A. (2023). Defusing Digital Disruption Through Creative Accumulation: Technology-Induced Innovation in Professional Service Firms. *Journal of Management Studies*, *62*(5), 1945–1990.

Pena, M. L. C., Carballal, A., Rodríguez-Fernández, N., Santos, I., & Romero, J.. (2021). Artificial intelligence applied to conceptual design. A review of its use in architecture. *Automation in Construction*, *124*, 103550.

Porter, M. E., & Heppelmann, J. E. (2014). How smart, connected products are transforming competition. *Harvard business review*, *92*(11), 64–88.

Rabetino, R., Kohtamäki, M., & Huikkola, T. (2024). Digital service innovation (DSI): a multidisciplinary (re) view of its origins and progress using bibliometric and text mining methods. *Journal of Service Management*, *35*(2), 176–201.

Richins, G., Stapleton, A., Stratopoulos, T. C., & Wong, C. (2017). Big data analytics: opportunity or threat for the accounting profession? *Journal of information systems*, *31*(3), 63–79.

Scott, W. R. (2013). *Institutions And organizations: Ideas, interests, And identities*. Sage publications.

Scott Kruse, C., Karem, P., Shifflett, K., Vegi, L., Ravi, K., & Brooks, M. (2018). Evaluating barriers to adopting telemedicine worldwide: a systematic review. *Journal of telemedicine and telecare*, *24*(1), 4–12.

Surden, H. (2019). Artificial intelligence and law: An overview. *Georgia State University Law Review*, *35*(4), 1305–1338.

Susskind, D. (2020). *A world without work: Technology, automation and how we should respond*. Penguin UK.

Susskind, R. (2019). *Online courts and the future of justice*. Oxford University Press.

Susskind, R., & Susskind, D. (2022). *The future of the professions: How technology will transform the work of human experts*. Oxford University Press.

Topol, E. (2019). *Deep medicine: How artificial intelligence can make healthcare human again*. Hachette UK.

Vial, G. (2019). Understanding digital transformation: A review and a research agenda. *The Journal of Strategic Information Systems*, *28*(2), 118–144.

Warschauer, M., & Matuchniak, T. (2010). New technology and digital worlds: Analyzing evidence of equity in access, use, and outcomes. *Review of research in education*, *34*(1), 179–225.

Westerman, G., Bonnet, D., & McAfee, A. (2014). *Leading digital: Turning technology into business transformation*. Harvard Business Press.

Wilson, H. J., & Daugherty, P. R. (2018). Collaborative intelligence: Humans and AI are joining forces. *Harvard Business Review*, *96*(4), 114–123.

World Economic Forum. (2020). The Future of Jobs Report 2020.

Yu, K. H., Beam, A. L., & Kohane, I. S. (2018). Artificial intelligence in healthcare. *Nature Biomedical Engineering*, *2*(10), 719–731.

Zuboff, S. (2023). The age of surveillance capitalism. In: *Social theory re-wired* (pp. 203–213). Routledge.

Part III

The Digital Transformation of Professions

6 The Digital Transformation of Professions

INTRODUCTION

Digital transformation refers to the fundamental reimagining of how organizations, industries, and institutions create and deliver value through the strategic integration of digital technologies (e.g., see Vial, 2019). Unlike simple digitization or automation, digital transformation involves comprehensive changes to business models, processes, culture, and stakeholder relationships (e.g. see Westerman et al., 2014). Digital transformation occurs at multiple levels—for example, at the organizational level (e.g., individual companies), at the industry level (e.g., entire sectors), at the institutional level (e.g., professions, education systems), and at the societal level (e.g., broad social structures) (Busulwa, 2022). When discussed in the context of professions, we are mostly concerned with digital transformation at the institutional level—specifically, with how digital technology advancements are driving fundamental changes in how professional acquire and apply knowledge and skills, fulfill particular roles, and create meaningful value for society (Susskind & Susskind, 2015). Digital transformation at this level encompasses changes to professionals' education, regulatory frameworks, ethical standards, and their social contract with the public (Abbott, 2014). At the individual professional level, digital transformation requires professionals to develop new digital or digitally enhanced competencies, adopt new digital tools, and to reinvent, adapt or enhance their value proposition in an increasingly digital, tech-rich future (Brynjolfsson & McAfee, 2014). Ultimately, professional digital transformation represents a strategic evolution of how professions maintain relevance, trust, and societal value in a digitally-mediated environment. In the remainder of this chapter, we distinguish digital transformation from digital disruption, unpack the aims of profession level digital transformation, and explore how digital transformation manifests itself at different levels of a profession (summarized in Table 6.1).

DIGITAL TRANSFORMATION AS A STRATEGIC CHOICE VS. FORCED ADAPTATION TO DIGITAL DISRUPTION

Digital transformation involves planned strategic changes where professions continuously explore the use of new digital technologies to improve how they work, the value they deliver, and their service delivery models. In contrast, digital disruption typically involves professionals being forced to change in ways they may not want or agree with, after digital technology advancements have already changed

DOI: 10.1201/9781003606604-9

TABLE 6.1
Examples of How Digital Transformation Manifests at Different Levels of a Profession

Level of Profession	Manifestation	Examples
Professional Services/Business Models	Shift to platform-enabled, outcome-focused, or subscription-based models.	Law firms offering AI-enhanced fixed-fee services.
Professional Roles, Processes, and Activities	Automation of routine tasks, integration of AI tools, and adoption of new digital workflows.	Radiologists using AI for preliminary screening; educators using LMS tools.
Professional Governance and Accreditation	Movement towards dynamic credentialing, real-time CPD monitoring, and data-informed regulatory oversight.	CPD systems that track competencies via blockchain-based learning records.
Public Trust and Societal Confidence	Increased demand for transparency, ethical AI use, and demonstrable human oversight in tech-enabled services.	Use of explainable AI in healthcare or finance to maintain public trust.

professional work (e.g., see Bharadwaj et al., 2013; Vial, 2019). The key difference is timing and choice: digital transformation happens when professions choose to proactively change before they have to, and to positively shape the change, while digital disruption happens when they are forced to change to survive (Christensen et al., 2015). Typically, professions that proactively transform and do it early get better results than those that wait. For example, radiology departments that started using AI to help read medical scans in 2018 can now complete this work 40% faster, giving doctors more time for complex cases that need human expertise (see Health Imaging, 2025). In contrast, many small law firms only started using digital tools for document review after courts required electronic filing. These firms now struggle to compete with new legal service companies that were built around digital technology from the start (see KPMG, 2024).

To shift from reactive responses to proactive digital transformation, professions need to develop capabilities for scanning new technologies and understanding their implications, experimenting with them safely, and continuously expanding how they are leveraged to offer better stakeholder value (e.g. Busulwa & Evans, 2021). This changes technology from being seen as a threat to being seen as a tool for professionals staying relevant and competitive.

Digital transformation as a strategic choice vs. Forced adaptation

Professions face a critical decision: embrace digital transformation as a strategic opportunity to enhance their value and relevance, or wait until external forces make adaptation not only a matter of survival but also one where the odds of survival are significantly reduced or survival comes with significant costs. Several key factors distinguish professions that embrace digital transformation as a strategic choice versus those that turn a blind eye to digital disruption, accept digital disruption but move glacially, or deny the significance and speed of digital disruption. The most significant differentiator is leadership quality (e.g. proactive, strategic leaders who can effectively engage members and devise/execute the right strategies), with forward-thinking professional bodies and educational institutions driving early adoption through strategic vision and resource allocation (e.g. see Westerman et al., 2014). Regulatory flexibility is also crucial—professions with adaptive governance structures can experiment with new technologies more readily than those constrained by rigid compliance frameworks (e.g. see Susskind & Susskind, 2015). Financial stability further influences transformation readiness, as professions facing immediate financial pressures often lack the resources for long-term strategic investment compared to those with sufficient financial reserves (e.g. see Christensen et al., 2015).

These different approaches to digital technology advancements and digital disruption produce dramatically different outcomes for professions and their members. Proactive professions consistently achieve superior results compared to fence sitters and reactive adapters. For example, early-adopting medical schools that integrated AI training into curricula now produce graduates better prepared for technology-enhanced healthcare delivery, while institutions that delayed adaptation struggle with outdated programs (e.g. see Topol, 2019). Similarly, accounting firms that proactively developed data analytics capabilities captured high-value advisory roles, whereas those forced to digitize basic services now compete primarily on price (Busulwa & Evans, 2021). Professional bodies, professional service firms, education institutions, and professionals themselves can each play a profound role in determining which approach is at play for a profession.

Given these stark differences in outcomes, the critical question becomes how professional leaders can systematically identify and effect transformation opportunities before market pressures force reactive and often painful changes. Strategic frameworks for early opportunity identification include systematic and continuous scanning of technology changes and their implications for professions, systematic and continuous stakeholder expectation analysis, and systematic and continuous refinements to the profession's digital transformation strategy as well as the strategy's execution (e.g. see Busulwa & Evans, 2021; Teece, 2018). Profession leaders should establish innovation committees, engage with technology providers early, and create pilot programs that test emerging tools before competitive necessity demands immediate implementation.

Impact of Digital Transformation on the Institutional Legitimacy of Professions and Their Social Contract

Understanding how digital transformation affects professional legitimacy requires examining the fundamental relationship between professions and society. Professional legitimacy traditionally rests on society's trust that professions possess exclusive expertise, maintain ethical standards, and serve the public interest (Abbott, 2014). Digital technology advances and digital transformation potentially challenge this legitimacy by democratizing access to professional knowledge, for example through AI tools and online platforms, raising questions about whether traditional professional gatekeeping remains necessary or valuable (Susskind & Susskind, 2015). Digital transformation can also fundamentally reconfigure how professions create and demonstrate value to society. Rather than relying on episodic expertise delivered at specific moments, digitally transformed professions increasingly provide proactive, transparent, data-driven stewardship through continuous monitoring and real-time insights (Schildt, 2022). For example, AI-enhanced diagnostic tools allow doctors to detect diseases earlier and more accurately, while legal technology enables lawyers to provide faster, more cost-effective services—for example with explainable AI-generated insights (Topol, 2019; McGinnis & Pearce, 2019).

To maintain their social contract while fundamentally changing their practices, professions' leaders must ensure they address three key priorities. First, they must develop clear ethical guidelines and monitoring systems that ensure the digital tools being used enable upholding of core professional values like competence, confidentiality, and putting clients' interests first (Gegenhuber et al., 2022). Without clear ethical guidelines for digital tools and workflows, professions risk losing public trust when use of these digital tools and workflows results in violation of public interests (e.g. through biased or even dangerous advice, breach of client privacy/confidentiality, supporting bad actors), potentially leading to regulatory intervention and loss of self-governance privileges. Second, they need to involve the public by being open about the professional issues technology is creating, by communicating how they are regulating professional use of technology, and by asking for public input on new digital services—to show they remain accountable to what the public expects. Failing to involve the public in technology decisions risks creating a disconnect between what professions offer and what society expects, potentially resulting in reduced public support and legitimacy. Third, professions need to create ongoing review processes where different groups—including students, practitioners, educators, and the public—can regularly assess new technologies and ensure they continue to serve society well. (Brynjolfsson & McAfee, 2014). Without ongoing review processes, professions risk adopting the wrong technologies, using the right technologies the wrong way, or offering new digital or digitally enhanced services not needed by the public or offering them in ways that gradually erode professional effectiveness or ethical standards—potentially leading to loss of professional relevance and public confidence.

KEY AIMS OF DIGITAL TRANSFORMATION

Having established what digital transformation means for professions and its impact on professional legitimacy, we now examine the specific aims of professional digital transformation efforts. Unlike the reactive responses characteristic of digital disruption, strategic digital transformation generally pursues seven interconnected aims that collectively reshape how digitally transformed professions operate and create value. These aims range from immediate operational improvements through efficiency breakthroughs to fundamental changes in professional identity and competitive positioning (see Table 6.2). Understanding these aims can help students prepare for digitally transformed professional careers, guide educators in their curriculum

TABLE 6.2
Example Aims that Guide and Motivate the Digital Transformation of Contemporary Professions

Aim	Explanation	Illustrative Examples
Achieving efficiency and effectiveness breakthroughs	Leveraging digital tools to streamline workflows, reduce costs, and improve service speed and accuracy.	AI-assisted medical diagnostics; real-time automated financial reporting.
Enhancing existing or creating new digital services	Delivering new value through services that are fully or partially digitally enabled.	Virtual legal consultations; interactive digital tax planning tools.
Embracing new digitally enhanced roles and workflows	Redesigning professional tasks and structures to integrate automation, data, and collaboration technologies.	Accountants shifting from compliance to data strategy advisory roles.
Cultivating new professional competencies	Equipping professionals with digital, data, and transformation skills required in a tech-rich work environment.	Competency frameworks updated to include cybersecurity, data literacy, and digital ethics.
Co-creating new or augmented professional identity	Reconstructing how professionals perceive and present their roles in a digital society.	Teachers transitioning from content deliverers to digital learning facilitators.
Maintaining or enhancing professional legitimacy and societal value	Ensuring that professions continue to serve the public good and uphold trust in a digitally transformed context.	Use of transparent, accountable AI in law and healthcare to uphold ethical standards.
Ensuring future relevance and sustainability of the profession	Supporting long-term survival, adaptability, and continued societal contribution of the profession.	Engineering bodies investing in AI-guided design and climate-resilient systems.
Enabling ecosystem integration and interprofessional collaboration	Supporting collaboration across disciplines and seamless operation in digital ecosystems.	Healthcare teams integrating AI tools, remote diagnostics, and cross-disciplinary input.

development efforts, assist practitioners in planning for new digital or digitally enhanced products/services, enable strategic leaders to design comprehensive transformation strategies, and provide researchers with future research directions in relation to profession digital transformation strategies and their impacts.

Achieving Efficiency and Effectiveness Breakthroughs

One of the primary aims driving transformation efforts is achieving significant efficiency and effectiveness improvements, such as streamlining repetitive tasks, enabling real-time data-driven decision-making, and fostering seamless, global collaboration. Digital transformation enables professions to reduce costs and improve speed—for example, by enabling leveraging of digital technology platforms and tools for automation of routine tasks, enhanced data collection and analytics capabilities, and streamlined workflows that move service delivery from episodic or "one-off" engagements to providing services continuously, using technology for real-time monitoring and support, and providing real-time/on-demand/any-device and personalized communication (e.g., see Davenport & Ronanki, 2018). For example, generative AI tools now reduce first-pass contract preparation time by 60% in early-adopter law firms, while AI-assisted continuous audit systems can cut substantive testing hours by up to 40% compared to traditional quarterly sampling methods (Thomson Reuters, 2025; Zhang & Vasarhelyi, 2022). Traditional inefficiencies that digital transformation enables professionals to address include manual document review, repetitive analytical tasks, and time-consuming hand-offs between different stages of professional work that previously stretched processes across days or weeks (McKinsey & Company, 2025a). Breakthrough gains extend beyond simple cost savings to include 25% faster or professional service project completion times and higher client experience scores—demonstrating that efficiency improvements can enhance rather than compromise service quality (Boston Consulting Group, 2025).

Effectiveness wise, digital transformation enables breakthroughs by allowing professionals to access and analyze vastly larger datasets than previously possible, leading to more accurate diagnoses, better legal precedent identification, and more comprehensive risk assessments (Topol, 2019). AI-powered pattern recognition can identify subtle trends and correlations that human analysis might miss, enabling earlier disease detection in healthcare, more precise legal case strategies, and more accurate financial forecasting (Davenport & Ronanki, 2018). Real-time data processing allows professionals to make decisions based on current rather than historical information, improving treatment outcomes, legal advice relevance, and financial recommendations (Brynjolfsson & McAfee, 2014). Additionally, digital tools enable personalized professional services at scale, allowing lawyers to tailor contracts to specific client needs, doctors to customize treatment plans based on individual patient data, and educators to adapt learning experiences to student requirements.

However, achieving these efficiency and effectiveness gains requires careful implementation of "human-in-the-loop" checkpoints (specific points in a digital workflow where a human professional must review, verify, or approve the output from an AI system before it moves to the next stage or is delivered to a client) and governance structures (e.g. mandating that all AI-generated diagnostic suggestions must be reviewed by a licensed physician). Professions must establish clear protocols for when human oversight is required, maintain quality assurance processes that verify automated outputs, and align performance metrics to speed, quality and ethical compliance (Wilson & Daugherty, 2018). The risk of prioritizing efficiency over accuracy and ethical compliance is the potential to undermine professional credibility and erode client/public trust—making it essential that breakthrough gains support rather than replace the fundamental judgment and expertise that professions provide to society.

Creating New Digital or Digitally Enhanced Services and Value

Beyond improving existing services, digital transformation enables professions to create entirely new service offerings that were previously impossible or impractical without the latest technology. These breakthrough services leverage digital technologies' unique capabilities to address stakeholder existing and new needs that traditional professional services could not meet (Vial, 2019). For example, "hospital-at-home" programs now allow clinicians to provide intensive medical monitoring and care in patients' homes using digital devices, achieving 30% lower readmission rates compared to traditional hospital stays (World Economic Forum & Boston Consulting Group, 2024). Architecture firms now offer virtual reality walkthroughs that allow clients to experience and modify building designs before construction begins, while forensic accountants use blockchain analysis to trace cryptocurrency transactions across global networks—services that were impossible without the digital technologies being leveraged (Russell, 2025). Similarly, digital twin technology (computer models that mirror real-world objects) allows engineers to simulate earthquake impacts on infrastructure and it allows teachers to create personalized learning environments that adapt to individual student progress in real-time (Toobler, 2025).

Digitally native professional services typically differ fundamentally from traditional offerings in that value is often delivered continuously, based on real-time data, and priced on subscription or outcome basis rather than hourly billing (Susskind & Susskind, 2015). Instead of episodic consultations, these services provide ongoing engagement and predictive insights. For instance, cybersecurity firms now offer continuous threat monitoring with instant response protocols, while traditional security consultants previously conducted periodic vulnerability assessments, and financial planners provide algorithm-driven portfolio rebalancing that responds to market changes within minutes rather than or in addition to quarterly review meetings (Brynjolfsson & McAfee, 2014).

Professions are employing a range of tools or methods to identify new digital and digitally enhanced product/services and value, for example "evidence-based imagination"—systematically mining transaction data for friction points, then using design thinking combined with data analytics to test solutions rapidly (Chhabra & Williams, 2019). Other tools/methods include Jobs-to-Be-Done interviews (structured conversations that uncover what clients are really trying to accomplish) to help identify unmet "jobs" that stakeholders need completed, pilot programs to test promising innovations before competitors enter the market, design thinking, and startup or corporate accelerators (e.g., see Busulwa et al., 2020; Fonstad, 2023).

Creating New Digital or Digitally Enhanced Professional Roles and Workflows

As digital disruption and digital transformation reshape service delivery, professional roles are evolving from single-discipline "doers"—such as nurses manually taking vital signs and documenting care—to hybrid "orchestrators" who steward data, AI systems, and ethical decision-making processes, managing automated monitoring systems while focusing on patient education and complex care decisions (Accenture, 2024). Many routine, repetitive, and data-intensive tasks are being automated, allowing professionals to focus on higher-order activities requiring judgment, creativity, and interpersonal skills (Wilson & Daugherty, 2018). For example, entry-level law associates now supervise AI review systems that pre-screen contracts, reducing first-read time by 65% and freeing humans for complex negotiation strategies (Thomson Reuters, 2025). Similarly, accounting staff are being redeployed as "insight translators" who validate automated outputs and craft narrative dashboards that help clients understand complex financial data, while AI platforms handle routine reconciliations and draft preliminary advisory reports (Business Insider, 2025). In healthcare, AI-powered triage systems assess patient symptoms and automatically direct simple cases (like prescription refills or basic health questions) to online pharmacy platforms or telehealth services, while routing more complex cases requiring human judgment to doctors and specialists, demonstrating how task reallocation elevates professional judgment rather than eliminating it (World Health Organization & International Telecommunication Union, 2024).

Workflows are being redesigned around strategic human-AI handoffs where digital systems capture structured data, algorithmic engines generate recommendations, and professionals apply contextual knowledge, empathy, and ethical filtering before final approval (Brynjolfsson & McAfee, 2014). This collaborative approach enables early adopters to complete professional services 20% faster—for example, finishing audits or legal cases more quickly—while achieving higher client satisfaction scores, because professionals can spend their time on activities that require human expertise (like strategic advice and relationship building) rather than routine data processing (The Australian Financial Review, 2025).

Successful transitions into digitally-enabled roles require structured support systems that help professionals learn new digital skills while maintaining confidence in their core professional values and purpose (Busulwa & Evans, 2021). Leading firms are currently pairing micro-credential pathways in areas like AI ethics and data analysis with protected "sandbox" rotations that allow professionals to practice new tools while maintaining their core professional duties and responsibilities. Mentoring circles and reflective practice approaches help professionals track their evolving competence while leaders use structured career development reviews to create new digital advancement pathways that honor traditional professional values while embracing technological capabilities (Susskind & Susskind, 2015).

Cultivating New Digital or Digitally Enhanced Professional Competencies

Digital competence now extends far beyond basic computer skills to encompass multiple interconnected areas: data literacy, digital collaboration, content creation, digital safety, and problem-solving, alongside critical competencies in AI literacy, responsible technology use, understanding the implications and limitations of different digital technologies for professional practice, and the practical ability to effectively use diverse digital tools and platforms in professional contexts (European Commission JRC, 2022; Busulwa, 2022; Busulwa et al., 2025). Employers rank analytical thinking (the ability to break down complex problems into smaller parts and examine evidence to make logical decisions), systems thinking (understanding how different parts of an organization or process connect and influence each other), and big-data fluency (the ability to work with large amounts of information to identify patterns and insights) as the fastest-growing professional needs, warning that 39% of today's skill sets will become obsolete by 2030 (World Economic Forum, 2025). For example, a social worker today needs to interpret data from multiple digital sources, collaborate through digital platforms, create digital case documentation, protect client information online, and solve problems using AI-powered tools while maintaining ethical standards (Davenport, 2018). However, 66% of managers report that recent graduates lack practical digital skills, revealing a significant gap between academic training and workplace requirements (Deloitte, 2025).

Professionals face the "T-shape" challenge: developing deep technical expertise in specific areas (like coding, data science, or AI) while maintaining broad digital literacy and ethical awareness across all technologies (Brynjolfsson & McAfee, 2014). The solution to the T-shape challenge is ensuring that professionals develop both broad knowledge and skills across many different technologies (the horizontal part of the T) AND deep expertise in specific technical areas relevant to their work (the vertical part of the T). For instance, a modern accountant might need broad knowledge of various digital tools—cloud computing, AI assistants, cybersecurity basics, data visualization—while also developing deep expertise in specific areas like advanced fraud detection analytics or automated audit systems. Tiered competency frameworks that progress from foundation level to specialist expertise help professionals understand clear career development pathways while ensuring everyone achieves basic digital fluency before pursuing specialized skills (e.g. see Busulwa, 2022; Busulwa et al., 2025b).

Some of the most effective professional competence cultivation approaches use blended, bite-sized learning that accommodates busy professional schedules. Micro-credentials (short certification programs focusing on specific skills) enjoy 97% endorsement from higher education leaders for improving job readiness (Coursera, 2024). Successful examples include Levi's eight-week machine learning bootcamp that successfully retrained non-technical staff for data roles, demonstrating that intensive, focused training can bridge skill gaps quickly (McDowell, 2021). Effective development pathways combine self-paced online courses, group projects, mentorship programs, and challenging work assignments that allow both beginners and experts to progress together. Professional organizations are integrating these approaches into continuing education requirements to keep workforces future-ready (Busulwa & Evans, 2021).

Co-creating New Digital or Digitally Enhanced Professional Identities

Digital disruption and digital transformation occurring across organizations, industries, and society compel professions, as part of each profession's digital transformation, to renegotiate their professional identity around a new blend of algorithmic fluency (understanding how to work with digital technologies like AI, data analytics/data science tools, robotics, IoT) and human judgment—fundamentally shifting the basis of professional credibility. Whereas traditional professional status has largely rested on exclusive knowledge and controlled access to expertise, credibility now also derives from effectively curating data, governing AI systems, and translating complex digital insights for stakeholders (Abbott, 2014). Teachers exemplify this identity tension as they navigate between their historic "sage on the stage" self-image and new roles as learning-experience designers, facilitators of AI-powered learning systems, and digital tool skill cultivators (e.g., see Crompton et al., 2024; Busulwa et al., 2025). Healthcare and legal professionals also struggle with how to behave professionally on social media and digital platforms, where it's harder to separate their personal and professional identities while maintaining client confidentiality and professional standards (Guraya et al., 2021).

To redefine identity constructively, some leading professional associations host open design workshops and multi-stakeholder forums that invite students, practitioners, clients, and policymakers to collaborate in crafting digital-era codes of conduct—such as guidelines for AI use in medical diagnosis, social media policies for lawyers, or data privacy standards for accountants—and developing new specialized roles within traditional professions, including AI ethicists in law firms, digital health coordinators in medical practices, and cybersecurity specialists in accounting firms (Susskind & Susskind, 2015). These participatory processes are proving effective for rebuilding professional identity by "bridging the digital gap" and giving those resistant to change a voice in shaping new identity narratives, thereby converting skeptics into advocates for evolved professional identities (Sun et al., 2025). For example, medical professional bodies have engaged in extensive consultations to understand how AI diagnostic tools should be integrated while preserving physicians' clinical judgment and patient relationship responsibilities (Topol, 2019).

Frameworks guiding the co-creation of new digital or digitally enhanced professional identities focus on preserving core fiduciary duties—such as competence, confidentiality, and serving the public interest—which remain key anchors of professional legitimacy (e.g. see Wilson & Daugherty, 2018). Elements needing adaptation include the symbols and workflows that demonstrate these duties, such as moving from paper signatures to blockchain-verified credentials or from face-to-face consultations to secure digital platforms. Professional rituals that create unnecessary complexity or delays can be retired, but the profession's moral purpose and evidence-based knowledge foundation remain central, ensuring continuity of public trust even as the tools, workflows, and professional self-concepts evolve (Brynjolfsson & McAfee, 2014).

Enhancing Professional Legitimacy and Public Trust Through Digital Excellence

Professional legitimacy today has been argued to live or die on *digital excellence*—the disciplined fusion of advanced tools with human expertise and ethical accountability. In medicine the American Medical Association's *Augmented Intelligence Principles* recast algorithms as instruments that *extend*—never supplant—clinical judgment, keeping physicians firmly accountable (AMA, 2025). Similar language now appears in law, engineering, and education codes, signaling a profession-wide pivot from *automation* to *augmentation*. However trust in professionals' augmented intelligence is greatly influenced by the extent to which digital reasoning is inspectable. For example, IFAC's *Public Trust in Tax 2024* survey found confidence in accountants increases when transparent e-filing platforms reveal calculation logic, helping citizens "see" professionalism in action (International Federation of Accountants, 2024). explainable-AI dashboards that translate complex algorithm logic into plain language that clients and stakeholders can understand; algorithm registers that disclose where, why, and under what safeguards AI systems are deployed; and independent audit trails that record data sources and decision pathways for accountability (National Academies of Sciences, Engineering, and Medicine, 2022). McKinsey & Company's *AI Trust Survey* (2025b) shows professionals or organizations implementing such measures are twice as likely to gain stakeholder confidence in AI outputs (McKinsey & Company, 2024). Many leading professional services firms now release quarterly Responsible-AI scorecards, providing profession boards, professionals, educators, students, and PhD researchers with live data on progress and remaining gaps (McKinsey & Company, 2025b).

Demonstrating that technology enhances rather than replaces professional judgment requires formal human-in-the-loop protocols where algorithms assist but licensed professionals retain final authority (Wilson & Daugherty, 2018). Veterinarians illustrate this approach by combining AI-assisted imaging with behavioral assessment to develop comprehensive treatment plans (Burti et al., 2024). Urban planners use AI-powered zoning models while maintaining citizen participation processes for final approvals (Lartey & Law, 2025). The breadth and depth of digital technologies leveraged, plus the extent and effectiveness to which transparency mechanisms, accountability frameworks, and human-centered protocols are used by professions constitute digital excellence—demonstrating to the public that professions have mastered the disciplined fusion of advanced tools with human expertise and ethical accountability. When professions achieve this digital excellence, they not only maintain but actually enhance their legitimacy and public trust, proving that thoughtful digital transformation of the professions strengthens rather than diminishes professional value to society.

Achieving Sustainable Competitive Advantage

Sustainable competitive advantage in the digital era comes from building dynamic capabilities (Teece, 2018). For professions, this means the ability to sense emerging technological opportunities (like identifying how AI can enhance diagnostic accuracy), to seize them quickly (by developing new competencies, service models, and workflows), and to reconfigure their expertise and resources faster than competitors—such as when the COVID-19 pandemic hit, some medical practices quickly reorganized their staff roles, converted physical consultation spaces into telehealth centers, and retrained doctors to provide effective remote care, while competitors closed or took months to adapt their traditional in-person models. An example of dynamic capabilities for law firms is their ability to rapidly integrate new legal technology platforms into legal workflows. An example for an accounting practice is their capacity to quickly adopt emerging blockchain auditing tools while maintaining client relationships. An example for a medical practice is their skill in implementing telemedicine platforms while preserving quality patient care. Professional organizations that direct approx. 8-10% of their revenue into ongoing exploration of optimal leveraging of digital technologies and data assets, and to related professional talent cultivation, have been argued to significantly outperform peers (Replicon, 2025). Leading professions are pairing proprietary data collections with specialized digital tools (e.g. algorithms, software) to create switching costs and knowledge advantages that late adopters struggle to replicate (e.g., see Weill & Woerner, 2015). For example, psychologists and therapists who develop comprehensive databases of treatment outcomes combined with AI-assisted therapy protocols create defensible positions that generic mental health apps cannot match. Similarly, clergy and religious professionals who build digital platforms combining spiritual guidance with community analytics develop unique value propositions that purely technological solutions cannot replicate.

Sustainable advantage increases when professions embrace platform thinking—orchestrating multi-sided ecosystems where clients, technology partners, educators, and regulators collaborate to create shared value rather than selling individual services (Gawer & Cusumano, 2014). Professional bodies can create platforms that draw multiple stakeholders into standards-based marketplaces that continuously improve while cementing the profession's central role (Boston Consulting Group, 2025). Surveyors, for instance, can develop platforms connecting property developers, architects, engineers, and regulatory bodies, positioning themselves as essential ecosystem coordinators. Such platforms can benefit from network effects where every new participant increases the platform's value for all users, creating barriers to entry that protect competitive advantage.

HOW THE DIGITAL TRANSFORMATION OF PROFESSIONS MANIFESTS AT DIFFERENT LEVELS

Transformation of Professional Roles and Activities

Digital technologies are fundamentally reshaping professional roles and activities by automating routine, repetitive activities, while enabling professionals to focus on complex analysis, relationship building, and strategic decision-making. However, this transformation is also leading to organizational restructuring and workforce reductions, particularly affecting traditional entry-level roles that previously provided career pathways for new professionals. Artificial intelligence in particular has been shown to automate tasks and shrink entry-level roles, requiring new graduates to operate at higher levels in order to enter the workforce (Deloitte, 2025). Additionally, professional job advertisements increasingly emphasize digital technology skills alongside traditional professional knowledge, requiring candidates to combine domain expertise with competencies in digital technologies (e.g., AI tools, data analytics, ERP systems, and digital collaboration platforms). These surface-level changes represent a fundamental shift from professionals executing tasks manually to orchestrating digital systems that enhance their capabilities and extend their reach (Brynjolfsson & McAfee, 2014).

Building on research into digital disruption and digital transformation, Busulwa and Evans (2021) identify six key ways professional roles and workflows are being digitally transformed. First, the volume, variety, and velocity of data available to professionals have expanded exponentially, enabling access to continuous streams of real-time information rather than periodic snapshots or just profession specific datasets (Busulwa & Evans, 2021). Second, the tools of work are being fundamentally recast, as new tools like AI-powered assistants, digital platforms, and machine learning systems replace traditional manual methods and provide enhanced decision support (Busulwa & Evans, 2021). Third, these enhanced tools enable entirely new forms of value creation, allowing professionals to offer, for example, predictive analytics, continuous monitoring, and personalized services at scale (Busulwa & Evans, 2021). Fourth, the optimal ways of working are changing, with digital systems often handling routine processing and escalating complex cases to human experts (Busulwa & Evans, 2021). Fifth, new digital or digitally enhanced competencies are required of professionals to use the new digital tools. Finally, professional impact increasingly depends on orchestrating workflows across multi-stakeholder ecosystems rather than working as isolated experts (Gawer & Cusumano, 2014).

Transformation of Professional Services Business Models

The digital transformation of professions is resulting in fundamental changes in how professional firms make money and operate, leading to five main shifts. First, there is a move towards subscription and outcome-based pricing. Instead of charging by the hour, firms are offering predictable monthly fees for ongoing services. This better aligns their goals with client needs, as seen in reports like the Deloitte (2024) analysis. Second, firms are becoming platform orchestrators. Think of them like digital marketplaces where clients can easily find services, access templates, and connect with professionals through one integrated online system. This allows firms to grow by connecting more users, much like how social media platforms gain value as more people join (Harvard Business School Online, 2024). Third, professional knowledge is being "productized." This means turning years of experience and methods into easy-to-use software products that clients can license directly. This creates repeatable, high-profit revenue streams and frees up professionals to focus on the truly complex, human-centered tasks (Vecteris, 2024). Fourth, hybrid human-AI delivery models are becoming common. Here, AI handles repetitive tasks like data analysis, while human professionals focus on interpreting information, building relationships, and making ethical decisions (Wilson & Daugherty, 2018). Lastly, service engagements are moving from one-off projects to continuous, data-driven monitoring relationships. This transforms professionals from occasional consultants into "always-on" advisors, using real-time data to provide ongoing guidance (MindBridge, 2025).

These changes significantly alter how firms price their services, how much they can scale, and how they deliver value. Fixed subscriptions and usage fees are replacing hourly billing. AI allows even smaller firms to serve clients globally without geographic limits (Brynjolfsson & McAfee, 2014). Digital platforms lower the extra cost of serving each new client, meaning firms can offer automated basic services alongside premium, tailored advice. Professionals can also manage many more clients thanks to automated routine tasks, while still offering personalized insights using data analytics (Busulwa & Evans, 2021). Leading firms manage the challenge of standardizing digital processes while keeping services personal through modular service designs. This means they use clear, automated digital "cores" for speed and consistency. On top of this, they add flexible layers that allow relationship managers to customize how they use data, communicate, and give recommendations to fit each client's specific situation (Vecteris, 2024). By doing this, firms can gain the efficiency benefits of digital standardization without losing the personal touch and deep professional judgment that clients expect and value (Topol, 2019).

Transformation of Professional Governance and Regulation

Digital technologies are forcing professional regulators to rethink everything from entry-level licensing to day-to-day oversight. Five key shifts currently dominate discussions. First, many boards are baking digital-competency standards into the right to practice; for example, the Law Society of New South Wales in Australia now tests graduates on e-discovery software, and comparable moves are appearing in medicine and engineering (Verhoef et al., 2021). Second, oversight is becoming risk-based: for example, regulators are classifying AI tools by their potential for harm and setting usage rules that match that risk. This approach, where more powerful or impactful systems (like AI systems) face stricter scrutiny, mirrors long-standing drug-safety regulations with different tiers of risk based on potential patient impact (Kraus et al., 2021). Third, professional codes of conduct now embed explicit digital-ethics rules; for example, the American Medical Association requires physicians to check algorithms for bias before deployment, aligning digital use with equity obligations (Zaidan & Ibrahim, 2024). Fourth, traditional confidentiality clauses are expanding into stringent data-protection mandates so that cloud workflows meet privacy law and professional confidentiality simultaneously (United Nations Commission on International Trade Law, 2019; Lynn et al., 2021). Fifth, inspection is shifting from annual audits to real-time supervision: for example, continuous-monitoring dashboards alert accounting bodies the moment an anomaly appears, replacing reactive spot checks with proactive risk management (Hanelt et al., 2021). Many jurisdictions add a sixth, cross-cutting element—collaborative governance-by co-designing rules with technology firms and public advocates to keep pace with rapid innovation (De Almeida et al., 2021).

Accreditation bodies are likewise broadening their mandate. They are writing digital skills into core curricula, partnering with EdTech and other technology vendors to co-create training, and revising continuing-professional-development so practitioners refresh competencies every renewal cycle (Papagiannidis et al., 2020). Several accreditation bodies host "regulatory sandboxes" that let universities, start-ups and practitioners trial AI applications under controlled conditions, generating evidence regulators can fold back into standards (Hanelt et al., 2021). Others accredit third-party auditors of AI systems, expanding assurance capacity without over-stretching internal staff (Taeihagh, 2021). Balancing heritage with change hinges on separating immutable principles from mutable mechanisms. For example, integrity, competence, and the primacy of the public interest remain non-negotiable, but the means of demonstration—such as data-lineage logs and version-controlled algorithms—evolve continuously. The transformation of professional governance hinges on balancing stability and innovation: institutions protect public trust by preserving core values in high-level statutes, while frequently updating technical guidelines for digital practices. This allows members the necessary regulatory freedom to experiment with, iterate, and expand digital services that were unfeasible under prior, less adaptable rule-making.

Transformation of Public Trust and Social Contract

Digital tools are fundamentally changing the relationship and social contract between professions and the public. A 2024 Pew study highlights this mixed impact: while 74% of patients valued tele-consultations for convenience, only 38% trusted AI-generated legal advice to be unbiased (Pew Research Center, 2025). This shows that digital transformation can either build or break public trust. Today, citizens expect more than just technical skill; they demand digital fluency and ethical innovation, wanting assurance that services are inclusive, explainable, and protect their privacy (European Commission, 2024). Professional organizations are responding by adding duties of digital competence and rules about algorithmic fairness to their codes of conduct (American Medical Association, 2025). Achieving trust in digitally transformed professional practices relies on three interconnected elements: transparency, accountability, and ethics. Transparency means showing how digital tools arrive at their conclusions. This is done through "model cards" (summaries of AI systems), simple explanations, and clear statements about how data is handled, allowing clients to understand the algorithms at work (McKinsey & Company, 2024). Accountability is maintained through "human-in-the-loop" systems. For instance, UK radiologists must personally approve every abnormality flagged by AI, with their signature and the AI's confidence score recorded in an unchangeable audit log (Royal College of Radiologists, 2024). Digital ethics becomes concrete through independent third-party audits. The International Federation of Accountants' draft "algorithm-ready" audit standard requires external checks of the data used to train AI and how its performance changes over time (International Federation of Accountants, 2024).

Professions can help advance society's digital evolution without losing their unique value by acting as trusted translators. For example, accountants can share open tax dashboards that simplify complex financial AI, while still offering personalized judgment on tricky "grey-area" cases. Engineers can release city-wide "digital twins" (virtual models of cities) under open licenses, letting communities test green-space ideas, but professionals still provide the final safety sign-off. Teachers can pilot AI literacy coaches in schools and openly share results, showing how to adopt technology effectively and ethically. In each case, professionals "open the black box" of technology for citizens, but they reserve the crucial work of interpretation, relationship-building, and ethical decision-making that justifies their licensure. By blending unchanging values like integrity, competence, and public interest with flexible digital practices, professions can show that mastering algorithms strengthens, rather than weakens, the trust that underpins their legitimacy.

Transformation of Professional Identity and Value

Digital transformation does more than just automate tasks—it actively redefines who professionals are and why society values them. Professional identity—the way people understand who they are as members of a profession and what roles, responsibilities, values, and behaviors that membership entails (Ellis & Hogard, 2020; Ibarra, 1999)—is shifting along three key areas. First, the idea of a knowledge-gatekeeper (someone who controls access to information) is changing into that of a data-steward and translator. For example, radiologists once primarily focused on individually reading images; today, they manage large collections of patient images, check the accuracy of AI tools that help sort cases, and explain complex AI findings to other doctors and patients (Royal College of Radiologists, 2024). Second, the craft-centric solo expert is becoming an orchestrator of hybrid intelligence. This means leading lawyers now oversee AI tools that screen legal clauses, guide tailored document rewrites using AI, and then apply their unique negotiation skills. They are blending machines' ability to spot patterns with human judgment (Ford & Ashkenazy, 2024). Third, the locally focused advisor—a professional whose work, client base, and reputation are tied to a specific geographic community—is evolving into an omnichannel relationship manager—a professional who orchestrates client or stakeholder interactions seamlessly across *all* available channels—face-to-face, video, phone, email, chatbots, mobile apps, data dashboards, even social media. Teachers, for instance, now combine their in-person coaching with AI-powered literacy bots that send parents daily updates on their child's progress. This makes the teacher's role part mentor and part data-driven sentiment analyst (OECD, 2025).

As professional identity evolves, so does the very definition of "value." Clients are increasingly rewarding continuous insight over one-time reports. For example, MindBridge's real-time audit streams flag financial anomalies daily, turning auditors into constant risk monitors rather than just annual inspectors (MindBridge, 2025). Predictive and personalized results are replacing backward-looking reports. For example, oncologists who can interpret AI-generated genetic risk scores get more referrals because they offer forward-looking guidance about a patient's future health (Maleki Varnosfaderani & Forouzanfar, 2024). Also, scalable, productized knowledge assets are becoming part of a firm's income. For example, KPMG's "Clara" audit platform generates high-profit licensing revenue, freeing up partners to focus on complex, exceptional cases (KPMG, 2024). Finally, transparent algorithmic assurance (proving how AI works) is now complementing traditional trust based on reputation. Things like "model cards" (descriptions of what a particular AI model is, where it came from, how well it performs, and when it should and shouldn't be trusted), open datasets, and independent checks for AI bias are now part of what clients expect and value (International Federation of Accountants, 2024).

Navigating these major shifts in professional identity and value requires a collective effort from an entire professional community. Leading professional bodies are using several strategies: they are issuing digital-competence badges that stand alongside traditional licenses, signaling new forms of authority; continuing professional development (CPD) providers are running "sandbox fellowships" where members can test new hybrid human-AI workflows under expert guidance; and "identity playbooks" are being created to document new success stories. These playbooks help students and early-career professionals visualize their future roles in the transformed professions. By securing timeless principles like integrity, public interest, and competence within agile digital practices, professions demonstrate that algorithms expand, rather than diminish, their inherent worth, strengthening a social contract that now highly values speed, inclusivity, and ethical transparency.

CONCLUSION

This chapter examines how digital transformation is reshaping professions, highlighting a shift, though uneven across professions, toward proactive, strategic engagement with technology rather than merely reacting to disruption. It distinguishes digital transformation from digital disruption by focusing on how professionals and organizations can proactively adopt digital tools to enhance, redesign, and innovate their work. Key changes include the automation and redistribution of tasks through AI and digital platforms; evolving tools and workflows; and shifts in professional values such as expertise, autonomy, and ethics. It discusses how professional identities are becoming more hybrid, combining diverse roles and skills, and becoming more individualized, with greater emphasis on flexibility and self-direction. It also discusses how client relationships are increasingly collaborative and mediated by digital systems. Education and career paths are adapting through micro-credentials, continuous learning, and alternative entry routes. The chapter also explores the evolving governance of professional work, particularly in regulating emerging technologies and ensuring ethical data use. Overall, it portrays digital transformation as a complex, ongoing redefinition of professional life.

DISCUSSION QUESTIONS

1. How is digital transformation conceptually different from digital disruption, and why is this distinction important for understanding professional change?
2. What are the key aims of digital transformation in the context of professional work and service delivery?
3. In what ways can digital transformation enable professionals to enhance, rather than replace, their core roles and relationships with clients or end users?
4. Why is it important for professions to actively shape digital transformation rather than simply adapt to it?
5. What challenges might arise when trying to integrate digital transformation at different levels of a profession (e.g., individual roles, service processes, governance, professional identity)?
6. How can professional bodies and accreditation institutions support the digital transformation of their professions?
7. What capabilities and mindsets do professionals need to develop in order to thrive in a digitally transformed professional landscape?

REFERENCES

Abbott, A. (2014). *The system of professions: An essay on the division of expert labor.* University of Chicago Press.

Accenture. (2024). *Technology vision 2024: Human by design.* Accenture.

American Medical Association. (2025). *Principles for augmented intelligence development, deployment, and use.* AMA. Retrieved from https://www.ama-assn.org/system/files/ama-ai-principles.pdf

Bharadwaj, A., El Sawy, O. A., Pavlou, P. A., & Venkatraman, N. (2013). Digital business strategy: Toward a next generation of insights. *MIS Quarterly, 37*(2), 471–482.

Boston Consulting Group. (2025). *GenAI tools in professional services.* BCG.

Brynjolfsson, E., & McAfee, A. (2014). *The second machine age: Work, progress, and prosperity in a time of brilliant technologies.* W. W. Norton & Company.

Burti, S., Banzato, T., Coghlan, S., Wodzinski, M., Bendazzoli, M., & Zotti, A. (2024). Artificial intelligence in veterinary diagnostic imaging: Perspectives and limitations. *Research in Veterinary Science, 175*, 105317.

Business Insider. (2025, March). Big Four bet on agentic AI that can "liberate" staff. Retrieved from: https://www.businessinsider.com/deloitte-ey-launch-agentic-ai-platforms-big-four-competition2025-3

Busulwa, R. (2022). *Navigating digital transformation in management.* Routledge.

Busulwa, R., Birdthistle, N., & Dunn, S. (2020). *Startup accelerators: A field guide.* John Wiley & Sons.

Busulwa, R., Birt, J., Gepp, A., & Oates, G. (2025b). Current state of Accountants' knowledge of digital technologies: Evidence from Australia and New Zealand. *Accounting & Finance, 65*(3), 2649–2664.

Busulwa, R., & Evans, N. (2021). *Digital transformation in accounting.* Routledge.

Busulwa, R., Pathiranage, N. W., & Pickering, M. E. (2025). Integration of critical digital technologies into hospitality and tourism curricula: Evidence from QS-ranked universities. *Journal of Hospitality and Tourism Technology.* https://doi.org/10.1108/JHTT-06-2024-0388

Chhabra, A., & Williams, S. (2019). *Fusing data and design to supercharge innovation—in products and processes. McKinsey & Company.*

Christensen, C. M., Raynor, M. E., & McDonald, R. (2015). What is disruptive innovation? *Harvard Business Review, 93*(12), 44–53.

Coursera. (2024). *Micro-Credentials Impact Report 2024.* Retrieved from: https://www.coursera.org/enterprise/resources/ebooks/micro-credentials-report-2024

Crompton, H., Edmett, A., Ichaporia, N., & Burke, D. (2024). AI and English language teaching: Affordances and challenges. British Journal of Educational Technology, 55(6), 2503–2529.

Davenport, T. H. (2018). *The AI advantage: How to put the artificial intelligence revolution to work.* MIT Press.

Davenport, T. H., & Ronanki, R. (2018). Artificial intelligence for the real world. *Harvard Business Review, 96*(1), 108–116.

De Almeida, P. G. R., dos Santos, C. D., & Farias, J. S. (2021). Artificial intelligence regulation: A framework for governance. *Ethics and Information Technology, 23*(3), 505–525.

Deloitte. (2024). *Pricing your as-a-service solutions.* Retrieved from https://www.deloitte.com/be/en/services/tax/services/pricing-your-as-a-service-solutions.html

Deloitte. (2025). *2025 Global Human Capital Trends: Closing the experience gap.* Retrieved from: https://www.deloitte.com/us/en/insights/topics/talent/human-capital-trends/2025/closing-the-experience-gap-through-talent-development.html

Ellis, R., & Hogard, E. (2020). Professional identity in the caring professions. *London: Routledge*. https://doi.org/10.4324/9781003025610
European Commission. (2024). *Proposal for a regulation laying down harmonised rules on artificial intelligence (AI Act)*. https://digital-strategy.ec.europa.eu/
European Commission Joint Research Centre. (2022). *DigComp 2.2: The Digital Competence Framework for Citizens*. Retrieved from: https://publications.jrc.ec.europa.eu/repository/handle/JRC128415
Fonstad, N. O. (2023). *Strategic value from digital innovations. MIT Center for Information Systems Research.*
Ford, C., & Ashkenazy, Q. (2024). The Legal Innovation Sandbox. *The American Journal of Comparative Law*, *72*(3), 557–600.
Gawer, A., & Cusumano, M. A. (2014). Industry platforms and ecosystem innovation. *Journal of Product Innovation Management*, *31*(3), 417–433.
Gegenhuber, T., Dobusch, L., & Kremp, P. A. (2022). Institutional perspectives on digital transformation. *Research in the Sociology of Organizations*, *83*, 1–17.
Guraya, S. S., Guraya, S. Y., & Yusoff, M. S. B. (2021). Preserving professional identities, behaviors, and values in digital professionalism using social networking sites; A systematic review. *BMC Medical Education*, *21*, 1–12.
Hanelt, A., Bohnsack, R., Marz, D., & Antunes Marante, C. (2021). A systematic review of the literature on digital transformation: Insights and implications for strategy and organizational change. *Journal of Management Studies*, *58*(5), 1159–1197.
Harvard Business School Online. (2024). Traditional vs. platform-based business models: 4 key differences. Retrieved from https://online.hbs.edu/blog/post/platform-based-business-models
Health Imaging. (2025, March 15). Generative AI increases efficiency and quality of radiology reports. Retrieved from https://healthimaging.com/topics/artificial-intelligence/generative-ai-increases-efficiency-quality-radiology-reports
Ibarra, H. (1999). Provisional selves: Experimenting with image and identity in professional adaptation. *Administrative Science Quarterly*, *44*(4), 764–791.
International Federation of Accountants. (2024). *Public trust in tax 2024: Latin America and beyond*. IFAC. Retrieved from *https://www.accaglobal.com/content/dam/ACCA_Global/professional-insights/public-trust-tax-2024/PI-PTIT-2024-GLOBAL-FINAL.pdf*
KPMG. (2024). *Three forces driving change in legal services*. KPMG International.
Kraus, S., Jones, P., Kailer, N., Weinmann, A., Chaparro-Banegas, N., & Roig-Tierno, N. (2021). Digital transformation: An overview of the current state of the art of research. *Sage Open*, *11*(3), 21582440211047576.
Lartey, D., & Law, K. M. (2025). Artificial intelligence adoption in urban planning governance: A systematic review of advancements in decision-making, and policy making. *Landscape and Urban Planning*, *258*, 105337.
Lynn, T., Mooney, J. G., van der Werff, L., & Fox, G. (2021). Data privacy and trust in cloud computing: Building trust in the cloud through assurance and accountability (p. 149). Springer Nature.
Maleki Varnosfaderani, S., & Forouzanfar, M. (2024). The role of AI in hospitals and clinics: Transforming healthcare in the 21st century. *Bioengineering*, *11*(4), 337.
McDowell, M. (2021, November 8). *Exclusive: Lessons from Levi's data science bootcamp. Vogue Business.*
McGinnis, J. O., & Pearce, R. G. (2019). The great disruption: How machine intelligence will transform the role of lawyers in the delivery of legal services. Actual Probs. Econ. & L., 1230.
McKinsey & Company. (2024). *Building AI trust: The key role of explainability*. McKinsey Digital. Retrieved from: https://www.mckinsey.com/capabilities/quantumblack/our-insights/building-ai-trust-the-key-role-of-explainability

McKinsey & Company. (2025a). *Superagency in the workplace: Empowering people to unlock AI's full potential.* McKinsey Digital. Retrieved from: https://www.mckinsey.com/capabilities/tech-and-ai/our-insights/superagency-in-the-workplace-empowering-people-to-unlock-ais-full-potential-at-work

McKinsey & Company. (2025b). *Insights on responsible AI: Global AI trust maturity survey.* McKinsey Digital. Retrieved from: https://www.mckinsey.com/capabilities/tech-and-ai/our-insights/tech-forward/insights-on-responsible-ai-from-the-global-ai-trust-maturity-survey

MindBridge. (2025). Continuous auditing: Real-time accountability with AI-powered decision intelligence. Retrieved from https://www.mindbridge.ai/blog/continuous-auditing-real-time-accountability-with-ai-powered-decision-intelligence/

National Academies of Sciences, Engineering, and Medicine. (2022). Human-AI teaming: State-of-the-art and research needs. Washington, DC: The National Academies Press. Retrieved from: https://www.amazon.com.au/Human-AI-Teaming-State-Art-Research/dp/0309270170

Papagiannidis, S., Harris, J., & Morton, D. (2020). WHO led the digital transformation of your company? A reflection of IT related challenges during the pandemic. *International Journal of Information Management*, *55*, 102166.

Pew Research Center. (2025). *How the U.S. Public and AI Experts View Artificial Intelligence.* https://www.pewresearch.org/

Replicon. (2025). *2025 professional services maturity benchmark.* Service Performance Insight.

Royal College of Radiologists. (2024). AI deployment fundamentals for medical imaging. Retrieved from: https://www.rcr.ac.uk/media/sbdhwnfl/ai-deployment-fundamentals-for-medical-imaging-2024.pdf

Russell, M. (2025, May 26). *Legaltech startups have raised over $1 billion this year—10 companies to watch. Business Insider.*

Schildt, H. (2022). The institutional logic of digitalization. In: *Digital transformation and institutional theory* (pp. 235–251). Emerald Publishing Limited.

Sun, X., Wang, H., & Qian, Y. (2025). Promote the digital transformation of traditional enterprise by resetting organizational identification. *Asia Pacific Journal of Management*, 1–27.

Susskind, R., & Susskind, D. (2015). *The future of the professions: How technology will transform the work of human experts.* Oxford University Press.

Taeihagh, A. (2021). Governance of artificial intelligence. *Policy and Society*, *40*(2), 137–157.

Teece, D. J. (2018). Business models and dynamic capabilities. *Long Range Planning*, *51*(1), 40–49.

The Australian Financial Review. (2025, August). How AI saves consultants lots of time (to do more work) https://www.afr.com/companies/professional-services/how-ai-saves-consultants-lots-of-time-to-do-more-work-20250731-p5mj9i

Thomson Reuters. (2025). *Generative AI in professional services report.* Thomson Reuters.

Toobler. (2025, March 20). *Top 7 digital twin consulting services in 2025. Toobler Blog.*

Topol, E. (2019). *Deep medicine: How artificial intelligence can make healthcare human again.* Basic Books.

United Nations Commission on International Trade Law. (2019). *Notes on the main issues of cloud computing contracts.* Retrieved from **https://uncitral.un.org/en/cloud/drafting%20a%20contract**

Vecteris. (2024). Ten key steps to standardize and scale professional services. Retrieved from https://www.vecteris.com/blog/ten-key-steps-to-standardize-and-scale-professional-services

Verhoef, P. C., Broekhuizen, T., Bart, Y., Bhattacharya, A., Dong, J. Q., Fabian, N., & Haenlein, M. (2021). Digital transformation: A multidisciplinary reflection and research agenda. *Journal of Business Research*, *122*, 889–901.

Vial, G. (2019). Understanding digital transformation: A review and a research agenda. *The Journal of Strategic Information Systems*, *28*(2), 118–144.

Weill, P., & Woerner, S. L. (2015). Thriving in an increasingly digital ecosystem. *MIT sloan Management Review*, *56*(4), 27.

Westerman, G., Bonnet, D., & McAfee, A. (2014). *Leading digital: Turning technology into business transformation*. Harvard Business Press.

Wilson, H. J., & Daugherty, P. R. (2018). Collaborative intelligence: Humans and AI are joining forces. *Harvard Business Review*, *96*(4), 114–123.

World Economic Forum. (2025). *The Future of Jobs Report 2025*. Retrieved from: https://www.weforum.org/publications/the-future-of-jobs-report-2025/

World Economic Forum & Boston Consulting Group. (2024, January 9). Transforming healthcare: Navigating digital health with a value-driven approach. Retrieved from: https://www.weforum.org/publications/transforming-healthcare-navigating-digital-health-with-a-value-driven-approach/

World Health Organization & International Telecommunication Union. (2024). *Implementation toolkit for accessible telehealth services*. Retrieved from: https://www.who.int/publications/i/item/9789240094161

Zaidan, E., & Ibrahim, I. A. (2024). AI governance in a complex and rapidly changing regulatory landscape: A global perspective. *Humanities and Social Sciences Communications*, *11*(1), 1–18.

Zhang, C. A., Cho, S., & Vasarhelyi, M. (2022). Explainable artificial intelligence (XAI) in auditing. *International Journal of Accounting Information Systems*, *46*, 100572.

7 Profession Digital Transformation Strategies

INTRODUCTION

Having discussed the aims of profession level digital transformation and its implications for professional roles, business models, governance, and public trust, this chapter addresses the flow on questions: How do professions effect this digital transformation, what roles do key profession stakeholders need to play, and how will professions know if they are succeeding in their digital transformation efforts? Digital transformation is not a passive wave to ride; it demands deliberate, well-crafted strategies that require strategic, iterative, and continuous execution. We begin by examining ten most common profession level digital transformation strategies—ranging from system-wide reskilling programs to emerging technology credentialing—that professions are deploying to build digital capacity and resilience. Next, we identify the key actors—from individual practitioners to professions' strategic leaders, to government bodies and technology providers—whose decisions and collaborations drive digital transformation. Finally, we turn to measuring success, introducing performance metrics, maturity models, and trust indicators that reveal whether transformation efforts are delivering intended outcomes. Concluding with core principles for designing future-ready professions, this chapter equips readers with a strategic lens to ensure that professions not only survive the digital age but thrive—continuing to deliver indispensable value to society.

DIGITAL TRANSFORMATION STRATEGIES AND APPROACHES

Successful digital transformation requires deliberate, well-defined strategies. Here, we explore a range of innovative approaches professions are using—from targeted skill development and agile policy frameworks to collaborative ecosystems and robust data governance. Each strategy is designed to address specific facets of the digital transformation of professions, ensuring that professions can proactively adapt, innovate, and maintain trust while delivering enhanced value in an increasingly digital, tech-rich future. Understanding these strategies is crucial for anyone involved in shaping the future of the professions.

System-wide Upskilling and Reskilling Programs

System-wide upskilling and reskilling programs represent coordinated profession-wide initiatives to systematically develop digital competencies across entire professional communities, shifting members from manual, outdated roles and workflows to technology-augmented roles and workflows. These programs contribute to a

DOI: 10.1201/9781003606604-10

profession's digital transformation by creating shared digital literacy baselines, facilitating knowledge transfer between early adopter members and mainstream practitioners, and enabling professionals to harness digital tools to improve service quality, efficiency, and innovation (e.g., see World Economic Forum, 2020). Professionals with sufficient digital competence represent the ultimate enabler of the digital transformation of professions, as without digitally fluent workforces, even advanced technologies remain underutilized.

Implementation of this strategy typically involves professional governing boards leading skills-gap analyses, partnering with academics and technology vendors to design modular courses, and integrating digital competency requirements into licensure renewal cycles through continuing professional development mandates (e.g., see Busulwa & Evans, 2021). For example, the Association of Chartered Certified Accountants has integrated data analytics and cybersecurity into its global qualification programs, enabling member firms to have the talent resources required to pivot to higher-value advisory services (ACCA, 2020).

Digital Competency Frameworks and Stackable Micro-Credentials

Digital competency frameworks define the specific digital skills, knowledge, and behaviors professionals need at various career stages, while stackable micro-credentials are bite-sized, verifiable qualifications for specific competencies that can be accumulated toward larger qualifications or competence levels. By keeping their competence frameworks for all career stages up to date with digital technology changes and having micro credentials addressing critical parts of those competence frameworks, professions are providing structured pathways for skill development that create a common language for digital skills across professions, help close emerging skill gaps at the rapid pace technology demands, and ensure workforce competencies continuously evolve with technological advancements (Vuorikari et al., 2022). Frameworks such as SFIA (Skills Framework for the Information Age) break down digital competencies into discrete levels—from foundational digital literacy to advanced expertise—enabling professionals to demonstrate competencies through rigorous assessment processes while maintaining flexibility for personalized learning journeys.

Implementation of this strategy typically involves professional governing boards or competency committees leading development or updating of customized frameworks that reflect technology changes as well as regulatory environments and client expectations, then partnering with accredited education providers—such as universities, MOOCs, or industry-recognized organizations—to develop stackable micro-credential programs mapped directly to framework competence areas and levels (e.g. see Digital Promise, 2024). Professional organizations can integrate these requirements into continuing professional development mandates, create badge registries for transparency and portability, and utilize senior "digital mentors" to guide cohorts through project-based assessments.

The Education and Training Foundation's Digital Teaching Professional Framework exemplifies successful implementation, providing structured competency development for further education of professionals through bite-sized training modules that offer digital credentials and support professional development pathways (Education and Training Foundation, 2023). Similarly, professional bodies across sectors are integrating digital competency requirements into talent management and performance reviews, demonstrating how systematic approaches to digital competence building enhance collective professional adaptability and competitive advantage of professions (Sánchez-Canut et al., 2023).

Regulatory Sandboxes and Policy Experimentation Zones

Regulatory sandboxes and policy experimentation zones create controlled environments where professionals can test digital innovations—such as AI audits, blockchain recordkeeping, or telehealth services—without immediately breaching existing regulations. In doing so, they accelerate learning and de-risk early deployment, while enabling professions to develop best practices before broad rollout (Digital Regulation Platform, 2024). These frameworks contribute to profession digital transformation by helping reduce regulatory uncertainty that often stifles innovation (Just et al., 2024), by creating dynamic feedback loops between innovators and regulators, and by informing development of agile, future-proof policies that keep pace with rapid technological change (OECD, 2023). Sandboxes allow regulators to base their regulatory response to innovations on results of live experiments, helping them make faster and better informed decisions on how to appropriately regulate new professional services and workflows (CGAP, 2020).

Implementation of this strategy typically involves professional regulatory bodies collaborating with government policymakers to define clear eligibility criteria, to establish time-boxed pilots with regular progress reporting requirements, and to create multi-stakeholder oversight committees including board members, consumer advocates, and technologists to review findings and issue interim guidance (Digital Regulation Platform, 2024). Successful pilots often result in updated regulations or no-action letters certifying approved practices as compliant post-study (West Virginia University, 2024). Singapore's Ministry of Health established the Licensing Experimentation and Adaptation Programme (LEAP) enabling community pharmacists to provide influenza vaccination services after additional training, demonstrating controlled expansion of professional scope through structured testing (Ministry of Health Singapore, 2024). Similarly, Utah's legal regulatory sandbox has enabled over 2,500 people to receive legal services from innovative delivery models, demonstrating how time-boxed experimentation can address access challenges while maintaining service quality (IAALS, 2024).

Open-innovation Ecosystems and Strategic Tech Partnerships

Open-innovation ecosystems are collaborative networks where professions work with external partners—such as technology companies, universities, startups, and other industries—to jointly develop new digital solutions, rather than creating them independently. And strategic tech partnerships are formal, long-term collaborations in which a profession and one or more technology providers pool resources, expertise, and funding to create tools or platforms tailored to professional needs. By leveraging external technical know-how—such as AI algorithms, blockchain security, or extended-reality interfaces—professions can accelerate innovation, reduce development costs through shared investment, and overcome "not invented here" resistance (Sassanelli et al., 2021).

Implementation involves professional associations establishing innovation committees that issue calls for collaboration—for instance, a nursing association inviting healthcare technology startups to develop patient monitoring apps. Partners then draft agreements specifying intellectual property sharing (such as joint ownership of software code), data protection measures (like anonymizing patient information), and ethical standards (ensuring AI algorithms are bias-free). Steering groups comprising professional representatives, technology executives, and user advocates oversee development—for example, doctors, software engineers, and patient representatives jointly evaluating a telemedicine platform (Multishoring, 2025). The International Telecommunication Union's Digital Innovation Ecosystems program demonstrates this approach, connecting telecommunications professionals with software developers to create network optimization tools, while engineering bodies collaborate with environmental scientists to develop smart city monitoring systems (ITU, 2024). These partnerships enable professions to leverage external expertise while maintaining professional standards and ethical oversight.

Data-driven Governance and Member Analytics

Data-driven governance and member analytics empower professional bodies to base decisions on empirical evidence rather than intuition, transforming governance from reactive, process-focused models into proactive, insight-led approaches (Jo & Ahn, 2024). Data-driven governance involves systematically collecting and analyzing information such as continuing professional development participation, licensing metrics, and engagement data to enhance decision-making around professional standards, compliance monitoring, and strategic direction (De Reuver et al., 2018). Member analytics specifically focuses on analyzing data about members' digital engagement patterns, learning preferences, career progression pathways, and technology adoption behaviors to enable more targeted professional development initiatives (Shahbaznezhad et al., 2021). These analytical approaches contribute to profession digital transformation by enabling agile regulation, early identification of emerging ethical dilemmas or competency gaps, and ensuring initiatives being implemented by a profession precisely address members' evolving needs (Jobin et al., 2019). Organizations utilizing comprehensive data analytics for member engagement demonstrate significantly improved decision-making capabilities and resource allocation efficiency compared to those relying primarily on traditional feedback mechanisms (Shahbaznezhad et al., 2021).

Implementation of data driven governance and member analytics typically begins with governing boards establishing data governance committees or strategic analytics task forces responsible for designing comprehensive member data strategies (De Reuver et al., 2018). These committees identify relevant data sources including from customer relationship management systems, learning management platforms, event registrations, online forums, and digital engagement metrics—often partnering with cloud providers to build centralized data warehouses or member data lakes (Jo & Ahn, 2024). Dedicated analytics teams then develop interactive dashboards tracking key performance indicators such as engagement scores, renewal predictors, and continuing professional development completion rates, while establishing access controls to maintain member confidentiality and regulatory compliance (De Reuver et al., 2018).

There is evidence of the benefits of these implementations so far being promising (e.g., see CPA Australia, 2024). CPA Australia has developed comprehensive member analytics capabilities to assess digital skill proficiency and continuing professional development engagement, enabling more targeted educational programming and advocacy initiatives, as demonstrated in their integrated reporting approach (CPA Australia, 2024). The Engineering Council and affiliated professional engineering institutions maintain sophisticated continuing professional development tracking systems that monitor member engagement with digital learning modules and regulatory compliance requirements, enabling more responsive updates to competency standards and professional development frameworks (Jobin et al., 2019). Success in implementing data-driven governance requires ongoing investment in technological infrastructure, analytical capabilities, and staff training while maintaining strong ethical frameworks for member data protection and privacy (Jo & Ahn, 2024).

Sector-specific Digital-Ethics and Trust Frameworks

Sector-specific digital-ethics and trust frameworks are specialized sets of ethical principles, guidelines, and best practices tailored to address the unique risks and responsibilities that different professions encounter when integrating digital technologies into practice (Jobin et al., 2019). These frameworks explicitly address critical issues such as algorithmic bias, data privacy, accountability for AI-driven outcomes, transparency in automated decision-making, and the maintenance of human professional judgment in digitally augmented workflows (; Brookings Institution, 2019; Reisman et al., 2018).

Implementation of these frameworks typically involves leadership from digital-ethics task forces, convened by professional governing bodies, collaborating with regulators, technology developers, and stakeholder representatives (UNESCO, 2021). The process typically begins by mapping sector-specific digital risks, such as biased algorithms in healthcare diagnostics or unauthorized data access in telehealth platforms (Vayena et al., 2018). Task forces then draft comprehensive digital-ethics codes specifying requirements- for example, requirements for explainable AI in clinical decision-support systems or secure data-sharing protocols in infrastructure projects (Floridi et al., 2018). Profession entities have begun implementing such frameworks across diverse sectors. The American Medical Association released principles for augmented intelligence in December 2023, emphasizing transparency, oversight, and accountability in healthcare AI applications (American Medical Association, 2023). Multiple Canadian law societies have issued guidance on generative AI use, addressing technological competence, confidentiality, and bias mitigation requirements (Law Society of Alberta, 2023; Bennett Jones, 2024). The University of Leeds launched Engineering Ethics 2028, a ten-year plan to embed ethical considerations into engineering practice, particularly regarding climate change and public engagement (Baxter, 2020).

Member-centric Digital Service Platforms

Member-centric digital service platforms represent a strategic approach for professional organizations to enhance member engagement through user-friendly portals, mobile applications, and virtual communities that provide on-demand access to continuing professional development, mentoring, and peer support. These platforms place member needs at the center of service design, aiming to enhance engagement, streamline resource access, and foster community connections crucial for member retention and cultivation of new digital or digitally enhanced competencies (De Reuver et al., 2018).

Implementation of this strategy typically involves digital services teams conducting comprehensive needs assessments through surveys and focus groups to identify desired features such as CPD registration systems, discussion forums, and mentorship matching capabilities. They then select vendors or develop in-house solutions, prioritizing intuitive user experience design, mobile responsiveness, and secure authentication systems (e.g., see Shahbaznezhad et al., 2021). Following prototype development and testing by early adopters, platforms are launched then through promotional strategies including newsletters, social media channels, and regional events, while governing boards establish policies addressing content moderation, data privacy, and technical support. Digital engagement within professional communities serves multiple functions beyond information sharing, creating opportunities for sustained professional development and networking (Lane et al., 2024).

Many profession entities have implemented such platforms with promising results. The American Institute of Architects operates AIAU, a digital learning platform providing on-demand courses, networking opportunities, and certificate programs that received recognition from the American Society of Association Executives with a Power of Associations Silver Award in 2024 (American Institute of Architects, 2024). The Royal College of Nursing has invested in digital member services including online continuing education resources, professional development tools, and virtual networking opportunities to support their diverse membership base (Silverbear, 2021). These initiatives reflect broader trends where digital platforms serve strategic functions including accessible service delivery, strengthened community bonds, and comprehensive member support. Success requires ongoing measurement through analytics tracking engagement metrics while maintaining focus on user experience optimization and continuous platform evolution.

Blockchain-enabled Credentialing and License Verification

Blockchain-enabled credentialing leverages distributed ledger technology to create secure, immutable, and easily verifiable records of professional qualifications, including licenses, certifications, and continuing professional development credentials (Raimundo & Rosário, 2021). Unlike traditional paper-based or centralized digital systems prone to fraud, delays, and administrative burden, decentralized blockchain models empower both professional bodies and practitioners by enabling selective credential sharing while maintaining cryptographic verification capabilities (Turkanović et al., 2018). This approach strengthens public trust through transparency, prevents falsification, and accelerates global verification processes, particularly beneficial for internationally mobile professionals and cross-border practice recognition (Nguyen et al., 2020).

Implementation of this strategy typically involves professional regulatory bodies partnering with blockchain technology providers to establish permissioned ledger architectures (Raimundo & Rosário, 2021). Governing boards first define which credentials will be tokenized, such as initial licensure, specialty certificates, or continuing professional development badges, while ensuring compliance with regional data protection regulations (Turkanović et al., 2018). Blockchain infrastructure is then designed that maintains data privacy while providing shared cryptographic verification capabilities, often utilizing smart contracts to automate renewal processes when continuing education requirements are digitally verified (Nguyen et al., 2020). Several institutions around the world have leveraged this strategy to improve assurance of professional education, providing meaningful case studies for profession entities. The Massachusetts Institute of Technology pioneered blockchain diploma issuance in 2017, enabling graduates to share tamper-proof academic credentials with employers worldwide through their Blockcerts Wallet application, which utilizes Bitcoin's blockchain technology for verification (MIT News, 2017). In Canada, eCampusOntario has partnered with BCdiploma to implement blockchain-based micro-credential systems, enabling secure, portable digital credentials for continuing education and professional development programs across Ontario's postsecondary institutions (eCampusOntario, 2023). The University of Melbourne has similarly piloted blockchain credential verification systems, while Malta's Ministry for Education and Employment has tested distributed ledger technology for academic certification tracking (Jirgensons & Kapenieks, 2018). These initiatives demonstrate blockchain technology's capacity to enhance credential portability, reduce verification timeframes, and strengthen trust in digital certification systems across diverse regulatory environments (Nguyen et al., 2020).

Data-interoperability and Reporting-Standards Initiatives

Data-interoperability and reporting standards initiatives establish common taxonomies, data formats, and exchange protocols that enable digital systems across organizations and jurisdictions to seamlessly share professional data. By adopting established standards such as XBRL (eXtensible Business Reporting Language) for financial reporting, HL7 FHIR (Fast Healthcare Interoperability Resources) for healthcare records, and GRI Standards for sustainability metrics, professions can eliminate data silos, enable automated analytics, and support real-time decision-making (Health Level Seven International, 2023; XBRL International, 2023). This strategy helps drive profession digital transformation by ensuring that disparate platforms "speak the same language," reducing manual data re-entry and minimizing errors, expanding data availability, and accelerating cross-organization collaboration—thereby improving the quality of data and analytics related tools used by professionals.

Implementation of this strategy is typically led by the profession's standards committee or data-governance committee, often partnering with industry consortia and vendor coalitions. The process usually begins with a gap analysis to identify legacy data formats and reporting requirements. Next, committees select or adapt an interoperability standard, then draft implementation guidelines and mapping guides that translate local data fields to standard taxonomies (XBRL International, 2023). Professions then organize pilot implementations with willing member organizations to test data exchange between systems, such as transmitting audited financial statements from accounting practices to regulatory portals using XBRL tags. Training modules and developer toolkits help IT teams modify existing software for compliance, while conformance testing and certification processes ensure member systems validate against standards before full adoption (Health Level Seven International, 2023; XBRL International, 2009).

In financial services, XBRL has become the standard for structured business reporting, with approximately 6,000 public companies using the US GAAP Taxonomy maintained by the Financial Accounting Standards Board since 2010 (Financial Accounting Standards Board, 2019). In healthcare, HL7 FHIR uses modern web-based technologies including RESTful protocols to enable quick and efficient health data exchange, with organizations reporting improved data sharing capabilities and reduced duplicate diagnostic testing (Health Level Seven International, 2023). For sustainability reporting, the GRI Standards are used by over 10,000 companies from more than 100 countries, with 78% of the world's largest companies adopting these standards (Global Reporting Initiative, 2023; KPMG, 2022). The European Sustainability Reporting Standards achieved high interoperability with GRI Standards through collaboration confirmed in September 2023 (Grant Thornton, 2024). By institutionalizing data-interoperability and reporting standards, professions create unified data ecosystems that enhance transparency, support data-driven insights, and enable efficient collaboration across platforms and borders.

Digital-maturity Assessment and KPI Frameworks

Digital-maturity assessment frameworks and Key Performance Indicator (KPI) models provide professions with structured methodologies to evaluate current digital capabilities and competence levels, and to monitor progress towards execution of digital transformation strategies. These measurement and assessment frameworks represent systematic approaches to understanding professions' digital evolution, typically defining progressive stages from initial adoption of digital technologies to advanced digital integration across multiple dimensions of the profession (e.g., see Busulwa, 2022; Hanelt et al., 2021). Core assessment dimensions commonly include technology infrastructure in place, data management capabilities, digital competence levels, client/member digital experience, and innovation processes (Kane, 2019). By establishing baseline profession digital transformation maturity assessments, these frameworks illuminate profession strengths and gaps while fostering accountability for achieving strategic digital transformation goals. Complementing maturity assessments, KPI frameworks specify quantifiable metrics that measure execution success and return on digital investments, these in turn help guide resource allocation decisions and refinements of digital transformation strategy (e.g., see Singh & Hess, 2020). Examples of these metrics include digital tool adoption rates, digital product/service prevalence, member digital literacy progression, cybersecurity resilience indicators, and client/member satisfaction with digital services. Effective digital transformation requires systematic measurement approaches that align with digital transformation strategic objectives (Singh & Hess, 2020).

Implementing this strategy typically begins with profession leadership teams selecting appropriate maturity models suited to the profession and its unique context. Comprehensive surveys and focus groups are then usually undertaken with members and other stakeholders, generating data that highlight capability gaps and development priorities. Concurrently, leadership teams will lead the identification of specific KPI targets—such as achieving defined percentages of members completing digital competency certifications within specified timeframes or expanding the number and diversity of digital/digitally enhanced services offered. Interactive dashboards are usually developed to monitor these metrics, enabling real-time tracking of digital transformation progress (Li et al., 2018). The systematic implementation of digital-maturity assessments and KPI frameworks enables professions to develop data-driven digital transformation roadmaps. This approach allows governing bodies to identify quick wins, address capability gaps systematically, and maintain momentum toward developing future-ready professions that serve stakeholder needs effectively.

KEY ACTORS WHO CAN DRIVE DIGITAL TRANSFORMATION

While digital transformation strategy is often discussed in terms of technologies, products/tools, and strategies, its successful execution fundamentally depends on human agency. This section shifts focus to the diverse array of actors whose active participation is indispensable for driving and sustaining this profound change across professions. From the individual practitioner integrating new tools into daily work, to educational institutions shaping future talent, and regulatory bodies setting the governance framework, each actor plays a distinct yet interconnected role (see Table 7.1). Their collective engagement—or lack thereof—directly determines the pace, direction, and ultimate success of a profession's digital transformation, making understanding of these different actors and their roles of paramount importance.

Regulatory/Oversight and Advocacy Bodies

Regulatory and oversight bodies—such as national medical boards, accounting oversight councils, or legal licensing agencies—hold legal authority to set and enforce professional standards, license practitioners, and investigate misconduct,

TABLE 7.1
Key Actors and Their Example Roles in Enabling Profession Digital Transformation

Actor	Example Roles in Digital Transformation	Examples Initiatives Actors have taken
Regulatory / Oversight Bodies	Set and enforce digital competency and ethical standards; enable experimentation and innovation	Embedding AI-ethics in licensure; establishing regulatory sandboxes for telehealth or fintech experimentation
Professional Bodies	Define digital competencies, accredit programs, provide ethical guidance, issue micro-credentials	Issuing blockchain credentialing standards; integrating cybersecurity into CPD requirements
Universities / Education Providers	Deliver digitally infused curricula, provide lifelong learning, research digital transformation of the professions	Offering blockchain or AI ethics micro-credentials; embedding data analytics across degree programs
Professional Service Firms	Adopt and operationalize technologies; model best practices; invest in upskilling	Law firms using automated research tools; accounting firms upskilling staff in robotic process automation
Individual Professionals	Adopt digital tools; mentor peers; provide grassroots feedback and use-case innovation	Doctors piloting telemedicine; engineers refining BIM tools; teachers sharing tech-enhanced pedagogies
Students	Serve as early adopters and co-creators of new digital practices; influence curriculum and digital tool adoption	Nursing students pushing for use of VR simulations in curricula; law students pushing for integration of hackathons in curricula; students proactively contributing to digital curriculum design
Governments / Policymakers	Legislate ethical tech use, fund digital infrastructure, incentivize innovation	EU implementing AI Act; telehealth laws in Korea; fintech sandbox in Singapore
Technology Providers	Co-develop profession-aligned tools; provide support, training, and updates	Legal tech firms collaborating with tech firms on compliant AI platforms; technology vendors working with engineering firms to build digital twins
Advocacy Bodies / Unions	Represent member interests; lobby for digital inclusion and resourcing; negotiate vendor partnerships	Negotiating group software discounts; lobbying for digital CPD funding

thereby safeguarding the public interest (Abbott, 1988; Hanelt et al., 2021). Advocacy bodies—such as bar associations, nursing unions, or engineering societies—represent members' interests by providing resources, conducting research, and lobbying for favorable policies, even though they may lack direct licensing power. Together, these entities shape the external environment within which professions operate and evolve.

By updating standards to include digital competencies, establishing regulatory sandboxes, and funding innovation grants, these bodies can help accelerate digital transformation of the professions. For example, a medical board embedding AI-ethics requirements into licensure ensures clinicians adopt explainable-AI tools safely (Jobin et al., 2019). And advocacy associations can support digital adoption by collecting member input on technology needs, negotiating group discounts with software vendors, and providing profession-specific training programs that help practitioners integrate new digital tools into their daily work. (Parviainen et al., 2017). If regulatory or advocacy bodies fail to act, professions' digital transformation can stall, if it is able to even genuinely begin. Regulatory lag—when rules do not keep pace with technological change—creates uncertainty, stifles innovation, and allows digital risks such as unchecked algorithmic bias to emerge (Taeihagh, 2021). Without advocacy bodies championing policy changes and resources, practitioners lack guidance and infrastructure, resulting in fragmented adoption and persistent skills gaps. Ultimately, absent proactive oversight and advocacy, professions risk losing competitive footing and public trust in a rapidly digitizing world.

Professional Bodies

Professional bodies—such as the Institute of Electrical and Electronics Engineers (IEEE), the International Federation of Social Workers, and the Chartered Institute of Marketing—serve as collective custodians of professional standards, ethics, and public trust (Abbott, 1988; Vial, 2019). They define core competencies, accredit educational programs, administer licensure or certification, and oversee continuing professional development requirements, ensuring that members maintain the skills and ethical frameworks necessary for quality practice. These organizations also lobby for member needs, issue best-practice guidelines, and convene stakeholders to shape policy and resource allocation for the profession (Verhoef et al., 2021).

To support digital transformation of the professions, professional bodies can update competency frameworks to embed digital skills such as data analytics, digital ethics, and knowledge of established and emerging technologies into core qualifications and continuing professional development (Papagiannidis et al., 2020). They can endorse and issue micro-credentials that validate specific digital proficiencies, creating flexible upskilling pathways for members across diverse fields from engineering to social work to marketing. Professional bodies can also provide essential digital ethics and cybersecurity guidance—For example, international engineering associations develop and issue guidelines for autonomous systems design, which instructs practitioners on safety protocols and human oversight requirements (Jobin et al., 2019). They can host innovation sandboxes or knowledge-sharing platforms, they can enable members to experiment with digital tools collaboratively and share best practices, and they can take a diverse range of other activities to normalize technology adoption across different professional contexts globally.

Professional bodies are a critical driver of professions' digital transformation. If they fail to fulfill their role, this can result in outdated accreditation and continuing professional development requirements, it can leave graduates ill-equipped for their digital and tech rich future, widening digital skills gaps and diminishing the profession's relevance worldwide. If they fail to engage it can also result in absent or questionable guidance on emerging technologies use—exposing members and the public to unaddressed risks, eroding trust and professional credibility across international markets.

Education Providers

Education providers—including universities, colleges, and vocational institutions—deliver foundational knowledge, skills, and ethical grounding to future professionals across professions and geographies (Abbott, 1988; Verhoef et al., 2021). They design and get curricula accredited, ensuring graduates meet core competency standards, whether at South Africa's University of Cape Town, India's Indian Institutes of Technology, or Brazil's Universidade de São Paulo. By convening academic experts, industry practitioners, and regulatory bodies, they maintain academic rigor and practical relevance, sustaining a profession's human capital need and societal credibility.

Education providers can accelerate a profession's digital transformation by embedding digital competencies—such as data analytics, AI ethics, and cybersecurity—across all degree programs and subjects (Papagiannidis et al., 2020). For example, Mexico's Tecnológico de Monterrey offers micro-credentials in blockchain for business students, while Singapore's National University integrates AI ethics modules across engineering and medical curricula. Education providers can also deliver flexible lifelong learning—online courses, stackable certificates, and executive education—that upskills existing professionals, from Kenyan teachers learning e-pedagogy to German engineers mastering digital manufacturing systems (Jobin et al., 2019). If education providers do not participate in a profession's digital transformation, the profession's digital competence is likely to gradually become outdated. For example, if education providers don't engage in professions' digital transformation efforts, this can result in outdated curricula—producing graduates lacking requisite digital skills, creating talent mismatches and forcing costly retraining by employers. Without education providers' research on emerging technologies, professions may lack evidence-based guidance for ethical tool integration. And without education providers' collaboration with industry, misaligned graduate competencies may result—undermining the profession's collective capacity to innovate and eroding public trust in the profession (Vial, 2019).

Professional Services Firms

Professional services firms—including law practices, accounting firms, engineering consultancies, and healthcare clinics—are the primary entities through which individual practitioners deliver specialized services to clients (Verhoef et al., 2021; Wirtz & Daiser, 2017). These firms translate complex professional knowledge into practical solutions, manage client relationships, and often employ a significant portion of the professional workforce. Their importance lies in setting internal standards, mentoring junior staff, and shaping operational workflows that reflect and reinforce broader professional norms across diverse industries from legal services to engineering consulting.

Professional service firms can play a critical role in professions' digital transformation. For example, they can invest in and integrate cutting-edge technologies—such as AI-powered analytics, automation platforms, and collaborative cloud solutions—into their daily operations (Papagiannidis et al., 2020). A mid-sized engineering consultancy in South Korea, for example, might deploy digital-twin simulations to optimize infrastructure projects, while a large law firm in India might adopt AI-driven legal-research tools to accelerate case preparation. They can also invest in the development of digital competencies of professionals. For example, accounting firms in Brazil and the UK have established in-house digital training programs to upskill staff in data visualization and robotic process automation. Further, they can develop new digital or digitally enhanced professional services products.

If professional service firms don't adopt the latest tech, don't train professionals, and don't develop new digital services or products, the entire profession risks losing its authority and market position. When leading firms fail to offer required digital capabilities, clients may turn to technology companies or other professions that offer faster, more efficient solutions—such as legal tech platforms handling contract work or AI diagnostic tools competing with traditional medical consultations (Vial, 2019). This professional displacement may erode the profession's exclusive jurisdiction over its traditional domain of expertise. Additionally, regulatory bodies may respond to lagging digital innovation within professional services firms by allowing non-professionals to perform services previously restricted to licensed practitioners, fundamentally weakening professional status. Without unified digital leadership from major professional service firms, professions may lose their ability to shape how emerging technologies are integrated into practice, ceding control to external technology vendors and ultimately diminishing professional autonomy and public trust.

Individual Professionals

Individual professionals—such as doctors in Nigeria, teachers in Poland, lawyers in India, and engineers in Canada—are the frontline practitioners who apply a profession's specialized knowledge to serve clients and communities. They maintain professional standards, exercise judgment, and uphold ethical obligations (Susskind & Susskind, 2015). As the primary interface between technology and practice, their daily decisions determine whether digital tools are used effectively, safely, and responsibly. Without their engagement, advanced systems (e.g., AI diagnostics, virtual classrooms, automated contract analysis) remain abstract concepts rather than practical solutions.

To support their profession's digital transformation, individual professionals can act as change champions by adopting new technologies, providing user feedback, and mentoring peers. For example, a Nigerian physician pilot-testing telemedicine platforms can refine workflows and demonstrate patient outcomes; a Polish teacher integrating AI-driven lesson customization can showcase improved student engagement (Fitzgerald et al., 2014; Hanelt et al., 2021). By embracing change, sharing successes and lessons learned—via webinars, professional forums, or social media—individual professionals can help reduce resistance to change and accelerate collective adoption of new digital or digitally enhanced roles and tools. Professionals can also co-design digital workflows (such as e-filing systems for Indian attorneys or BIM tools for Canadian architects), ensuring tools meet practical needs rather than being misguided top-down mandates. Without grassroots participation, digital initiatives risk becoming siloed experiments; firms and institutions lose momentum, and clients migrate to more digitally proficient competitors. Ultimately, absent active engagement from individual professionals, professions lose their collective capacity to innovate and risk diminished relevance in an increasingly digital, tech-rich future.

Students

Students represent the future professional workforce and are critical stakeholders in a profession's digital transformation (Van Laar et al., 2017; Verhoef et al., 2021). As emerging practitioners, students bridge academic learning and professional practice, cultivating foundational knowledge and nascent digital competencies. Their role is essential because today's students will become tomorrow's professionals; their openness to technology and fresh perspectives can catalyze change within entrenched professional cultures. Students can advance digital transformation by serving as early adopters and co-creators of digital workflows. When students engage in project-based learning—such as law students using e-discovery platforms or nursing students training on virtual-reality simulators—they validate tool effectiveness, provide user feedback, and help refine pedagogy (Papagiannidis et al., 2020). Student-led hackathons and digital innovation clubs often generate prototypes that professional bodies can pilot. Furthermore, students' digital fluency enables them to collaborate with faculty and industry partners in research—for example research on ethical AI use, data analytics in practice, and tele-services design—bringing fresh perspectives to traditional professional challenges (Jobin et al., 2019; Van Laar et al., 2017).

If students are not empowered to engage with new and emerging digital tools, practices, and critical thinking, professions risk a widening skills mismatch. For example, graduates may lack practical experience with contemporary platforms—such as AI-driven legal-research tools or building information modeling for architects—forcing firms to invest in costly retraining rather than innovation. A lack of student participation in curriculum co-design and pilot programs may yield outdated learning outcomes, weakening the talent pipeline's readiness for digital challenges. Consequently, professions can face stagnation in their digital transformation efforts, eroded competitiveness, and diminished public confidence as incoming practitioners struggle to meet contemporary digital demands.

Governments and Other Policy Makers

Government and policy makers—including national legislatures, regulatory agencies, and local authorities in countries ranging from Germany to Ghana—create the legal and institutional frameworks that govern professional practice. They enact laws on data privacy, cybersecurity, intellectual property, and liability to safeguard public interest and set boundaries for ethical, secure digital practice. By investing in national digital infrastructure and funding research, they also influence the ecosystem in which professions operate, whether enabling telemedicine in rural Australia or incentivizing e-governance for legal services in Estonia (e.g. Lember et al., 2018).

To support professions' digital transformation, governments and other policy makers can draft forward-looking legislation and adapt existing regulations to accommodate new technologies. For example, South Korea's Ministry of Health and Welfare has developed various initiatives for telehealth services, including demonstration projects and regulatory frameworks to enable physicians to deliver remote care while upholding patient-data safeguards (Kim et al., 2015; Oh et al., 2015). Similarly, the European Union's AI Act provides a risk-based framework that guides legal, healthcare, and engineering professions in adopting AI responsibly (European Commission, 2021; Taeihagh, 2021). The AI Act categorizes AI systems into four risk levels—unacceptable, high, limited, and minimal—with proportionate regulatory requirements for each category (EU AI Act, 2024). Governments and other policy makers can further catalyze change through targeted incentives—such as tax credits for professional firms investing in AI tools—or by establishing regulatory sandboxes that allow controlled experimentation with digital services. Singapore's Monetary Authority, for instance, launched the FinTech Regulatory Sandbox in 2016, enabling financial institutions and fintech startups to test innovative solutions within a controlled environment with relaxed regulatory requirements (MAS, 2016; Chia, 2020).

Technology Providers

Technology providers—including global software vendors, niche start-ups, cloud infrastructure firms, and open-source communities—supply the digital tools, platforms, and services essential for modern professional practice (Yoo et al., 2010; Nambisan et al., 2017). Whether developing AI-powered diagnostic systems for hospitals in Singapore, legal research platforms for firms in South Africa, or virtual classroom environments for schools in Finland, these providers drive innovation by creating scalable, secure, and user-friendly digital solutions (Wirtz & Daiser, 2017). Their deep technical expertise and ongoing R&D investments enable professions to extend capabilities—transforming how services are delivered, from remote patient monitoring in Canada to blockchain-verified certification in India.

Technology providers can support digital transformation of professions by co-designing or customizing solutions with professional bodies and professional service firms to ensure domain-specific fit (Rai & Tang, 2010; Münch et al., 2022). For example, European engineering firms collaborate with software vendors to build digital twins for infrastructure planning, while Australian legal-tech start-ups work with bar associations to develop automated contract-analysis tools. Technology providers can also offer training, support, and updates, ensuring that new tools evolve with professions' regulatory and ethical requirements. By fostering "digital ecosystems"—where APIs, modules, and services interoperate—technology providers can underpin seamless workflows, enabling professionals to leverage data analytics, collaboration suites, and automation in fields as diverse as architecture and accounting (Hanelt et al., 2021).

CONCLUSION

This chapter outlined strategic approaches that professional bodies and stakeholders can adopt to guide proactive digital transformation within their profession. It presents a set of emerging strategies, such as system-wide upskilling, micro-credentialing, and the development of digital competency frameworks. The chapter also explores experimental tools like regulatory sandboxes, which allow limited testing of new policies in controlled environments. Emphasizing collaboration, the chapter highlights the importance of open-innovation ecosystems, strategic partnerships with technology providers, and data-informed governance to enhance transparency and responsiveness. Addressing ethical challenges through sector-specific digital trust frameworks is also discussed. The chapter further discusses the exploratory use of technologies like blockchain for credential verification and digital platforms for delivering services. A dedicated section examines the distinct roles of regulators, professional bodies, educators, professional service firms, individual professionals, and governments, stressing that their coordinated efforts are essential for maximizing the odds of success. Ultimately, the chapter argues that inclusive, strategic action is critical for professions to adapt, remain relevant, and meet evolving societal and competitiveness demands.

DISCUSSION QUESTIONS

1. How is digital transformation different from digital disruption, and why is this distinction important for understanding professional change?
2. What are the key aims of digital transformation in the context of professional work and service delivery?
3. In what ways can digital transformation enable professionals to enhance, rather than replace, their core roles and relationships with clients or end users?
4. Why is it important for professions to actively shape digital transformation rather than simply adapt to it?
5. What challenges might arise when trying to integrate digital transformation at different levels of a profession (e.g., individual roles, service processes, governance, professional identity)?
6. How can professional bodies and accreditation institutions support the digital transformation of their professions?
7. What capabilities and mindsets do professionals need to develop in order to thrive in a digitally transformed professional landscape?

REFERENCES

Abbott, A. (1988). *The system of professions: An essay on the division of expert labor.* University of Chicago Press.

ACCA. (2020). *The digital accountant: Digital skills in a transformed world.* Association of Chartered Certified Accountants.

American Institute of Architects. (2024). AIA receives 2024 Power of Associations Silver Award for online learning platform. Press release. Retrieved from https://www.aia.org/

American Medical Association. (2023). Principles for augmented intelligence development, deployment, and use. Retrieved from https://www.ama-assn.org/

Baxter, J. (2020). How ethical are you? Institute of Civil Engineering. Retrieved from https://www.ice.org.uk/news-views-insights/inside-infrastructure/how-ethical-are-you

Brookings Institution. (2019). Algorithmic bias detection and mitigation: Best Practices and policies to reduce consumer harms. Washington, DC: Brookings Institution Press.

Busulwa, R. (2022). *Navigating digital transformation in management.* Routledge.

Busulwa, R. & Evans, N. (2021). *Digital transformation in accounting.* Routledge.

CGAP. (2020). How to Build a Regulatory Sandbox: A Practical Guide for Policy Makers. Retrieved from: https://www.cgap.org/research/publication/how-to-build-regulatory-sandbox-practical-guide-for-policy-makers

CPA Australia. (2024). *Integrated Report 2024.* Retrieved from https://www.cpaaustralia.com.au/

De Reuver, M., Sørensen, C., & Basole, R. C. (2018). The digital platform: A research agenda. *Journal of Information Technology, 33*(2), 124–135.

Digital Promise. (2024). The role of micro-credentials in lifelong learning and development: Empowering learners, empowering organizations. Digital Promise.

Digital Regulation Platform. (2024). A case for ICT regulatory sandbox. Digital Regulation Platform.

eCampusOntario. (2023). *Free webinar: Benefits of issuing micro-credentials on a blockchain technology.* Retrieved from https://ecampusontario.ca/

Education and Training Foundation. (2023). *Digital teaching professional framework.* The Education and Training Foundation.

EU AI Act. (2024). *Regulation (EU) 2024/1689 of the European Parliament and of the Council of 13 June 2024 laying down harmonised rules on artificial intelligence.* Official Journal of the European Union.

European Commission. (2021). *Laying down harmonised rules on artificial intelligence (artificial intelligence act) and amending certain union legislative acts. Proposal for a regulation of the European parliament and of the council.*

Financial Accounting Standards Board. (2019). *Harmonizing accounting and data standards.* XBRL US. https://xbrl.us/harmonizing-accounting-data-standards/

Fitzgerald, M., Kruschwitz, N., Bonnet, D., & Welch, M. (2014). Embracing digital technology: A new strategic imperative. *MIT Sloan Management Review, 55*(2), 1.

Floridi, L., Cowls, J., Beltrametti, M., Chatila, R., Chazerand, P., Dignum, V., & Vayena, E. (2018). AI4People—an ethical framework for a good AI society: Opportunities, risks, principles, and recommendations. *Minds and Machines, 28*, 689–707.

Global Reporting Initiative. (2023). *About GRI.* https://www.globalreporting.org/about-gri/

Grant Thornton. (2024). *Round-up of 2023 sustainability reporting.* https://www.grantthornton.global/en/insights/articles/sustainability-reporting-2023-roundup/

Hanelt, A., Bohnsack, R., Marz, D., & Antunes Marante, C. (2021). A systematic review of the literature on digital transformation: Insights and implications for strategy and organizational change. *Journal of Management Studies, 58*(5), 1159–1197.

Health Level Seven International. (2023). *HL7 FHIR overview.* https://www.hl7.org/fhir/overview.html

IAALS. (2024). Data from Utah's sandbox shows extraordinary promise, refutes fears of harm. Institute for the Advancement of the American Legal System.

ITU. (2024). *Digital innovation for sustainable development.* International Telecommunication Union.

Jirgensons, M., & Kapenieks, J. (2018). Blockchain and the future of digital learning credential assessment and management. *Journal of Teacher Education for Sustainability, 20*(1), 145–156.

Jo, H., & Ahn, H. Y. (2024). Understanding digital engagement: Factors influencing awareness and satisfaction of digital transformation. *Discover Computing, 27*(1), 23.

Jobin, A., Ienca, M., & Vayena, E. (2019). The global landscape of AI ethics guidelines. *Nature Machine Intelligence*, *1*(9), 389–399.

Jones, B. (2024). *Unchartered territories: Canadian Courts and law societies grapple with the use of generative artificial intelligence tools.* Bennett Jones Legal Update.

Just, S. N., Sivertsen, M. F., & Lewin, S. (2024). Open for business: The discursive diffusion of regulatory sandboxes for fintech innovation. *Journal of Cultural Economy*, *17*(3), 360–378.

Kane, G. (2019). The technology fallacy: People are the real key to digital transformation. *Research-Technology Management*, *62*(6), 44–49.

Kim, H. S., Kim, H., Lee, S., Lee, K. H., & Kim, J. H. (2015). Current clinical status of telehealth in Korea: Categories, scientific basis, and obstacles. *Healthcare Informatics Research*, *21*(4), 244–250.

KPMG. (2022). *Survey of sustainability reporting 2022.* Global Reporting Initiative.

Lane, J. N., Leonardi, P. M., Contractor, N. S., & DeChurch, L. A. (2024). Teams in the digital workplace: technology's role for communication, collaboration, and performance. *Small Group Research*, *55*(1), 139–183.

Law Society of Alberta. (2023). *Gen AI rules of engagement for Canadian lawyers.* Professional Conduct Guidelines.

Lember, V., Kattel, R., & Tõnurist, P. (2018). Technological capacity in the public sector: The case of Estonia. *International Review of Administrative Sciences*, *84*(2), 214–230.

Li, L., Su, F., Zhang, W., & Mao, J. Y. (2018). Digital transformation by SME entrepreneurs: A capability perspective. *Information Systems Journal*, *28*(6), 1129–1157.

MAS. (2016). *MAS issues "regulatory sandbox" guidelines for FinTech experiments* [Press release]. Monetary Authority of Singapore.

Ministry of Health Singapore. (2024). *Regulatory sandbox.* Ministry of Health Singapore.

MIT News. (2017). *Digital diploma debuts at MIT.* Massachusetts Institute of Technology. Retrieved from https://news.mit.edu/

Multishoring. (2025). Technology partnerships meaning & examples. Multishoring.

Münch, C., Marx, E., Benz, L., Hartmann, E., & Matzner, M. (2022). Capabilities of digital servitization: Evidence from the socio-technical systems theory. *Technological Forecasting and Social Change*, *176*, 121361.

Nambisan, S., Lyytinen, K., Majchrzak, A., & Song, M. (2017). Digital innovation management: Reinventing Innovation management research in a digital world. *MIS Q. 41*(1), 223–238.

Nguyen, B. M., Dao, T. C., & Do, B. L. (2020). Towards a blockchain-based certificate authentication system in Vietnam. *PeerJ Computer Science*, *6*, e266.

OECD. (2023). *Regulatory sandboxes in artificial intelligence.* OECD Publishing.

Oh, J. Y., Park, Y. T., Jo, E. C., & Kim, S. M. (2015). Current status and progress of telemedicine in Korea and other countries. *Healthcare Informatics Research*, *21*(4), 239–243.

Papagiannidis, S., Harris, J., & Morton, D. (2020). WHO led the digital transformation of your company? A reflection of IT related challenges during the pandemic. *International Journal of Information Management*, *55*, 102166.

Parviainen, P., Tihinen, M., Kääriäinen, J., & Teppola, S. (2017). Tackling the digitalization challenge: How to benefit from digitalization in practice. *International Journal of Information Systems and Project Management*, *5*(1), 63–77. https://doi.org/10.12821/ijispm050104

Rai, A., & Tang, X. (2010). Leveraging IT capabilities and competitive process capabilities for the management of interorganizational relationship portfolios. *Information Systems Research*, *21*(3), 516–542.

Raimundo, R., & Rosário, A. (2021). Blockchain system in the higher education. *European Journal of Investigation in Health, Psychology and Education*, *11*(1), 276–293.

Reisman, D., Schultz, J., Crawford, K., & Whittaker, M.. (2018). *Algorithmic impact assessments: A practical framework for public agency accountability.* AI Now Institute.

Sánchez-Canut, S., Usart-Rodríguez, M., Grimalt-Álvaro, C., Martínez-Requejo, S., & Lores-Gómez, B. (2023). Professional digital competence: Definition, frameworks, measurement, and gender differences: A systematic literature review. *Human Behavior and Emerging Technologies*, *2023*(1), 8897227.

Sassanelli, C., Terzi, S., Panetto, H., & Doumeingts, G. (2021). Digital innovation hubs supporting SMEs digital transformation. In *2021 IEEE international conference on engineering, technology and innovation (ICE/ITMC)* (pp. 1–8). IEEE.

Shahbaznezhad, H., Dolan, R., & Rashidirad, M. (2021). The role of social media content format and platform in users' engagement behavior. *Journal of Interactive Marketing*, *53*(1), 47–65.

Silverbear. (2021). RCN Case Study: Silverbear technology support Royal College of Nursing's vital work during the COVID-19 pandemic and beyond. Retrieved from https://silverbear.com/Customers/Case-Studies/RCN

Singh, A., & Hess, T. (2020). How chief digital officers promote the digital transformation of their companies. In: *Strategic information management* (pp. 202–220). Routledge.

Susskind, R., & Susskind, D. (2015). *The future of the professions: How technology will transform the work of human experts*. Oxford University Press.

Taeihagh, A. (2021). Governance of artificial intelligence. *Policy and Society*, *40*(2), 137–157. https://doi.org/10.1080/14494035.2021.1928377

Turkanović, M., Hölbl, M., Košič, K., Heričko, M., & Kamišalić, A. (2018). EduCTX: A blockchain-based higher education credit platform. *IEEE access*, *6*, 5112–5127.

UNESCO. (2021). Recommendation on the ethics of artificial intelligence. Paris: UNESCO Publishing.

Van Laar, E., Van Deursen, A. J., Van Dijk, J. A., & De Haan, J. (2017). The relation between 21st-century skills and digital skills: A systematic literature review. *Computers in human behavior*, *72*, 577–588.

Vayena, E., Blasimme, A., & Cohen, I. G. (2018). Machine learning in medicine: addressing ethical challenges. *PLoS medicine*, *15*(11), e1002689.

Verhoef, P. C., Broekhuizen, T., Bart, Y., Bhattacharya, A., Dong, J. Q., Fabian, N., & Haenlein, M. (2021). Digital transformation: A multidisciplinary reflection and research agenda. *Journal of business research*, *122*, 889–901.

Vial, G. (2019). Understanding digital transformation: A review and a research agenda. *Journal of Strategic Information Systems*, *28*(2), 118–144. https://doi.org/10.1016/j.jsis.2019.01.003

Vuorikari, R., Kluzer, S., & Punie, Y. (2022). *DigComp 2.2: The digital competence framework for citizens—with new examples of knowledge, skills and attitudes*. Publications Office of the European Union.

West Virginia University. (2024). *What are regulatory sandboxes? Science and Technology Policy Notes.*

Wirtz, B. W., & Daiser, P. (2017). Business model innovation: An integrative conceptual framework. *Journal of Business Models*, *5*(1), 1–25. https://doi.org/10.5278/ojs.jbm.v5i1.1923

World Bank. (2022). Consultative group to assist the poor (CGAP) Annual Report 2022 (English). Washington, D.C.: World Bank Group. http://documents.worldbank.org/curated/en/099011624152041148

World Economic Forum. (2020). The Future of Jobs Report 2020. Retrieved from: https://www.weforum.org/publications/the-future-of-jobs-report-2020/

XBRL International. (2009). *XBRL 2.1 conformance suite 1.0*. https://www.xbrl.org/2008/xbrl-conf-cr4-2008-07-02.htm

XBRL International. (2023). *What is XBRL?* https://www.xbrl.org/the-standard/what/what-is-xbrl/

Yoo, Y. (2010). Computing in everyday life: A call for research on experiential computing. *MIS quarterly*, 213-231.

8 Agents of Change or Guardians of Tradition

Professionals' Roles in the Digital Transformation of the Professions

INTRODUCTION

The rapid evolution of digital technologies has profoundly reshaped professional landscapes across industries, compelling professionals to navigate the dual forces of digital disruption and digital transformation. Digital disruption refers to the upheaval caused by emerging technologies that fundamentally alter how industries, organizations, and professions operate; often rendering traditional practices obsolete (Susskind & Susskind, 2022). Digital transformation, conversely, involves the strategic integration of digital technologies to enhance processes, deliver value, and foster innovation within organizations and professions (Schallmo et al., 2024). For professionals, these phenomena present both challenges and opportunities, requiring them to actively adapt to remain relevant in their fields (Pemer, 2021). This chapter explores the pivotal role professionals play in shaping their professions (summarized in Table 8.1), their capacity to accelerate or impede digital transformation, the current shortcomings in their engagement with these changes, the necessary shifts in mindset and skills to support transformation, and specific strategies they can adopt to optimize the digital evolution of their professions.

TABLE 8.1
Professional Roles in Digital Transformation

Role	Description
Catalyst	Drives adoption of digital tools and fosters innovation.
Gatekeeper	Resists change due to identity, ethics, or tradition.
Interpreter	Translates digital tools into professional standards.
Mentor	Guides peers in digital adaptation and ethical use.
Change Agent	Leads transformation initiatives within organizations.

DOI: 10.1201/9781003606604-11

THE ROLE OF PROFESSIONALS IN SHAPING THE PROFESSIONS

Professionals are not merely passive recipients of institutional norms or technological change; rather, they are active agents in constructing and evolving the contours of their own professions (Kluttz & Mulligan, 2019). Through their specialized knowledge, commitment to ethical practice, and engagement with both formal and informal professional networks, they shape the values, norms, and boundaries that define their fields (Fitzgerald, 2020). This agency becomes particularly salient during periods of technological disruption, when traditional practices are unsettled, and new competencies and models of practice emerge (Becher, 2018). In such contexts, professionals do more than adopt new tools—they interpret, contest, and redefine what these tools mean for the standards of competence, responsibility, and service that underlie their professional identities (Susskind & Susskind, 2022).

A historical example of such agency is found in the actions of American dentists during the early twentieth century. Rather than waiting for state regulation or academic reform to define their occupation, U.S. dentists actively constructed their profession by establishing national associations, such as the American Dental Association, and by shaping the educational curricula, licensing procedures, and ethical codes that would distinguish dentistry as a recognized and autonomous profession (Fejerskov et al., 2018). In doing so, they asserted authority not only over technical practice but also over the moral and civic dimensions of their work (Holland, 2009). This self-definition was a proactive response to broader shifts in science, medicine, and public expectations, and it exemplifies how professionals can institutionalize change on their own terms.

By contrast, the case of psychologists in the United Kingdom offers insight into how professionals may resist changes they perceive as misaligned with professional identity or values (Kwiatkowski & Jackson, 2021). When the U.K. government introduced reforms to standardize psychological services within the National Health Service, many psychologists expressed concern that managerial logics and bureaucratic quantification would undermine the relational and interpretive aspects of their practice (Kwiatkowski & Jackson, 2021). Their resistance was not merely oppositional; it was an attempt to negotiate the meaning of professional expertise in an environment increasingly shaped by performance metrics and digital diagnostics (Petrakaki et al., 2025). This underscores how professionals exercise interpretive authority, not just by embracing innovation, but by discerning which changes uphold or erode the core commitments of their field.

In both cases, professionals have shaped the transformation of their fields by participating in professional associations and regulatory bodies that establish and revise educational standards, licensing requirements, and ethical codes. These structures provide a platform through which professionals mediate the tension between conserving the values of the profession and responding to technological and institutional change (Kwiatkowski & Jackson, 2021). They do not merely comply with disruption; they interpret it, negotiate it, and often lead its institutionalization in ways that align with public trust and professional integrity.

Moreover, the authority of professionals extends into mentorship, research, and public discourse, where they help define the relevance of their professions in an increasingly digital world (Holmes & Douglass, 2022). As digital infrastructures intersect with human services, through automation, algorithmic decision-making, and AI-assisted diagnostics, professionals are tasked with navigating the boundary between human judgment and machine logic (Susskind & Susskind, 2022). Their involvement ensures that technological transformation is not divorced from the ethical, experiential, and relational foundations of professional life (Faulconbridge et al., 2025).

Ultimately, professionals are not only shaped by their professions but are instrumental in shaping them. Their role is both reflective and anticipatory—they safeguard the identity and social function of the profession while embedding new digital competencies into its core (Susskind & Susskind, 2018). In doing so, they do not merely adapt to technological change; they co-author the future of their professions in ways that preserve public legitimacy and social responsibility.

HOW PROFESSIONALS CAN ACCELERATE OR IMPEDE DIGITAL TRANSFORMATION

Professionals as Catalysts of Digital Transformation

Professionals occupy a critical juncture in the digital transformation of the professions, possessing the agency to either catalyze or constrain technological progress (Vähäsantanen, 2015). When professionals exhibit a forward-looking mindset and a commitment to lifelong learning, they become active enablers of digital transformation. This proactive orientation often translates into the integration of emerging digital tools, data-driven decision-making, and novel service delivery models that redefine traditional professional boundaries (Susskind & Susskind, 2022). For instance, the adoption of artificial intelligence, machine learning, and digital platforms by accountants, engineers, and legal practitioners is reshaping how professional judgments are formed and services are rendered, often leading to improvements in accuracy, scalability, and client engagement (Faulconbridge et al., 2025).

Organizational Drivers of Professional Change

Organizational norms, practices, and benchmarks play a significant role in influencing professionals to adopt new technologies and shift their mindsets. For instance, accountants who implement cloud-based software streamline financial reporting processes, enabling real-time decision-making and enhancing their firms' competitiveness in a dynamic market (Kroon et al., 2021). These tangible benefits help overcome initial resistance, encouraging broader adoption and adaptation of emerging technologies within the profession. Similarly, educators who integrate digital learning platforms foster more interactive and personalized learning environments, driving pedagogical innovation (Alam & Mohanty, 2023). Today, academics around the world find themselves in an implicit competition to embrace technology-enhanced teaching methods, reflecting a global shift toward digitally empowered education.

Barriers to Digital Adoption Among Professionals

However, the transformative potential of digital technologies is not uniformly realized across all sectors or among all individuals. In many instances, professionals themselves become impediments to digital progress—not out of deliberate opposition, but due to cognitive inertia, perceived threats to professional identity, or the influence of institutional conservatism (Petrakaki et al., 2025). This resistance is often reinforced by organizational cultures that valorize established practices and frame technological innovation as a disruption rather than an opportunity. For example, in the medical field, reluctance among some practitioners to adopt electronic health records (EHRs) has impeded the shift toward data-driven care, limiting both interoperability and improvements in patient outcomes (Petrakaki et al., 2025). Such resistance not only delays transformation but also places professionals at risk of marginalization, as clients and organizations increasingly value digital fluency and adaptability. This dynamic can lead to a form of passive inertia, wherein digital tools are either underutilized or misapplied, ultimately stalling broader systemic innovation (Ferguson et al., 2021). The uneven distribution of digital literacy across professional cohorts further compounds this issue, particularly in legal professions where analog methods are deeply entrenched (Kluttz & Mulligan, 2019).

The Role of Leadership and Culture in Overcoming Resistance

Addressing this divide requires intentional leadership. Professionals in senior roles are uniquely positioned to catalyze transformation by cultivating a culture of innovation, allocating resources for upskilling, and modeling openness to technological change (Becher, 2018). The boundary between acceleration and impediment often lies in the willingness to engage in constructive dialogue about the risks, trade-offs, and ethical implications of digital tools (Susskind & Susskind, 2018). Professionals who proactively surface concerns—about data privacy, algorithmic bias, or unintended consequences—do not necessarily impede progress; rather, they anchor transformation in robust governance and social responsibility (Yang et al., 2024)). The key differentiator is whether such critique is coupled with openness to experimentation and co-design, or whether it defaults to obstruction and skepticism. In environments where critical questioning is integrated into agile pilots and iterative roll-outs, potential pitfalls are identified early, solutions are refined collaboratively, and stakeholder buy-in deepens (Faulconbridge et al., 2025).

Institutional Support and the Future of Professional Practice

The capacity of professionals to influence digital transformation is therefore deeply contingent upon institutional support, professional education, and regulatory adaptation. Change management efforts must not only provide technical upskilling but also address the cultural and epistemic dimensions of transformation—challenging entrenched norms while articulating a shared vision of future practice. Professionals who can reconcile technological change with professional values are more likely to view digital transformation as an enhancement rather than an erosion of their roles

(Fraser-Arnott, 2019). Ultimately, whether digital transformation proceeds smoothly or faces friction depends in large part on how professionals navigate the tension between tradition and innovation within their own domains.

CURRENT SHORTCOMINGS OF PROFESSIONALS IN RELATION TO DIGITAL TRANSFORMATION

Despite the accelerating pace of digital transformation across industries, many professionals continue to face significant shortcomings in adapting to technological change. Foremost among these is the persistent digital skills gap (Ferguson et al., 2021). Although digital technologies are becoming increasingly embedded in the practice of professions—ranging from algorithmic diagnostics in healthcare to data-driven pedagogy in education—many professionals lack the requisite technical competencies to leverage these tools effectively (Kluttz & Mulligan, 2019). This gap is particularly pronounced in professions that have historically prioritized tacit knowledge, interpersonal engagement, and manual processes (Faulconbridge et al., 2025). For instance, in architecture, professionals may find it difficult to fully utilize building information modeling (BIM) software, thereby limiting their capacity to collaborate on complex, multi-stakeholder projects (Jeong & Kim, 2022).

The problem is further exacerbated by a lack of professional development programs specifically designed to address digital upskilling, particularly for mid-career professionals whose initial training did not encompass these emerging technologies (Vähäsantanen, 2015). In Australia, for instance, there is an anticipated shortage of over 370,000 digital experts and digitally enabled workers by 2026, underscoring the urgency for upskilling initiatives (Digital Skills Organisation, 2023). This gap is not confined to technical roles; even in fields like sustainability, professionals struggle to harness the potential of artificial intelligence due to limited digital competencies (Digital Skills Organisation, 2023). As a result, professionals may struggle to integrate digital tools into their workflows in meaningful ways, often relying on outdated practices that undermine both efficiency and service quality.

Beyond the acquisition of technical skills, digital transformation presents a deeper epistemological challenge, this is, the absence of a digital mindset (Susskind & Susskind, 2022). It is not merely about mastering new tools, but about reimagining how value is conceptualized, created, and delivered within professional domains (Faulconbridge et al., 2025). Many professionals, however, remain anchored in traditional logics of practice, displaying skepticism or ambivalence toward emerging technologies. For example, legal practitioners frequently express doubt about the reliability and ethical implications of AI-generated information (Armour & Sako, 2020). This resistance is not unfounded; it often arises from concerns that digital tools may erode professional autonomy, compromise expert judgment, or disrupt long-standing ethical frameworks (Kluttz & Mulligan, 2019). As a result, some professionals underinvest in the time, effort, and learning necessary to adapt to technological change, thereby reinforcing the inertia that impedes meaningful digital innovation.

Organizational culture and leadership also contribute to these shortcomings (Ferguson et al., 2021). In many professional settings, digital transformation is perceived as a peripheral initiative rather than a strategic priority. The absence of clear

TABLE 8.2
Shortcomings Hindering Digital Adaptation

Shortcoming	Impact
Digital Skills Gap	Limits effective use of emerging technologies.
Lack of Digital Mindset	Hinders innovation and openness to change.
Institutional Conservatism	Discourages experimentation and adaptation.
Siloed Identities	Restricts interdisciplinary collaboration.
Weak Leadership Support	Fails to prioritize digital transformation.

leadership and institutional commitment to digital change can leave professionals without the guidance, incentives, or support structures necessary to experiment with and embrace digital innovations (Susskind & Susskind, 2018). This is compounded by siloed professional identities, which may limit cross-disciplinary learning and collaboration—an essential feature of digital ecosystems (Kroon et al., 2021). As professions face mounting pressure to modernize, addressing these interrelated shortcomings is critical not only to their sustainability but also to the continued legitimacy of professional expertise in the digital age (Table 8.2).

HOW PROFESSIONALS NEED TO CHANGE TO BEST SUPPORT DIGITAL TRANSFORMATION

The digital transformation of the professions is not merely a technological shift but a profound reconfiguration of how expertise, trust, and value are produced and delivered (Faulconbridge et al., 2025). In this context, professionals are not only consumers of new technologies but also central agents in shaping how these technologies are integrated into professional practice (Armour & Sako, 2020). Supporting digital transformation requires more than acquiring technical competencies; it demands a reorientation of professional identity, a rethinking of ethical responsibilities, and a commitment to fostering adaptive and resilient organizational cultures (Susskind & Susskind, 2022).

Central to this reorientation is the cultivation of a digital mindset—a disposition that embraces uncertainty, experimentation, and cross-disciplinary collaboration (Valta et al., 2024). Professionals must be willing to interrogate their established methods and assumptions, recognizing that digital tools do not simply automate tasks but can redefine what constitutes professional judgment, service delivery, and even client relationships (Imjai et al., 2024). For example, the integration of algorithmic decision-making tools in law, healthcare, and finance requires professionals to critically assess both the capabilities and limitations of such systems, ensuring that technological efficiency does not come at the cost of fairness or accountability (Petrakaki et al., 2025).

Moreover, supporting digital transformation requires professionals to adopt new and evolving roles within their organizations (Singh et al., 2019). They must increasingly act as digital advocates and change agents, serving as intermediaries between technical experts and domain-specific practitioners (Faulconbridge et al., 2025).

This role extends beyond participating in decisions related to technology procurement and implementation; it also involves shaping how digital systems are integrated in ways that uphold the core values and ethical commitments of their profession (Valta et al., 2024). Ensuring this alignment is essential to prevent digital tools from undermining professional judgment or diminishing public trust.

In addition, professionals must cultivate adaptability and resilience. Digital transformation is rarely a linear process; it involves experimentation, iterative learning, and the capacity to adjust strategies in response to setbacks or shifting contexts (Faulconbridge et al., 2025). This is particularly evident in dynamic fields such as marketing, where professionals must continuously respond to evolving digital platforms and consumer behaviors (Singh et al., 2019). Finally, successful digital transformation depends on interdisciplinary collaboration. Professionals need to engage with technologists, policymakers, and other stakeholders to co-create solutions that are not only technically effective but also aligned with professional standards and broader societal expectations (Petrakaki et al., 2025).

Finally, professionals must engage in ongoing, reflexive learning—not as a response to obsolescence, but as an intrinsic feature of modern professional life (Curran et al., 2019). Lifelong learning in this context extends beyond acquiring software skills; it includes understanding data governance, digital ethics, cybersecurity, and the socio-political impacts of emerging technologies (Susskind & Susskind, 2022). Institutions responsible for professional accreditation and training will need to redesign curricula and continuing education pathways to support this broader, more integrated model of professional development (Leocádio et al., 2025). Said that, professionals who aim to support digital transformation must evolve as critical thinkers, collaborative leaders, and ethical stewards of technology. Their transformation is not ancillary to digital change—it is a foundational condition for its success.

SPECIFIC STRATEGIES OR ACTIONS FOR OPTIMIZING DIGITAL TRANSFORMATION

In the context of digital disruption, optimizing digital transformation is not simply a matter of adopting new technologies; it requires a deliberate, sustained engagement with structural, cultural, and professional change (Pribadi & Nasution, 2021). For professionals, this entails a reconfiguration of traditional roles and competencies, as well as a strategic orientation toward adaptability, learning, and innovation (Kroon et al., 2021). One of the foundational actions is professionals must undertake the continuous development of digital literacy and technological fluency (Tsakissiris & Grant-Smith, 2021). Digital transformation is inherently dynamic and therefore necessitates a commitment to lifelong learning—whether through formal education, industry certifications, or informal and experiential learning environments (Curran et al., 2019). This investment in knowledge capital enables professionals not only to remain relevant but also to actively shape the contours of digital change within their respective fields.

A complementary strategy lies in cultivating a digital mindset. Unlike technical competence alone, a digital mindset reflects an attitudinal shift: an openness to experimentation, an acceptance of ambiguity, and a willingness to embrace failure as part of the innovation process (Valta et al., 2024). This orientation empowers professionals to engage critically with emerging tools while recognizing the strategic and ethical implications of their use (Imjai et al., 2024). Importantly, the transformation is not only technological but cultural. Professionals must become advocates and enablers of change within their organizational contexts (Khawaja & Hamdan, 2023.). By participating in conversations about technology adoption, offering informed perspectives, and supporting the integration of new systems, they help create a more inclusive and participatory approach to transformation (Susskind & Susskind, 2022).

Furthermore, professionals must reimagine collaboration as a key enabler of digital optimization (Goto, 2021).). In contrast to the siloed knowledge structures of traditional professional domains, digital ecosystems thrive on cross-functional and interdisciplinary exchange (Booth et al., 2021). Active knowledge sharing, both within and beyond organizational boundaries, fosters a culture of innovation and collective learning (Faulconbridge et al., 2025). Engaging in professional networks, be they formal associations, conferences, or virtual communities, enhances visibility into emerging trends, tools, and regulatory developments, equipping professionals to anticipate rather than merely react to technological shifts (Brice & Almond, 2020.).

Equally vital is a resolute focus on customer-centric value creation (Singh et al., 2019). As digital technologies redefine service delivery and user expectations, professionals must reorient their practices to prioritize the evolving needs of clients, stakeholders, and end-users (Petrakaki et al., 2025). This involves leveraging digital tools not only for efficiency, but for responsiveness, personalization, and strategic insight (Holmes & Douglass, 2022). The capacity to translate digital affordances into meaningful, value-adding solutions becomes a hallmark of professional excellence in a digital age.

Finally, professionals must integrate principles of effective change management into their transformation strategies (Faulconbridge et al., 2025). Digital disruption can provoke resistance, uncertainty, and cultural friction (Susskind & Susskind, 2022). Professionals are well positioned to bridge these divides by communicating clearly, building trust, and facilitating inclusive participation in the change process (Goto, M. (2021). Evaluation and feedback mechanisms should also be embedded throughout digital initiatives, ensuring that transformation efforts are not only implemented, but also measured, refined, and aligned with broader professional and organizational goals (Holmes & Douglass, 2022). this discussion thus entails that optimizing digital transformation requires a multifaceted and proactive approach that blends technical proficiency with strategic foresight, collaborative ethos, and ethical responsibility. Professionals who embrace this complexity are more likely to lead, rather than follow, in the unfolding digital landscape.

CONCLUSION

This chapter explored the complex role professionals play in digital transformation, acting as both enablers and, at times, sources of resistance within their fields. It examines how professionals influence change by interpreting, adopting, or challenging digital innovations in light of their values, identities, and expertise. Transformation efforts can gain momentum when professionals are supported by strong leadership, a culture of innovation, and institutional alignment. However, progress may be slowed by skill shortages, legacy practices, and organizational inertia. To contribute effectively, professionals are increasingly expected to engage in lifelong learning, to cultivate a digital mindset, and to collaborate across disciplines. The chapter encourages professionals to embrace new roles as digital advocates, mentors, and ethical stewards. It also outlines strategies such as promoting innovation cultures, focusing on user-centered value, and applying change management principles. Ultimately, it argues that the future of professional work depends on professionals' willingness to evolve and collectively shape technology-integrated, socially responsible practices.

DISCUSSION QUESTIONS

1. In what ways do professionals serve as both catalysts and gatekeepers of digital transformation, and how can this dual role be constructively managed to balance innovation with professional ethics and identity?
2. How can professional associations and regulatory bodies be reimagined to support continuous digital upskilling and mindset transformation among practitioners, particularly mid-career professionals?
3. What cultural and epistemological barriers within professional environments most significantly hinder digital transformation, and what leadership strategies can effectively address them?
4. In what ways does the integration of AI, algorithmic decision-making, and digital platforms challenge traditional notions of professional judgment, and how should professionals navigate these tensions?
5. To what extent should professionals be expected to engage in interdisciplinary collaboration and co-design in the digital age, and how might this reshape their sense of autonomy, accountability, and authority?

REFERENCES

Alam, A., & Mohanty, A. (2023). Educational technology: Exploring the convergence of technology and pedagogy through mobility, interactivity, AI, and learning tools. *Cogent Engineering, 10*(2), 2283282.

Armour, J., & Sako, M. (2020). AI-enabled business models in legal services: from traditional law firms to next-generation law companies? *Journal of Professions and Organization, 7*(1), 27–46.

Becher, T. (2018). *Professional practices: Commitment and capability in a changing environment.* Routledge.

Booth, R. G., Strudwick, G., McBride, S., O'Connor, S., & López, A. L. S. (2021). How the nursing profession should adapt for a digital future. *BMJ, 373*, n1190. https://doi.org/10.1136/bmj.n1190

Brice, S., & Almond, H. (2020). Health professional digital capabilities frameworks: a scoping review. *Journal of multidisciplinary healthcare, 13*(1), 1375–1390.

Curran, V., Fleet, L., Simmons, K., Lannon, H., Gustafson, D. L., Wang, C., & Wetsch, L. (2019). Adoption and use of mobile learning in continuing professional development by health and human services professionals. *Journal of Continuing Education in the Health Professions, 39*(2), 76–85.

Digital Skills Organisation, 2023, Growing Australia's digital workforce digiworkforce. https://digiworkforce.futureskillsorganisation.com.au/

Faulconbridge, J., Sarwar, A., & Spring, M. (2025). How professionals adapt to artificial intelligence: The role of intertwined boundary work. *Journal of Management Studies*, *62*(5), 1991–2024.

Fejerskov, O., Uribe, S., & Mariño, R. J. (2018). Dentistry in a historical perspective and a likely future of the profession. In: Mariño, R., Morgan, M., Walmsley, A. (eds) Career paths in Oral health. pp. 3–19, Springer, Cham. https://doi.org/10.1007/978-3-319-89731-8_1

Ferguson, S. L., Smith, C., & Kietzmann, J. (2021). Hands-off? Lessons from high-touch professionals about going virtual. *Business Horizons*, *65*(3), 303.

Fitzgerald, A. (2020). Professional identity: A concept analysis. *Nursing forum*, *55*(3), 447–472.

Fraser-Arnott, M. A. (2019). Evolving practices and professional identity: How the new ways we work can reshape us as professionals and a profession. *IFLA journal*, *45*(2), 114–126.

Goto, M. (2021). Collective professional role identity in the age of artificial intelligence. *Journal of Professions and Organization*, *8*(1), 86–107.

Holland, L. M. (2009). *The development of professional services in nineteenth century county towns: a case study of the county towns of Stafford* (Doctoral dissertation, University of Leicester).

Holmes, A. F., & Douglass, A. (2022). Artificial intelligence: Reshaping the accounting profession and the disruption to accounting education. *Journal of Emerging Technologies in Accounting*, *19*(1), 53–68.

Imjai, N., Promma, W., Usman, B., & Aujirapongpan, S. (2024). The intertwined effects of digital literacy, agile mindset on design thinking skill and management control competency: Insights from Thai young accountants. *International Journal of Information Management Data Insights*, *4*(2), 100244.

Jeong, D. Y., & Kim, H. J. (2022). The Advent of the New Architectural Profession through BIM. *Buildings*, *12*(8), 1134.

Khawaja, N., & Hamdan, A. (2023). The moderation effect of digital leadership on the relationship between artificial intelligence and accounting profession: A review. In: El Khoury, R., Nasrallah, N. (eds) *Emerging trends and innovation in business and finance. Contributions to management science.* Springer, Singapore.

Kluttz, D. N., & Mulligan, D. K. (2019). Automated decision support technologies and the legal profession. *Berkeley technology law journal*, *34*(3), 853–890.

Kroon, N., do Céu Alves, M., & Martins, I. (2021). The impacts of emerging technologies on accountants' role and skills: Connecting to open innovation—a systematic literature review. *Journal of Open Innovation: Technology, Market, and Complexity*, *7*(3), 163.

Kwiatkowski, R., & Jackson, C. (2021). Professional identity, behaviour and values: A partial and provocative history of the code of ethics of the British psychological society. In: *Handbook of international psychology ethics* (pp. 143–173). Routledge.

Leocádio, D., Malheiro, L., & Reis, J. C. G. D. (2025). Auditors in the digital age: a systematic literature review. *Digital Transformation and Society*, *4*(1), 5–20.

Pemer, F. (2021). Enacting professional service work in times of digitalization and potential disruption. *Journal of Service Research*, *24*(2), 249–268.

Petrakaki, D., Chamakiotis, P., Russell, E., & Charlwood, A. (2025). Resistance, tensions and consent to digital working in healthcare. *Social Science & Medicine*, *368*, 117691.

Pribadi, A., & Nasution, N. (2021). Digital transformation to the sustainability of public relations profession in the era of disruption. *Commicast*, *2*(1), 52–57.

Schallmo, D., Baiyere, A., Gertsen, F., Rosenstand, C., & Williams, C. A. 2024, *Digital disruption and transformation: Case studies, approaches, and tools (*1st *ed.),* Cham: Springer International Publishing.

Singh, J., Flaherty, K., Sohi, R. S., Deeter-Schmelz, D., Habel, J., Le Meunier-FitzHugh, K., & Onyemah, V. (2019). Sales profession and professionals in the age of digitization and artificial intelligence technologies: concepts, priorities, and questions. *Journal of Personal Selling & Sales Management*, *39*(1), 2–22.

Susskind, D., & Susskind, R. (2018). The future of the professions. *Proceedings of the American Philosophical Society*, *162*(2), 125–138.

Susskind, R., & Susskind, D. (2022). *The future of the professions: How technology will transform the work of human experts*. Oxford University Press.

Tsakissiris, J., & Grant-Smith, D. (2021). The influence of professional identity and self-interest in shaping career choices in the emerging ICT workforce. *International Journal of Work-Integrated Learning*, *22*(1), 1–15.

Vähäsantanen, K. (2015). Professional agency in the stream of change: Understanding educational change and teachers' professional identities. *Teaching and teacher education*, *47*, 1–12.

Valta, M., Hildebrandt, Y., & Maier, C. (2024). Fostering the digital mindset to mitigate technostress: an empirical study of empowering individuals for using digital technologies. *Internet Research*, *34*(6), 2341–2369.

Yang, J., Amrollahi, A., & Marrone, M. (2024). Harnessing the potential of artificial intelligence: affordances, constraints, and strategic implications for professional services. *The Journal of Strategic Information Systems*, *33*(4), 101864.

9 How Professionals Can Future-Proof Their Careers

INTRODUCTION

As professions are being continuously disrupted and transformed due to rapid technological advancement and constantly evolving demands, the idea of "future-proofing" a career has become essential, not just an option. Future-proofing means actively and continuously improving your skill set, knowledge/understanding, and mindset to adapt to evolving needs and to stay relevant, valuable, and strong in the face of future changes (e.g. see Bowles et al., 2020; Busulwa & Evans, 2021; Vial, 2019). Unlike older, more predictable professions roles and career paths, professionals today must navigate a world where digital technologies like Artificial Intelligence (AI), the Internet of Things, and quantum computing, as well as global connectivity and competition, and changing client expectations are not only fundamentally transforming professional roles, workflows, and products/services, but also entire professional fields operate (Susskind & Susskind, 2022). Digital disruption and digital transformation at all levels bring both significant challenges, as they drive many routine tasks to become automated, but they also drive exciting opportunities for those who can effectively use new technologies. A key part of this adaptation is the ability to "keep up" with digital technologies, which has been conceptualized as an accelerated and adaptable learning practice (Busulwa & Evans, 2021). This means professionals must proactively and continuously align their learning rate with the rapid pace of technological change. This ability is crucial for maintaining expertise and remaining competitive in a world undergoing significant digital transformation (Busulwa, 2022).

This chapter aims to provide clear, actionable strategies relevant to professionals, and even more so to students and other prospective professionals. We unpack how to develop vital skills—both digital and those unique to humans—and discuss effective approaches to accelerated and continuous learning (Busulwa & Evans, 2021; World Economic Forum, 2020). By understanding these approaches, you can not only reduce career risks but also unlock new possibilities for making an impact, growing, and finding satisfaction in your career, ensuring it remains valuable and relevant for the future.

CULTIVATING ESSENTIAL FUTURE-PROOFING COMPETENCIES

To effectively future-proof their careers, professionals must proactively cultivate a diverse set of competencies that extend beyond traditional qualifications. In this section, we delve into the core skills and attributes essential for thriving in the digitally transformed professional setting (see examples in Table 9.1). We will explore

DOI: 10.1201/9781003606604-12

TABLE 9.1
Examples of Competencies for Future-Proofing Professional Careers

Competency Category	Description	Example skills/abilities
Advanced Digital Fluency	Strategic use and understanding of digital tools, platforms, and data to enhance value creation.	Data analytics, AI literacy, digital privacy awareness, cybersecurity, cloud technologies.
Human-Centric Skills	Essential interpersonal, ethical, and emotional capabilities that cannot be automated.	Empathy, ethical judgment, emotional intelligence, communication, cultural competence.
Adaptability and Resilience	Capacity to embrace change, recover from setbacks, and thrive in dynamic environments.	Reframing failure, adopting new workflows, staying engaged in uncertain situations.
Accelerated and Lifelong Learning	Commitment to continuously acquiring new, relevant knowledge and skills at pace.	Pursuing micro-credentials, learning on demand, unlearning outdated approaches.
Ethical and Responsible Tech Use	Ability to anticipate, evaluate, and respond to ethical dilemmas in tech-enabled professional settings.	Understanding algorithmic bias, informed consent in digital health, secure data handling.
Collaboration in Digital Environments	Effective teamwork and communication across virtual and hybrid professional contexts.	Using Microsoft Teams, Slack, Zoom; coordinating across asynchronous digital workflows.
Strategic and Interdisciplinary Thinking	Understanding systems and synthesizing insights across domains to drive innovation.	Blending legal, technical, and social perspectives; applying systems thinking to solve problems.
Career Self-Management and Personal Branding	Taking ownership of one's career path, visibility, and positioning in a digital labor market.	Maintaining a professional portfolio, LinkedIn strategy, articulating digital value proposition.

the critical need for advanced digital fluency, moving beyond basic technology tool usage to strategic leveraging of technology. We discuss the equally important unique human-centric skills that remain irreplaceable by digital technology tools and automation—such as critical thinking and emotional intelligence. Finally, we will examine the foundational importance of adaptability, resilience, and a continuous, accelerated learning mindset—qualities that enable professionals to continuously evolve alongside technological advancements, and in line with the demands of digitally transforming professional roles and workflows.

Advanced Digital Fluency: Beyond Basic Tech Skills

Advanced digital fluency is the sophisticated and strategic ability to understand, critically evaluate, and responsibly leverage established and emerging digital technologies to solve complex problems and create value within professional contexts, while also finding imaginative and effective ways to apply new tools or platforms to solve problems, improve processes, or create new value, even in ways that might not have been their original purpose (e.g., see University of Mary Washington, n.d.). For professionals in digitally transforming contexts, this concept extends far beyond basic software and digital tool competency. The World Economic Forum (2020) highlights how technological advancements have accelerated organizational demand for sophisticated digital competencies that fundamentally reshape industries. This encompasses deeper understanding and practical application of established and emerging technologies (e.g., see Busulwa et al., 2022; Busulwa et al., 2024).

As a subset of digital fluency, there are some essential digital competencies that are increasingly important across diverse professions. One example of these competencies is data literacy—the knowledge, skills, and abilities to understand, analyze, and communicate insights from data effectively, with 86% of business leaders considering it essential for daily work (DataCamp, 2025). Another example is AI literacy—knowledge, skills, and abilities to understand how artificial intelligence systems work, their applications, limitations, and ethical implications, as well as how to optimally use them. Almost 70% of leaders now rank AI literacy as essential (DataCamp, 2025). Yet another is cybersecurity awareness—encompassing knowledge of digital threats and protective measures, particularly critical as geopolitical tensions increase cyber risk concerns around the world (World Economic Forum, 2025). Additional essential competencies include cloud proficiency and digital collaboration skills for distributed work environments (Busulwa & Evans, 2021).

The critical challenge involves transitioning from passive technology consumption to strategic leverage. This requires developing competencies in understanding how digital tools can innovate workflows, automate processes, and derive strategic insights. For example, accountants develop competencies in AI-powered anomaly detection for fraud identification, while legal professionals build skills in natural language processing for contract analysis (Susskind & Susskind, 2022). This shift demands critical thinking competencies about how technology solves complex problems and creates opportunities within professional domains (Vial, 2019).

Developing these professional competencies requires structured approaches combining formal learning through specialized courses and certifications, experiential opportunities like hackathons and cross-functional projects, and continuous development through industry engagement (Yang et al., 2025). As nearly 40% of workforce skills will change within five years, continuous learning remains essential for professional success (World Economic Forum, 2025).

Human-Centric Skills: The Irreplaceable Edge

As digital technologies automate routine and even some analytical tasks, professionals are increasingly distinguished not by their technical capabilities alone, but by their uniquely human attributes. Skills such as critical thinking, creativity, ethical judgment, emotional intelligence, and the ability to engage clients empathetically are emerging as essential complements to digital fluency (Deming, 2017; Xing & Marwala, 2017). These competencies are less susceptible to automation because they rely on context, nuance, and interpersonal understanding—domains in which machines continue to lag significantly behind humans. As Autor (2015) demonstrates, while automation substitutes for routine tasks, it also complements human labor by amplifying the comparative advantage of human workers' problem-solving skills, adaptability, and creativity.

Professionals who cultivate uniquely human skills are more likely to remain indispensable as work environments become more collaborative, interdisciplinary, and digitally mediated. Emotional intelligence, for instance, is critical for effective leadership, conflict resolution, and client trust, particularly in high-stakes professional domains such as healthcare, law, and consulting (Goleman, 1995). Similarly, ethical reasoning and values-sensitive judgment are crucial as professionals are increasingly tasked with overseeing the design and deployment of technologies that raise moral and social implications, such as AI and predictive analytics (Floridi et al., 2018). The World Economic Forum's Future of Jobs Report (World Economic Forum, 2025) reinforces this trend, highlighting that human-centric skills such as creative thinking, resilience, flexibility and agility, curiosity and lifelong learning, and leadership and social influence are among the top ten skills rising in demand.

Deliberate practice, reflective learning, and interdisciplinary engagement are key to cultivating these human-centric competencies. Project-based learning, professional mentoring, and exposure to diverse work cultures can further strengthen them (Andrews & Higson, 2008). Research demonstrates that employers increasingly value graduates who possess soft skills over those with purely technical knowledge, as these interpersonal and cognitive abilities enable adaptation to organizational culture and contribute to long-term success. For students and early-career professionals, showcasing these capabilities through authentic client engagement, leadership roles, and problem-solving contributions can significantly enhance employability and long-term relevance in an automated, yet deeply human-centered professional future.

Adaptability, Resilience, Continuous/Accelerated Learning, and a Growth Mindset

Given relentless and accelerating digital disruption and digital transformation of the professions, adaptability, resilience, continuous learning, and a growth mindset are becoming indispensable competencies for professionals seeking long-term career viability. Adaptability refers to professionals' ability to adjust effectively to new ways of working and demands on professionals, while resilience reflects professionals' capacity to maintain performance, motivation, and psychological well-being in the face of disruptions, setbacks, and overwhelm (Lengnick-Hall et al., 2011). Central to both is a growth mindset—the belief that required knowledge, skills, and abilities can be developed through effort, feedback, and learning—which encourages persistence, openness to change, and a proactive stance towards competence development (Dweck, 2006). Equally critical is professionals' ability to unlearn or put aside outdated methods and assumptions. As digital technologies evolve rapidly, professionals must actively discard obsolete knowledge and behaviors that hinder the adoption of new tools and practices (Senge, 2006). This process of unlearning supports accelerated learning—the capacity to rapidly acquire, apply, and adapt new competencies in response to dynamic changes in professional roles, workflows, and employer or client expectations. Recent research emphasizes that professionals can keep up with digital technologies to the extent that they can accelerate or align their learning rate to the rate of change in digital technologies (Busulwa & Evans, 2021).

In addition to adaptability, resilience, a growth mindset, and continuous and accelerated learning, professionals who cultivate intellectual curiosity and embrace ambiguity are more likely to explore new ideas and technologies rather than resist them. Being comfortable with uncertainty and imperfect information is a hallmark of agile decision-makers in today's complex professional contexts. The World Economic Forum's Future of Jobs Report 2025 reinforces this trend, identifying resilience, flexibility and agility, and curiosity and lifelong learning as among the top ten skills rising in demand globally. Moreover, psychological resilience is essential for coping with stress and remaining engaged during ongoing transitions, particularly given the accelerated pace of change experienced during disruptions such as the COVID-19 pandemic (Ratten, 2020).

As the pace of technological change intensifies, professionals who embrace these competencies will not only safeguard their careers but contribute meaningfully to their organizations' competitiveness and sustainability. This represents a fundamental shift from static skill acquisition to dynamic competency development that enables professionals to thrive amid continuous change.

STRATEGIES FOR LIFELONG AND ACCELERATED LEARNING AND SKILL ACQUISITION

Given the relentless pace of technological change and evolving professional demands, continuous learning is no longer optional but a strategic imperative. This section outlines actionable strategies for professionals to engage in effective lifelong and accelerated learning, ensuring their skill sets remain relevant and dependable. We will explore diverse pathways for acquiring new knowledge, from formal certifications to informal learning networks. Emphasis will be placed on proactive skill auditing and developing personalized learning roadmaps, alongside the critical role of experiential learning in cementing new competencies. Ultimately, this section provides a framework for cultivating an agile and accelerated learning habit that empowers professionals to continuously adapt and excel throughout their careers.

Navigating Diverse Accelerated Learning Pathways

Accelerated learning requires that professionals embrace a mix of formal, informal, and self-directed learning strategies to remain future-ready. Flexible formal learning options—including modular online courses, micro-credentials, executive education, and short-cycle professional certifications—are particularly well-suited to busy professionals and students alike. These formats offer targeted, industry-relevant competencies without the extended time commitments of traditional degrees, enabling rapid upskilling aligned with evolving professional demands (Ifenthaler et al., 2016; World Economic Forum, 2020). Equally essential are informal or non-formal learning avenues. Peer networks, online forums, webinars, podcasts, and curated newsletters provide real-time access to diverse perspectives, while mentorship and reverse mentorship facilitate valuable two-way knowledge transfer across generations and disciplines (Eraut, 2004; Westerman et al., 2014). These avenues allow learners to stay current with emerging trends and refine their competencies through contextual, experience-driven engagement.

To enhance learning efficiency, professionals can cultivate active learning habits—such as setting learning goals, reflecting on learning effectiveness, and experiential application—that accelerate competence acquisition. Recent research emphasizes that professionals can keep up with digital technologies to the extent that they can accelerate or align their learning rate to the rate of change in digital technologies, highlighting the importance of developing competence in "learning how to learn" effectively (Busulwa & Evans, 2021). Professional bodies and education providers can play a catalytic role by curating accredited resources, recognizing and offering easily accessible micro-credentials, and supporting lifelong learning strategies that align with professional standards and workforce needs. Ultimately, professionals who strategically combine diverse learning approaches—and develop competencies in how to learn efficiently—are best positioned to navigate technological change and continuously align their expertise with the evolving demands of the digital transformation of professions.

Proactive Skill Auditing and Personalized Development

Future-proofing a career depends, in large part, on professionals' ability to routinely audit their competencies against emerging demands in their field. This involves systematically identifying current strengths and skill gaps by benchmarking against evolving job roles, professional body standards, digital transformation roadmaps, and sector-specific technology trends (e.g., see World Economic Forum, 2020; OECD, 2021). Engaging in this type of self-audit enables professionals to prioritize what to learn, when to learn it, and how best to learn it. Professionals can utilize a range of tools to structure this process, including professional body competency frameworks, skill-mapping templates, digital self-assessment platforms, and structured development plans (e.g., see Ifenthaler et al., 2016). Increasingly, online assessment tools and CPD tracking dashboards offer tailored feedback and suggest precise learning pathways based on real-time market needs. These tools can help identify both technical and human-centric competencies requiring immediate financial and or effort investment.

Once skill gaps are identified, the next step is to translate insights into a *personalized, agile learning roadmap.* This living document can align learning efforts with individual career goals and rapidly shifting employer expectations. It should be revised regularly and prioritize high-impact competencies such as AI fluency, data fluency, digital ethics, communication, and collaboration. The OECD Skills Outlook 2021 (OECD, 2021) emphasizes that creating a habit of lifelong learning empowers individuals to better manage change. It also emphasizes the importance of developing "meta-learning" skills – i.e. skills in learning how to learn effectively. Professionals who proactively manage their learning and development in this way are more likely to remain employable, credible, and impactful job roles, workflows, and work tools continue to be digitally transformed.

Experiential Learning and Demonstrating Competence

Acquiring real-world experience is essential for demonstrating digital and human-centric competencies. Experiential learning allows professionals to apply theoretical knowledge of digital technologies and related tools in practice, facilitating deep learning, adaptability, and confidence with both established and emerging technologies (Kolb, 2015). Kolb's experiential learning cycle—comprising concrete experience, reflective observation, abstract conceptualization, and active experimentation—provides a framework for professionals to develop competencies through hands-on engagement. Opportunities for experiential learning of technologies and related tools include leading internal innovation pilots, joining digital transformation initiatives, volunteering in tech-enabled roles, or participating in side projects and hackathons. These settings foster problem-solving under real constraints, enhancing both technical and interpersonal competencies.

Professionals are increasingly expected to showcase demonstrated competence rather than rely solely on formal qualifications. A dynamic professional portfolio—featuring project artifacts, outcomes, and reflections—offers tangible evidence of a professional's ability to create impact in real-world scenarios (Ifenthaler et al., 2016). Unlike static résumés, portfolios communicate competency, relevance, growth, and applicability, aligning more closely with the expectations in digital or digitally enhanced professional roles. Effectively communicating these competencies involves more than listing skills. Professionals can strategically narrate their experiences through project write-ups, client success stories, or public contributions such as blog posts or open-source work. Digital platforms like LinkedIn, GitHub, and personal websites enable professionals to curate and market their learning journey and illustrate their readiness for future challenges (Susskind & Susskind, 2022). Technology vendors enable professionals to undertake and credibly market technology related certifications. For students, this portfolio-based approach can provide a powerful entry point into competitive job markets and serve as a springboard for continuous learning, demonstrating both technical competencies and the meta-learning competencies essential for thriving in a digital tech-rich future (Table 9.2).

TABLE 9.2
Strategies for Lifelong and Accelerated Professional Learning

Strategy Type	What It Involves	Illustrative Examples
Formal Learning	Structured courses leading to credentials aligned with professional needs.	Online certifications in data science, AI micro-credentials, executive short courses.
Informal and Peer Learning	Flexible, contextual, and social learning through professional communities.	LinkedIn learning, podcasts, peer mentoring, discussion groups, reverse mentoring.
Experiential Learning	Hands-on application of knowledge through projects and reflective practice.	Innovation pilots, hackathons, side projects, interdisciplinary collaboration.
Proactive Skill Auditing	Regular evaluation of current competencies vs. future needs to guide learning.	Using CPD dashboards, digital skill self-assessments, creating personalized learning plans.
Professional Portfolio Building	Documenting, showcasing, and communicating applied competencies to signal readiness and value.	Sharing project outcomes, maintaining an online portfolio or personal website.

NAVIGATING AND SHAPING PROFESSIONAL CAREER TRAJECTORIES

The traditional, linear career path is increasingly becoming a relic of the past. Today and in future, professionals must proactively navigate and shape their career trajectories rather than passively following past routes. This section explores essential strategies for professionals to proactively design their career journeys in an era of rapid change. We will delve into embracing agile career models like portfolio careers and intrapreneurship, which offer flexibility and opportunities for innovation within or across organizations. Additionally, the critical importance of strategic networking and personal branding will be discussed, empowering professionals to build visibility and influence in their chosen fields.

Embracing Agile Career Models: Portfolio Careers and Intrapreneurship

Agile career models have also become essential for maintaining long-term professional relevance and adaptability. The traditional linear career path—characterized by progression within a single organization or field—is increasingly being replaced by more flexible, multifaceted approaches that better align with modern workplace realities and technological disruption. One prominent approach is the portfolio career, where professionals simultaneously or sequentially engage in multiple roles across different projects, disciplines, or organizations (Hall, 2004). This approach enables continuous skill acquisition, exposure to varied work contexts, and greater adaptability during digital disruption (Susskind & Susskind, 2022). Portfolio careers offer particular advantages for students and early-career professionals by providing practical ways to explore different fields, build diverse networks, and develop what researchers call "career agility"—the ability to quickly adapt to changing market demands and technological advances (Haapakorpi, 2022). This flexibility has proven especially valuable during periods of economic uncertainty and rapid technological change.

Closely aligned with portfolio careers is intrapreneurship—acting entrepreneurially within established organizations. Intrapreneurs lead internal initiatives such as pilots to develop and commercialize new digital or digitally enhanced products, artificial intelligence-enabled service redesign, or cross-functional process innovation. These professionals identify opportunities by staying attuned to technological trends and organizational or customer needs, then drive change from within existing structures (Pinchot, 1985; Westerman et al., 2014). Intrapreneurship builds not only digital competence but also leadership, creativity, and strategic influence—critical capabilities for thriving in digitally transformed workplaces. Unlike traditional entrepreneurship, professionals do not risk their own capital and do not depend entirely on their own infrastructure—instead, they have the organization's capital and infrastructure to leverage. Former General Electric CEO Jack Welch used to say that in such situations, professionals can swing for the fences—if they miss, the impact on them is minimal compared to traditional entrepreneurs (Welch & Welch, 2005).

Finally, cross-functional and interdisciplinary experiences deepen career agility by broadening understanding of how different domains intersect. Taking on hybrid roles, rotating through departments, or co-leading collaborative ventures between departments or organizations allows professionals to develop systems thinking and anticipate diverse stakeholder needs (e.g. see Welch & Welch, 2005). Interdisciplinary collaboration competencies are increasingly valued, as organizations seek professionals who can bridge traditional silos and drive innovation across organizational or professional boundaries. Such versatility increases a professional's capacity to innovate and adapt while enhancing their perceived value in complex, evolving workplaces.

These agile career approaches—portfolio careers, intrapreneurship, and interdisciplinary experiences—provide essential levers for professional success in digitally transforming professions. They enable continuous learning, adaptability, and innovation, making professionals more resilient and valuable in environments where traditional career paths may no longer guarantee long-term success.

Strategic Networking and Personal Branding in the Digital Age

As digital transformation of the professions accelerates, the professional world is becoming an increasingly interconnected one. As a result, strategic networking and intentional personal branding are becoming critical for future-proofing careers. These complementary practices enable professionals to build meaningful relationships, establish credibility, and create opportunities in environments where traditional career advancement pathways are being disrupted by technological change and shifting organizational structures. Strategic networking involves building mutually beneficial relationships that provide opportunities for knowledge exchange, mentorship, visibility, and collaborative growth (Ibarra & Hunter, 2007). Today's networks span digital and physical spaces, with professionals attending conferences, joining professional associations, and engaging in online forums such as LinkedIn, GitHub, or field-specific communities as part of a deliberate effort to remain connected, informed, and relevant. Networking plays a crucial role in career success, with studies showing that more and more professionals are finding positions through networking of various forms, with LinkedIn being the most effective platform for professional connections (Porter et al., 2023). Effective networking requires developing what researchers call "strategic networking skills"—the ability to identify key relationships, maintain meaningful connections, and leverage networks for mutual benefit rather than simple relationship accumulation.

At the same time, personal branding—the ongoing articulation of one's unique professional identity—enables students and professionals to position themselves effectively in the employment market. A strong digital presence, built by publishing insights, curating an active portfolio, and engaging in industry debates, reinforces one's credibility and values (Montoya & Vandehey, 2008). Recent research emphasizes that personal branding has become essential for career advancement, significantly influencing hiring decisions, job satisfaction, and earning potential (Gorbatov et al., 2019; Kucharska, 2024). For students and early-career professionals, this might mean sharing reflections on internships, undertaking side projects, or doing course-based work to signal readiness and initiative while building authentic professional narratives that differentiate them from other graduates.

When combined, networking and personal branding form a powerful engine for learning and opportunity creation. They help professionals remain visible, attract meaningful collaborations, and navigate lateral or unconventional career trajectories. Research shows that these practices are particularly valuable for building social capital and adapting flexibly to evolving job markets, especially for graduates entering uncertain economic environments (Trang et al., 2024).

RISKS OF FAILING TO FUTURE-PROOF CAREERS

Failing to future-proof one's career amid accelerating digital transformation can result in serious and multifaceted risks that extend beyond individual consequences to affect entire professional ecosystems. Professionals who do not actively update their skills and mindsets may experience job displacement, particularly as automation and artificial intelligence absorb both routine and analytical tasks. Research indicates that almost half of jobs are at risk of computerization, with lower-wage and lower-education occupations being disproportionately vulnerable (Frey & Osborne, 2017). This technological disruption, accelerated by the COVID-19 pandemic, has created what the World Economic Forum (2025) describes as a "double-disruption" scenario, where 92 million jobs are expected to be displaced by 2030, even as 170 million new roles emerge.

When professionals don't keep up with changing workplace demands, three main problems occur: their income potential decreases, they have limited options for career advancement, and they face greater risk of unemployment. Over time, these pressures can compound into more severe consequences: reduced career satisfaction, feelings of professional stagnation, and burnout—especially for professionals unprepared for the pace and complexity of technological change (Edú-Valsania et al., 2022). Recent research highlights the emergence of "digital burnout," where professionals struggle to adapt to rapidly evolving technological demands, resulting in chronic workplace stress that affects both productivity and well-being (da Silva et al., 2024).

The consequences extend beyond individual professionals. If workforces fail to evolve, entire professional fields risk losing societal relevance, competitive advantage, and public trust. A static workforce inhibits innovation, diminishes the collective value proposition of professions, and leaves them ill-equipped to tackle emerging societal challenges (Busulwa & Evans, 2021). As the expectations of employers, clients, and regulators shift toward digital competency and adaptability, failure to adapt could mean marginalization or exclusion from strategic conversations that shape the future of professional practice.

Moreover, professionals who resist future-proofing strategies may find themselves trapped in declining industry segments or obsolete skill sets, facing what researchers term "technological unemployment"—joblessness resulting from technological advancement outpacing human adaptability (Chang et al., 2022). Recognizing these risks underscores the urgency of continuous learning and strategic career development, not merely for survival, but to remain influential, fulfilled, and valued contributors in a digitally transforming professional landscape.

CONCLUSION

This chapter offers professionals and aspiring professionals practical strategies to strengthen career resilience amid ongoing digital disruption and digital transformation. It emphasizes the need for cultivating digital fluency tailored to specific professional contexts, including competencies in data, AI, cybersecurity, and cloud technologies, alongside essential human-centric skills such as emotional intelligence, ethical judgment, and critical thinking. Adaptability, resilience, and a growth mindset are highlighted as vital for staying relevant in rapidly evolving environments. The chapter outlines approaches for lifelong and accelerated learning, including formal courses, informal networks, mentorship, and experiential learning. It also underscores the importance of personalized skill audits and dynamic development plans. Agile career strategies, such as portfolio careers, intrapreneurship, and participation in hackathons/accelerators, or interdisciplinary initiatives, are presented as increasingly relevant for navigating shifting roles. Strategic networking and personal branding are also emphasized as tools for career visibility and opportunity. Finally, the chapter highlights risks of inaction, including job displacement and professional obsolescence, emphasizing the urgency of continuous, proactive learning.

DISCUSSION QUESTIONS

What does it mean to "future-proof" a career, and why is this concept particularly urgent in digitally transforming professions?

How are the competencies needed for future-proofing evolving, and why are both digital fluency and human-centric skills critical?

What are the key mindsets that support accelerated learning, adaptability, and career resilience?

Which formal and informal learning pathways are most effective for professionals aiming to keep up with digital change?

How can professionals assess and respond to their own evolving skill gaps in a personalized and agile way?

In what ways does experiential learning, including innovation projects and side ventures, enhance professional competence and visibility?

What risks do professionals face if they fail to engage with future-proofing strategies, both personally and at the level of their profession?

REFERENCES

Andrews, J., & Higson, H. (2008). Graduate employability, 'soft skills' versus 'hard' business knowledge: A European study. *Higher Education in Europe*, *33*(4), 411–422.

Autor, D. H. (2015). Why are there still so many jobs? The history and future of workplace automation. *Journal of Economic Perspectives*, *29*(3), 3–30.

Bowles, M., Ghosh, S., & Thomas, L. (2020). Future-proofing accounting professionals: Ensuring graduate employability and future readiness. *Journal of Teaching and Learning for Graduate Employability*, *11*(1), 1–21.

Busulwa, R. (2022). *Navigating digital transformation in management*. Routledge.

Busulwa, R., & Evans, N. (2021). *Digital transformation in accounting.* Routledge.

Busulwa, R., Pickering, M., & Mao, I. (2022). Digital transformation and hospitality management competencies: Toward an integrative framework. *International Journal of Hospitality Management, 102*, 103132.

Busulwa, R., Pickering, M., & Pathiranage, N. W. (2024). Readiness of hospitality and tourism curricula for digital transformation. *Journal of Hospitality, Leisure, Sport & Tourism Education, 35*, 100519.

Chang, C. C., Tamers, S. L., & Swanson, N. (2022). The role of technological job displacement in the future of work. *NIOSH Science Blog, Centers for Disease Control and Prevention.*

da Silva, F. P., Jerónimo, H. M., Henriques, P. L., & Ribeiro, J. (2024). Impact of digital burnout on the use of digital consumer platforms. *Technological Forecasting and Social Change, 200*, 123172.

DataCamp. (2025). *The state of data & AI literacy report 2025.* DataCamp Inc.

Deming, D. J. (2017). The growing importance of social skills in the labor market. *The Quarterly Journal of Economics, 132*(4), 1593–1640.

Dweck, C. S. (2006). *Mindset: The new psychology of success.* Random house.

Edú-Valsania, S., Laguía, A., & Moriano, J. A. (2022). Burnout: A review of theory and measurement. *International Journal of Environmental Research and Public Health, 19*(3), 1780.

Eraut, M. (2004). Informal learning in the workplace. *Studies in Continuing Education, 26*(2), 247–273.

Floridi, L., Cowls, J., Beltrametti, M., Chatila, R., Chazerand, P., Dignum, V., & Vayena, E. (2018). AI4People—an ethical framework for a good AI society: Opportunities, risks, principles, and recommendations. *Minds and Machines, 28*, 689–707.

Frey, C. B., & Osborne, M. A. (2017). The future of employment: How susceptible are jobs to computerisation? *Technological forecasting and social change, 114*, 254–280.

Goleman, D. (1995). *Emotional intelligence: Why it can matter more than IQ.* Bantam Books.

Gorbatov, S., Khapova, S. N., & Lysova, E. I. (2019). Get noticed to get ahead: The impact of personal branding on career success. *Frontiers in psychology, 10*, 2662.

Haapakorpi, A. (2022). The quality of a professional portfolio career in the post-industrial era. *Journal of education and work, 35*(4), 441–454.

Hall, D. T. (2004). The protean career: A quarter-century journey. *Journal of vocational behavior, 65*(1), 1–13.

Ibarra, H., & Hunter, M. (2007). How leaders create and use networks. *Growth, 35*(1), 101–103.

Ifenthaler, D., Bellin-Mularski, N., & Mah, D. K. (Eds.). (2016). *Foundation of digital badges and micro-credentials: Demonstrating and recognizing knowledge and competencies.* Springer.

Kolb, D. A. (2015). *Experiential learning: Experience as the source of learning and development.* FT press.

Kucharska, W. (2024). Self-perceived personal brand equity of knowledge workers by gender in light of knowledge-driven organizational culture: Evidence from Poland and the united states. *SAGE Open, 14*(1), 21582440241227280.

Lengnick-Hall, C. A., Beck, T. E., & Lengnick-Hall, M. L. (2011). Developing a capacity for organizational resilience through strategic human resource management. *Human resource management review, 21*(3), 243–255.

Montoya, P., & Vandehey, T. (2008). *The brand called you: Make your business stand out in a crowded marketplace.* McGraw Hill Professional.

OECD. (2021). OECD Skills Outlook 2021. Retrieved from: https://www.oecd.org/en/publications/2021/06/oecd-skills-outlook-2021_6f4da936.html

Pinchot, G. III. (1985). Intrapreneuring: Why you don't have to leave the corporation to become an entrepreneur. *University of Illinois at Urbana-Champaign's Academy for Entrepreneurial Leadership Historical Research Reference in Entrepreneurship.*

Porter, C. M., Woo, S. E., Alonso, N., & Snyder, G. (2023). Why do people network? Professional networking motives and their implications for networking behaviors and career success. *Journal of Vocational Behavior, 142*, 103856.

Ratten, V. (2020). Coronavirus (Covid-19) and the entrepreneurship education community. *Journal of Enterprising Communities: people and places in the global economy, 14*(5), 753–764.

Senge, P. M. (2006). *The fifth discipline: The art and practice of the learning organization.* Broadway Business.

Susskind, R., & Susskind, D. (2022). The future of the professions: How technology will transform the work of human experts (Updated ed.). Oxford University Press.

Trang, N. M., McKenna, B., Cai, W., & Morrison, A. M. (2024). Personal branding in the digital era: Social media strategies for graduates. *International Journal of Contemporary Hospitality Management, 36*(4), 1123–1145.

Vial, G. (2019). Understanding digital transformation: A review and a research agenda. *The Journal of Strategic Information Systems, 28*(2), 118–144.

Welch, J., & Welch, S. (2005). *Winning.* New York: HarperCollins.

Westerman, G., Bonnet, D., & McAfee, A. (2014). *Leading digital: Turning technology into business transformation.* Harvard Business Review Press.

World Economic Forum. (2020). *The future of jobs report 2020.* World Economic Forum.

World Economic Forum. (2025). *The future of jobs report 2025.* World Economic Forum.

Xing, B., & Marwala, T. (2017). Implications of the fourth industrial age on higher education. *arXiv preprint arXiv:1703.09643.*

Yang, Y., Zhang, Y., Sun, D., He, W., & Wei, Y. (2025). Navigating the landscape of AI literacy education: insights from a decade of research (2014–2024). *Humanities and Social Sciences Communications, 12*(1), 1–12.

Part IV

Case Studies of the Digital Transformation Journeys of Different Professions

10 Case Study of the Digital Transformation of General Practice

INTRODUCTION

General practice, also known as family medicine or a core component of primary care, depending on the region, is currently undergoing a significant digital transformation. This digital transformation is driven by a range of advanced technologies, including telehealth, AI-driven diagnostic tools, electronic health records (EHRs), wearable Internet of Things (IoT) devices, robotics, integrated data platforms, and Large Language Models (LLMs). These innovations are fundamentally reshaping how healthcare is delivered, how clinicians interact with patients, how healthcare teams collaborate, and ultimately, the efficiency and effectiveness of general practitioners (GPs). Unlike earlier waves of healthcare reform - which often centered on financing (how healthcare services are funded) or workforce distribution (how healthcare professionals are allocated across different areas or specialties), and that were driven by economic, equity/access, and quality/safety concerns, the current transformation is distinctively technology-driven (Topol, 2019). Specifically, digital technologies are changing how GPs acquire and apply clinical knowledge, how they coordinate care, how they engage with patients, and how they contribute to population health. The COVID-19 pandemic significantly accelerated these changes. For instance, telehealth consultations in Australia experienced a dramatic increase in 2020, a trend observed globally (Halcomb et al., 2023). However, this rapid adoption also highlighted considerable disparities when it came to technology. Some GP clinics didn't have the ability to leverage digital technologies to offer telehealth services, the infrastructure for digital health wasn't available in some regions (e.g. broadband internet, appropriate telehealth devices), and equitable access to telehealth was driven by consumer digital literacy. But digital transformation in general practice extends far beyond simply adopting and integrating new digital tools into practice. It necessitates a fundamental reimagining of professional roles, clinician-patient relationships, and the foundational values underpinning care (Car & Sheikh, 2020).

This chapter will provide a comprehensive examination of how digital disruption is occurring in general practice, the threats and opportunities it presents for different aspects of the profession, and the change imperative it demands. We then provide a comprehensive review of what digital transformation means for general practice, how it is manifested at different levels of the profession, what it requires of different stakeholders of the profession, and the strategies being used by different

DOI: 10.1201/9781003606604-14

profession stakeholders to ensure safe and efficient digital transformation of the profession. As a profession that interacts with nearly all health conditions and population groups, general practice offers a unique vantage point for understanding the scope, complexity, and implications of digitally mediated healthcare. Through comparative case studies, evidence-based analysis, and stakeholder mapping, this chapter will explore how GPs and GP clinics are navigating the inherent tensions between innovation and equity, autonomy and standardization, and tradition and disruption. It will offer a framework for understanding how digital transformation is redefining not only clinical workflows but also the broader assumptions that shape professional expertise in medicine. Finally, we invite readers from outside of general practice to consider the implications of these changes for their own professions and to reflect on the societal responsibilities that accompany the digital evolution of professional services in an increasingly digital and technology-rich future.

DIGITAL DISRUPTION OF GENERAL PRACTICE

The digital disruption of general practice is multifaceted, affecting nearly every aspect of how care is delivered, experienced, and conceptualized. Unlike the incremental reforms of earlier decades, this digital shift is redefining the boundaries of what it means to be a general practitioner (GP). To understand this transformation systematically, this section examines five critical dimensions that, together, reflect the most fundamental changes occurring in general practice. These dimensions are informed by established frameworks for analyzing professional disruption (e.g., see Abbott, 1988; Susskind & Susskind, 2015) and analyzing digital transformation in healthcare (e.g., see Car & Sheikh, 2020; Topol, 2019), which identify the key channels through which digital technologies reshape professional work. The first of these involves how patients engage with services - for example, digital tools reshape expectations of care access, care responsiveness, and care personalization. The second concerns the competitive landscape - for example, non-traditional actors, such as health tech startups, telehealth platforms, AI-powered services, and even other healthcare professionals who effectively leverage digital technologies, are increasingly challenging the exclusive domain of GPs. The third addresses the democratization of information - for example, health knowledge once confined to professionals becomes widely available to patients and third parties. The fourth highlights the rise of platform-based models that reconfigure how healthcare services are organized, coordinated, and delivered. The fifth focuses on professional identity itself - for example, core markers of expertise, autonomy, and authority are being redefined in the digital era.

Taken together, these five interrelated dimensions - the transformation of patient expectations, the emergence of digital health competitors, the increasing accessibility of health data, the platformization of care delivery, and the shifting contours of professional identity - offer a useful framework for understanding how digital disruption is fundamentally reshaping the practice, purpose, and positioning of general practice within modern healthcare systems (Greenhalgh et al., 2020; Reed et al., 2019).

Changing Patient Expectations

One key way digital technology advancements disrupt professions is by significantly changing consumer expectations of the services offered by that profession (e.g. see Vial, 2019; Busulwa, 2022). In healthcare, digital technology advancements are rapidly changing patient expectations regarding healthcare service quality, access, convenience, and engagement. Patients increasingly approach healthcare with consumer-like expectations, demanding new digital or digitally enhanced services, seamless service delivery, immediate access to information, personalization of care, convenience, and expanded value for money (e.g., see Reed et al., 2019). This shift is particularly pronounced among early technology adopters and digital natives who have grown up with on-demand digital services and expect similar responsiveness from healthcare providers. Evidence of these changing expectations is visible across multiple developed countries. In the United Kingdom, the NHS App has evolved into a comprehensive digital front door to the healthcare system, with over 30 million registered users by the end of 2023, providing patients with tools to book appointments, access medical records, order repeat prescriptions, receive health advice, manage hospital appointments, book vaccinations, and receive direct messages from healthcare providers (NHS Digital, 2023). Similarly, in Australia, the My Health Record system has achieved high coverage with over 90% of Australians having a record as of 2023, largely due to the opt-out system implemented in 2019 - although it is worth noting that active usage remains a work in progress and patient expectations about accessing and controlling health information are still evolving, with ongoing concerns about privacy and security affecting usage (Australian Digital Health Agency, 2022).

The change in patient expectations is even more dramatic in rapidly growing digital health markets where a diverse array of digital health services is already on offer. For example, in China, many patients have access to access revolutionalizing platforms like WeDoctor and Ping An Good Doctor. WeDoctor alone serves over 270 million registered users and processes more than 29 million consultations annually (WeDoctor, 2022). These platforms integrate virtual consultations, prescription services, home diagnostics, and health monitoring into seamless digital experiences that far exceed traditional healthcare service models in terms of convenience and accessibility. Offerings like these expand patient expectations, creating both opportunities and challenges for GPs and GP clinics. Aside from these access revolutionalizing platforms, patients increasingly arrive at consultations with substantial amounts of self-generated health data from wearable devices, smartphone applications, online health assessments, and artificial intelligence (AI) tools (Piwek et al., 2016). While this can enhance patient engagement and provide valuable clinical insights, it also requires GPs to develop new skills in data interpretation, digital health literacy education, and managing patient concerns about potentially inaccurate or anxiety-provoking self-generated health information.

Emergence of Digital Health Competitors

Digital disruption has introduced dynamic and scalable new entrants into primary care, ranging from well-funded startups to large multinational technology companies.

These digital health competitors offer services that were traditionally provided only by GPs, but do so using scalable, efficient, and often more user-friendly digital platforms (Susskind & Susskind, 2015). Companies such as Babylon Health (UK), Teladoc (USA), Kry (Sweden), and Halodoc (Indonesia) have developed comprehensive digital health platforms that combine AI-driven triage, virtual consultations, and integrated care pathways (Parker & Van Alstyne, 2018). These services often provide extended operating hours, reduced wait times, and provide greater flexibility for patients who may struggle to attend traditional in-person appointments. For example, Babylon Health's AI-powered chatbot can conduct initial patient assessments 24/7, while their network of clinicians provides follow-up care as needed. While some digital services increase demand for GP clinics by streamlining referrals or broadening access, others divert certain types of presentations away from general practice. For example, mental health platforms like BetterHelp handle low-to-moderate psychological concerns directly and connect users with clinicians globally, offering 24/7 access - though often outside traditional regulatory or care integration frameworks.

The competitive threat is particularly acute in regions where traditional healthcare access is limited. In Brazil, companies like Dr. Consulta have developed vertically integrated models that combine digital scheduling, low-cost diagnostics, and access to medical professionals, effectively bypassing traditional GP gatekeeping structures (Marques & Ferreira, 2020). Similar models are emerging across Latin America, Southeast Asia, and parts of Africa, where digital-first healthcare providers can often deliver more accessible and affordable care than traditional practice models. These new entrants present significant challenges to traditional GP practices, particularly smaller independent practices that lack the talent or financial resources to leverage digital technologies to compete on convenience, cost, or technological sophistication. The convenience and perceived value offered by digital health providers can divert patient volume away from traditional GPs, threatening both their financial sustainability and their role as coordinators of comprehensive care (Greenhalgh et al., 2020).

Digital technologies are also enabling other health professionals, such as pharmacists, to expand into areas traditionally managed by GPs. With access to shared electronic health records, clinical decision support tools, and telehealth platforms, and LLMs, pharmacists can now provide services such as medication reviews, chronic disease management, and limited prescribing in some jurisdictions (Anderson et al., 2020; Cadogan & Hughes, 2021). These digitally supported capabilities not only extend pharmacists' scope of practice but also challenge traditional professional boundaries, potentially reshaping patient care pathways and redistributing responsibilities within primary care systems (Mossialos et al., 2015).

Democratization of Health Data and Tools

Digital technology innovations have enabled patients to collect, store, and analyze their own health data, marking a fundamental shift from centralized medical knowledge toward patient empowerment. Consumer wearable devices, smartphone health applications, and home diagnostic tools have made health monitoring and basic health assessment accessible to millions of people worldwide (Piwek et al., 2016). Modern wearable devices such as the Apple Watch, Fitbit, and Oura Ring can continuously monitor heart rate, sleep patterns, physical activity, blood oxygen levels, and even detect irregular heart rhythms. The Apple Watch's electrocardiogram feature has been credited with detecting atrial fibrillation in previously undiagnosed patients, while continuous glucose monitors originally designed for diabetes management are increasingly being used by healthy individuals to optimize their metabolic health (Perez et al., 2019).

Home diagnostic capabilities have expanded dramatically, particularly following the COVID-19 pandemic. Devices like TytoCare enable remote physical examinations including heart, lung, and throat assessments; while companies have developed laboratory-quality testing for various conditions from home settings, though regulatory challenges remain as seen with Cue Health's recent FDA warnings and subsequent closure (Kvedar et al., 2021). This democratization of diagnostic capabilities represents a fundamental shift in the traditional model where such assessments were exclusively within the domain of healthcare professionals. However, this democratization creates new challenges for GPs. Patient-generated health data is often vast in quantity but variable in quality and clinical relevance. For example, a GP might receive continuous glucose monitoring data from a diabetic patient's sensor, daily blood pressure readings from a home monitor, sleep pattern data from a fitness tracker, and symptom logs from a smartphone app - all requiring interpretation alongside traditional clinical assessments. GPs must develop new competencies in evaluating and interpreting data from diverse sources, distinguishing between clinically significant trends and normal variations, while helping patients understand the limitations and appropriate use of self-monitoring technologies. Additionally, the integration of patient-generated data into clinical workflows requires new technical infrastructure and clinical protocols that many practices are still developing. This includes EHR systems capable of importing and displaying data from multiple device manufacturers, secure cloud storage for continuous data streams, interoperability standards to ensure devices can communicate with practice management systems, automated alert systems to flag concerning patterns requiring immediate attention, and workflow protocols for staff to review and triage the constant flow of patient-generated information between scheduled appointments (Gordon & Hornbrook, 2016).

Platformization of Care Ecosystems

Healthcare is increasingly organizing around integrated digital platforms that consolidate administrative, clinical, and communication functions into unified ecosystems. This platformization represents a fundamental shift from fragmented, provider-centric systems toward patient-centric, interoperable networks that can coordinate care across multiple providers and settings (Parker & Van Alstyne, 2018). Leading examples of this trend include Singapore's HealthHub platform, which enables patients to access services across the entire national healthcare system through a single digital interface, and Estonia's digital health infrastructure, which provides seamless integration of health records, prescription management, and care coordination across all healthcare providers (Lember et al., 2018). These platforms demonstrate the potential for digital integration to improve care coordination, reduce administrative burden, and enhance patient experience. In Australia, the My Health Record system aims to provide similar integration, though implementation has been more gradual and faced greater resistance from both providers and patients (Australian Digital Health Agency, 2022). The United States presents a more fragmented picture, with multiple competing platforms and limited interoperability so far, though initiatives like the 21st Century Cures Act are driving greater data sharing and platform integration (Office of the National Coordinator for Health Information Technology, 2020).

Platformization presents both opportunities and challenges for GPs. While these systems can improve care coordination and reduce administrative burden, they also require significant investment in new technologies, digital or digitally enhanced processes/workflows, and GP clinic competencies. Independent practices may struggle to integrate with platform ecosystems, potentially excluding them from patient-preferred systems and threatening their long-term viability. Similarly, some GPs may struggle with maintaining required competence in new technology tools and digital or digitally enhanced processes, constraining their attractiveness to GP clinics and their income potential relative to peers.

Transformation of Professional Identity and Authority

Perhaps the most profound impact of digital disruption is its challenge to traditional concepts of professional identity and clinical authority. Historically, GPs have served as trusted gatekeepers and interpreters of medical knowledge, with their professional authority rooted in specialized training, clinical experience, and privileged access to diagnostic tools and medical information (Abbott, 1988). Digital technologies are challenging these traditional sources of professional authority in multiple ways. AI diagnostic tools increasingly match or exceed human performance in specific clinical tasks, while patient access to medical information and self-diagnostic tools reduces the information asymmetry that has traditionally underpinned the doctor-patient relationship (Topol, 2019). Additionally, clinical decision support systems and evidence-based protocols are shifting the basis of clinical authority from individual expertise toward adherence to standardized, algorithm-driven recommendations.

However, digital technologies are also creating opportunities for GPs to redefine and enhance their professional roles. The most successful digitally-enabled GPs are developing new competencies in data interpretation, technology evaluation, and digital health coaching - while maintaining their core strengths in relationship building, clinical reasoning, and holistic care coordination (Greenhalgh et al., 2020). This shift requires GPs to leverage digital technologies not just as tools, but as platforms for delivering enhanced patient care - using AI-assisted diagnostics to inform rather than replace clinical judgment, employing patient-generated data to enrich rather than overwhelm clinical assessments, and utilizing digital communication channels to strengthen rather than replace therapeutic relationships.

THE DIGITAL TRANSFORMATION OF GENERAL PRACTICE: DEFINITION AND KEY AIMS

The digital transformation of general practice represents more than the adoption of digital tools - it is a systemic reconfiguration of how general practitioners (GPs) deliver care, interact with patients, manage workflows, and sustain their professional identity. Drawing from the broader theoretical foundations outlined in Chapter 6, this section applies the conceptual understanding of digital transformation to the specific case of general practice. In particular, we explore the 7 key aims of digital transformation as applied to general practice. These include achieving care delivery efficiency and effectiveness breakthroughs, offering new digital or digitally enhanced services and value, effectively fulfilling new digital or digitally enhanced professional roles and workflows, cultivating required new digital or digitally enhanced professional competencies, co-creating new digital or digitally enhanced professional identities, enhancing professional legitimacy and public trust through digital excellence, and achieving sustainable competitive advantage for the profession's role in society. We discuss each of these aims in more detail below.

Achieving Care Delivery Efficiency and Effectiveness Breakthroughs

GPs around the world are increasingly leveraging digital tools to achieve significant improvements in service efficiency and clinical effectiveness, though the magnitude of these gains depends heavily on implementation quality. Examples of these advances include AI-assisted triage systems, clinical decision support systems (CDSS), and automated booking and follow-up solutions that work together to streamline both administrative and clinical workflows. For example, in the UK, the NHS e-Referral Service (e-RS) has streamlined appointment coordination between primary and secondary care providers. According to NHS implementation data, secondary care providers have experienced a 50% reduction in missed appointments when patients manage their own referrals through e-RS (CGI,2020). Similarly, AI-based diagnostic tools are demonstrating meaningful improvements in clinical accuracy, particularly when used to assist rather than replace clinical judgment. Research demonstrates that AI algorithms achieve a sensitivity of 87.0% and specificity of 77.1% for skin cancer diagnosis, compared to clinicians' sensitivity of 79.78% and specificity of 73.6% (Salinas et al., 2024). More significantly, AI assistance improves diagnostic accuracy across all clinical experience levels, with non-dermatologists benefiting most from AI support, showing improvements of +13 points in sensitivity and +11 points in specificity (Krakowski et al., 2024). However, efficiency gains are not automatic. Poor implementation—such as systems that disrupt established workflows, lack integration with existing electronic health records, or are introduced without adequate training—can increase clinician burden, reduce patient trust, and exacerbate digital divides (Greenhalgh et al., 2020). Achieving sustainable improvements requires careful integration into GP workflows, alignment with regulatory frameworks, and adequate digital literacy among both providers and patients.

Offering New Digital or Digitally Enhanced Services and Value

Digital transformation is enabling the creation of new service modalities such as virtual consultations, digital therapeutics, and AI-powered symptom checkers. For instance, Australia's Healthdirect Symptom Checker is a government-supported service that allows patients to self-assess before contacting a GP, providing triage advice about whether patients should see a doctor, care for themselves at home, or seek emergency care (Australian Government Department of Health and Aged Care, 2022). In sub-Saharan Africa, SMS-based health interventions and WhatsApp consultations are emerging as viable services in areas with limited healthcare access. Research demonstrates that two-way text messaging interventions are being successfully implemented across sub-Saharan Africa for healthcare delivery, with 31 trials involving 28,563 participants showing benefits for medication adherence, though effects on appointment attendance were uncertain (Ødegård et al., 2022). For example, in Nigeria, SMS messages substantially increased patient adherence to rapid diagnostic test (RDT) results for malaria. RDTs are point-of-care tests that quickly detect diseases without laboratory equipment—critical in areas with limited healthcare infrastructure. The SMS reminders helped ensure patients followed appropriate treatment: taking antimalarial medication if the test was positive, or avoiding unnecessary treatment if negative, thereby improving health outcomes and reducing drug resistance.

Additionally, mobile instant messaging tools such as WhatsApp are being used to support rural community health workers. For example, WhatsApp groups enabled health workers to organize campaigns, coordinate meetings, manage drug distribution efforts across dispersed communities, and mobilize health resources more efficiently. The platform also provided participatory support by fostering empathetic connections among professionally isolated workers, enhancing communication quality, and increasing the speed of task completion. Implementation was received positively by health workers as a useful tool to support distributed rural health work (Pimmer et al., 2017). These care delivery innovations are examples of new opportunities for expanding healthcare reach and supporting patient engagement, though their integration with traditional GP services varies by context. Unfortunately, uneven access to technology infrastructure and weak digital literacy among patients can limit impact, requiring careful consideration of local contexts and capabilities when implementing these new service models.

Effectively Fulfilling New Digital or Digitally Enhanced Professional Roles and Workflows

Digital transformation is creating new digital roles and digitally enhancing existing roles within general practice settings. Examples of new digital roles include telehealth coordinators who manage virtual care platforms and coordinate remote consultations, digital patient care coordinators who handle online patient portals and virtual appointment scheduling, and remote patient monitoring coordinators who oversee technology-enabled patient surveillance systems (Indeed, 2024). Traditional general practitioner roles are also becoming digitally enhanced through advanced diagnostic tools and clinical decision support systems. AI-powered stethoscopes are being rolled out to GP clinics across the NHS, enabling physicians to detect heart failure with 91% sensitivity and 80% specificity, providing immediate diagnostic support that was previously only available through expensive hospital tests (Imperial College Healthcare NHS Trust, 2024). Clinical decision support systems powered by artificial intelligence are being integrated into GP workflows to accelerate diagnosis and improve decision-making, particularly for patients with unclear symptoms or complex conditions (Schmieding et al., 2025). Digital stethoscopes with wireless connectivity enable seamless integration with electronic health records, allowing GPs to automatically capture examination findings and share them across care teams, while also supporting remote consultations through high-fidelity audio transmission (Bellet, 2024). These technological enhancements are transforming the traditional GP services and roles from primarily manual diagnostic approaches to AI-assisted, data-driven, and digital workflow facilitated services and roles.

Effectively Cultivating Required New Digital or Digitally Enhanced Professional Competencies

General practitioners must now develop competencies beyond traditional clinical knowledge, including digital literacy, cybersecurity awareness, digital ethics, data interpretation, and familiarity with AI-assisted diagnostic tools. Professional body competency frameworks are increasingly recognizing the importance of technology-related skills. The Royal College of General Practitioners (RCGP) curriculum includes working with data, technology, and systems as a specific competency area, requiring GPs to be make competent across a range of IT skills and to develop knowledge of the benefits for their practices and patients, as well as an understanding of the potential pitfalls, in order to perform effectively in the modern healthcare environment (RCGP, 2025). In North America, the Canadian CanMEDs framework has developed specific eHealth competencies, with working groups creating "key and enabling competencies under the core CanMEDs roles" to address digital health skills (Royal College of Physicians and Surgeons of Canada, 2015). The Accreditation Council for Graduate Medical Education (ACGME) has established clinical informatics as a subspecialty with specific program requirements, while broader competency frameworks expect physicians to "use information technology to optimize learning". The 2015 CanMEDs update explicitly stated that "competence in health care informatics is viewed as crucial for medical leaders and managers and vital to the delivery of health care" (Royal College of Physicians and Surgeons of Canada, 2015).

The integration required new digital or digital and digitally enhanced competencies into professional body competence frameworks remains inconsistent across regions, with some countries or some specific professional bodies being well advanced, while others have very little integrated. Many current and prospective GPs want greater institutional support for acquiring and keeping up with these evolving digital competencies, despite growing evidence of the need for them (e.g. see Neves & Burgers 2022).

Co-creating New Digital or Digitally Enhanced Professional Identities

The integration of digital technologies is prompting GPs to reflect on and renegotiate their professional identities. No longer limited to face-to-face consultations and traditional diagnostics, modern GPs may be seen as digital integrators, patient empowerment agents, and data stewards. This shift challenges traditional values of "hands-on" care and personalized medicine but also opens up new possibilities for professional identity formation grounded in innovation, accessibility, and evidence-based practice. Professional bodies are critical to this co-creation process. In Australia, the Royal Australian College of General Practitioners (RACGP) has developed position statements on telehealth that frame digital practice as aligned with core values of comprehensive, continuous, and coordinated primary care (Royal Australian College of General Practitioners, 2023). Professional medical organizations in other countries, including the UK Royal College of General Practitioners and various European GP associations, are developing similar frameworks to prevent digital marginalization of GPs and support professional identity evolution in the digital age.

Enhancing Professional Legitimacy and Public Trust through Digital Excellence

As patients increasingly interact with healthcare through digital means, the perceived legitimacy of GPs hinges on their ability to deliver safe, ethical, and high-quality digital care. Public trust is closely tied to how well GPs handle data privacy, navigate algorithmic decisions, and preserve continuity of care. In the USA, the American Academy of Family Physicians (AAFP) has developed digital health guidance to support clinicians in using technology in ways that maintain trust and quality (AAFP, 2020). Conversely, when digital tools are used poorly - such as AI misdiagnoses or privacy breaches - the profession's legitimacy may suffer. Excellence in digital practice, then, is not just a technical issue but a reputational imperative.

Achieving Sustainable Competitive Advantage for the Profession's Place in Society

Finally, the profession must ensure it remains indispensable and influential in healthcare systems increasingly disrupted by non-traditional players such as tech companies, retail health providers, and AI platforms. Digital transformation offers GPs a chance to embed themselves in high-value, patient-centered ecosystems. Those who do not evolve risk being sidelined. In some regions, such as Scandinavia and Singapore, GPs are leading digital innovation and setting benchmarks that influence national health strategy. In others, the risk of professional obsolescence is real. Competitive advantage will come from proactive engagement, ethical leadership, and digital innovation stewardship (Topol, 2019).

HOW THE DIGITAL TRANSFORMATION OF GENERAL PRACTICE MANIFESTS AT DIFFERENT LEVELS

Digital transformation within the general practice (GP) profession is not a monolithic change - it manifests differently across multiple levels, including individual practitioners, general practice clinics or services, educational institutions, professional bodies, and government regulators (see Table 10.1). Understanding its manifestation at these levels helps illuminate the interdependencies and gaps that shape the overall digital maturity of the profession. This section unpacks how digital transformation is occurring so far at each level of the profession and the flow on implications.

Transformation of Professional Roles and Activities

At the practitioner level, the most visible transformation is the evolution of the GP's role. Traditional tasks like diagnosis, prescription, and follow-up are now increasingly supported - or partially replaced - by digital tools. AI-powered symptom checkers and automated triage systems are being developed, though research shows that appropriate triage advice is provided in only 57% of evaluations, rising to 80% for emergency cases (Summerton & Cansdale, 2019). Digital prescribing platforms and decision support tools are changing how clinical judgment is applied and how time is allocated. In some healthcare systems, GPs are beginning to operate as digital navigators - guiding patients through complex ecosystems of digital apps, platforms,

TABLE 10.1
Manifestations of Digital Transformation in General Practice

Aspect of General Practice	How Digital Transformation Manifests	Example manifestations
Patient Access	Shift to digital and hybrid models of care delivery	Telehealth, asynchronous messaging platforms, patient portals
Clinical Workflow	Automation and digital augmentation of diagnosis, referrals, and follow-ups	AI-enabled triage, e-referral systems, predictive analytics for care coordination
Practice Operations	Digitization of administrative processes and data infrastructure	Electronic medical records (EMRs), digital booking systems, integrated billing
Professional Roles and Skills	Emergence of new digital competencies and hybrid clinical-technological tasks	GPs learning to interpret AI outputs; digital literacy becoming core to patient care
Professional Identity	Redefinition of what it means to be a GP in a tech-augmented, data-driven environment	GPs as coordinators of digital care teams; data custodians; remote-first clinicians
Governance and Trust	Evolving regulatory, ethical, and legal standards to ensure responsible tech use and protect public trust	Guidelines for AI-assisted decisions; digital consent practices; cybersecurity standards

and monitoring devices. This role requires both digital fluency and the ability to maintain clinical leadership in increasingly collaborative, interdisciplinary teams. Simultaneously, administrative burdens have also shifted. While some digital tools reduce paperwork, others create new demands - primary care physicians spend more than one-half of their workday, nearly 6 hours, interacting with electronic health records during and after clinic hours (Arndt et al., 2017). Managing digital alerts, overseeing telehealth logistics, and updating electronic health records represent significant new time commitments, with inbox management alone accounting for substantial portions of physicians' daily workflow (Dymek et al., 2021). Proficiency in well-designed digital tools and platforms can enhance individual GPs' efficiency and effectiveness in specific areas, though implementation challenges and new administrative burdens may offset some benefits. The net impact varies significantly based on the specific tools, implementation quality, and individual GP digital literacy.

Transformation of Professional Services Business Models

Digital transformation has also begun to occur in the business models underpinning general practice services. Telehealth services, virtual clinics, subscription-based care models, and mobile health platforms are introducing new pathways for delivering primary care. Direct-to-consumer telemedicine models, where patients access physicians via telephone or video conferencing, are growing rapidly and may increase access to care; although they may not decrease overall healthcare spending, as increased convenience may tap into unmet demand for healthcare (Ashwood et al., 2017; Mehrotra et al., 2017). These direct-to-consumer services often operate outside traditional Medicare systems and raise the need for navigation of care fragmentation issues, as patients typically lack existing relationships with providers and care episodes may not be communicated to their regular GP (Foo et al., 2023). Meanwhile, hybrid models are emerging in various healthcare systems where traditional clinics augment in-person care with digital consultations and asynchronous services. These models are more likely to be financially viable when supported by updated reimbursement policies and stable digital infrastructure. Business model transformation has also accelerated in developing regions, where mobile health innovations are enabling new models of practice delivery in underserved areas. For example, in Kenya, organizations like Living Goods recruit community health workers on a micro-entrepreneurship model to sell health commodities door-to-door, while Healthy Entrepreneurs trains community health workers to become "health entrepreneurs" by providing business management training, loans, and mobile phones to order health commodities online for rural communities (Ameso & Prince, 2025). However, regulatory frameworks for these innovations often need to catch up to technological developments, to ensure accountability, quality standards, and long-term sustainability.

Transformation of Professional Governance and Regulation

Regulatory bodies and professional associations have had to evolve to keep pace with emerging digital health realities. In countries such as Singapore and the Netherlands, regulators have embraced "regulatory sandboxes" to test new digital services within safe, monitored environments (PPC Land, 2025). For example, Singapore's Ministry of Health has established regulatory sandboxes that create controlled environments for testing innovative healthcare services while maintaining appropriate safeguards, such as allowing community pharmacists to administer influenza vaccinations under specific protocols (Ministry of Health Singapore, 2024). These structures allow general practice innovators to trial novel tools while ensuring ethical and clinical oversight.

Professional bodies like the RACGP, the RCGP (UK), and the AMA (USA) are increasingly publishing digital health guidelines, endorsing tools, and advocating for inclusive policy development. These actions help standardize digital practice and provide practitioners with the legitimacy and confidence to innovate. However, progress remains uneven. In many countries, professional regulation still lags behind digital innovation. The absence of clear standards for AI use, data sharing, or teleconsultation reimbursement creates uncertainty for GPs and exposes them to regulatory and legal risks. Coordinated efforts across international and national bodies are essential for ensuring the safe and equitable governance of digital general practice.

Transformation of Public Trust and Social Contract

Public trust is a cornerstone of the GP profession, and digital transformation puts that trust to the test. As interactions become more mediated by algorithms and platforms, patients may question the role, necessity, and reliability of their GPs. Research on public perspectives during the COVID-19 pandemic found that while patients identified benefits of virtual primary care including improved access and timeliness, they also expressed concerns about healthcare equity and the impact on care quality (Neves et al., 2021). Additionally, studies show that patients report varying comfort levels with digital health tools, with particular concerns about data privacy and the potential impact on the patient-provider relationship. However, well-implemented digital transformation can actually strengthen the social contract. Digital health initiatives have demonstrated potential to improve access to care, particularly for underserved populations, and can enhance the visibility and relevance of primary care services. When designed thoughtfully, telehealth initiatives can help rebuild trust in care systems, particularly when they address cultural and linguistic barriers that historically excluded certain patient groups. To preserve trust, digital tools must be seen as enhancing - not replacing - empathy, continuity, and clinical expertise. This requires ethical AI design, transparent data policies, and ongoing patient engagement to ensure that technological advances serve to strengthen rather than undermine the fundamental relationship between patients and their GPs.

Transformation of Professional Identity and Value

As digital transformation changes clinical practice, it influences how GPs understand their professional roles and how society values their contribution. The rapid shift toward remote care delivery, particularly accelerated during COVID-19, has created new challenges for general practice. Video consultations and other digital modalities have been rolled out at unprecedented speed (Greenhalgh et al., 2020), creating ongoing pressures to change traditional models of care delivery. Research indicates that the implementation of digital technologies in healthcare is a complex change that disrupts long-established processes and routines. Some clinicians express concerns about technical and clinical quality, privacy, safety, and accountability when using new digital tools (Greenhalgh et al., 2020). These technological changes challenge traditional professional boundaries and may influence how GPs perceive their role in patient care.

Professional identity is also affected by the evolution of healthcare roles, with nurse practitioners and other healthcare professionals taking on expanded responsibilities that may overlap with traditional GP functions. In healthcare systems adopting new care delivery models, questions arise about the unique value proposition of different professional roles. To navigate these challenges, professional bodies, educators, and clinics must support reflective practice, interprofessional dialogue, and career development paths that help clarify the evolving value of general practice in the digital age. Clear guidance on appropriate use of digital technologies, attention to workflow redesign, and proper training for clinical and non-clinical staff are essential for successful adaptation (Greenhalgh et al., 2020). By maintaining focus on patient-centered care while embracing technological capabilities, GPs can continue to demonstrate their essential role in contemporary healthcare delivery.

CHALLENGES TO DIGITALLY TRANSFORMING GENERAL PRACTICE

The digital transformation of general practice brings with it a complex mix of promise and pressure. While digital tools and processes offer significant opportunities to enhance diagnosis, treatment, efficiency, access, patient engagement, and more, their integration into GP workflows, systems, and professional identity is neither seamless nor universally beneficial. This section examines some of the diverse challenges the profession faces in navigating its digital transformation, including infrastructural and interoperability barriers, digital ethics and privacy concerns, financial and organizational constraints, impacts on health equity, and effects on clinician wellbeing and professional identity.

Digital Infrastructure and Interoperability Challenges

Digital infrastructure encompasses the foundational technological architecture required for modern healthcare delivery, including telecommunications networks (particularly broadband connectivity), data centers, cloud computing platforms, cybersecurity frameworks, and the hardware and software systems that enable digital health services. This infrastructure provides the foundational technological platform that supports electronic health records, telehealth platforms, clinical decision support systems, and other health information technologies. Inadequate digital infrastructure poses significant barriers, particularly in rural, remote, and under-resourced healthcare settings. For example, reliable broadband internet connectivity remains inconsistent across many healthcare settings globally, limiting access to cloud-based health systems, telehealth services, and real-time data sharing capabilities (World Health Organization, 2021). Research demonstrates that in the United States, approximately 35% of rural populations lack access to high-speed broadband, and nearly 39% of rural healthcare facilities lack adequate broadband services, substantially constraining telehealth implementation and creating digital health disparities (Graves et al., 2021). This infrastructure deficit limits access to cloud-based health information systems, real-time clinical data exchange, and telemedicine services.

Interoperability refers to the technical and semantic capability of disparate health information systems to exchange, interpret, and utilize shared data across organizational and technological boundaries. This includes both syntactic interoperability (the ability to exchange data formats) and semantic interoperability (the ability to interpret the meaning of exchanged data), as well as organizational interoperability (the alignment of processes and governance structures to enable effective data sharing). Substantial progress has been made in overcoming interoperability challenges in recent years, though gaps persist. In the US, Office of the National Coordinator for Health Information Technology data indicates that 88% of hospitals participate in electronic health data exchange as of 2021, with 70% of hospitals engaging in routine interoperable exchange by 2023 (Office of the National Coordinator for Health Information Technology, 2023). However, significant barriers remain in achieving seamless data sharing across all care settings, particularly among smaller rural hospitals, long-term care facilities, and behavioral health providers. Canada exemplifies the complexity of interoperability in federated healthcare systems. While individual provinces have developed sophisticated health information infrastructures, limited cross-jurisdictional integration creates discontinuities in care coordination when patients receive services outside their home province. This systemic fragmentation diminishes the potential benefits of electronic health records and creates inefficiencies in care transitions.

Estonia and Denmark provide good examples of success at overcoming digital infrastructure and interoperability challenges (e.g., see Nøhr et al., 2017). Estonia's X-Road platform, operational since 2001, provides a secure, decentralized data exchange layer that connects over 450 public and private organizations while maintaining data sovereignty and privacy protections. Denmark's sundhed.dk portal, launched in 2003, offers a unified patient and provider interface for health information access, integrating data from multiple national health registries and clinical systems. These implementations illustrate the importance of national-level strategic coordination, standardization, and governance frameworks in achieving comprehensive digital health transformation.

Privacy, Security, and Digital Ethics Concerns

The digitization of health information creates significant privacy and security risks that disproportionately affect general practice settings. Unlike large hospital systems with dedicated cybersecurity teams, many GP practices lack the resources and expertise to implement robust security measures, making them attractive targets for cyberattacks (Kruse et al., 2017). Healthcare cybersecurity incidents have increased dramatically in recent years, with ransomware attacks particularly problematic for smaller healthcare providers. The 2017 WannaCry ransomware attack affected 200,000 - 300.000 computers across more than 150 countries, causing significant disruptions to healthcare services, including the UK's National Health Service (Ghafur et al., 2019). Similar attacks have targeted GP practices and smaller healthcare providers who often lack the security infrastructure and incident response capabilities of larger organizations.

Beyond cybersecurity concerns, the integration of AI and algorithmic decision-support tools raises complex ethical questions about clinical responsibility, transparency, and bias. Many AI diagnostic tools have been trained primarily on data from specific populations, potentially leading to reduced accuracy or biased recommendations for patients from different demographic groups (Rajkomar et al., 2018). GPs must navigate these ethical complexities often without institutional support or clear professional guidance. The proliferation of health apps and digital tools also creates challenges related to data governance and patient privacy. With a proliferation in volume and diversity of health apps available across major app stores, patients increasingly use tools that may not meet clinical standards for privacy protection or data security. GPs may need to help patients navigate these tools while managing potential privacy and safety risks.

Financial and Resource Constraints

Digital transformation requires significant financial investment in technology, training, and organizational change. For many GP practices, particularly smaller independent practices, these costs represent substantial barriers to digital transformation of services. Electronic health record implementation involves substantial upfront and ongoing costs for software licensing, hardware, maintenance, and technical support - though specific costs vary significantly by practice size and system complexity. The challenge is particularly acute in lower-income countries and regions where healthcare resources are already constrained. A study of digital health adoption in Sub-Saharan Africa found that cost was the most significant barrier to implementation, followed by lack of technical expertise and inadequate infrastructure (Mehl et al., 2018). Even in higher-income countries, rural and remote practices often struggle with the costs and complexity of digital transformation.

Training and workflow adaptation represent additional resource requirements that are often underestimated. Successful implementation of digital health tools requires not only initial training but ongoing support and workflow optimization. Research has documented various challenges with EHR implementation, including workflow disruptions and adaptation periods as staff learn new systems. Policy responses to these financial barriers vary significantly across jurisdictions, with some providing public funding support while others rely primarily on market mechanisms.

Impact on Health Equity and Access

While digital health technologies hold significant promise for improving health access and outcomes, their implementation can also exacerbate existing health inequities. The "digital divide" affects healthcare access along multiple dimensions including socioeconomic status, age, education level, geographic location, and cultural background (Benda et al., 2020). Older adults, individuals with lower incomes, and those with limited education are less likely to have access to digital devices, reliable internet connectivity, and the digital literacy skills necessary to effectively use digital health tools (Gordon & Hornbrook, 2016). During the COVID-19 pandemic, these disparities became particularly pronounced as healthcare systems rapidly shifted to telehealth delivery models. Language and cultural barriers also affect the equitable implementation of digital health tools. Digital health platforms and applications often lack adequate language and cultural adaptation for diverse populations. AI diagnostic tools may demonstrate reduced accuracy for patients from minority populations if training data is not representative (Rajkomar et al., 2018). Geographic disparities in digital infrastructure also affect health equity, with rural and remote communities often facing limited broadband access that can restrict the effectiveness of telehealth and digital health interventions.

Effects on Clinician Wellbeing and Professional Satisfaction

The impact of digital transformation on GP wellbeing and professional satisfaction is complex and often contradictory. While digital tools can enhance clinical capabilities and reduce some administrative burdens, they can also contribute to increased workload, cognitive burden, and professional stress (Shanafelt et al., 2015). Electronic health record systems, while providing important clinical benefits, have been associated with increased documentation burden and reduced face-to-face time with patients. Research has documented significant EHR-related workload challenges for primary care physicians, with substantial time spent on documentation and administrative tasks that can contribute to professional burnout and reduced job satisfaction (Arndt et al., 2017).

Alert fatigue represents another significant challenge, with clinicians receiving numerous automated alerts and notifications that may reduce attention to truly important clinical information. The high volume of alerts creates cognitive burden for clinicians, and research has shown that this can lead to frequent overriding of safety alerts, potentially reducing their clinical effectiveness (Van Der Sijs et al., 2006). However, when implemented thoughtfully, digital tools can actually enhance professional satisfaction by reducing routine administrative tasks, improving access to clinical information, and enabling more effective care coordination. The key appears to be ensuring that digital tools are designed with clinician workflow and user experience as primary considerations rather than treating these as secondary concerns.

THE PROFESSION'S STRATEGIC RESPONSES TO DRIVE PROACTIVE DIGITAL TRANSFORMATION

The successful digital transformation of general practice requires coordinated strategic responses across multiple levels and stakeholder groups. Individual practices, professional organizations, educational institutions, and health systems must work in concert to create supportive environments for digital adoption, while ensuring that digital transformation aligns with the core values and objectives of primary care. This section examines key strategic approaches currently being implemented to drive digital transformation in general practice globally.

Integration of Digital Health Education and Training

A critical driver of the digital transformation of general practice is developing digital health competencies among current and future general practitioners. Medical schools and training programs are increasingly recognizing the need to integrate digital health topics into core curricula, though implementation varies significantly across institutions and regions; and comprehensive digital health competency frameworks have been developed to guide curriculum design (Car et al., 2025). Similarly, various institutions have begun pioneering innovative approaches to training clinicians in digital health innovation and implementation. Professional development for practicing GPs presents greater challenges, as busy practitioners often have limited time for formal training programs. Professional medical colleges have begun offering flexible online learning modules covering digital health topics that can be integrated into continuing professional development requirements. Australia's Royal Australian College of General Practitioners has implemented digital health initiatives for GP leaders, including guidance on telehealth implementation (Royal Australian College of General Practitioners, 2023). However, significant gaps remain in digital health education globally, particularly regarding resource availability and access to high-quality continuing education in digital health topics.

Development of Interoperable Digital Infrastructure

The GP profession has strategically prioritized the development of interoperable digital infrastructure, as exemplified by the Royal College of General Practitioners' 2019 "All Systems GP" manifesto which called for "the joining up of IT systems across the NHS to be prioritized" and stated that "all GP practices should have fully interoperable IT systems" and "access to a single shared electronic patient record which documents patient interactions throughout the NHS" (Digital Health, 2020). This proactive focus drives digital transformation by ensuring that technological investments create seamless information flow rather than additional administrative burden, enabling GPs to access comprehensive patient information at the point of care. The anticipated benefits include reduced duplicate testing, improved care coordination across providers, enhanced clinical decision-making through comprehensive patient data access, and more efficient GP workflows that allow more time for direct patient care.

Digital health systems work best when different technologies can communicate and share information with each other - this is called "interoperability" (Office of the National Coordinator for Health Information Technology, 2023). Strategic investment in interoperable digital health infrastructure is essential for realizing the full benefits of digital transformation in general practice because it allows patient information to flow seamlessly between GPs, hospitals, specialists, and other healthcare providers. Without this connectivity, digital systems become isolated "islands" that can actually make healthcare coordination more difficult rather than easier (Car & Sheikh, 2020). Interoperability requires standards-based approaches (e.g., see World Health Organization, 2021), which aim to get all healthcare organizations to use the same technical rules and formats for storing and sharing health information - similar to how all email systems (e.g. Gmail, Outlook, Hotmail) can communicate with each other because they follow standard internet protocols like SMTP.

Leading examples demonstrating the importance of coordinated, standards-based approaches to interoperable digital health infrastructure development include Estonia and Denmark. Estonia's digital health system exemplifies successful national-level coordination of digital health infrastructure. The country's X-Road platform enables secure data sharing across all healthcare providers while maintaining patient privacy and system security. This means that when an Estonian patient visits any doctor or hospital, their complete medical history is immediately available, reducing duplicate tests and improving care quality. Estonia has achieved high levels of health data digitization through its coordinated national approach (Lember et al., 2018). Denmark has also implemented comprehensive digital health infrastructure through its national health portal and shared electronic health record system, enabling coordination across healthcare providers and patient access to health information (Danish Health Data Authority, 4).

In contrast, countries with more fragmented healthcare systems face greater challenges in developing interoperable infrastructure. For example, in a fragmented system, a patient's GP might not be able to see test results from a hospital visit in a timely manner, forcing the patient to repeat tests or to carry physical copies of records between providers, or alternatively forcing the patient's GP to ring the hospital. The United States has made significant investments in health information technology through initiatives like the HITECH Act and 21st Century Cures Act, but achieving comprehensive interoperability remains challenging due to system fragmentation and business practices where technology companies design systems that don't easily communicate with competitors' products.

Innovation Facilitation and Regulatory Adaptation

The GP profession has strategically focused on both facilitating digital innovation (e.g., facilitating the creation of new digital or digitally enhanced infrastructure, products/services, processes/workflows, job roles) and advocating for progressive regulatory frameworks, because such facilitation ensures innovations address real practice needs and workflow requirements, while appropriate regulatory frameworks enable safe adoption of beneficial technologies and practices within general practice. Success in these areas drives digital transformation of the profession by actively shaping/accelerating digital innovation of clinical practice, while ensuring its safety. An example of the profession facilitating digital innovation include dedicated initiatives such as the RCGP's Clinical Innovation and Research Centre, which works with clinical champions to develop materials addressing identified clinical priorities. Another example is the Research Engagement Hub, created in collaboration with the NIHR School for Primary Care Research to connect academics and practitioners in developing primary care innovations (RCGP, n.d.-a). The RCGP also maintains an innovation platform that shares examples of good practice and innovations in general practice, enabling peer-to-peer learning and dissemination of successful digital innovations across the profession (RCGP, n.d.-b).

GP professional organizations have also strategically advocated for regulatory frameworks that support digital health adoption while maintaining safety standards. The Royal Australian College of General Practitioners (RACGP) has developed comprehensive position statements advocating for appropriate telehealth regulations, stating that "telehealth has become a critical part of Australia's healthcare system" while calling for regulations that support "continuity of care between a patient and their usual GP" rather than fragmented direct-to-consumer models (RACGP, 2023). Similarly, the RCGP has developed position statements on AI in primary care, advocating that "AI and digital health will likely have an important role to play in the future of general practice" while calling for integration that ensures "appropriate safeguards" and secure data handling (RCGP, 2024). These professional advocacy efforts have influenced policy development, with the RACGP's telehealth position contributing to Australia's permanent adoption of Medicare-funded telehealth services beyond the COVID-19 pandemic.

Patient-Centered Digital Health Design

Patient-centered digital health design involves actively engaging patients and communities in the development, testing, and implementation of new digital or digitally enhanced healthcare products/services, processes/workflows, and roles, so as to ensure these tools address real patient needs, are easy to use, and fit into patients' daily lives and healthcare experiences. GP professional organizations recognized that patient centered digital health design can drive its digital transformation by accelerating demand for and adoption of new digital or digitally enhanced products/services, processes/workflows, and roles in general practice. The profession's key entities have begun incorporating patient perspectives into their digital health design/redesign initiatives through established patient engagement structures. For example, the Royal College of General Practitioners maintains a Patient and Carers Partnership Group (PCPG) that contributes to the College's policy development and strategic direction, including digital health considerations (RCGP, n.d.-c). The RCGP also operates patient groups across its devolved nations that "share similar aims, values and goals" and work to "enhance the quality of services delivered by GPs," including input on digital service delivery (RCGP, n.d.-d).

Addressing digital health literacy represents another critical area where the profession has taken action in relation to patient-centered digital health design. Since digital health literacy varies significantly among patient populations - with particular challenges for older adults, those with lower socioeconomic status, and patients from diverse linguistic backgrounds - the profession has sought ways to better engage these groups in care design and delivery. GP practices have increasingly implemented digital inclusion initiatives, such as engaging patients as digital health design/redesign advisors, and employing digital ambassadors within Primary Care Networks to provide patient training on digital health tools and build partnerships with local organizations to support patients who struggle with digital access or skills (Good Things Foundation, 2024). The profession acknowledges that patient involvement in digital health design is essential for offering relevant, usable, and effective products/services that patients will embrace, and thus that GPs and GP practices will adopt.

Financial Models and Incentives Alignment

Financial models and incentives alignment involves ensuring that payment and reimbursement systems support rather than hinder the adoption of digital health innovations in general practice. The GP profession has strategically focused on advocating for payment model reforms because traditional fee-for-service models often fail to adequately reimburse the time and resources required for digital health implementation or the additional value created. Often, payment models designed for traditional practice can unintentionally disincentivize digital innovation by underpaying for related outputs. This, in turn, can create financial barriers to the adoption of new digital or digitally enhanced products/services, process/workflows, or roles. Some GP professional organizations have successfully advocated and continue to advocate for expanded reimbursement for digital health services. The Royal Australian College of General Practitioners (RACGP) played a key role as "principal partner" with the Australian government in advocating for permanent telehealth funding under Medicare, with Minister for Health and Aged Care Greg Hunt acknowledging that "the RACGP has been our principal partner" in making telehealth transformational to Australia's healthcare system (RACGP, 2021). This advocacy resulted in over $100 million being allocated to facilitate permanent telehealth services and the inclusion of telehealth consultations in general practice funding calculations through the Workforce Incentive Program. Similarly, the Royal College of General Practitioners has advocated for funding reforms to support digital transformation of primary care, calling for "urgent reform funding to address widening health inequalities" and emphasizing the need for "fairer general practice funding" that accounts for the changing nature of practice in the digital age (RCGP, 2024). The RCGP has also welcomed government funding for expanded digital service models, stating that "funding must follow the patient" when supporting community-based digital care delivery.

KEY STAKEHOLDERS AND THEIR CONTRIBUTIONS TO THE PROFESSION'S DIGITAL TRANSFORMATION

The digital transformation of general practice requires the involvement of multiple stakeholder groups, each with distinct roles, capabilities, and interests. Understanding the potential contributions, limitations, and interests of these different stakeholders is essential for ensuring they all optimally support the profession's digital transformation. This section discusses each of these key stakeholder groups (see summary in Table 10.2).

TABLE 10.2
Key Actors in the Digital Transformation of General Practice

Actor	Role in Transformation	Examples
GPs and Practice Staff	Adopt digital tools, redefine roles, and guide patients through digital care models	Use of telehealth, wearable data, and digital clinical decision support
Government Bodies	Fund and regulate digital health initiatives; manage national health IT infrastructure	Australia's My Health Record; UK NHS app; Japan's digital health roadmap
Technology Vendors	Develop clinical platforms, EMRs, telehealth tools, and AI decision-support systems	GP software (Best Practice, MedicalDirector), triage bots, prescribing apps
Patients and Communities	Shape demand and engagement patterns; co-produce health value in digitally enabled systems	Use of remote monitoring, online consultations, health data contribution
Professional Colleges and Regulators	Set digital competency standards, certify tools, update ethical frameworks	RACGP digital readiness programs; telehealth prescribing guidelines
Medical Educators	Prepare current and future GPs with digital capabilities	Inclusion of digital health training in undergraduate and CPD programs

Professional Bodies and Regulatory Organizations

Professional bodies serve as the bridge between individual practitioners and the broader healthcare system, contributing to digital transformation of the profession through standards development, education, and advocacy. The Royal College of General Practitioners (UK), Royal Australian College of General Practitioners, American Academy of Family Physicians, and similar organizations globally have begun integrating digital health competencies into their professional standards and educational requirements. The RCGP requires members to undertake a minimum of 50 credits of CPD per year, covering a broad range of general practice topics over five years, with eLearning modules available on topics relevant to contemporary general practice including telehealth and digital technologies (RCGP, 2023). These organizations also provide guidance on the appropriate use of digital health tools and frameworks for evaluating new technologies, while serving as advocates for appropriate regulatory frameworks that support digital innovation in general practice while maintaining safety standards. However, professional bodies face inherent tensions in their role as key facilitators of the profession's digital transformation. While they are motivated by ensuring member competence and welfare, maintaining professional standards that protect public trust, and demonstrating the profession's continued relevance in an increasingly digital healthcare environment (American Medical Association, 2024), they simultaneously struggle with significant operational challenges. These include resource constraints in developing comprehensive digital health guidance, the rapid pace of technological change that makes it difficult to provide timely preparatory guidance, and potential resistance from members who may be hesitant to adopt new technologies (Med-Tech Innovation, 2024). The global nature of digital health innovation compounds these challenges, as technologies and practices developed in one country may quickly spread to others, requiring complex international coordination and standardization efforts.

Regulatory bodies face a parallel but distinct set of challenges in supporting the profession's digital transformation. Their primary roles include ensuring the safety and efficacy of digital health tools and practices in general practice, while also enabling digital innovation through appropriate regulatory frameworks for primary care settings. For example, regulatory bodies have developed telehealth licensing requirements that allow GPs to provide virtual consultations across jurisdictional boundaries, established data privacy regulations that govern how GP practices handle electronic health records and patient information sharing, and created reimbursement frameworks that determine which digital health services GPs can bill for and under what conditions. Professional medical boards have also updated licensing requirements to include digital health competencies, ensuring GPs maintain appropriate skills for technology-enabled care delivery. But regulatory bodies must navigate the fundamental "pacing problem" in the context of general practice - the gap between rapid digital innovation in primary care (i.e. new, better, more adopted digital or digitally enhanced products/services, processes/workflows) and regulatory frameworks designed for traditional practice models. This places them on a constant learning curve with new technologies and practices such as AI-enabled diagnostic tools for primary care, digital prescription management systems, and remote monitoring platforms that GPs use to manage chronic conditions (Torous, 2022). This creates a tension between their core interests of prioritizing patient safety in primary care settings while simultaneously needing to enable GPs to adopt beneficial innovations that improve practice efficiency and patient outcomes. Resource constraints further complicate their ability to keep pace with rapidly evolving technologies used in general practice, requiring ongoing upskilling to understand both benefits and risks of innovations like clinical decision support systems, patient portal integrations, and digital workflow management tools (Med-Tech Innovation, 2024). The result is often lengthy approval processes for GP-relevant technologies, unclear guidance on digital health implementation in primary care settings, and regulatory uncertainty that may discourage GP practices from investing in beneficial digital innovations, even as regulators strive to maintain consistent standards while preserving their authority in an increasingly digital primary care environment.

Together, these stakeholders must navigate the complex interplay between digital innovation facilitation and appropriate oversight, balancing member/public interests with the practical realities of delivering high quality primary care services.

Educational Institutions and Training Programs

Medical schools and postgraduate training programs are fundamental to preparing current and future GPs for digitally-enabled practice. They serve as the primary pipeline for developing digitally-competent general practitioners, directly impacting the GP profession's long-term capacity for digital transformation and its ability to deliver technologically-enhanced primary care. Leading education institutions and training programs have begun integrating digital health topics throughout their curricula, rather than treating them as separate add-on courses, recognizing that future GPs must be equipped to practice in increasingly digital healthcare environments. Harvard Medical School offers executive education programs in digital health transformation and AI implementation, targeting GP leaders and primary care professionals seeking to drive technology-enabled change in their practices and organizations (Harvard Medical School, 2022). Harvard's programs include "Leading Digital Transformation in Health Care," which provides frameworks for implementing digital technologies in primary care settings, and "AI in Healthcare: From Strategies to Implementation," which focuses on practical AI deployment strategies relevant to general practice (Harvard Medical School, 2025a, 2025b). These programs emphasize real-world application through case studies of digital transformation in primary care networks and capstone projects that require participants to develop actionable plans for modernizing GP practices. Similarly, the University of Toronto has developed specialized graduate programs that prepare healthcare informatics professionals who support GP digital transformation initiatives. The Master of Health Informatics program trains leaders capable of driving substantial change in primary care systems through AI and information technology-based solutions, covering advanced subjects such as electronic health record optimization, telehealth implementation, and digital health policy development - all critical areas for supporting GP practice modernization (Institute of Health Policy, Management and Evaluation, 2024). The Digital Health Technologies specialization focuses on data science and machine learning applications that can enhance GP diagnostic capabilities and practice management efficiency (University of Toronto, 2024).

However, many medical schools globally often lack the faculty expertise in technology and access to the technological resources necessary to provide comprehensive digital health education specifically tailored to general practice needs. This gap is particularly pronounced in lower-income countries where medical education resources are already constrained and where GP training programs may receive less investment than other specialist medical education. Additionally, most existing programs focus on graduate-level or executive education rather than integrating digital health competencies into undergraduate medical curricula, creating potential gaps in foundational digital literacy for future GPs entering practice. The rapid pace of technological advancement also presents challenges for curriculum development, as educational institutions struggle to keep pace with emerging technologies relevant to primary care while maintaining rigorous academic standards that meet GP professional accreditation requirements.

Educational institutions are motivated by their mission to maintain relevance and prepare GP graduates for evolving primary care environments. They seek to differentiate their programs in competitive markets by demonstrating their graduates' readiness for modern GP practice, to attract high-quality students interested in technologically-enhanced general practice, and to secure research funding for primary care digital health initiatives. They also aim to establish themselves as thought leaders in GP digital health education, enhancing their reputation and attracting partnerships with GP professional organizations, primary care networks, and health technology companies focused on general practice solutions. However, they must balance these pursuits with GP professional accreditation requirements, university resource constraints, and the need to ensure graduates meet licensing standards for general practice.

Technology Companies and Digital Innovation Partners

Technology companies serve as critical partners in the GP profession's digital transformation, but their commercial priorities can conflict with the profession's goals, requiring strategic navigation by GP professional organizations. Established healthcare technology companies like Epic, Cerner, and Allscripts provide the foundational electronic health record systems that many GP practices depend on for core clinical workflows (Becker's Hospital Review, 2024). These vendors increasingly bundle telehealth, patient engagement, and clinical decision support tools specifically marketed to primary care practices, promising to streamline GP workflows and improve patient access (Becker's Hospital Review, 2024). However, these integrated platforms can impose rigid workflow structures that may not align with optimal GP consultation patterns, potentially forcing practitioners to adapt their clinical approach to accommodate software limitations rather than vice versa. Additionally, there can be substantial implementation costs including customization, training, and ongoing support that create financial barriers that particularly burden smaller GP practices, while vendor lock-in arrangements limit practices' ability to switch systems or adopt innovative technologies from other providers (Converted Media Ltd, 2025; TechnologyAdvice, 2023).

Major technology companies like Google, Microsoft, and Amazon are introducing AI-powered tools that could significantly alter GP diagnostic and triage processes. While these innovations offer the promise of improved clinical decision-making and practice efficiency, they often come with attempts by technology companies to capture value from GP consultations and patient data - which can pose ethical risks. But smaller startup companies developing GP-specific solutions often lack understanding of the complexities of general practice, and lack the big resources often necessary for digital innovation in healthcare. They often end up designing tools that may increase rather than reduce administrative burden for practitioners and risks for patients. The fundamental challenge for the GP profession is how to collaborate with technology companies primarily motivated by scalability and profitability considerations while ensuring that support for the therapeutic relationship and preservation of GP professional autonomy do not take a back seat. This creates tension between commercial imperatives and professional values, particularly around patient privacy, clinical judgment, and the holistic approach central to general practice. GP professional organizations must therefore develop sophisticated strategies for engaging with technology partners, establishing standards that ensure digital tools and practices genuinely enhance rather than commoditize general practice, and maintaining professional control over how technology shapes the future of primary care delivery.

Health Systems and Practice Organizations

National, state, and regional health systems and practice organizations serve as crucial intermediaries in the GP profession's digital transformation, wielding significant influence over how or whether new digital/digitally enhanced products/services, processes/workflows, and roles are implemented and whether they enhance or constrain GP professional autonomy as well as patient experience. Large integrated health systems possess substantial potential influence on digital transformation of the profession due to their scale, resources, and ability to invest in comprehensive technology platforms. In the United States, Kaiser Permanente, as a large integrated health system serving over 8.6 million patients, has invested substantially in comprehensive digital transformation across its network of medical facilities, demonstrating both the advantages of organizational scale and the potential for standardized digital workflows to reshape clinical practice (Bornstein, 2012; IEEE Spectrum, 2012). In England's health system, the Primary Care Network (PCN) model enables smaller GP practices to share resources and coordinate digital health initiatives, with over 99% of practices joining one of approximately 1,250 PCNs each serving populations of 30,000 to 50,000 patients (NHS England, 2025; The King's Fund, 2024). Through the Additional Roles Reimbursement Scheme, PCNs have recruited over 34,000 new patient-facing staff and provide funding for enhanced services that individual practices could not afford independently (The King's Fund, 2024).

The strategic challenge for GP professional organizations is that health systems and practice organizations are mainly motivated by institutional sustainability, regulatory compliance, and operational efficiency. This can create potential tensions when their priorities for standardization and efficiency conflict with GP goals of individualized care and clinical judgment. GP professional organizations must therefore develop strategies for influencing how these health systems and practice organizations support the profession's digital transformation, ensuring that technological change supports rather than undermines the core values and practices that define effective general practice.

Government and Policy Makers

Government and policy makers play crucial roles in shaping the pace and direction of digital transformation in general practice. National digital health strategies and regulatory frameworks significantly influence the adoption of new digital or digitally enhanced products/services, processes/workflows, and roles in general practice, as well as GPs roles in their adoption. Australia's National Digital Health Strategy 2023-2028 provides a framework for digital health transformation including initiatives for general practice such as expanded My Health Record capabilities and continued telehealth support, though implementation depends on state and territory government cooperation and funding commitments (Australian Digital Health Agency, 2024). Singapore's Smart Nation initiative includes substantial investments in digital health infrastructure and has established regulatory sandboxes through the Ministry of Health's Licensing Experimentation and Adaptation Program, enabling innovation while maintaining safety standards (Ministry of Health Singapore, 2024).

Further, the National Electronic Health Record system provides integration across Singapore's healthcare providers, though this comprehensive data sharing raises questions about GP professional control over patient information and clinical decision-making autonomy (Digital Regulation Platform, 2020).

However, government policy priorities often emphasize cost containment, administrative efficiency, and population health outcomes rather than necessarily supporting GP professional development or preserving the therapeutic relationship. Policy challenges include balancing innovation with safety, ensuring equitable access to digital health benefits, and managing the disruption that government-mandated digital transformation can create for existing GP workflows and practice models. The tension between government desires for standardized, measurable healthcare delivery and GP professional values emphasizing individualized, relationship-based care creates ongoing challenges for how digital technologies are implemented and regulated.GP professional organizations must therefore develop sophisticated advocacy strategies to influence government policy direction, ensuring that digital health policies support rather than undermine professional autonomy and clinical effectiveness. This includes engaging with policy development processes, demonstrating the value of GP-led digital transformation approaches, and advocating for regulatory frameworks that preserve professional judgment while enabling technological innovation to enhance rather than replace the therapeutic relationship central to effective general practice.

Patients and Communities

Patients and communities are increasingly important stakeholders in digital health transformation, both as users of digitally enhanced care innovations and as participants in shaping the direction of change. Patient acceptance and engagement are crucial factors in the success of digital health initiatives. Patient organizations and advocacy groups play important roles in ensuring that digital health development considers patient needs and preferences. Organizations like Patients Like Me and the Society for Participatory Medicine advocate for patient-centered approaches to digital health innovation (Society for Participatory Medicine, 2025).

Community engagement is particularly important for addressing health equity concerns and ensuring that digital transformation of the profession does not exacerbate existing disparities. Successful initiatives involve community representatives in the design and implementation of digital health programs.

FUTURE-PROOFING GP CAREERS IN THE DIGITAL AGE

As digital transformation accelerates across healthcare systems globally, general practitioners must develop new competencies and adapt their professional approaches to remain relevant and effective in an increasingly digital healthcare environment. Future-proofing GP careers requires understanding both the opportunities and challenges that the profession's digital transformation presents, as well as developing and executing strategies to leverage technology in service of better patient care. In the remainder of this chapter, we discuss some critical strategies for future proofing GP careers.

Essential Digital Competencies for Modern GPs

The digitally competent GP of the future will require a broad set of technical and cognitive skills that complement traditional clinical competencies. These include foundational digital literacy skills such as proficiency with electronic health records, telehealth platforms, and data analytics tools, as well as more advanced competencies in AI interpretation, digital health coaching, and technology evaluation (Topol, 2019). Data literacy represents a particularly critical competency as patients increasingly generate health data through wearable devices, smartphone applications, and home monitoring tools. GPs must develop skills in interpreting and contextualizing this data while helping patients understand its clinical significance and limitations (Gordon & Hornbrook, 2016). AI literacy is becoming increasingly important as AI-enabled diagnostic and decision support tools become more prevalent in clinical practice. GPs need to understand how these tools work, their strengths and limitations, and how to integrate AI recommendations with clinical judgment and patient preferences (Rajkomar et al., 2018).

Digital communication skills are essential for effective telehealth delivery and patient engagement through digital channels. These include technical proficiency with various platforms, as well as adapted communication techniques that work effectively in digital environments (Reed et al., 2019). Cybersecurity awareness and digital ethics understanding are crucial for protecting patient information and navigating the ethical challenges that arise from use of digital health technologies. GPs must understand their responsibilities for data protection and be able to evaluate the ethical implications of different digital health tools and practices (Kruse et al., 2017).

Strategies for Continuous Learning and Adaptation

The rapid pace of digital health innovation requires GPs to develop strong capabilities for continuous learning and adaptation. Traditional continuing medical education models may not be sufficient for keeping pace with technological change, requiring new approaches to professional development. Peer learning networks and communities of practice can provide valuable opportunities for GPs to share experiences and learn from colleagues who are implementing digital health innovations. Organizations like the Digital Health Society and various online physician communities provide platforms for knowledge sharing and collaborative learning (Digital Health Society, 2021). Partnerships with technology companies and academic institutions can provide GPs with access to cutting-edge developments and opportunities to participate in pilot programs and research studies. These partnerships can help GPs gain hands-on experience with new technologies while contributing to their development and evaluation.

Formal technology focused education programs specifically designed for practicing physicians are increasingly available through medical schools and professional organizations. These programs range from short courses on specific technologies to comprehensive certificates and degrees in digital health and health informatics. Self-directed learning through online resources, conferences, and professional publications remains important for staying current with digital health developments.

However, the volume of information available requires developing skills in information evaluation and synthesis to focus on the most relevant and reliable sources.

Building Resilient and Adaptive Practice Models

Future-proofing also requires developing practice models that can adapt to changing technological and market conditions. This includes adopting technological infrastructure that can evolve with changing primary care requirements while developing organizational capabilities for managing change and innovation. Practice integration with larger networks or health systems can provide access to digital health capabilities and resources that would be difficult for individual practices to develop independently. However, this integration must be managed carefully to preserve the autonomy, patient relationships, and patient experience that are central to effective general practice, as standardized care delivered by interprofessional teams must maintain professional autonomy while ensuring smooth transitions of patients from one type of care to another (Leutz, 2005).

Developing diverse revenue streams and service offerings can help practices adapt to changing market conditions and patient preferences. This might include offering specialized digital health services, participating in remote monitoring programs, or providing digital health coaching and education services. Digital health technologies offer new opportunities for practices to provide services tailored to individual needs, from applications in general wellness to specialized medical applications that can widen access to healthcare provision while reducing costs (Awad et al., 2021). They also offer talent attraction and retention opportunities - e.g. enabling GPs to work anywhere, anytime, any device. Practices that maintain focus on patient-centered care, community health, and GP job satisfaction, while embracing appropriate technologies are likely to be most successful in the long term.

Collaborative Approaches to Professional Development

Individual GPs and practices cannot navigate digital transformation in isolation. Successful implementation requires collaborative approaches that involve GP professional organizations, educational institutions, technology partners, governments, and peer networks. Interdisciplinary collaboration with informaticians, data scientists, and technology developers can help GPs contribute to the development of primary care-specific digital health tools while expanding their understanding of technological possibilities and limitations for general practice workflows. Professional mentorship programs that pair experienced technologists or digital health leaders with general practitioners or practices who are early in their digital transformation journey can accelerate learning and reduce transformation risks (Scandiffio et al., 2024). These programs can be organized through GP professional associations or primary care networks, with structured initiatives providing mentorship for emerging GP leaders progressing toward roles such as GP practice partners, medical directors, or primary care network clinical directors.

Digital innovations in healthcare require interdisciplinary cooperation between professionals with different educational backgrounds, particularly for the development of new technical achievements such as healthcare technologies that serve primary care needs (Krause-Jüttler et al., 2022). GP professional organizations can facilitate partnerships between practicing general practitioners and technical experts to ensure digital innovations support rather than disrupt the therapeutic relationship central to effective primary care. Clinical informaticians can collaborate with GPs to assess information needs specific to general practice, develop clinical decision support systems tailored to primary care workflows, and lead procurement and implementation of clinical information systems that enhance rather than burden GP practice efficiency (American Medical Informatics Association, 2025).

Participation in primary care research and quality improvement initiatives related to digital health can provide opportunities for GP professional development while contributing to the evidence base for digital health implementation specifically in general practice settings. GP professional advocacy for appropriate policies and regulations that support beneficial digital transformation while protecting patient-practitioner relationships is an important professional responsibility that can help shape the future environment for primary care digital health practice. These collaborative approaches ensure that GP professional development in digital health occurs within supportive networks that combine clinical expertise with technical knowledge, ultimately strengthening the profession's capacity to lead rather than merely respond to technological change.

CONCLUSION

This chapter presents a comprehensive case study of digital transformation in general practice, illustrating how technological change is reshaping patient care, clinical workflows, and professional identity. It begins by examining sector-specific digital disruption, including increasing patient demand for flexible, digital-first access to care, the rise of hybrid models that blend in-person and virtual services, and growing responsibilities around data management and security. The chapter explores how technologies such as remote consultations, digital triage tools, and integrated platforms are altering how care is delivered and how general practitioners (GPs) work. It highlights changes in clinical decision-making and accountability, with greater emphasis on data-driven and outcomes-based practices. GP identity is evolving as well, with new competency expectations and educational frameworks emerging. Governance structures, from practice-level management to national policy, are also adapting to better support technology integration. This case offers valuable insights for other professions navigating digital transformation while seeking to uphold service quality and professional standards.

DISCUSSION QUESTIONS

1. Analyze how the five dimensions of digital disruption in general practice interact to create opportunities and challenges for GPs.
2. Compare the contributions, limitations, and interests of two key stakeholder groups in GP digital transformation. How should GP professional organizations manage these relationships?

3. Select three of the seven key aims of digital transformation for general practice and explain how they interconnect to drive meaningful change.
4. Which digital transformation challenge (out of infrastructure, privacy, financial, or equity) is the biggest challenge for general practice? What multi-stakeholder approach would address it?
5. Evaluate how the profession's strategic responses (education integration, infrastructure development, patient-centered design) address key digital transformation challenges.
6. How does digital transformation manifest across different levels of the profession? What coordination mechanisms are needed for coherent change?
7. What key actions should GP professional organizations and individual GPs prioritize to future-proof the profession? Justify your recommendations.

REFERENCES

Abbott, A. (1988). *The system of professions: An essay on the division of expert labor.* University of Chicago Press.

American Academy of Family Physicians (AAFP). (2020). A toolkit for building and growing a sustainable telehealth program in your practice. Retrieved from https://www.aafp.org/dam/AAFP/documents/practice_management/telehealth/2020-AAFP-Telehealth-Toolkit.pdf

American Medical Association. (2024, February 26). Driving the future of digital health. Retrieved from https://www.ama-assn.org/practice-management/digital-health/driving-future-digital-health

American Medical Informatics Association. (2025). Informatics: Research and practice. Retrieved from https://amia.org/about-amia/why-informatics/informatics-research-and-practice

Ameso, E. A., & Prince, R. J. (2025). Visions of Community Health and the Social Good in Kenya: Turning Community Health Workers into Entrepreneurs. Development and Change.

Anderson, C., Zhan, K., Boyd, M., & Mann, C. (2020). The role of pharmacists in general practice: A realist review. *Research in Social and Administrative Pharmacy, 16*(3), 321–330. https://doi.org/10.1016/j.sapharm.2019.05.014

Arndt, B. G., Beasley, J. W., Watkinson, M. D., Temte, J. L., Tuan, W. J., Sinsky, C. A., & Gilchrist, V. J. (2017). Tethered to the EHR: Primary care physician workload assessment using EHR event log data and time-motion observations. *Annals of Family Medicine, 15*(5), 419–426. https://doi.org/10.1370/afm.2121

Ashwood, J. S., Mehrotra, A., Cowling, D., & Uscher-Pines, L. (2017). Direct-to-consumer telehealth may increase access to care but does not decrease spending. *Health Affairs, 36*(3), 485–491

Australian Digital Health Agency. (2022). *My health record system operator annual report 2021–22.* Commonwealth of Australia.

Australian Digital Health Agency. (2024). Australia's National Digital Health Strategy 2023–2028. Retrieved from https://www.digitalhealth.gov.au/sites/default/files/documents/national-digital-health-strategy-2023-2028.pdf

Australian Government Department of Health and Aged Care. (2022). Healthdirect symptom checker. Retrieved from https://www.health.gov.au/resources/apps-and-tools/healthdirect-symptom-checker

Awad, A., Trenfield, S. J., Pollard, T. D., Ong, J. J., Elbadawi, M., McCoubrey, L. E., ... Basit, A. W. (2021). Connected healthcare: Improving patient care using digital health technologies. *Advanced drug delivery reviews*, *178*, 113958.

Becker's Hospital Review. (2024). *EHR telehealth breakdown: 14 things to know about features from allscripts.* Cerner, Epic & Meditech.

Benda, N. C., Veinot, T. C., Sieck, C. J., & Ancker, J. S. (2020). Broadband internet access is a social determinant of health! *American Journal of Public Health*, *110*(8), 1123–1125.

Busulwa, R. (2022). *Navigating digital transformation in management.* Routledge.

CGI. (2020). A modern e-referral service for the NHS. Retrieved from https://www.cgi.com/uk/en-gb/case-study/health/modern-e-referral-service-nhs

Bornstein, S. (2012). An integrated EHR at Northern California Kaiser Permanente: Pitfalls, challenges, and benefits experienced in transitioning. *Applied Clinical Informatics*, *3*(3), 318–325.

Cadogan, C. A., & Hughes, C. M. (2021). On the frontline against COVID-19: Community pharmacists' contribution during a public health crisis. Research in Social and Administrative Pharmacy, 17(1), 2032–2035.

Car, J., Ong, Q. C., Fox, T. E., Leightley, D., Kemp, S. J., Švab, I., ... Obadiel, Y. A. (2025). The digital health competencies in medical education framework: An international consensus statement based on a Delphi study. *JAMA Network Open*, *8*(1), e2453131.

Car, J., & Sheikh, .A. (2020). Digital health: A revolution in progress. *BMJ*, *368*, m1126. 10.1016/j.hrthm.2020.03.012

Collins, F. S., & Varmus, H. (2015). A new initiative on precision medicine. *New England Journal of Medicine*, 372(9), 793–795.

Converted Media Ltd. (2025). Epic EHR vs Oracle Health (formerly Cerner) 2025 comparison. Retrieved from https://www.ehrinpractice.com/epic-ehr-vs-cerner-ehr-comparison.html

Danish Health Data Authority. (2024). Digitalisation in Danish healthcare. Retrieved November 27, 2025, from https://healthcaredenmark.dk/media/sghmh0in/digitalisation_2024_onlineversion.pdf

Digital Health. (2020). Investment in digital 'is a building block for world class GP services'. Retrieved from https://www.digitalhealth.net/2020/01/investment-in-digital-is-a-building-block-for-world-class-gp-services/

Digital Health Society. (2021). *Building digital health communities.* https://www.linkedin.com/company/the-digital-health-society/?originalSubdomain=ie

Digital Regulation Platform. (2020). Singapore: Regulatory collaboration in support of the Smart Nation program. Retrieved from https://digitalregulation.org/singapore-regulatory-collaboration-in-support-of-the-smart-nation-program/

Dymek, C., Kim, B., Melton, G. B., Payne, T. H., Singh, H., & Hsiao, C. J. (2021). Building the evidence-base to reduce electronic health record–related clinician burden. *Journal of the American Medical Informatics Association*, *28*(5), 1057–1061.

Foo, D., Spanos, S., Dammery, G., Ellis, L. A., Willcock, S. M., & Braithwaite, J. (2023). The rise of direct-to-consumer telemedicine services in Australia: Implications for primary care and future research. *Medical Journal of Australia*, *219*(8), 344–347. https://doi.org/10.5694/mja2.52097

Ford, E., Edelman, N., Somers, L., Shrewsbury, D., Lopez Levy, M., Van Marwijk, H., & Porat, T. (2021). Barriers and facilitators to the adoption of electronic clinical decision support systems: A qualitative interview study with UK general practitioners. *BMC Medical Informatics and Decision Making*, *21*(1), 193.

Ghafur, S., Kristensen, S., Honeyford, K., Martin, G., Darzi, A., & Aylin, P. (2019). A retrospective impact analysis of the WannaCry cyberattack on the NHS. *NPJ Digital Medicine*, *2*(1), 1–7. https://doi.org/10.1038/s41746-019-0161-6

Good Things Foundation. (2024). A year of progress in fixing the digital divide. Retrieved from https://www.goodthingsfoundation.org/discover/digital-inclusion-insights/digital-inclusion-insights-2024/a-year-of-progress-impact-review-2024

Gordon, N. P., & Hornbrook, M. C. (2016). Differences in access to and preferences for using patient portals and other eHealth technologies based on race, ethnicity, and age: A database and survey study of seniors in a large health plan. *Journal of Medical Internet Research*, *18*(3), e4758. https://doi.org/10.2196/jmir.5105

Graves, J. M., Abshire, D. A., Amiri, S., & Mackelprang, J. L. (2021). Disparities in technology and broadband internet access across rurality: Implications for health and education. *Family & Community Health*, *44*(4), 257–265.

Greenhalgh, T., Wherton, J., Shaw, S., & Morrison, C. (2020). Video consultations for covid-19. *BMJ*, *368*, m998. https://doi.org/10.1136/bmj.m998

Halcomb, E. J., Ashley, C., Dennis, S., McInnes, S., Morgan, M., Zwar, N., & Williams, A. (2023). Telehealth use in Australian primary healthcare during COVID-19: A cross-sectional descriptive survey. *BMJ Open*, *13*(1), e065478.

Harvard Medical School. (2022). Technology and innovation in medicine program. Retrieved from https://hms.harvard.edu/departments/global-health-social-medicine/education/technology-innovation-medicine

Harvard Medical School. (2025a). AI in health care: From strategies to implementation program. Retrieved from https://execonline.hms.harvard.edu/artificial-intelligence-in-health-care-from-strategies-to-implementation

Harvard Medical School. (2025b). Leading digital transformation in health care. Retrieved from https://execonline.hms.harvard.edu/leading-digital-transformation-in-healthcare

IEEE Spectrum. (2012). Kaiser Permanente marks completion of its electronic health records implementation. Retrieved from https://spectrum.ieee.org/kaiser-permanente-marks-completion-of-its-electronic-health-records-implementation

Imperial College Healthcare NHS Trust. (2024). AI stethoscope rolled out to GP clinics in north west London to help diagnose heart failure. Retrieved from https://www.imperial.nhs.uk/about-us/news/ai-stethoscope-rolled-out-to-gp-clinics-in-north-west-london-to-help-diagnose-heart-failure

Indeed. (2024). Telehealth operations coordinator jobs. Retrieved from https://www.indeed.com/q-Telehealth-Operations-Coordinator-jobs.html

Institute of Health Policy, Management and Evaluation. (2024). *Master of health informatics*. University of Toronto. Retrieved from https://ihpme.utoronto.ca/programs/health-informatics/

Kaylor, A. (2024). Exploring digital stethoscope technology for improved diagnostics. TechTarget. Retrieved from https://www.techtarget.com/pharmalifesciences/feature/Exploring-digital-stethoscope-technology-for-improved-diagnostics

Krakowski, I., Kim, J., Cai, Z. R., Daneshjou, R., Lapins, J., Eriksson, H., & Linos, E. (2024). Human-AI interaction in skin cancer diagnosis: A systematic review and meta-analysis. *NPJ Digital Medicine*, *7*(1), 78.

Krause-Jüttler, G., Weitz, J., & Bork, U. (2022). Interdisciplinary collaborations in digital health research: Mixed methods case study. *JMIR Human Factors*, *9*(2), e36579.

Kruse, C. S., Frederick, B., Jacobson, T., & Monticone, D. K. (2017). Cybersecurity in healthcare: A systematic review of modern threats and trends. *Technology and Health Care*, *25*(1), 1–10. https://doi.org/10.3233/THC-161263

Kvedar, J., Coye, M. J., & Everett, W. (2021). Connected health: A review of technologies and strategies to improve patient care with telemedicine and telehealth. *Health Affairs*, *33*(2), 194–199. https://doi.org/10.1377/hlthaff.2013.0992

Lember, V., Kattel, R., & Tõnurist, P. (2018). Technological capacity in the public sector: The case of Estonia. *International Review of Administrative Sciences*, *84*(2), 214–230.

Leutz, W. (2005), Reflections on integrating medical and social care: Five laws revisited. *Journal of Integrated Care*, 13(5), 3–12. https://doi.org/10.1108/14769018200500034

Marques, I. C., & Ferreira, J. J. (2020). Digital transformation in the area of health: Systematic review of 45 years of evolution. *Health and Technology, 10*(3), 575–586. https://doi.org/10.1007/s12553-019-00402-8

Med-Tech Insights. (2024). Trying to keep pace: Technology and regulation. Rapid Medtech Communications Ltd. Retrieved from https://www.med-technews.com/medtech-insights/medtech-regulatory-insights/trying-to-keep-pace/

Mehl, G., Vasudevan, L., Gonsalves, L., Jhaveri, M., Hinton, N., Peddle, K., & Labrique, A. (2018). Harnessing mHealth in low-resource settings to overcome health system constraints and achieve universal access to healthcare. *Global Health Action, 11*(sup3), 1495604.

Mehrotra, A., Huskamp, H. A., Souza, J., Uscher-Pines, L., Rose, S., Landon, B. E., & Busch, A. B. (2017). Rapid growth in mental health telemedicine use among rural Medicare beneficiaries, wide variation across States. *Health Affairs, 36*(5), 909–917.

Ministry of Health Singapore. (2024). Regulatory sandbox - Singapore. Retrieved from https://www.moh.gov.sg/others/health-regulation/regulatory-sandbox

Mossialos, E., Naci, H., & Courtin, E. (2015). Expanding the role of community pharmacists: Policymaking in the absence of policy-relevant evidence? *Health Policy, 119*(5), 629–633. https://doi.org/10.1016/j.healthpol.2015.02.010

Neves, A. L., & Burgers, J. (2022). Digital technologies in primary care: Implications for patient care and future research. *European Journal of General Practice, 28*(1), 203–208.

Neves, A. L., Li, E., Gupta, P., Fontana, G., & Darzi, A. (2021). Virtual primary care in high-income countries during the COVID-19 pandemic: Policy responses and lessons for the future. *European Journal of General Practice, 27*(1), 241–247. https://doi.org/10.1080/13814788.2021.1965120

Royal Australasian College of General Practitioners (RACGP). (2021). 'A wonderful day': telehealth to become permanent. Retrieved from https://www1.racgp.org.au/newsgp/professional/a-wonderful-day-telehealth-to-become-permanent

NHS Digital. (2023). *NHS App Management Information.* Retrieved from https://digital.nhs.uk/data-and-information/publications/statistical/nhs-app-statistics#latest-statistics

NHS England. (2025). Primary care networks (PCNs). Retrieved from https://www.england.nhs.uk/long-read/primary-care-networks-pcns/

Nøhr, C., Parv, L., Kink, P., Cummings, E., Almond, H., Nørgaard, J. R., & Turner, P. (2017). Nationwide citizen access to their health data: Analyzing and comparing experiences in Denmark, Estonia and Australia. *BMC Health Services Research, 17*(1), 11.

Ødegård, E. S., Langbråten, L. S., Lundh, A., & Linde, D. S. (2022). Two-way text message interventions and healthcare outcomes in Africa: Systematic review of randomized trials with meta-analyses on appointment attendance and medicine adherence. *PloS One, 17*(4), e0266717.

PPC Land. (2025). Netherlands regulatory sandbox to launch by 2026 as EU clarifies AI rules. Retrieved November 27, 2025, from https://ppc.land/netherlands-regulatory-sandbox-to-launch-by-2026-as-eu-clarifies-ai-rules/

Office of the National Coordinator for Health Information Technology. (2020). *Strategy on reducing regulatory and administrative burden relating to the use of health IT and EHRs.* U.S. Department of Health and Human Services. Retrieved from https://www.healthit.gov/sites/default/files/page/2020-02/BurdenReport_0.pdf

Office of the National Coordinator for Health Information Technology. (2023). Interoperable exchange of patient health information among U.S. Hospitals: 2023. Washington, DC: U.S. Department of Health and Human Services.

Parker, G. G., & Van Alstyne, M. W. (2018). Innovation, openness, and platform control. *Management Science, 64*(7), 3015–3032. https://doi.org/10.1287/mnsc.2017.2757

Perez, M. V., Mahaffey, K. W., Hedlin, H., Rumsfeld, J. S., Garcia, A., Ferris, T., & Turakhia, M. P. (2019). Large-scale assessment of a smartwatch to identify atrial fibrillation. *New England Journal of Medicine, 381*(20), 1909–1917. https://doi.org/10.1056/NEJMoa1901183

Pimmer, C., Mhango, S., Mzumara, A., & Mbvundula, F. (2017). Mobile Instant messaging for rural community health workers: A case from Malawi. *Global Health Action, 10*(1), 1368236. https://doi.org/10.1080/16549716.2017.1368236

Piwek, L., Ellis, D. A., Andrews, S., & Joinson, A. (2016). The rise of consumer health wearables: Promises and barriers. *PLoS Medicine, 13*(2), e1001953. https://doi.org/10.1371/journal.pmed.1001953

Rajkomar, A., Hardt, M., Howell, M. D., Corrado, G., & Chin, M. H. (2018). Ensuring fairness in machine learning to advance health equity. *Annals of Internal Medicine, 169*(12), 866–872. https://doi.org/10.7326/M18-1990

Reed, S., Shell, R., Kassis, K., Tartaglia, K., Wallihan, R., Smith, K., & Hurtubise, L. (2019). Applying adult learning practices in medical education. *Current Problems in Pediatric and Adolescent Health Care, 49*(4), 109–112. https://doi.org/10.1016/j.cppeds.2019.03.004

Royal Australian College of General Practitioners (RCGP). (n.d.-a). Research at RCGP. Retrieved from https://www.rcgp.org.uk/clinical-and-research/our-programmes/innovation

Royal Australian College of General Practitioners (RCGP). (n.d.-b). Innovation at RCGP: Bright ideas from general practice. Retrieved from https://www.rcgp.org.uk/representing-you/innovation-at-rcgp

Royal Australian College of General Practitioners (RCGP). (n.d.-c). Area of capability: Working well in organisations and systems of care. Retrieved from https://www.rcgp.org.uk/mrcgp-exams/gp-curriculum/working-organisations-systems-care

Royal Australian College of General Practitioners (RACGP). (2023). The RACGP position on the use of telehealth in general practice. Retrieved from https://www.racgp.org.au/advocacy/position-statements/view-all-position-statements/clinical-and-practice-management/racgp-position-telehealth-general-practice

Royal College of General Practitioners (RCGP) (2023). The Royal College of General Practitioners (RCGP). Retrieved from https://directory.cpdstandards.com/sectors/the-royal-college-of-general-practitioners-rcgp/

Royal College of General Practitioners (RCGP). (2024a). RCGP calls on the government to reform GP funding to tackle health inequalities. Retrieved from https://www.rcgp.org.uk/News/reform-funding-health-inequalities

Royal College of General Practitioners (RCGP). (2024b). AI has 'potential' in general practice - but is not the panacea for GP pressures. Retrieved from https://www.rcgp.org.uk/News/ai-general-practice-gp-pressures

Royal College of General Practitioners. (2025). The RCGP curriculum: Being a general practitioner. Retrieved from https://www.rcgp.org.uk/getmedia/8437edbc-1960-4eac-89d9-f657e2f28753/being-general-practitioner-2025.pdf

Royal College of Physicians and Surgeons of Canada. (2015). CanMEDS 2015 Physician Competency Framework. Retrieved from https://www.royalcollege.ca/en/standards-and-accreditation/canmeds.html

Salinas, M. P., Sepúlveda, J., Hidalgo, L., Peirano, D., Morel, M., Uribe, P., & Navarrete-Dechent, C. (2024). A systematic review and meta-analysis of artificial intelligence versus clinicians for skin cancer diagnosis. *NPJ Digital Medicine, 7*(1), 125.

Scandiffio, J., Zhang, M., Karsan, I., Charow, R., Anderson, M., Salhia, M., & Wiljer, D. (2024). The role of mentoring and coaching of healthcare professionals for digital technology adoption and implementation: A scoping review. Digital Health, 10, 20552076241238075.RetryClaude can make mistakes. Please double-check responses.

Schmieding, M. L., Kopka, M., Bolanaki, M., Napierala, H., Altendorf, M. B., Kuschick, D., ... Slagman, A. (2025). Impact of a Symptom Checker App on Patient-Physician Interaction Among Self-Referred Walk-In Patients in the Emergency Department: Multicenter, Parallel-Group, Randomized, Controlled Trial. *Journal of Medical Internet Research, 27*, e64028.

Shanafelt, T. D., Hasan, O., Dyrbye, L. N., Sinsky, C., Satele, D., Sloan, J., & West, C. P. (2015). Changes in burnout and satisfaction with work-life balance among physicians and the general population between 2011 and 2014. *Mayo Clinic Proceedings, 90*(12), 1600–1613. https://doi.org/10.1016/j.mayocp.2015.08.023

Society for Participatory Medicine. (2025). *About Us*. Retrieved from https://participatory-medicine.org/about/

Summerton, N., & Cansdale, M. (2019). Artificial intelligence and diagnosis in general practice. *British Journal of General Practice, 69*(684), 324–325.

Susskind, R., & Susskind, D. (2015). *The future of the professions: How technology will transform the work of human experts*. Oxford University Press.

TechnologyAdvice. (2023). Cerner vs. Epic: Comparing the biggest EHR vendors. Retrieved from https://technologyadvice.com/blog/healthcare/cerner-vs-epic/

The King's Fund. (2024). Primary care networks explained. Retrieved from https://www.kingsfund.org.uk/insight-and-analysis/long-reads/primary-care-networks-explained

Topol, E. (2019). *Deep medicine: How artificial intelligence can make healthcare human again*. Basic Books.

Torous, J., Stern, A. D., & Bourgeois, F. T. (2022). Regulatory considerations to keep pace with innovation in digital health products. *NPJ Digital Medicine, 5*, 121. https://doi.org/10.1038/s41746-022-00668-9

UK Government. (2022). *Software and AI as a medical device change programme*. Retrieved from https://www.gov.uk/government/publications/software-and-ai-as-a-medical-device-change-programme/software-and-ai-as-a-medical-device-change-programme-roadmap.

University of Toronto. (2024). U of T launches new digital health technologies specialization. Retrieved from https://www.utoronto.ca/news/u-t-launches-new-digital-health-technologies-specialization

Van Der Sijs, H., Aarts, J., Vulto, A., & Berg, M. (2006). Overriding of drug safety alerts in computerized physician order entry. *Journal of the American Medical Informatics Association, 13*(2), 138–147. https://doi.org/10.1197/jamia.M1809

WeDoctor. (2022). *Annual report 2021*. WeDoctor Holdings Limited.

World Health Organization. (2021). *Global strategy on digital health 2020-2025*. World Health Organization.

11 Case Study of the Digital Transformation of the Accounting Profession

INTRODUCTION

Accounting, as a profession rooted in public trust, accountability, and the stewardship of financial information, is experiencing unprecedented disruption driven by rapid advancements in digital technology (Busulwa & Evans, 2021). The integration of artificial intelligence (AI), blockchain, robotic process automation (RPA), big data analytics, and cloud computing is not simply enhancing traditional accounting functions; it is fundamentally transforming them (Accounting Insights, 2025; Baldwin, 2024; Kanaparthi, 2024). These technologies are reshaping the role of accountants, shifting their focus from routine transactional processing towards strategic advisory, data-driven decision-making, and the ethical oversight of complex digital systems (Baldwin, 2024).

Aligned with the overarching aim of this volume to provide a research-informed understanding of digital disruption and transformation across professions, this chapter critically examines the evolving landscape of the accounting profession. It explores how digital technologies are redefining professional roles, processes, and required competencies, while assessing the capacity of strategic leadership bodies, educators, and practitioners to respond effectively to these changes. In doing so, it underscores the importance of cultivating a digitally capable, ethically grounded, and future-focused accounting workforce.

Drawing on recent empirical studies, global and national policy initiatives, and emerging best practices, the chapter evaluates the current state of the profession's digital transformation journey. It highlights structural and cultural barriers inhibiting progress, the risks associated with inaction, and the uneven pace of change across different sectors and regions. Furthermore, it proposes actionable strategies for professional bodies, tertiary institutions, and individual accountants to strengthen their roles in enabling meaningful and inclusive transformation.

Ultimately, this chapter argues that the sustainability and societal relevance of the accounting profession depend on its ability to adapt purposefully and inclusively to digital disruption. This adaptability is critical to ensuring the profession remains not only technically proficient but also strategically agile and ethically resilient in a rapidly evolving digital economy.

DOI: 10.1201/9781003606604-15

HOW THE ACCOUNTING PROFESSION IS BEING DIGITALLY DISRUPTED

The accounting profession is experiencing profound digital disruption that is reshaping not only how accounting work is conducted but also the competencies accountants require and the value they are expected to deliver. This disruption is largely driven by the adoption of emerging technologies, including artificial intelligence (AI), robotic process automation (RPA), blockchain, big data analytics, cloud computing, and cognitive computing (Table 11.1) (Accounting Insights, 2024; Busulwa & Evans, 2021). These tools have become integral to day-to-day operations in many accounting environments and are fundamentally altering the nature of the profession.

Artificial Intelligence (AI), in particular, has emerged as a transformative force within accounting. It is now widely used for fraud detection, anomaly spotting, forecasting, and interpreting large volumes of unstructured data. Audit firms increasingly embed AI platforms, such as MindBridge, into their workflows, enabling them to analyze entire datasets rather than relying solely on traditional sample based testing. This integration enhances both the accuracy and efficiency of audit procedures (Holmes & Douglass, 2022).

Similarly, RPA is playing a key role in automating routine and rules-based tasks, including invoice processing, reconciliations, and tax filings (Harrast, 2020). As Busulwa and Evans (2021) note, this automation allows accountants to redirect their focus towards higher-value activities such as strategic advisory services and risk analysis.

TABLE 11.1
Example of Key Digital Technologies Disrupting Accounting, Their Applications and Their Impacts

Digital Technology	Example Applications in Accounting	Example Impact on accounting practice
Artificial Intelligence	Fraud detection, anomaly detection, forecasting, audit analytics (e.g., MindBridge)	Automates complex tasks; enhances audit scope, speed, and precision
Robotic Process Automation (RPA)	Invoice processing, reconciliations, tax filing	Reduces manual workload; redirects focus to value-added services
Blockchain	Secure audit trails, real-time verification, immutable ledgers	Enhances trust, transparency, and fraud resistance
Big Data Analytics	Financial forecasting, risk modeling, strategic insight generation	Shifts role from reporter to business advisor
Cloud Computing	Real-time collaboration, SME platforms (e.g., Xero, MYOB, QuickBooks)	Increases accessibility, flexibility, and real-time decision-making
Cognitive Technologies	NLP, sentiment analysis, report automation	Improves interpretive insights and stakeholder communication

Blockchain technology is also gaining traction, particularly in audit and financial reporting. Its capacity to provide secure, real time, and immutable records supports increased trust and efficiency in verification processes (Nasir & Mohamed, 2024). Yermack (2017) highlights blockchain's potential to enhance transparency, reduce fraud, and facilitate real-time verification through its tamper proof ledger system.

The growing use of big data represents another major shift within the profession. Accountants are now expected to engage with large and often unstructured datasets to generate insights that inform strategic business decisions (Warren et al., 2015). This transition moves their role beyond retrospective reporting towards a proactive function in shaping organizational strategy (Nasir & Mohamed, 2024).

Cloud computing continues to transform how accounting services are delivered by facilitating real time collaboration and seamless data access for firms and clients (Bhimani & Willcocks, 2014). In the Australian context, platforms such as Xero and QuickBooks have enabled small and medium-sized enterprises (SMEs) to adopt more agile and responsive accounting practices (Busulwa & Evans, 2021).

Cognitive technologies, including natural language processing and machine learning, are also advancing the profession. These tools are being applied to monitor compliance, assess sentiment in financial disclosures, and generate dynamic reports (Appelbaum et al., 2017). By increasing the accessibility and interactivity of financial information, they are expanding the ways accountants engage with both data and stakeholders (Busulwa & Evans, 2021).

Furthermore, stakeholder expectations are evolving rapidly. Clients, regulators, and the broader public now demand that accountants contribute to areas such as sustainability reporting, digital risk management, and the ethical governance of emerging technologies. This shift reflects a broader transformation of the profession from a compliance focused model to one that is increasingly strategic, forward looking, and grounded in ethical leadership (Busulwa & Evans, 2021).

In summary, the digital disruption affecting accounting is not simply about adopting new tools but about redefining what it means to be an accountant. As traditional roles become automated, new roles are emerging that emphasize insight generation, ethical oversight, and adaptability. To remain relevant, the profession must prioritize continuous learning, curriculum reform, and a renewed focus on digital ethics and governance.

NEED FOR THE ACCOUNTING PROFESSION TO DIGITALLY TRANSFORM

Digital transformation in accounting extends far beyond the adoption of new tools and software; it requires a fundamental rethinking of what it means to be an accountant in a rapidly evolving technological landscape. As technologies such as artificial intelligence (AI), blockchain, robotic process automation (RPA), and data analytics continue to disrupt traditional tasks, the profession must evolve in both practice and mindset. Accountants are increasingly expected to move beyond routine number crunching and assume strategic advisory roles that demand digital fluency, ethical awareness, and critical thinking (Busulwa & Evans, 2021).

A critical area requiring attention is the development of digital capability. As Busulwa and Evans (2021) and Lajnef (2025) argue, accountants must acquire a working knowledge of emerging technologies such as cloud platforms, AI applications, and blockchain systems. However, technical expertise alone is insufficient. Professionals must also develop the ability to critically evaluate the risks and limitations of these technologies and apply them responsibly across diverse contexts (Holmes & Douglass, 2022).

Education plays a pivotal role in supporting this transformation. Unfortunately, many accounting programs still lag behind industry expectations and fail to adequately prepare graduates for modern roles (Lajnef, 2025). Baroudi and El Sayary (2024) emphasize the importance of embedding digital literacy and fostering lifelong learning within accounting curricula to address these gaps. Similarly, Tiron-Tudor et al. (2025) highlight the need for ethical training alongside technical content, particularly given the increasing use of AI in audit and decision making contexts. Saleem et al. (2023) further note that effective integration of big data and AI into accounting workflows has the potential to enhance reporting quality, forecasting accuracy, and overall decision making processes.

In Australia, professional bodies such as CPA Australia and Chartered Accountants ANZ (CA ANZ) have taken important steps by developing digital competency frameworks and promoting professional development initiatives in areas such as cybersecurity and sustainability reporting (CPA Australia, 2024; CAANZ, 2025). However, significant challenges remain, particularly for small and mid-sized firms that face barriers in accessing training resources and implementing advanced systems (Busulwa & Evans, 2021).

In practice, a shift in focus is also necessary. With RPA and AI automating many transactional tasks, accountants have an opportunity to move towards higher value added services such as sustainability assurance, risk modeling, and long term strategic planning. As Saleem et al. (2023) suggest, AI-enabled tools can improve accuracy and efficiency by reducing the time spent on routine activities, but this potential can only be realized if workflows are redesigned to accommodate these technologies.

Moreover, digital transformation must be inclusive to ensure that all students and professionals regardless of their backgrounds or geographic locations can meaningfully participate in the evolving profession. Universities and professional bodies have a critical role in narrowing the digital divide by ensuring equitable access to digital tools, practical training opportunities, and partnerships with industry. Tiron-Tudor et al. (2025) highlight that addressing these disparities through curriculum reform, mentorship programs, and lifelong learning initiatives is essential for preparing future ready graduates who are equipped to navigate and shape a technologically advanced profession.

Ultimately, digital transformation in accounting is not solely about technology; it represents a broader shift in professional identity, culture, and leadership. To remain relevant and resilient, the accounting profession must embrace continuous learning, ethical engagement, and a proactive stance in shaping its future trajectory

CURRENT STATE OF THE ACCOUNTING PROFESSION'S DIGITAL TRANSFORMATION JOURNEY

The accounting profession is steadily advancing in its digital transformation, yet this progress remains uneven across sectors and regions. Large multinational firms and proactive professional bodies are leading the charge, integrating advanced technologies and redefining professional competencies. In contrast, many smaller firms, public sector organizations, and educational institutions continue to face significant challenges, including limited financial and technological resources, resistance to change, and inconsistent integration of digital skills within curricula. Lajnef (2025) highlights these disparities, noting a persistent gap in digital readiness between well-resourced firms and those still in the early stages of adoption. This divide is particularly pronounced in the educational sector, where digital competencies are not uniformly embedded in accounting programs. Similarly, Argento et al. (2025) emphasize that the impacts of digital transformation are distributed unevenly across the profession, with public sector auditing and smaller institutions often constrained by structural and social barriers that hinder technological uptake.

Globally, the Big Four accounting firms PwC, Deloitte, EY, and KPMG, have emerged as frontrunners in adopting and integrating advanced digital technologies into their audit and consulting practices. Tools such as artificial intelligence (AI), robotic process automation (RPA), blockchain, and advanced data analytics are now widely utilized to streamline audit workflows, enhance risk detection, and support real time decision making. Saleem et al. (2023) report that these firms have implemented AI-powered risk engines and blockchain-based systems to modernize assurance functions, thereby improving both efficiency and accuracy. Lajnef (2025) also observes that the Big Four are perceived as key drivers of digitalization within the profession, leveraging their global infrastructure and strategic foresight to lead technological adoption. Similarly, Argento et al. (2025) highlight the influence of these firms in shaping digital transformation trends, particularly through their impact on professional expectations and regulatory innovation. Tiron-Tudor et al. (2025) further note that early investments in AI and blockchain by these firms have allowed them to reframe traditional assurance models and establish new standards for digital competence within the profession.

In Australia, both public and private sectors have demonstrated significant strides in digital adoption. Accounting firms of varying sizes, along with financial service providers, increasingly rely on platforms such as Xero, MYOB, and cloud-based enterprise resource planning (ERP) systems to enhance operational efficiency and improve client services. The Australian Taxation Office (ATO) has also been a leader in this space, introducing initiatives such as Single Touch Payroll (STP), e-invoicing, and the myID digital identity platform to modernize compliance and reporting infrastructures (Australian Taxation Office, 2023).

Despite these advancements, small and medium-sized enterprises (SMEs), particularly in rural and regional areas, face considerable obstacles in adopting digital tools. These challenges include limited access to high speed internet, financial constraints, and a shortage of digital literacy and training opportunities (Marshall et al., 2021). Busulwa and Evans (2021) point out that while urban SMEs are rapidly adopting digital technologies, their regional counterparts lag behind due to infrastructural and educational disparities. Resistance to change and the complexity of integrating new technologies with legacy systems further inhibit adoption (Phoung, 2024).

In the education sector, progress has also been uneven. While some universities have introduced modules on data analytics, cloud accounting, and automation into their programs, these digital components often remain optional rather than being systematically integrated throughout the curriculum (Lajnef, 2025; Qasim & Kharbat, 2020). Research by Tiron-Tudor et al. (2025) indicates that many graduates still enter the workforce without the digital readiness employers now expect, exacerbating the skills gap. Lajnef (2025) also reports that although students value digital skills, they often feel underprepared to apply them in practice. This misalignment between curriculum design and industry expectations underscores an urgent need for comprehensive reform in accounting education. Without embedding digital competencies as core components of programs, students risk being left behind in a profession that is rapidly evolving through technological innovation.

There is growing recognition of the need for systemic reform in accounting education to align with the demands of a digitally transformed profession. Lajnef (2025) argues that curricula must go beyond simply incorporating digital tools to also cultivate critical thinking, ethical reasoning, and adaptability traits essential in a rapidly changing environment. Tiron-Tudor et al. (2025) emphasize that accounting graduates require a combination of technical digital skills and soft skills to thrive in technology driven workplaces. Marrone and Hazelton (2019) further contend that accounting research has not kept pace with real world innovation, creating a gap between academic outputs and professional practice that limits the development of timely, relevant educational strategies. Consequently, students are often underprepared for industry expectations, and universities risk falling behind unless programs evolve in tandem with technological and societal shifts.

Beyond education, many smaller firms continue to rely on outdated systems and manual processes. Restrepo-Morales et al. (2024) identify key barriers to digital adoption among SMEs, including limited financial resources, a shortage of qualified staff, complex IT integration challenges, and concerns about cybersecurity. Rombaldo Junior et al. (2023) add that many small firms lack the awareness and literacy required to implement effective cybersecurity measures. Evans (2023) similarly notes that the complexity of integrating new technologies with legacy systems often deters small businesses from adopting digital tools. Without targeted support and policy driven initiatives, these firms risk falling further behind in an increasingly digitized economy.

Professional organizations such as CPA Australia and Chartered Accountants ANZ (CA ANZ) have introduced digital capability frameworks and professional development initiatives focusing on AI, ESG reporting, and cybersecurity (CAANZ, 2025). While these are important steps, Busulwa and Evans (2021) argue that they must be complemented by stronger incentives, funding, and support mechanisms to achieve widespread impact across the profession.

In summary, while the accounting profession is progressing in its digital transformation, the pace and extent of this change remain uneven. Bridging these gaps will require greater collaboration among universities, professional bodies, regulators, and firms to ensure that all accountants regardless of organizational size or geographic location are equipped to succeed in a digitally enabled future.

KEY ISSUES AND CHALLENGES THE ACCOUNTING PROFESSION IS FACING IN ITS DIGITAL TRANSFORMATION JOURNEY

While the accounting profession has made significant strides towards digital transformation, several persistent challenges continue to hinder its full potential. These obstacles vary across firm size, geographic regions, access to resources, and institutional capacity. Broadly, they encompass technological and educational barriers, ethical concerns, and cultural resistance, each posing unique risks to the profession's long term relevance and resilience.

Digital Capability Gaps and Resource Constraints

Small and medium-sized practices (SMPs), particularly those operating in regional or resource constrained environments, often struggle to adopt advanced digital tools such as robotic process automation (RPA), blockchain, and artificial intelligence (AI). The International Federation of Accountants (IFAC, 2024) highlights how the digital divide between large and small firms continues to grow, driven by disparities in access to talent, infrastructure, and investment capacity. In Australia, this divide is particularly visible, with metropolitan firms increasingly leveraging cloud-based platforms and AI-driven analytics, while many smaller or regional practices continue to rely on legacy systems (Busulwa & Evans, 2021). High implementation costs, cybersecurity concerns, and limited access to digital training further exacerbate these challenges. Restrepo-Morales et al. (2024) identify insufficient financial resources and gaps in digital knowledge as major barriers for SMEs undergoing digitalization. Without targeted interventions, including government grants, professional body initiatives, and industry collaborations, SMPs risk marginalization in an increasingly digital economy.

Cybersecurity and Risk Management Deficiencies

The shift towards digital systems has amplified cybersecurity risks across the accounting profession. Accountants now manage sensitive financial data using cloud services and mobile applications, making them vulnerable to cyberattacks. Haapamäki and Sihvonen (2019) note that smaller firms, in particular, often lack the expertise and resources to establish robust cybersecurity frameworks. Cybercriminals frequently target these firms due to their weaker security protocols, exposing them to potential data breaches. Rombaldo Junior et al. (2023) further highlight that limited cybersecurity literacy and constrained budgets hinder the adoption of effective protections. Even large firms are not immune; Litt et al. (2023) demonstrate that breaches can severely damage auditor reputations and erode client trust. Without proactive strategies and targeted support, the profession remains highly exposed to both financial and reputational risks.

Educational and Training Shortfalls

Many accounting graduates enter the workforce without sufficient exposure to essential digital tools. Although universities are beginning to integrate content on cloud accounting, AI, and data analytics, these subjects are often treated as electives rather than core curriculum components (Holmes & Douglass, 2022; Lajnef, 2025). As a result, graduates often lack the practical digital competencies employers expect. Holmes and Douglass (2022) argue that the rapid integration of AI in professional practice is not being matched by curriculum updates, leaving students underprepared for real world demands. Similarly, Lajnef (2025) highlights through cognitive mapping that fragmented digital learning pathways inhibit students' ability to engage meaningfully with technological changes in the profession.

Ethical and Governance Challenges with AI and Automation

The growing integration of AI and automation into accounting workflows introduces complex ethical and governance challenges (Sutton et al. 2022). As AI systems take on roles in fraud detection, client risk assessments, and financial forecasting, concerns arise regarding algorithmic bias, lack of transparency, and diminished human oversight. Tang and Karim (2023) emphasize that biases embedded in AI tools can perpetuate inequities, while Munoko et al. (2020) warn that the opaque nature of AI systems makes it difficult to audit or explain decisions. Mokander (2023) highlights that auditing AI requires the development of legal, ethical, and technical safeguards. Without robust governance structures and consistent ethical guidelines, the adoption of AI risks undermining stakeholder trust and professional integrity.

Resistance to Change and Cultural Inertia

Cultural resistance within the profession is another significant barrier to transformation. Holmes and Douglass (2022) found that some senior accountants remain reluctant to engage with digital tools, often due to discomfort with technology or the belief that they will retire before significant changes fully take effect. This contributes to a generational divide, where younger professionals embrace digital tools while older cohorts persist with traditional methods. Busulwa et al. (2024) highlight how negative attitudes and skepticism towards technology can delay firm wide transformation. Venokur (2024) suggests that bridging these generational gaps requires purpose driven strategies that foster innovation, mentorship, and continuous learning across all age groups.

Regulatory and Compliance Ambiguity

Rapid technological innovation has outpaced the evolution of regulatory frameworks in accounting and auditing. While blockchain provides benefits such as real time and immutable recordkeeping, many jurisdictions have yet to update audit and assurance standards to address such innovations (Holmes & Douglass, 2022). This regulatory lag creates uncertainty for practitioners and increases compliance risks. The UK's Financial Reporting Council (FRC) recently reported that major accounting firms lack formal mechanisms to assess AI's impact on audit quality, underlining the need for clearly defined metrics and oversight (Kissin, 2025). Without coordinated global efforts to modernize standards, firms face significant challenges in adopting emerging technologies confidently and responsibly.

Lack of Unified Strategic Direction

Although professional bodies such as CPA Australia and Chartered Accountants ANZ have developed frameworks to guide digital competency development, the profession lacks a unified roadmap for digital transformation. This has resulted in inconsistent practices and a fragmented approach to technological adoption. Busulwa and Evans (2021) argue that greater collaboration between universities, professional associations, and regulators is needed to align efforts and build a stronger, future-ready profession.

SUFFICIENCY OF THE ACCOUNTING PROFESSION'S STRATEGIC LEADERSHIP ENTITIES, CURRICULA, AND PROFESSIONALS'S ROLES IN THE PROFESSION'S DIGITAL TRANSFORMATION

The accounting profession's response to digital transformation has been uneven, reflecting a mix of progress and persistent gaps. While there have been notable advances in professional frameworks, educational initiatives, and technological adoption, challenges remain in achieving consistency, scale, and strategic alignment. Some segments of the profession are moving forward rapidly, while others continue to lag behind.

Strategic Leadership Bodies: Good Intentions, Uneven Impact

Strategic leadership organizations such as CPA Australia, Chartered Accountants ANZ (CA ANZ), and the International Federation of Accountants (IFAC) have taken important steps in articulating a vision for the profession in the digital era. IFAC's concept of "future-ready" accountants outlines evolving roles such as digital technology enabler, data navigator, and sustainability analyst, reflecting the profession's expanding responsibilities (IFAC, 2024). Similarly, CPA Australia and CA ANZ have developed digital competency frameworks and roadmaps focusing on data analytics, cybersecurity, and climate related financial disclosures.

However, while these initiatives demonstrate strong intent, their practical impact across the profession has been inconsistent. Many small and medium-sized practices (SMPs), particularly in regional and resource constrained settings, face significant challenges in accessing the tools, training, and support required to implement these frameworks effectively (Busulwa & Evans, 2021). High level frameworks from organizations such as IFAC and ACCA provide clear guidance on desired competencies but often fail to account for the operational realities of firms with limited infrastructure or investment capacity. Argento et al. (2025) stress that digital transformation in accounting involves not only technological adoption but also structural and cultural change. Similarly, Abad et al. (2023) identify critical enablers and barriers to technology adoption, highlighting that sustained change depends on tailored implementation strategies, contextual responsiveness, and professional support structures. Without comprehensive support including funding, tailored continuing professional development (CPD), and mentorship programs, these strategies risk falling short of their transformative potential. Professional bodies must move beyond issuing guidance documents and take a more active role in capacity building and monitoring adoption, especially among underserved segments of the profession (ACCA, 2023).

Accounting Curricula: Still Catching Up

Despite growing awareness of the importance of digital transformation, university accounting programs often remain anchored in traditional content. Lajnef (2025) emphasizes the need to integrate digital skills such as AI literacy, data analytics, and cloud accounting into core curricula rather than treating them as peripheral electives. Progress in curriculum reform has been slow, hindered by limited educator preparedness and access to training resources. Holmes and Douglass (2022) highlight that unless academia aligns more closely with industry expectations, graduates will continue to enter the workforce without the digital readiness employers increasingly demand. Addressing these gaps requires not only curriculum redesign but also investment in faculty development and stronger collaboration between universities and professional bodies.

Practicing Professionals: A Divided Landscape

Among practicing accountants, engagement with digital transformation varies considerably. Professionals in large, digitally progressive firms are leveraging automation, AI, and data analytics to streamline workflows and deliver value added insights. In contrast, many in smaller or traditional firms encounter barriers such as high implementation costs, limited technical expertise, and time constraints (Busulwa & Evans, 2021). Holmes and Douglass (2022) identify a generational divide, with younger professionals more willing to embrace digital tools while senior accountants often resist change. This divide aggravates uneven adoption across firms and regions.

Ethical awareness presents another challenge. Argento et al. (2025) note that many accountants remain uncertain about how to manage ethical risks associated with AI and automation, including algorithmic bias, data security, and accountability in automated decision-making processes. Without robust digital ethics training and clearer professional guidance, these risks could undermine public trust and professional standards.

Industry-Academia Collaboration: Room for Growth

Partnerships between universities and accounting firms, such as internships, guest lectures, and joint training initiatives, are emerging but remain largely ad hoc. This lack of long-term strategic focus contributes to misalignments between academic curricula and the rapidly evolving needs of the profession. Wahyudi and Andriani (2025) argue that embedding practitioner input into course design and assessments could significantly enhance the relevance of accounting education in a digitized world. Structured collaborations can give students exposure to real world applications and ensure curricula remain aligned with industry practices. Without these linkages, universities risk producing graduates who are theoretically proficient but lack practical digital competencies (INAA, 2022).

In summary, although progress has been made, the accounting profession still faces significant challenges in aligning leadership, education, and practice with the demands of digital transformation. Coordinated action is needed to reform curricula, expand access to professional development, build educator capability, and strengthen industry academia partnerships to ensure the profession remains resilient and relevant in an increasingly digital economy.

IMPLICATIONS OF SHORTCOMINGS OF THE ACCOUNTING PROFESSION'S STRATEGIC LEADERSHIP ENTITIES, CURRICULA, AND PROFESSIONALS

The accounting profession's inability to adapt effectively to digital transformation carries both immediate and long term consequences. These shortcomings compromise the profession's capacity to address current challenges and threaten its ability to remain relevant and valuable in the future. Delayed action may erode trust in the profession, weaken its strategic role within organizations, and diminish its attractiveness to new entrants. Moreover, failure to modernize risks exacerbating disparities across firms, particularly disadvantaging smaller practices and professionals who lack access to upskilling opportunities. The implications are evident across key areas such as credibility, workforce readiness, strategic positioning, and innovation.

Erosion of Professional Relevance and Credibility

Without evolving alongside technological advancements, the profession risks appearing outdated. As automation and digital tools become more sophisticated, organizations may increasingly turn to professionals from other disciplines such as data analysts or IT specialists to perform tasks that accountants traditionally managed. Holmes and Douglass (2022) observe a shift in hiring practices, with many firms now favoring graduates from science, technology, engineering, and mathematics (STEM) backgrounds over traditional accounting graduates for technology enabled roles. Similarly, Fisher (2023) highlights that accountants are under mounting pressure to keep pace with technological and regulatory change, with those unable to do so facing marginalisation within their own field.

Employment and Skills Mismatch

Graduates entering the job market without relevant digital skills may struggle to secure meaningful employment or advance in their careers. Baroudi and El Sayary (2024) highlight a widening gap between what accounting graduates are taught and what the profession requires, particularly in data analytics, technological fluency, and critical thinking. Elo et al. (2025) similarly identify misalignments between the skills practitioners possess and employers' expectations, emphasizing the need for universities to align curricula more closely with industry demands. This disconnect not only hampers individual career progression but also weakens the profession's ability to adapt to technological advancements in an increasingly competitive business environment.

Heightened Exposure to Ethical and Cybersecurity Risks

Inadequate understanding of the ethical and governance implications of AI and other digital tools presents significant risks for the profession. Without robust frameworks for AI accountability and ethical data use, accountants may inadvertently contribute to biased, opaque, or non-compliant practices. This is particularly concerning given the profession's duty to uphold public trust and ensure the integrity of financial reporting. Fülöp et al. (2023) found that many accountants still possess only a superficial understanding of AI technologies, limiting their ability to identify or address ethical challenges. Additionally, the Kissin (2025) reported that large accounting firms have yet to establish consistent frameworks for assessing AI's impact on audit quality, exposing a systemic governance gap in how these technologies are evaluated and regulated. Such deficiencies undermine trust in AI assisted accounting processes and expose firms to legal, reputational, and operational risks.

Loss of Strategic Influence

As business decisions increasingly rely on predictive analytics, scenario modeling, and real time data, accountants must be equipped to engage with these tools to maintain their strategic relevance. If they fail to do so, they risk being replaced by professionals with stronger digital skills. Olagoke (2025) emphasizes that predictive analytics not only enhances operational efficiency but also strengthens strategic foresight critical qualities for accountants seeking to influence executive level decision-making. Similarly, Mulyadi (2025) notes that firms increasingly expect finance professionals to provide forward looking insights by interpreting complex data trends and assessing risk scenarios. Without upskilling in these areas, accountants may lose their traditional advisory roles to more tech savvy professionals from other fields.

Marginalisation of Small and Mid-Tier Firms

Small and mid-tier accounting firms face disproportionate challenges in adopting digital tools due to limited financial resources, insufficient in house IT expertise, and inadequate support from professional bodies. Without targeted initiatives for training and implementation, these firms risk falling further behind, deepening the profession's digital divide (Busulwa & Evans, 2021). Restrepo-Morales et al. (2024) report that SMEs often encounter high investment costs, skills shortages, and uncertainty about technology providers, all of which hinder meaningful digital transformation. Bridging this gap requires coordinated interventions from professional associations and policymakers to provide funding, training, and tailored strategic support.

Fragmented Educational Response

A lack of coordination between universities, professional bodies, and industry stakeholders has resulted in fragmented and inconsistent curriculum reforms. Digital skills are often partially integrated into programs or treated as optional, leaving graduates underprepared for modern accounting roles. Lajnef (2025) argues that curriculum development frequently lacks alignment with the technological competencies demanded in practice, contributing to a gap between graduate output and employer expectations. Birt et al. (2023) similarly found that varying levels of ICT and data analytics integration across universities have created inconsistencies in graduate readiness. Saad (2025) warns that unless universities rapidly adapt to the demands of AI and automation, accounting graduates will remain ill-equipped to navigate an increasingly digital profession.

In summary, these gaps present risks not only for individual professionals and firms but also for the credibility and long term sustainability of the entire accounting profession. Addressing these challenges will require coordinated efforts across educational institutions, professional bodies, and regulators to ensure that the profession evolves in line with technological and societal change.

WHAT THE ACCOUNTING PROFESSION'S STRATEGIC LEADERSHIP ENTITIES, CURRICULA, AND PROFESSIONALS DO TO MAXIMIZE THEIR CONTRIBUTION TO THE PROFESSION'S DIGITAL TRANSFORMATION EFFORTS

For the accounting profession to remain relevant and resilient in a digitally driven world, a proactive and coordinated approach to digital transformation is essential. Strategic leadership bodies, educators, and individual professionals each have a critical role to play, not only in addressing existing gaps but also in preparing for the challenges and opportunities that lie ahead.

Strategic Leadership Entities: Leading with Vision and Support

Strategic leadership bodies such as the International Federation of Accountants (IFAC), CPA Australia, and Chartered Accountants ANZ (CA ANZ) have made significant strides in defining the future of the profession in the digital age. IFAC's *Future-Fit Accountants* initiative outlines evolving roles including digital technology enabler, data navigator, and sustainability analyst that reflect the expanding responsibilities of modern accountants (IFAC, 2019). Similarly, CPA Australia and CA ANZ have developed digital competency frameworks and roadmaps, highlighting the importance of skills in areas such as data analytics, cybersecurity, and climate-related financial disclosures (CAANZ, 2025).

While these efforts demonstrate strong intent, their practical impact has been uneven across the profession. Many small and mid-sized practices (SMPs), especially in regional or resource limited contexts, face challenges in accessing the tools, training, and support needed to implement these frameworks effectively (Busulwa & Evans, 2021). High level frameworks from organizations like IFAC and ACCA often fail to account for the operational realities of firms with limited resources or infrastructure. Argento et al. (2025) emphasize that digital transformation in accounting requires not only technological innovation but also structural and cultural change. Without sustained funding, tailored continuing professional development (CPD), and regional mentorship programs, even the most well-intentioned strategies risk falling short. Professional bodies must move beyond issuing guidance documents to actively building capacity and monitoring adoption, particularly in underserved areas (ACCA, 2023; Chartered Accountants Worldwide, 2025).

Curricula: Making Digital Skills a Core Competency

Tertiary institutions also play a pivotal role in preparing future accountants for the demands of a digital economy. Digital literacy, ethical awareness, and adaptability must move from peripheral considerations to central pillars of accounting education. Embedding digital competencies such as data analytics, blockchain, AI ethics, and accounting information systems into core curricula ensures students engage with these skills early and often, making them part of their professional identity rather than optional enhancements (Lajnef, 2025). Linking these competencies to real world applications and assessments can further improve retention and practical readiness.

Educator readiness is equally critical. Universities must invest in upskilling faculty to ensure emerging technologies are taught effectively and in alignment with evolving industry expectations. Building partnerships with industry through guest lectures, internships, and collaborative capstone projects can also strengthen the connection between academic learning and professional practice (Baroudi & El Sayary, 2024).

Accounting Professionals: Embracing Lifelong Learning and New Roles

Practicing accountants must embrace lifelong learning to remain competitive in a fast-changing environment. This involves engaging in short courses, earning digital credentials, and gaining hands on experience with AI tools and cloud platforms. As Lee et al. (2024) note, critical digital skills such as data analytics and AI system interfacing are now baseline expectations for accounting professionals.

The role of the accountant is also shifting dramatically. As Busulwa and Evans (2021) highlight, accountants must move beyond compliance focused tasks to take on roles as data stewards, strategic advisors, and ethics champions. Jayashree and Jayakani (2025) further argue that digital transformation necessitates a proactive, consultative mindset, requiring both technical expertise and strong professional judgment to navigate emerging challenges effectively.

Building Stronger Ecosystems Through Collaboration

Successful digital transformation depends on robust collaboration across sectors. Professional bodies must work closely with universities to co-develop curriculum standards and align them with industry needs. Governments also have a vital role in funding digital infrastructure and supporting skills development, particularly in regional and underrepresented areas. Employers, meanwhile, should create opportunities for early career professionals and students to gain hands on exposure to digital tools and real world projects.

Tiron-Tudor et al. (2025) emphasize that bridging the gap between market demands and student expectations requires multi-stakeholder ecosystems where professional associations, educators, and employers co-create digitally rich learning experiences. Similarly, structured university-industry partnerships have been shown to enhance graduate employability, improve curriculum relevance, and accelerate knowledge transfer (Weagle et al., 2022). Building these collaborative ecosystems will be essential to prepare future accountants and ensure equitable digital transformation across the profession.

Tracking Progress and Encouraging Accountability

To ensure meaningful progress, it is critical to establish clear metrics for digital transformation. Professional bodies and educational institutions should monitor key performance indicators (KPIs) such as CPD completion rates, software adoption, and curriculum integration to assess digital maturity over time. A comprehensive study by the International Accounting Education Standards Board (IAESB) provides models for output-based CPD measurement, offering insights into tracking learning outcomes and professional development. Zou et al. (2024) also highlight the importance of KPI frameworks covering adoption rates, productivity gains, and return on investment (ROI) to guide continuous improvement and sustain transformation momentum. Regular assessments can help identify gaps, direct targeted support, and hold leadership accountable for progress. These efforts require collective action across the profession (Table 11.2) outlines key actors, their roles in driving digital transformation, and examples of practical actions they can take to support accountability and sustained progress.

TABLE 11.2
Examples of Actors, Roles They can Play, and Actions They can Take to Advance Accounting's Digital Transformation

Example Actors	Example Roles in Digital Transformation	Examples of specific Actions to Take
Strategic Leadership Bodies	Set national/global vision, develop digital frameworks, drive equitable capacity building	Expand CPD access, offer funded upskilling programs, track adoption KPIs
University Educators	Redesign curricula, upskill educators, embed digital and ethical capabilities as core competencies	Integrate AI/data/cloud into core courses; foster partnerships with industry
Practicing Professionals	Embrace lifelong learning; adapt to evolving roles such as strategic advisor and digital steward	Gain digital credentials; adopt AI/cloud tools; stay abreast of ethical risks
Professional Associations	Bridge academia and industry; provide guidance on digital ethics and transformation pathways	Co design curricula; fund innovation hubs; mentor under-resourced firms
Employers	Provide hands-on training opportunities, internships, and internal CPD for staff	Sponsor certifications; encourage cross-generational tech mentoring
Governments	Support infrastructure and equitable access in underserved regions	Fund SME digital adoption; promote regional partnerships; reduce digital inequality

CONCLUSION

This chapter has examined how digital disruption is reshaping the accounting profession and considered the implications of this transformation for its future. It begins by discussing the technologies driving change such as artificial intelligence (AI), blockchain, and cloud computing and highlights how these innovations are fundamentally altering traditional accounting roles, workflows, and service delivery models. The analysis underscores that meaningful digital transformation requires more than the adoption of new tools; it necessitates a reimagining of professional competencies, ethical frameworks, and the ways in which accountants create value in a dynamic and interconnected environment.

While large firms and progressive institutions have made significant strides in embracing digital innovation, the profession's transformation remains uneven. Smaller practices and educational providers, in particular, face notable barriers including limited financial resources, outdated curricula, cybersecurity vulnerabilities, ethical challenges, and cultural resistance to technological change. These challenges, if unaddressed, may result in a loss of professional relevance, widening skills gaps, and missed opportunities for innovation and strategic influence.

The chapter also critically evaluates the roles of professional bodies, universities, and individual practitioners in driving and supporting digital transformation. While there have been positive initiatives such as the development of digital competency frameworks and professional development programs these efforts often lack consistency, scale, and alignment across the profession. Strengthening collaboration among stakeholders, setting clearer strategic priorities, and investing more deeply in education and training are identified as key enablers for future progress.

In conclusion, the chapter calls for a coordinated and forward thinking approach to digital transformation. Such an approach will be essential to ensure that all segments of the profession regardless of size, location, or available resources are equipped to engage with technological disruption and contribute to shaping the profession's future in a manner that is both responsible and ethically grounded.

DISCUSSION QUESTIONS

1. In what ways are technologies like AI, blockchain, and cloud computing changing the nature of accounting work?
2. What does digital transformation really involve for the accounting profession? Is it just about learning new tools, or does it require a deeper shift in how accountants think, work, and add value?
3. The chapter discusses uneven progress in digital transformation across the profession. What do you think contributes to this unevenness, and how can the profession support those who are being left behind?
4. What are some of the main challenges accounting firms and educators face when trying to keep up with digital change?
5. Do you think professional bodies and universities are doing enough to prepare the profession for a digital future? Where have they made progress, and where is there still room for improvement?

6. The chapter outlines some serious consequences if the profession doesn't adapt. Which of these risks do you think are most urgent, and why?
7. How important is collaboration between universities, employers, and professional associations in shaping accounting education and professional development? Can you think of any examples where this collaboration has worked well or where it has fallen short?
8. Looking ahead, what practical steps should the accounting profession take to make sure digital transformation is inclusive, ethical, and future-ready? What role can individual accountants play in shaping that future?

REFERENCES

Abad, C., de Haro, D., & Robson, K. (2023). Enablers, barriers, and strategies for adopting new technology in accounting. *International Journal of Accounting Information Systems*, 51, 100624. https://doi.org/10.1016/j.accinf.2023.100624

ACCA. (2023). *Digital horizons: Technology, innovation and the future of accounting.* Association of Chartered Certified Accountants. https://www.accaglobal.com/content/dam/ACCA_Global/professional-insights/digital-horizons2023/PI-DIGITAL-HORIZONS%20v5.pdf

Accounting Insights. (2024). *Trends Transforming the Future of the Accounting Profession.* Accounting Insights. https://accountinginsights.org/trends-transforming-the-future-of-the-accounting-profession/

Accounting Insights. (2025). *Transforming accounting with AI, blockchain, and cloud technology.* https://accountinginsights.org/transforming-accounting-with-ai-blockchain-and-cloud-technology

Appelbaum, D., Kogan, A., Vasarhelyi, M., & Yan, Z. (2017). Impact of business analytics and enterprise systems on managerial accounting. *International Journal of Accounting Information Systems, 25*, 29–44. https://doi.org/10.1016/j.accinf.2017.03.003

Argento, D., Dobija, D., Grossi, G., Marrone, M., & Mora, L. (2025). The unaccounted effects of digital transformation: Implications for accounting, auditing, and accountability. *Accounting, Auditing & Accountability Journal.* https://doi.org/10.1108/AAAJ-01-2025-7670

Australian Taxation Office. (2023). *ATO digital strategy 2022–25.* https://www.ato.gov.au/about-ato/managing-the-tax-and-super-system/ato-digital-strategy/ato-digital-strategy-2022-25

Baldwin, R. (2024). *How emerging technologies are enhancing the accounting profession.* AICPA & CIMA. https://www.aicpa-cima.com/professional-insights/article/how-emerging-technologies-are-enhancing-the-accounting-profession

Baroudi, S., & El Sayary, .A. (2024). Driving transformation in higher education: Exploring the process and impact of educational innovations for sustainability through interdisciplinary studies. *Higher Education Quarterly*, 1–23.

Bhimani, A., & Willcocks, L. (2014). Digitisation, 'Big Data' and the transformation of accounting information. *Accounting and Business Research*, *44*(4), 469–490. https://doi.org/10.1080/00014788.2014.910051

Birt, J., Safari, M., & de Castro, V. B. (2023). Critical analysis of integration of ICT and data analytics into the accounting curriculum: A multidimensional perspective. *Accounting & Finance*, *63*(4), 4037–4063. https://doi.org/10.1111/acfi.13084

Busulwa, R., Birt, J., Gepp, A., & Oates, G. (2024). Accountants' attitudes to digital technology: a barrier to the digital transformation of accounting? In *Digital Transformation in Accounting and Auditing: Navigating Technological Advances for the Future* (pp. 153–182). Cham: Springer International Publishing. https://doi.org/10.1007/978-3-031-46209-2_6

Busulwa, R., & Evans, N. (2021). *Digital transformation in accounting*. Routledge.

Chartered Accountants Australia and New Zealand. (2025). *A capability model to help shape profession of the future*. Retrieved from https://www.charteredaccountantsanz.com/learning-and-events/learning/capability-model

Chartered Accountants Worldwide. (2025). *AI and the future of the global chartered accountancy profession*. https://charteredaccountantsworldwide.com/wp-content/uploads/2025/04/CAW_AI-in-Accountancy-web.pdf

CPA Australia. (2024). *New micro-credentials to prepare accountants for the opportunities of a sustainable future*. Retrieved from https://www.cpaaustralia.com.au/about-cpa-australia/media/media-releases/new-micro-credentials-to-prepare-accountants-for-the-opportunities-of-a-sustainable-future

Elo, T., Puumalainen, K., Sjögrén, H., & Pätäri, S. (2025). Skill gaps in accounting: Contrasting stakeholder expectations with perceived skill

Evans, M. (2023). *Small-medium businesses face barriers to technology adoption*. AI Business. Retrieved from https://aibusiness.com/verticals/small-medium-businesses-face-barriers-to-technology-adoption

Kissin, E. (2025). Big accounting firms fail to track AI impact on audit quality, says regulator. Financial Times, Retrieved from https://www.proquest.com/trade-journals/big-accounting-firms-fail-track-ai-impact-on/docview/3233654824/se-2

Fisher, L. (2023). *Professionals under pressure*. AB Magazine. Retrieved from https://abmagazine.accaglobal.com/global/articles/2023/oct/careers/professionals-under-pressure.html

Fülöp, M. T., Topor, D. I., Ionescu, C. A., Cifuentes-Faura, J., & Măgdaş, N. (2023). Ethical concerns associated with artificial intelligence in the accounting profession: A curse or a blessing? *Journal of Business Economics and Management*, *24*(2), 387–404. https://doi.org/10.3846/jbem.2023.19251

Phuong, K. T. (2024). *Top 7 challenges Australian SMEs face in digital transformation and how to overcome them*. Glinteco. Retrieved from https://glinteco.com/en/post/top-7-challenges-australian-smes-face-in-digital-transformation-and-how-to-overcome-them/

Haapamäki, E., & Sihvonen, J. (2019). Cybersecurity in accounting research. *Managerial Auditing Journal*, *34*(7), 808–834. https://doi.org/10.1108/MAJ-09-2018-2004

Harrast, S. A. (2020). Robotic process automation in accounting systems. *Journal of Corporate Accounting & Finance*, *31*(4), 209–213.

Holmes, A. F., & Douglass, .A. (2022). Artificial intelligence: Reshaping the accounting profession and the disruption to accounting education. *Journal of Emerging Technologies in Accounting*, *19*(1), 53–68.

International Federation of Accountants. (2019). *Future-Fit Accountants: Roles for the Next Decade*. Retrieved from https://www.ifac.org/knowledge-gateway/discussion/future-fit-accountants-roles-next-decade

International Federation of Accountants. (2024). *Digital transformation and the future of the accounting profession*. Retrieved from https://www.ifac.org

Jayashree, R., & Jayakani, S. (2025). Study on impact of digital transformation within the accounting domain and evolving responsibilities of accountants: A data-driven exploration. *AIP Conference Proceedings*, *3306*(1), 030028. https://doi.org/10.1063/5.0276496

Kanaparthi, V. (2024). Exploring the Impact of Blockchain, AI, and ML on Financial Accounting Efficiency and Transformation. In: Vimal, V., Perikos, I., Mukherjee, A., Piuri, V. (eds), *Multi-strategy learning environment*. Springer, Singapore. https://doi.org/10.1007/978-981-97-1488-9_27

Lajnef, K. (2025). How does accounting education shape the digitalization of the accounting profession? A cognitive mapping investigation. *Quality & Quantity*, 59, 3441–3460. https://doi.org/10.1007/s11135-025-02131-9

Lee, A. S., Chin, Y. M., Foo, P. Y., Loh, C. T. I., & Ng, Y. H. (2025). Upskilling and Retraining of Accounting Professionals in the Digitalized Era. In *Proceedings of the 12th International Conference on Business, Accounting, Finance and Economics (BAFE 2024)* (pp. 391–401). Atlantis Press.

Litt, B., Tanyi, P., & Watson, M. W. (2023). Cybersecurity breach at a big 4 accounting firm: Effects on auditor reputation. *Journal of Information Systems, 37*(2), 77–100. https://doi.org/10.2308/ISYS-2022-006

Marrone, M., & Hazelton, J. (2019). The disruptive and transformative potential of new technologies for accounting, accountants and accountability. *Meditari Accountancy Research, 27*(5), 677–694.

Mokander, J. (2023). Auditing of AI: Legal, ethical and technical approaches. *Digital Society, 2*, 49. https://doi.org/10.1007/s44206-023-00074-y

Mulyadi, M. (2025). Predictive analytics will transform accounting. *Accounting Today.* Retrieved from https://www.accountingtoday.com/opinion/predictive-analytics-will-transform-accounting

Munoko, I., Brown-Liburd, H., & Vasarhelyi, M. A. (2020). The ethical implications of using artificial intelligence in auditing. *Journal of Business Ethics, 167*(2), 209–234.

Nasir, M., & Mohamed, .A. (2024). Blockchain technology, business data analytics, and artificial intelligence use in the accounting profession: Trends and integration. *International Journal of Accounting and Information Management, 32*(2), 101–118.

Olagoke, M. F. (2025). The role of predictive analytics in enhancing financial decision-making and risk management. *Journal of Financial Risk Management, 14*(1), 47–65. https://doi.org/10.4236/jfrm.2025.141004

Qasim, A., & Kharbat, F. F. (2020). Blockchain technology, business data analytics, and artificial intelligence: Use in the accounting profession and idea for inclusion into the accounting curriculum. *Journal of Emerging Technologies in Accounting, 17*(1), 107–117.

Marshall, A., Babacan, H., & Dale, A. (2021). *Leveraging digital development in regional and rural Queensland: Policy discussion paper.* Rural Economies Centre of Excellence. Retrieved from https://www.ruraleconomies.org.au/media/1309/recoe_paper_june-2021-digital-connectivity-final-paper-web-version.pdf

Restrepo-Morales, J. A., Ararat-Herrera, J. A., López-Cadavid, D. A., & Camacho-Vargas, .A. (2024). Breaking the digitalization barrier for SMEs: A fuzzy logic approach to overcoming challenges in business transformation. *Journal of Innovation and Entrepreneurship, 13*(1), 1–18.

Rombaldo Junior, A., Manchini, J. A., Viana, R. F., & Geronimo, G. D. (2023). Cybersecurity challenges faced by SMEs: A systematic review. *arXiv.* Retrieved from https://arxiv.org/abs/2309.17186

Saad, A. M. A. M. (2025). Adapting accountants to the AI revolution: University strategies for skill enhancement, job security and competence in accounting. *Higher Education, Skills and Work-Based Learning, 15*(2), 290–305. https://doi.org/10.1108/HESWBL-10-2023-0295

Saleem, I., Abdeljawad, I., & Nour, A. I. (2023). Artificial intelligence and the future of accounting profession: implications and challenges. In *Artificial Intelligence, Internet of Things, and Society 5.0* (pp. 327–336). Cham: Springer Nature Switzerland

Sutton, S. G., Holt, M., & Arnold, V. (2022). The expanding role of artificial intelligence in accounting: Implications for audit and ethics. *Journal of Information Systems, 36*(2), 5–18.

Tang, Y., & Karim, K. E. (2023). Algorithmic bias and the ethics of AI in accounting. *Journal of Emerging Technologies in Accounting, 20*(1), 45–68. https://doi.org/10.2308/JETA-2022-003

Tiron-Tudor, A., Cordos, G., & Deliu, D. (2025). Future-ready digital skills in the AI era: Bridging market demands and student expectations in the accounting profession. *Technological Forecasting and Social Change*, *215*, 124105. https://doi.org/10.1016/j.techfore.2025.124105

Venokur, A. (2024). Bridging the accounting profession's generational gap requires purpose-driven strategy steeped in innovation and adaptability. *CPA Practice Advisor.* Retrieved from https://www.cpapracticeadvisor.com/2024/11/20/bridging-the-accounting-professions-generational-gap-requires-purpose-driven-strategy-steeped-in-innovation-and-adaptability/152254/

Wahyudi, I., & Andriani, P. D. (2025). Digital revolution in accounting education: Bridging the academia–industry gap in the era of technological disruption. *Proceedings of the International Student Conference on Business Education, Economics, Accounting and Management (ISC-BEAM)*, *3*(1), 2449.

Warren, J. D., Moffitt, K. C., & Byrnes, P. (2015). How big data will change accounting. *Accounting Horizons*, *29*(2), 397–407. https://doi.org/10.2308/acch-51069

Weagle, A., Dalrymple, A., & Smith, B. (2022). University–industry collaboration in business curriculum co-creation: Benefits and barriers. *International Journal of Management Education*, *20*(3), 100645. https://doi.org/10.1016/j.ijme.2022.100645

Yermack, D. (2017). Corporate governance and blockchains. *Review of Finance*, *21*(1), 7–31.

Zou, L., Li, W., Wu, H., Liu, J., & Gao, P. (2024). Measuring corporate digital transformation: Methodology, indicators and applications. *Sustainability*, *16*(10), 4087. https://doi.org/10.3390/su16104087

12 Case Study of the Digital Transformation of Teaching

INTRODUCTION

The teaching profession is undergoing an unprecedented transformation due to rapid advancements in digital technology. Digital disruption has significantly altered traditional teaching and learning methods, shifting educational practices from predominantly face-to-face instruction to technology driven environments. This transformation has been accelerated by the Fourth Industrial Revolution and global challenges such as the COVID-19 pandemic, which forced institutions to rapidly adapt to online and hybrid learning models (Mhlanga, 2024). While digital transformation presents numerous opportunities to enhance teaching effectiveness, it also introduces significant challenges, including digital literacy gaps, unequal access to technology, and the need for revised pedagogical frameworks (Oliveira & Souza, 2022). Moreover, the sudden shift to remote education during the pandemic exposed deep infrastructural inequalities particularly in rural areas where limited electricity, internet access, and device availability hindered effective online delivery (Magocha et al., 2025; Srinivasan et al., 2021). Concurrently, both students and teachers have begun to demand more personalized, interactive learning experiences reminiscent of consumer grade digital applications, placing new pressures on educators to cultivate advanced digital literacies and pedagogical adaptability (Magocha et al., 2025). This chapter delves into the digital disruption of teaching, outlines the necessary steps for meaningful transformation, assesses the current state of digital education, identifies key challenges, evaluates the role of strategic leadership entities, and projects the future trajectory of the profession.

HOW THE TEACHING PROFESSION IS BEING DIGITALLY DISRUPTED

The Acceleration of Digital Learning

The transition to digital learning has been driven by advances in technology and the imperative for flexible education models. The adoption of Learning Management Systems (LMS), video conferencing platforms, and smart classroom technologies has reshaped how educators deliver content and interact with students (Díaz-García et al., 2022). This shift coincides with the emergence of learner centered models, which leverage technology to accelerate learning and help close longstanding educational disparities (Digital Promise, 2023; Zheng et al., 2022). Mobile learning applications have also facilitated continuous education beyond the traditional classroom

DOI: 10.1201/9781003606604-16

setting. During the COVID-19 pandemic, mobile devices emerged as critical tools providing easy, flexible, and unlimited access to learning opportunities both inside and outside the classroom (Liu & Chen, 2022). While the sudden shift to digital platforms during the COVID-19 pandemic exposed technological barriers, digital literacy[1] gaps, and engagement difficulties (Kasımoğlu et al., 2022), it also presented opportunities for more flexible learning models and expanded access to education through online platforms (Otto et al., 2023).

The rise of Massive Open Online Courses (MOOCs) has further democratized education globally. Many universities and schools have integrated e-learning platforms with adaptive learning technologies, enabling teachers to monitor student progress, identify learning gaps, and tailor instruction accordingly (Cobos et al., 2023; Schleicher, 2024). Adaptive systems powered by artificial intelligence (AI) now offer timely feedback, dynamically adjust content difficulty, and promote personalized learning paths. Intelligent tutoring systems and AI-enabled platforms can monitor student progress in real time, diagnose learning gaps, and deliver individualized instruction without constant teacher intervention (Luckin et al., 2016; Bui & Nguyen, 2023; Schleicher, 2024). However, despite these advancements, questions remain regarding equitable implementation, digital infrastructure, and pedagogical readiness across diverse educational contexts (Bui & Nguyen, 2023). Table 12.1 provides examples of major types of digital disruption in teaching, including shifts toward AI-driven personalization, immersive learning, mobile learning, and data-driven instructional models.

TABLE 12.1
Examples of Types of Digital Disruption in Teaching

Type of Disruption	Description	Examples changes in teaching practice
Shift to Digital Learning Environments	Replaces face-to-face teaching with technology-enabled formats	Use of LMSs, video conferencing, smart classrooms
AI-Driven Personalization	Adapts content and teaching pace based on real-time learner data	Use of AI platforms, intelligent tutoring, adaptive learning systems
Mobile and Anytime Learning	Extends learning beyond traditional settings through mobile devices and applications	Resilience of COVID-era mobile learning, continuous access outside classrooms
Rise of MOOCs and Micro-Credentials	Offers scalable, flexible alternatives to traditional degrees	Growth of MOOCs, micro-credentialing systems in higher education
Data-Driven Instruction and Analytics	Uses data to identify gaps, customize instruction, and predict performance	Integration of predictive analytics, AI chatbots, personalized student feedback
Immersive and Gamified Learning	Enhances engagement via virtual environments and game-like features	Use of VR/AR classrooms, gamified flipped learning strategies

Artificial Intelligence and Data Analytics in Teaching

AI-powered tools such as adaptive learning platforms and intelligent tutoring systems have begun to play a critical role in delivering personalized education. AI applications can provide real time feedback, automate administrative tasks, and enhance student engagement through data driven insights (Schleicher, 2024). Moreover, these systems analyze students' learning behaviors, identify knowledge gaps, and suggest tailored learning pathways to ensure a more individualized educational experience (Luckin et al., 2016; Schleicher, 2024).

Beyond personalization, predictive analytics is increasingly used to forecast student performance and recommend timely interventions for learners at risk of falling behind (Bui & Nguyen, 2023). AI chatbots and virtual assistants also support students by answering routine questions, providing resources, and offering tutoring services on demand, thereby reducing the workload for human instructors (Mhlanga, 2024). These developments underscore the transformative potential of AI in creating more effective, inclusive, and responsive education systems (Schleicher, 2024).

Challenges of Digital Literacy and Professional Development

Despite the benefits of digital transformation, many educators face difficulties adapting to digital teaching methods. Research underscores that professional development programs are essential in equipping teachers with the digital competencies needed to integrate new technologies meaningfully (Badiozaman et al., 2022). These programs must go beyond theory to include immersive, hands-on experiences with instructional design for online learning, classroom management in digital settings, and frameworks like TPACK[2] or DigCompEdu[3] to be effective (Bećirović & Dervić, 2022; Smith & Johnson, 2022). Evidence from professional learning communities, including online certification courses and peer-mentorship networks, shows significant improvements in teacher confidence and pedagogical efficacy (Bećirović & Dervić, 2022).

The global shift to digital classrooms has also surfaced a range of new challenges. Meinokat and Wagner (2024) found that online teaching introduced disruptions such as student disengagement, technical interruptions, and heightened demands on teacher administrative oversight. Similarly, Bećirović and Dervić (2022) identify persistent barriers: lack of adequate infrastructure, insufficient formal training, and limited institutional support. These dual internal and external obstacles must be addressed through comprehensive professional development and ongoing support to prevent inequality and educator burnout (Schleicher, 2024; Bui & Nguyen, 2023). These professional challenges are deeply intertwined with systemic inequities in digital access, where infrastructure deficits and resource gaps further complicate teachers' ability to adopt and sustain digital pedagogies effectively. This aligns with evidence that even when digital tools are available, many educators struggle with limited technical training, insufficient institutional support, and a lack of pedagogical guidance for technology integration (Atabek, 2019).

The Digital Divide and Equity Issues

Access to digital tools and resources remains uneven, especially in rural and low-income communities. This disparity is primarily driven by inadequate infrastructure, high costs of broadband connectivity, and limited availability of devices, which collectively hinder the implementation of effective digital education strategies (Mhlanga, 2024; Miras et al., 2023).

The COVID-19 pandemic brought these inequities into sharper focus and accelerated efforts to bridge the divide. National governments and non-for-profit organizations introduced initiatives such as device lending programs, community Internet hubs, and targeted digital literacy campaigns to address access issues (Coman et al., 2020). However, gaps persist. Salas-Pilco et al., (2022) highlight how students in Latin America faced significant barriers to online learning due to unreliable connectivity, insufficient access to hardware, and a lack of tailored institutional support. They emphasize that the shift to remote learning often amplified preexisting socioeconomic disparities, particularly for marginalized groups.

To address these challenges, researchers recommend comprehensive strategies that combine infrastructure investment, targeted professional development for teachers, and equity focused policies. Without such systemic interventions, digital transformation risks further exacerbating educational inequalities instead of alleviating them (OECD, 2023; Salas-Pilco et al., 2022).

NEED FOR THE TEACHING PROFESSION TO DIGITALLY TRANSFORM

Rethinking Pedagogical Approaches

Digital transformation in education demands a significant shift from traditional, lecture based instruction to interactive and student centered learning models. Blended learning, flipped classrooms, and gamification have demonstrated strong potential in improving student engagement, motivation, and learning outcomes (Schleicher, 2024; Zainuddin et al., 2024). For example, Zainuddin et al. (2024) highlight that gamified flipped classroom strategies not only increased student participation but also enhanced learning retention in diverse higher education settings.

In addition, microlearning has gained prominence as an effective method for delivering focused and flexible learning content. Designed to be accessible on mobile platforms, microlearning enables learners to engage in "bite-sized" learning activities that fit seamlessly into their daily routines. Studies have shown that optimized microlearning materials can support just-in-time learning and enhance learner confidence and comprehension (Kohnke, 2021).

Competency based education (CBE) is another pedagogical innovation gaining traction in digitally transformed classrooms. This model emphasizes student mastery of specific skills and concepts rather than time spent in class. Sölch et al. (2023) report that integrating CBE frameworks into interactive learning systems, such as Artemis, enables adaptive and personalized learning pathways while providing real-time feedback to both students and instructors. These approaches demonstrate how digital tools, and adaptive platforms can empower teachers to design mastery-driven environments tailored to individual learners' needs.

Integration of Digital Tools and AI in Curriculum Design

Educational institutions need to embed digital tools and AI-driven approaches within curricula to ensure students acquire essential digital competencies for the modern workforce. AI-powered assessment methods, virtual simulations, and collaborative online learning platforms create opportunities for more interactive and adaptive teaching methods, supporting differentiated instruction and personalized feedback (Oliveira & Souza, 2022).

Moreover, immersive technologies such as virtual reality (VR) and augmented reality (AR) are increasingly used to enhance experiential learning. Recent developments in AR and VR highlight their potential to create interactive environments that engage students in exploring complex concepts and real world scenarios (Al-Ansi et al., 2023). These tools are being applied across disciplines, allowing learners to conduct simulated science experiments, visualize historical events in three dimensions, and participate in practical problem solving exercises. Such approaches foster critical thinking, creativity, and collaboration while making learning more accessible and engaging.

However, effective integration of these technologies requires careful curriculum design, sufficient investment in infrastructure, and robust professional development for educators. Without these foundational supports, there is a risk of widening the digital divide, particularly in under resourced educational contexts (Nyaaba et al., 2024).

Strengthening Teacher Training Programs

Continuous professional development is essential for teachers to stay current with rapidly evolving educational technologies. Institutions should invest in comprehensive upskilling programs that emphasize digital pedagogy, AI literacy, and cybersecurity awareness (Bui & Nguyen, 2023). A recent integrative review supports the importance of AI-focused teacher training, emphasizing both theoretical understanding and hands-on activities with generative AI tools to build competence (Author et al., 2024). Training should not only include practical experience with emerging educational technology tools but also offer structures for teachers to collaborate on innovative teaching techniques through online learning communities (Author et al., 2024; Hori & Fujii, 2021).

To support lifelong learning among educators, online professional networks and communities of practice should be established. Studies show that digital professional learning communities mediate the relationship between teacher training and successful technology integration, especially among (Science, Technology, Engineering, and Mathematics (STEM) professionals (Hori & Fujii, 2021). By engaging collaboratively in these communities, teachers benefit from peer support, shared resources, and reflective practices that reinforce classroom implementation of digital methods (Author et al., 2024).

CURRENT STATE OF THE TEACHING PROFESSION'S DIGITAL TRANSFORMATION JOURNEY

The digital transformation of the teaching profession is progressing at varying speeds across regions, institutions, and educational levels. While some educational institutions have fully embraced digital tools, others continue to struggle with implementation due to insufficient infrastructure, low levels of digital literacy, and inadequate policy support (Díaz-García et al., 2022). The COVID-19 pandemic accelerated technology adoption, but many institutions continue to struggle with integrating these tools sustainably into everyday teaching practices.

At present, many schools and universities have adopted hybrid and blended learning models, leveraging Learning Management Systems (LMS) such as Canvas, Moodle, and Google Classroom to organize coursework and facilitate communication between teachers and students (Bui & Nguyen, 2023). In addition, AI-powered adaptive learning platforms have increasingly been integrated to personalize student learning experiences, providing real time feedback and targeted instruction (Schleicher, 2024). However, the level of digital adoption remains uneven. Research in Latin America has shown that students and educators in low income regions continue to face significant challenges related to device availability, stable internet access, and limited teacher readiness for digital pedagogies, contributing to inequities in education delivery (García-Martín & García-Sánchez, 2022).

Emerging trends in higher education include a dramatic rise in online degree programs and micro-credentialing systems that support lifelong learning and workforce adaptability. A systematic review on micro-credential implementation highlights their potential to disrupt traditional degree models, though institutional capacity and equitable access remain critical for success (Ahsan et al., 2023). Additionally, VR classroom use is gaining traction: a recent review of 95 empirical studies indicates that immersive virtual environments support active learning and engagement, but standardization and scalable models are still in early stages (Stracke et al., 2025). At the same time, concerns around data privacy and digital fatigue among students have prompted educators to consider ethical guidelines and balanced delivery models (McGreal, 2024).

Teacher preparedness remains a central issue. Many educators feel underprepared to integrate these advanced digital tools into their teaching practices, and ongoing professional development often remains fragmented or inaccessible (Badiozaman et al., 2022). Strengthening teacher training, improving access to digital infrastructure, fostering global partnerships, and establishing data governance policies will be essential to narrowing the digital divide and ensuring all learners reap the benefits of educational innovation.

KEY ISSUES AND CHALLENGES THE TEACHING PROFESSION IS FACING IN ITS DIGITAL TRANSFORMATION JOURNEY

The digital transformation of the teaching profession presents several critical challenges that must be addressed to ensure its effectiveness and sustainability. One of the most pressing issues is the digital divide, which continues to create significant disparities in access to technology and reliable internet connectivity among students and educators. In many rural and low-income communities, inadequate infrastructure particularly broadband access and device availability prevents meaningful engagement in digital learning environments (Mhlanga, 2024). A systematic review by Sithole and Mbukanma (2024) examining rural South African universities highlights that lack of technical support, poor connectivity, and limited institutional backing impede ICT adoption and reinforce systemic inequities. Furthermore, a localized survey in Mkatazo village (Mwansa et al., 2025) found that over half of residents lacked internet access, and two-thirds demonstrated insufficient digital literacy, findings that emphasize the layered nature of digital exclusion, which goes beyond infrastructure to include affordability, skills, and geographic isolation.

Another significant challenge is teacher preparedness and digital literacy. Although many educators recognize the importance of technology in education, a substantial number report feeling underprepared to integrate digital tools into their teaching practices (Badiozaman et al., 2022), resulting in inconsistent adoption and instructional quality. Professional development (PD) programs often focus heavily on theory, failing to offer hands-on, contextualized training that builds practical skills. Falloon (2020) argues that achieving digital competence, not just literacy, requires structured and sustained professional development that blends technical training with pedagogical strategies tailored to real classroom contexts. Supporting this, Tondeur et al. (2017) found that teachers participating in collaborative, practice based PD demonstrated significantly greater confidence and more meaningful integration of technology in their teaching. Without such immersive and ongoing training, educators remain ill-equipped to capitalize on the pedagogical potential of digital tools, limiting the effectiveness of digital transformation in education.

Additionally, the rapid accumulation of student data through learning management systems and AI-driven analytics has elevated data privacy and cybersecurity to critical concerns in digital education. As Oliveira and Souza (2022) highlight, the exponential growth of data necessitates strong institutional policies on data usage, security, and adherence to international privacy frameworks like GDPR. Complementing this, Amo Filva et al. (2021) advocate for the integration of local or decentralized technologies designed specifically to enhance privacy protections and reduce vulnerabilities associated with centralized data systems. Moreover, Sithole et al. (2024) emphasize that many educators and administrators currently have limited awareness of data protection protocols, increasing the risk of privacy breaches within educational institutions. Instituting comprehensive training initiatives and transparent data-governance policies is essential to build trust and ensure that the tools central to digital transformation are used responsibly.

Student engagement and well-being also pose significant challenges within digital learning environments. The rapid shift to online education has raised concerns about excessive screen time, reduced opportunities for social interaction, and increasing instances of digital fatigue. Empirical studies reveal that even well-designed digital tools can inadvertently lead to cognitive overload, contributing to emotional exhaustion, impaired focus, and reduced motivation when students engage with screens for extended periods (Chen & Qin, 2024). Chen and Qin (2024) further found that such fatigue diminishes participation and undermines the overall effectiveness of online teaching strategies. Similarly, Akpen et al. (2024), in a systematic review, report that while online platforms can enhance personalized learning and flexibility, they often fragment attention and reduce student engagement, especially in settings with limited teacher-student interaction. These findings underscore the importance of designing balanced learning environments that integrate screen breaks, combine synchronous and asynchronous modalities, and prioritize pedagogical strategies that foster self-regulation and social connection to mitigate the negative impacts of digital fatigue.

Furthermore, equity in digital transformation efforts remains a critical issue in education systems globally. Many schools and universities in under resourced areas lack sufficient funding to provide students with essential digital resources such as laptops, tablets, and reliable internet access. Without targeted government policies and sustained financial support, these institutions risk falling further behind in the rapidly evolving digital education landscape. Akiva et al. (2023) argue that building equitable learning ecosystems requires more than providing hardware; it also necessitates strong community partnerships, culturally responsive practices, and policies designed to address structural inequities. Similarly, the Molenaar and Sleegers (2023) emphasizes that equitable digital transformation depends on enabling conditions such as robust infrastructure, high quality teacher training, and inclusive digital content that ensures all learners benefit from technological advancements. Bishop et al. (2022) reinforce these concerns, noting that digital equity must go beyond access to devices and focus on fostering meaningful digital inclusion through localized solutions, community engagement, and sustained capacity building efforts. Without such comprehensive and coordinated strategies, the promise of digital transformation risks reinforcing existing disparities rather than bridging them.

Finally, institutional resistance to change is another barrier to successful digital transformation. Some educators and administrators remain skeptical about the effectiveness of digital tools and hesitate to abandon traditional teaching methods. Overcoming this challenge requires strong leadership, collaborative policy development, and a shift in institutional culture that embraces innovation in education.

Addressing these challenges will require a concerted effort from policymakers, educators, and technology providers to create an inclusive, secure, and effective digital learning ecosystem. By prioritizing digital literacy training, expanding infrastructure, and implementing policies that protect student data, the education sector can successfully navigate the complexities of digital transformation and enhance learning outcomes for all students.

SUFFICIENCY OF THE TEACHING PROFESSION'S STRATEGIC LEADERSHIP ENTITIES, CURRICULA, AND PROFESSIONALS'S ROLES IN THE PROFESSION'S DIGITAL TRANSFORMATION

The role of strategic leadership entities, curricula, and professionals in digital transformation is crucial in shaping the trajectory of modern education. While many stakeholders recognize the need for technological integration, the degree of engagement varies significantly across institutions and regions.

Strategic Leadership and Policy Development

Educational governing bodies and policymakers play a critical role in setting the framework for digital transformation. In some regions, proactive initiatives have been implemented to expand access to technology, develop teacher training programs, and establish data privacy regulations (Rêgo et al., 2024). For instance, UNESCO collaborates with national education ministries to develop inclusive, forward-looking digital learning policies that promote access, manage risks, and foster innovation (UNESCO, 2025). However, in many areas, a lack of cohesive policies and insufficient funding have slowed the pace of adoption. Numerous institutions still lack clear digital strategies, hindering the deployment of new tools and pedagogical innovations (Mhlanga, 2024). Rêgo et al. (2024) also highlight that while there is widespread acknowledgment of the need for digital skills development, gaps in institutional leadership and fragmented policy approaches continue to impede transformative change. Complementing these insights, Normén-Smith et al. (2024) introduce a six-pillar framework coordination, connectivity, cost, capacity, content, and data that underscores the need for holistic strategic planning in digital education policy.

Curriculum Reform and Digital Integration

Curricula must continually evolve to incorporate digital literacy, AI applications, and technology driven problem solving. Some educational institutions have successfully integrated coding, robotics, and data analytics into their courses, equipping students with future-ready skills (Grubišić & Crnokić, 2024). However, many curricula remain outdated and disconnected from the digital era's demands. Extensive reviews reveal a persistent gap between theoretical knowledge and practical digital skills: students often learn concepts without real world application, underscoring the need to overhaul teaching methodologies and assessment frameworks to emphasize experiential learning (Fantinelli et al., 2022). Moreover, educators struggle to design lessons that balance theoretical foundations with hands-on digital tool use, suggesting that effective digital integration hinges not only on curriculum design but also on sustained teacher training, sufficient resource allocation, and strong institutional support structures (Sailer et al., 2021).

Role of Educators and Professional Development

Teachers and education professionals are at the forefront of implementing digital transformation, yet many feel underprepared due to insufficient training and support (Joya et al., 2025). A systematic review by Joya et al. (2025) highlights that although there is increasing awareness about the need for digital competence among educators, significant gaps remain in hands-on experience with emerging technologies and their pedagogical integration. Professional development programs must therefore go beyond theoretical seminars to include guided, practical training on digital tools, evidence-based online teaching strategies, and ethical considerations in technology use.

Continuous learning opportunities through accredited workshops, formal certifications, and peer communities can empower educators to integrate digital methodologies effectively into their daily teaching practices. Ning and Danso (2025) confirm that while many educators acknowledge the benefits of digital tools, persistent barriers such as limited professional development and institutional support continue to hinder implementation. Additionally, teachers emphasize the importance of blended support across administrative, pedagogical, and technical domains to strengthen competency in digital environments (Ning & Danso, 2025).

Challenges in Stakeholder Collaboration

A major barrier to successful digital transformation is the lack of coordination among policymakers, educators, and technology providers. Many education institutions struggle with fragmented decision-making, where digital initiatives are introduced without a comprehensive strategy for sustainability (Oliveira & Souza, 2022). Indeed, Oliveira and Souza's study emphasizes that while isolated interventions such as one-off pilot programs may show initial impact, they frequently fail to implement the sustained organizational processes needed for long-term success. Bridging the gap between these stakeholders through structured collaboration, dedicated funding initiatives, and knowledge sharing platforms is essential for progress. According to Molenaar and Sleegers (2023), successful digital ecosystems depend heavily on multi-stakeholder co-creation mechanisms, where education ministries, private-sector tech firms, educators, and civil society share governance frameworks and resources.

Moving forward, digital transformation in education must be driven by collective efforts from leadership bodies, curriculum developers, and education professionals. By establishing clear policies, reforming curricula, and equipping teachers with essential digital skills, the education sector can create a resilient, future ready learning environment for all students (Table 12.2) synthesises these challenges by highlighting the specific gaps in contributions across key stakeholder groups and the implications of these shortcomings for the effective digital transformation of teaching.

TABLE 12.2
Gaps in Stakeholder Contributions to Teaching's Digital Transformation

Stakeholder Group	Current Shortcomings	Implications
Strategic Leadership	Fragmented policies, underinvestment, resistance to innovation	Delayed adoption, widened digital divide
Curricula Developers	Outdated content, limited integration of digital and AI skills	Students graduate without future-ready competencies
Educators	Low digital competence, inadequate professional development	Poor technology adoption, teacher burnout
Institutions	Inconsistent infrastructure, resistance to change	Unequal access, ineffective implementation
Policymakers	Insufficient coordination and equity focus	Reinforced socio-economic disparities in digital education
Technology Providers	Limited collaboration with educators and misaligned tools	Ineffective solutions, poor uptake in classrooms

IMPLICATIONS OF SHORTCOMINGS OF THE TEACHING PROFESSION'S STRATEGIC LEADERSHIP ENTITIES, CURRICULA, AND PROFESSIONALS

Shortcomings in the digital transformation efforts by strategic leadership entities, curricula developers, and professionals can have significant and lasting consequences for education. A lack of coordination, insufficient investment, and resistance to change can hinder the potential of digital education and exacerbate existing educational inequalities.

Widening the Digital Divide

One of the most pressing implications of leadership shortcomings is the exacerbation of the digital divide. If policymakers and education leaders fail to implement inclusive technology policies and infrastructure investments, students from disadvantaged backgrounds will continue to lack access to essential digital tools (Mhlanga, 2024). This disparity creates unequal learning opportunities, with students in well-funded schools benefiting from advanced digital tools while others struggle to access basic online resources. Mhlanga (2024) reports that in emerging economies, factors such as poverty, unreliable electricity, and poor internet access significantly impede equitable adoption of asynchronous digital education. A recent systematic review by Miras et al. (2023) further confirms that these persistent structural inequalities identified through over 500 analyzed studies, were aggravated during the COVID-19 pandemic, revealing substantial gaps in infrastructure and digital literacy across socio-economic groups. Without strategic leadership to address these systemic issues, such disparities risk becoming entrenched.

Declining Teacher Preparedness and Effectiveness

A failure to provide adequate training for educators results in a workforce unprepared to integrate digital tools into their teaching. Without ongoing professional development programs, teachers may struggle to use emerging technologies effectively, leading to inconsistent adoption and ineffective instruction (Joya et al., 2025). Teachers who lack digital competencies are less likely to engage students with interactive content, personalized learning platforms, and AI-driven assessments, reducing the potential benefits of digital transformation in education. Revuelta-Domínguez et al. (2022) emphasize that digital competence gaps persist globally, especially in regions where institutional support and structured training frameworks are limited. Similarly, Basilotta-Gómez-Pablos et al. (2022) highlight that even within higher education, teachers often lack the pedagogical and technological skills necessary to design innovative and inclusive digital learning environments.

Curriculum Stagnation and Irrelevance

An outdated curriculum that does not incorporate digital literacy and emerging technologies fails to prepare students for the modern workforce. If curricula do not evolve to include essential digital skills such as coding, data analysis, and AI literacy, graduates may find themselves ill-equipped for careers in technology-driven industries (Jaramillo & Chiappe, 2024). Indeed, their review highlights that embedding AI and digital problem-solving across subjects fosters critical thinking and contextual competence. Furthermore, a lack of emphasis on digital ethics and cybersecurity awareness can leave students vulnerable in an increasingly digitalized world (Oliveira & Souza, 2022).

Reduced Student Engagement and Learning Outcomes

Inadequate digital transformation strategies can negatively impact student engagement and learning outcomes. Poorly implemented technology can lead to cognitive overload, reduced motivation, and increased distractions in online and hybrid learning environments (Nabiem Akpen et al., 2024). This aligns with cognitive load theory, where poorly designed digital tools impose extraneous mental demands that interfere with learning (Skulmowski & Xu, 2021). If digital tools are not aligned with effective pedagogical strategies, they may become obstacles rather than enablers of student learning. Moreover, Singun (2025) demonstrates that systematic barriers such as lack of digital vision, leadership, and ethical frameworks consistently undermine student engagement and academic outcomes across higher education institutions globally.

Security and Privacy Risks

A lack of clear policies regarding data privacy and cybersecurity in digital education can put students and educators at risk. Institutions that do not enforce stringent security measures may expose student information to cyber threats, data breaches, and misuse of personal information (Oliveira & Souza, 2022). For instance, Easton Kelso et al. (2025) found that unsanctioned apps and tools used by instructors often bypass institutional vetting processes, increasing the risk of unauthorized access to sensitive data. Additionally, global reports highlight alarming trends: in 2023 alone, around 4.3 million student records were compromised in U.S. educational data breaches, underscoring the scale of vulnerability across both K–12 and higher education sectors (Comparitech, 2024 & StudentDPA, 2025). Recent research by Guillén-Gámez et al. (2024) underscores that addressing gaps in digital security education is critical to preparing students for safe and responsible participation in technology driven environments. Ensuring compliance with international data protection standards and educating stakeholders on best practices such as multi-factor authentication, privacy-by-design, and incident response is crucial for mitigating these risks (Comparitech, 2024).

Institutional Resistance and Slow Adoption

Without strong leadership and commitment to digital transformation, many educational institutions resist change due to bureaucratic inertia, fear of technology replacing traditional teaching methods, or budget constraints. Institutions that fail to embrace digital transformation risk becoming obsolete, leaving their students at a disadvantage in an increasingly competitive and technology-driven global landscape (Oliveira & Souza, 2022). Oliveira and Souza (2022) emphasize that without organizational processes aligned to digital goals, institutional inertia can stall even well-funded initiatives, reducing their impact and sustainability. Moreover, a recent analysis of European higher education systems highlights that cultural barriers and fragmented governance frequently delay the adoption of flexible learning models and structural digital policies (EduTimes, 2025).

To mitigate these issues, educational leadership entities must implement comprehensive digital strategies that prioritize equity, teacher training, and curriculum innovation. Collaboration among policymakers, educators, and technology providers is essential to create inclusive and effective digital learning environments. By addressing these shortcomings proactively, the education sector can maximize the benefits of digital transformation and ensure a more equitable and future-ready learning experience for all students.

WHAT THE TEACHING PROFESSION'S STRATEGIC LEADERSHIP ENTITIES, CURRICULA, AND PROFESSIONALS DO TO MAXIMIZE THEIR CONTRIBUTION TO THE PROFESSION'S DIGITAL TRANSFORMATION EFFORTS

Maximizing the contributions of strategic leadership entities, curricula developers, and professionals is crucial for ensuring the success of digital transformation in education. By taking a proactive and structured approach, these stakeholders can create an ecosystem that fosters innovation, inclusivity, and efficiency in digital education.

Enhancing Strategic Leadership and Policy Development

Leadership entities must establish clear digital transformation policies that promote equitable access to technology and digital literacy training for educators and students. Governments and education ministries should allocate funding for digital infrastructure, ensuring that all schools have the resources needed to implement technology-driven learning (Joya et al., 2025). As Molenaar and Sleegers (2023) argue, digital transformation requires not only financial investments but also robust governance frameworks and cross-sector collaboration to address systemic challenges and avoid fragmented implementations. Collaborative partnerships between public and private sectors can help scale edtech initiatives and bring cutting edge tools into classrooms, as demonstrated by OECD countries where such partnerships accelerated equitable access and innovation (Mhlanga, 2024).

Reforming Curricula to Integrate Digital Skills

Curricula must be continuously updated to reflect advancements in digital technology and industry needs. This includes integrating subjects such as coding, data science, cybersecurity, and AI literacy into the standard curriculum (Jaramillo & Chiappe, 2024). Jaramillo and Chiappe's systematic review of 130 curriculum-related articles confirms that embedding AI across subject areas fosters both technical and critical thinking competencies. Additionally, instructional methodologies should incorporate digital pedagogy strategies such as blended learning, gamification, and immersive technologies like virtual and augmented reality (Guillén-Gámez et al., 2024). Their findings indicate that using games and augmented reality not only boosts student engagement but also supports deeper conceptual learning. To be truly effective, such curriculum reforms need consistent alignment with teacher training, as even well designed content fails without teacher readiness and institutional support (Joya et al., 2025).

Investing in Professional Development for Educators

Teachers play a fundamental role in digital transformation, yet many lack the necessary training to effectively integrate technology into their teaching. Professional development programs should provide educators with hands-on experience in using digital tools, AI-powered learning platforms, and data analytics to assess student progress (Joya et al., 2025). Joya et al. (2025) highlight that teachers' digital competence directly influences their confidence and willingness to experiment with technology enhanced pedagogies. Offering ongoing workshops, peer mentoring, and online certification programs can help bridge the digital literacy gap among teachers and ensure effective adoption of technology enhanced learning practices. Furthermore, Basilotta-Gómez-Pablos et al. (2022) emphasize that institutional support and well-structured training strategies are essential for moving beyond superficial tool usage toward transformative pedagogical practices.

Fostering a Culture of Innovation and Collaboration

A culture that encourages innovation and experimentation is essential for the success of digital transformation efforts. Institutions should support research into emerging technologies in education and encourage educators to develop and test new teaching methodologies. Collaboration between universities, schools, and edtech companies can lead to the co-creation of digital learning solutions tailored to diverse educational needs (Oliveira & Souza, 2022). Oliveira and Souza (2022) emphasize that such partnerships enable knowledge sharing and accelerate the scaling of best practices across institutions. Furthermore, Molenaar and Sleegers (2023) highlight that multi-stakeholder ecosystems bringing together policymakers, educators, and technology providers are critical to building adaptive and resilient educational systems capable of continuous innovation.

Ensuring Digital Equity and Inclusion

Addressing disparities in access to digital resources is fundamental to achieving inclusive digital transformation. Leadership entities must implement policies that provide underprivileged schools with adequate funding for technology and internet access (Mhlanga, 2024). Mhlanga (2024) underscores that failing to address these structural inequities risks widening the digital divide and perpetuating systemic inequalities in education. Schools should also adopt universal design principles to ensure that digital content is accessible to students with disabilities, bridging the gap in digital learning opportunities for all learners. Furthermore, Joya et al. (2025) emphasize that fostering digital literacy programs for marginalized communities is equally critical, as it equips both students and teachers with the competencies required to meaningfully engage in digital learning environments.

Strengthening Cybersecurity and Data Privacy Policies

As education institutions increasingly rely on digital platforms for teaching and assessment, data security and privacy must be a top priority. Leadership entities must enforce robust data protection policies, ensuring compliance with international regulations on student data privacy (Guillén-Gámez et al., 2024). Guillén-Gámez et al. (2024) emphasize that institutions often lack standardized frameworks for safeguarding sensitive information, leaving students vulnerable to data misuse and cyberattacks. Educators and students should also be trained in digital safety practices to minimize risks associated with cyber threats and unauthorized data breaches. Moreover, Molenaar and Sleegers (2023) argue that integrating privacy-by-design principles into institutional digital strategies can enhance resilience against evolving cybersecurity challenges.

By implementing these strategies, strategic leadership entities, curricula developers, and professionals can drive the digital transformation of the teaching profession forward, ensuring an innovative, inclusive, and secure learning environment for future generations.

CONCLUSION

The teaching profession is undergoing profound digital transformation, driven by technological advancements and accelerated by global disruptions such as the COVID-19 pandemic. Digital technologies have reshaped traditional pedagogical methods, fostering new modes of instruction and interaction while simultaneously presenting significant challenges. This chapter examines the scope, opportunities, and obstacles of digital disruption in teaching, emphasizing the roles of educators, curricula, and strategic leadership entities in fostering meaningful transformation.

Digital disruption in education has been characterized by the rapid adoption of learning management systems (LMS), mobile learning applications, and artificial intelligence (AI)-enabled platforms. These innovations have facilitated personalized learning, expanded access through massive open online courses (MOOCs), and introduced adaptive technologies capable of tailoring instruction to individual learners' needs. However, equitable implementation remains elusive. Infrastructural limitations, particularly in rural and low income communities, have exacerbated existing educational disparities, highlighting a persistent digital divide. Governments and non-profit organizations have made efforts to address these inequities, yet gaps in device access, broadband connectivity, and teacher readiness persist.

Central to the transformation is the role of AI and data analytics in curriculum design and delivery. AI-powered systems provide real time feedback, automate administrative tasks, and support predictive analytics to identify at-risk learners.

Immersive technologies such as virtual and augmented reality (VR/AR) are enhancing experiential learning, enabling students to engage with content in novel, interactive ways. However, the integration of these tools necessitates significant investment in professional development and curriculum reform. Many educators report insufficient training to adopt digital tools effectively, emphasizing the need for sustained, hands-on professional learning opportunities that cultivate digital competence alongside pedagogical innovation.

Key challenges to digital transformation include data privacy and cybersecurity risks, student well-being concerns such as digital fatigue, and institutional resistance to change. The exponential growth of student data requires robust governance policies to safeguard privacy and ensure compliance with international standards. Simultaneously, balancing screen time and maintaining social interaction have emerged as critical priorities for fostering student engagement and motivation in online learning environments.

To overcome these barriers, strategic leadership entities must implement clear, equity driven policies, reform curricula to embed digital skills, and support teachers with comprehensive professional development. Collaborative partnerships between policymakers, educators, and technology providers are essential to creating inclusive and secure digital learning ecosystems. Without such coordinated efforts, digital transformation risks reinforcing existing inequalities rather than bridging them.

This chapter underscores that the success of digital transformation in teaching hinges on a holistic approach that addresses infrastructural, pedagogical, and cultural dimensions. By prioritizing equity, fostering innovation, and building institutional capacity, the education sector can harness technology's potential to create engaging, inclusive, and future ready learning environments.

DISCUSSION QUESTIONS

1. How has the COVID-19 pandemic accelerated digital disruption in the teaching profession, and what evidence does this chapter provide about its long-term impact on pedagogical practices?
2. What are the key distinctions between digital literacy and digital competence, and why does the chapter argue that moving from literacy to competence is critical for effective teaching in the digital era?
3. In what ways do artificial intelligence (AI) and data analytics enhance curriculum design and student learning outcomes, and what ethical considerations arise from their use in education?
4. How does the digital divide manifest across different socio-economic and geographical contexts, and what strategies does the chapter suggest to address these disparities in access and opportunity?
5. What challenges do teachers face in adopting and integrating digital tools into their practice, and how might professional development programs evolve to better support educators in this transformation?
6. To what extent do concerns about data privacy and cybersecurity affect the adoption of educational technologies, and how can institutions balance innovation with the need for robust data governance?

7. How does institutional culture influence the pace and success of digital transformation in education, and what leadership and policy approaches are recommended to overcome resistance to change?
8. Drawing from the chapter, what would an ideal "equitable digital learning ecosystem" look like, and what roles should governments, educational leaders, and technology providers play in building it?

NOTES

1 Digital literacy' refers to foundational skills such as navigating devices and accessing digital content, while 'digital competence' encompasses the broader ability to critically and creatively use technology in pedagogical contexts
2 The TPACK framework stands for Technological Pedagogical Content Knowledge, and it's a widely used model for understanding the knowledge teachers need to integrate technology effectively into their teaching.
3 The Digital Competence Framework for Educators (DigCompEdu) was developed by the European Commission's Joint Research Centre (JRC) in 2017. It provides a comprehensive framework for assessing and developing teachers' ability to use digital technologies effectively in professional practice and teaching.

REFERENCES

Ahsan, K., Akbar, S., Kam, B., & Abdulrahman, M. D.-A. (2023). Implementation of micro-credentials in higher education: A systematic literature review. *Education and Information Technologies*, *28*, 13505–13540. https://doi.org/10.1007/s10639-023-11739-z

Akiva, T., Delale-O'Connor, L., & Pittman, K. J. (2023). The promise of building equitable ecosystems for learning. *Urban Education*, *58*(6), 1271–1297. https://doi.org/10.1177/0042085920926230

Akpen, C. N., Asaolu, S., Atobatele, S., Okagbue, H., & Sampson, S. (2024). Impact of online learning on student's performance and engagement: A systematic review. *Discover Education*, *3*(1), 205. https://doi.org/10.1007/s44217-024-00253-0

Al-Ansi, A. M., Jaboob, M., Garad, A., & Al-Ansi, A. (2023). Analyzing augmented reality (AR) and virtual reality (VR) recent development in education. *Social Sciences & Humanities Open*, *8*(1), 100532. https://doi.org/10.1016/j.ssaho.2023.100532

Amo Filva, D., Prinsloo, P., Alier Forment, M., Fonseca Escudero, D., Torres Kompen, R., Canaleta Llampallas, X., & Herrero Martín, J. (2021). Local technology to enhance data privacy and security in educational technology. *International Journal of Interactive Multimedia and Artificial Intelligence*, *7*(2), 262–273. https://doi.org/10.9781/ijimai.2021.02.007

Atabek, O. (2019). *Challenges in integrating technology into education*. arXiv. https://arxiv.org/abs/1904.06518

Author, A. B., Cousin, C. D., & Walker, E. F. (2024). Professional development for teachers in artificial intelligence and data literacy. In V. Olari & T. Zoppke (Eds.), *Digitally transformed education: Are we there yet?* (IFIP AICT, Vol. 734, pp. 15–27). Springer. https://doi.org/10.1007/978-3-031-88744-4_2

Badiozaman, I., Peña-López, S., & Rincón-Flores, E. (2022). Development and strengthening of teachers' digital competence: A systematic review. *Contemporary Educational Technology*, *17*(1), Article ep555. https://files.eric.ed.gov/fulltext/EJ1460141.pdf

Basilotta-Gómez-Pablos, V., Matarranz, M., Casado-Aranda, L. A., & Otto, A. (2022). Teachers' digital competencies in higher education: A systematic literature review. *International Journal of Educational Technology in Higher Education*, *19*(1), 8. https://doi.org/10.1186/s41239-021-00312-8

Bećirović, S., & Dervić, M. (2022). Students' perspectives of digital transformation of higher education in Bosnia and Herzegovina. Electronic Journal of Information Systems in Developing Countries, *89*(2), e12243. https://doi.org/10.1002/isd2.12243

Bishop, S., Quintanilla-Muñoz, C., & Marshall, T. III. (2022). *Literature review: Digital equity and inclusion for education.* Intercultural Development Research Association. https://www.idra.org/publications/literature-review-digital-equity-and-inclusion-for-education/

Bui, T. T., & Nguyen, T. S. (2023). The survey of digital transformation in education: A systematic review. *International Journal of TESOL & Education*, *3*(4), 32–51. https://doi.org/10.54855/ijte.23343

Chen, Y., & Qin, X. (2024). Student fatigue and its impact on teaching effectiveness based on online teaching. *Education and Information Technologies*, *29*(8), 10177–10200. https://doi.org/10.1007/s10639-023-12197-3

Cobos, R., Sánchez, M., & López, T. (2023). Self-regulated learning and active feedback of MOOC learners supported by learning analytics. *Electronics*, *12*(15), 3368. https://doi.org/10.3390/electronics12153368

Coman, C., Țîru, L. G., Meseșan-Schmitz, L., Stanciu, C., & Bularca, M. C. (2020). Online teaching and learning in higher education during the coronavirus pandemic: Students' perspective. *Sustainability*, *12*(24), 10367.

Comparitech. (2024). *US schools leaked 37.6 million records in 3,713 data breaches.* Comparitech. Retrieved from https://www.comparitech.com/blog/vpn-privacy/us-schools-data-breaches/ Comparitech

Díaz-García, V., Montero-Navarro, A., Rodríguez-Sánchez, J.-L., & Gallego-Losada, R. (2022). Digitalization and digital transformation in higher education: A bibliometric analysis. *Frontiers in Psychology*, *13*, 108159. https://doi.org/10.3389/fpsyg.2022.1081595

Digital Promise. (2023, April 24). *Breaking with the past: Embracing digital transformation in education.* https://digitalpromise.org/2023/04/24/breaking-with-the-past-embracing-digital-transformation-in-education/

Easton Kelso, A., Soneji, A., Navid, S., Z, -H., Soshitaishvili, Y., Rahaman, S., & Hasan, R. (2025). Investigating the security & privacy risks from unsanctioned technology use by educators. *arXiv*. https://doi.org/10.48550/arXiv.2502.16739

EduTimes. (2025, March 7). *The urgent need for flexibility in higher education: Overcoming resistance and financial strain. The EduTimes.* Retrieved from https://edutimes.com/news/2025/03/20250318927

Falloon, G. (2020). From digital literacy to digital competence: The teacher digital competency (TDC) framework. *Educational Technology Research and Development*, *68*(5), 2449–2472. https://doi.org/10.1007/s11423-020-09767-4

Fantinelli, S., Cortini, M., Di Fiore, T., Iervese, S., & Galanti, T. (2022). Bridging the gap between theoretical learning and practical application: A qualitative study in the Italian educational context. *Education Sciences*, *14*(2), 198. https://doi.org/10.3390/educsci14020198

García-Martín, J., & García-Sánchez, J.-N. (2022). The digital divide of know-how and use of digital technologies in higher education: The case of a college in Latin America in the COVID-19 era. *International Journal of Environmental Research and Public Health*, *19*(6), 3358. https://doi.org/10.3390/ijerph19063358

Grubišić, V., & Crnokić, B. (2024). A systematic review of robotics' transformative role in education. In *Digital transformation in education and artificial intelligence application* (pp. 257–272). *Communications in Computer and Information Science, 2124.* Springer. https://doi.org/10.1007/978-3-031-62058-4_16

Guillén-Gámez, F. D., Tomczyk, Ł, Ruiz-Palmero, J., & Connolly, C. (2024). Digital security in educational contexts: Digital competence and challenges for good practice. *Computers in the Schools*, *41*(3), 257–262. https://doi.org/10.1080/07380569.2024.2390319

Hori, K., & Fujii, M. (2021). Leveraging professional learning communities to improve digital instructional integration: A PISA-based study. *International Journal of STEM Education*, *11*(56). https://doi.org/10.1186/s40594-024-00513-3

Jaramillo, J. J., & Chiappe, A. (2024). The AI-driven classroom: A review of 21st century curriculum trends. *Prospects*. https://doi.org/10.1007/s11125-024-09704-w

Joya, L. G., Merchán, M. A. M., & Barrera, E. A. L. (2025). Development and strengthening of teachers' digital competence: Systematic review. *Contemporary Educational Technology*, *17*(1), ep555. https://doi.org/10.30935/cedtech/15744

Kasımoğlu, S., Bahçelerli, N. M., & Çelik, M. U. (2022). Digital literacy during COVID-19 distance education: Evaluation of communication-based problems in line with student opinions. *Frontiers in Psychology*, *13*, 809171. https://doi.org/10.3389/fpsyg.2022.809171

Kohnke, L. (2021). Optimizing microlearning materials for mobile learning. In J. R. Corbeil, B. H. Khan, & M. E. Corbeil (Eds.), *Microlearning in the digital age: The design and delivery of learning in snippets* (pp. 80–94). Routledge. https://doi.org/10.4324/9780367821623-7

Liu, N. X., & Chen, Z. T. (2022). Collaborative learning during the pandemic: The role of mobile devices. In *Coping with COVID-19, the Mobile way* (pp. 259–280). Springer. https://doi.org/10.1007/978-981-19-5787-1_12

Luckin, R., & Holmes, W. (2016). Intelligence unleashed: An argument for AI in education.

Magocha, M., Munyaradzi, J., & Babalola, S. S. (2025). The impact of the pandemic on digital literacy skills for online teaching in Zimbabwean schools: A mixed-methods research approach. *Research in Social Sciences and Technology*, *10*(1), 310–331. https://doi.org/10.46303/ressat.2025.17 files.eric.ed.gov+1eric.ed.gov+1

McGreal, R. (2024). The AI revolution in micro-credentialing: Personalized learning paths. *Frontiers in Education*, *9*, 1445654. https://doi.org/10.3389/feduc.2024.1445654

Meinokat, P., & Wagner, I. (2024). Classroom disruptions in digital teaching during the pandemic: An interview study. *Frontiers in Education*, *9*. https://doi.org/10.3389/feduc.2024.1335249

Mhlanga, D. (2024). Digital transformation of education: The limitations and prospects of introducing fourth industrial revolution asynchronous online learning in emerging markets. *Discover Education*, *3*(1), Article 32. https://doi.org/10.1007/s44217-024-00115-9

Miras, S., Ruiz-Bañuls, M., Gómez-Trigueros, I. M., & Mateo-Guillen, C. (2023). Implications of the digital divide: A systematic review of its impact in the educational field. *Journal of Technology and Science Education*, *13*(3), 936–950. https://doi.org/10.3926/jotse.2249

Molenaar, I., & Sleegers, P. (2023). Country digital education ecosystems and governance: Multi-stakeholder collaboration and co-creation towards responsible application of AI in education. In OECD (Ed.), *Digital education outlook 2023* (pp. 318–348). OECD Publishing. https://doi.org/10.1787/c74f03de-en

Mwansa, G., Ngandu, M. R., & Mkwambi, Z. (2025). Bridging the digital divide: Exploring the challenges and solutions for digital exclusion in rural South Africa. *Discover Global Society*, *3*(1), 1–24. https://doi.org/10.1007/s44282-025-00189-2

Nabiem Akpen, C., Asaolu, S., Atobatele, S., Okagbue, H., & Sampson, S. (2024). Impact of online learning on student performance and engagement: A systematic review. *Education and information technologies*. Advance online publication. https://doi.org/10.1007/s44217-024-00253-0

Ning, Z., & Danso, K. (2025). Assessing pedagogical readiness for digital innovation: A mixed-methods study. *Educational Technology Research and Development*, *73*(1), 114–132. Retrieved from https://arxiv.org/abs/2502.15781

Normén-Smith, J., van, Cappelle, F., Atis, E., & Ghobashy, D. (2024, September 24). Launch of common framework to guide the digital transformation of education. *UNESCO*. https://www.unesco.org/en/articles/launch-common-framework-guide-digital-transformation-education

Nyaaba, M., Akanzire, B. N., & Nabang, M. (2024). Virtual reality in teacher education: Insights from pre-service teachers in resource-limited regions. *Frontiers in Education*. https://doi.org/10.48550/arXiv.2411.10225

OECD. (2023). *digital education outlook 2023: Shaping digital education—Enabling factors for quality, equity and efficiency*. OECD Publishing. https://doi.org/10.1787/bac4dc9f-en

Oliveira, K. K. S., & Souza, R. A. C. (2022). Digital transformation towards education 4.0. *Informatics in Education*, *21*(2), 283–309. https://doi.org/10.15388/infedu.2022.13

Otto, S., Bertel, L. B., Lyngdorf, N. E. R., Overgaard Markman, A., Andersen, T., & Ryberg, T. (2023). Emerging digital practices supporting student-centered learning environments in higher education: A review and lessons learned from the COVID-19 pandemic. *Education and Information Technologies*, *29*, 1673–1696. https://doi.org/10.1007/s10639-023-11789-3

Rêgo, B. S., Lourenço, D., Moreira, F., & Pereira, C. S. (2024). Digital transformation, skills and education: A systematic literature review. *Industry and Higher Education*, *38*(4), 336–349. https://doi.org/10.1177/09504222231208969

Revuelta-Domínguez, F. I., Guerra-Antequera, J., González-Pérez, A., Pedrera-Rodríguez, M. I., & González-Fernández, A. (2022). Digital teaching competence: A systematic review. *Sustainability*, *14*(11), 6428. https://doi.org/10.3390/su14116428

Sailer, M., Murböck, J., & Fischer, F. (2021). Digital learning in schools: What does it take beyond digital technology? *Teaching and Teacher Education*, *103*, 103346. https://doi.org/10.1016/j.tate.2021.103346

Salas-Pilco, S. Z., Yang, Y., & Zhang, Z. (2022). Student engagement in online learning in Latin American higher education during the COVID-19 pandemic: A systematic review. *British Journal of Educational Technology*, *53*(1), 1–27. https://doi.org/10.1111/bjet.13190

Schleicher, A. (2024). *Toward the digital transformation in education. Frontiers in Digital Education*, *1*(1), 4–25. https://doi.org/10.1007/s44366-024-0018-7

Singun, A. J. Jr. (2025). Unveiling the barriers to digital transformation in higher education institutions: A systematic literature review. *Discover Education*, *4*, 37. https://doi.org/10.1007/s44217-025-00430-9

Sithole, V. L., & Mbukanma, I. (2024). Prospects and challenges to ICT adoption in teaching and learning at rural South African universities: A systematic review. *Research in Social Sciences and Technology*, *9*(3), 178–193. https://doi.org/10.46303/ressat.2024.54

Skulmowski, A., & Xu, K. M. (2021). Understanding cognitive load in digital and online learning: A new perspective on extraneous cognitive load. *Educational Psychology Review*, *34*(2), 171–196. https://doi.org/10.1007/s10648-021-09624-7

Sölch, M., Aberle, M., & Krusche, S. (2023). Integrating competency-based education in interactive learning systems. In *Proceedings of the 18th European Conference on Technology Enhanced Learning* (pp. 457–469). Springer. https://doi.org/10.1007/978-3-030-77857-6_38

Srinivasan, M., Jishnu, D., & Shamala, R. (2021). COVID-19 and online education: Digital inequality and other dilemmas of rural students in accessing online education during the pandemic. *World of Media. Journal of Russian Media and Journalism Studies*, *4*, 34–54. https://doi.org/10.30547/worldofmedia.4.2021.2

Stracke, C. M., Bothe, P., Adler, S. et al. (2025). Immersive virtual reality in higher education: A systematic review. *Virtual Reality*, *29*, 415–437. https://doi.org/10.1007/s10055-025-01136-x

StudentDPA. (2025). *Case study: Lessons from major student data privacy breaches.* Retrieved from https://studentdpa.com/blog/case-study-student-data-privacy-breaches-edtech-03232025

Tondeur, J., van Braak, J., Ertmer, P. A., & Ottenbreit-Leftwich, A. (2017). Understanding the relationship between teachers' pedagogical beliefs and technology use in education: A systematic review of qualitative evidence. *Educational Technology Research and Development*, *65*(3), 555–575. https://doi.org/10.1007/s11423-016-9481-2

T. T, Bui,. & Nguyen, T. S. (2023). The survey of digital transformation in education: A systematic review. International Journal of TESOL & Education, 3(4), 32–51. https://doi.org/10.54855/ijte.23343.

UNESCO. (2025). *Digital learning and transformation of education. UNESCO.* https://www.unesco.org/en/articles/digital-learning-and-transformation-education

Zainuddin, Z., Chu, S. K. W., & Perera, C. J. (2024). Gamification in a flipped classroom: Strategies for enhancing engagement and motivation. In *Gamification in a flipped classroom* (pp. 115–165). Springer. https://doi.org/10.1007/978-981-97-2219-8_4

Zheng, L., Zhang, X., & Cui, P. (2022). Technology-facilitated personalized learning: A meta-analysis of 34 studies. *Education and Information Technologies*, *27*(9), 11805–11832. https://doi.org/10.1007/s10639-022-11092-7

13 Case Study of the Digital Transformation of Law

INTRODUCTION

The legal profession is undergoing a period of significant change as it responds to the challenges and opportunities presented by digital technologies. Tools such as artificial intelligence (AI), blockchain, cloud computing, and legal automation are beginning to reshape how legal services are delivered, how legal work is organized, and what skills are required from legal professionals. While some parts of the profession have started to adopt these technologies, overall progress has been uneven and cautious.

This chapter aims to examine the digital transformation of the law profession in depth. It begins by exploring the key ways in which the profession is being disrupted by digital technologies. It then considers how the profession needs to transform in response to these changes, and where it currently stands in its transformation journey. The chapter also discusses the main challenges the profession faces, such as ethical concerns, limited digital skills, and resistance to change. It evaluates the roles being played by legal educators, professional bodies, and individual practitioners, and considers the potential consequences of inaction or slow adaptation.

Using recent research, professional reports, and global developments in legal education and practice, the chapter highlights areas where change is needed and where progress is already being made. It concludes by offering suggestions for how the legal profession's key stakeholders can better support the process of digital transformation in a way that ensures continued relevance, efficiency, and public trust.

HOW IS THE LAW PROFESSION BEING DIGITALLY DISRUPTED?

The law profession has long been known for its reliance on tradition, precedent, and human expertise. However, in recent years, digital technologies have started to significantly disrupt how legal services are delivered, how lawyers work, and how clients access justice. Technologies such as artificial intelligence (AI), cloud computing, blockchain, and legal automation tools are changing the profession at a pace never seen before.

One major area of disruption is AI in legal research and analytics. In the past, legal research involved sifting through large volumes of case law, legislation, and commentary which is a time-consuming process. Now, AI-powered platforms like *Lexis+*, *Westlaw Edge*, and previously *ROSS Intelligence* allow lawyers to conduct legal research faster and more accurately. These tools use natural language processing (NLP) to understand queries and retrieve relevant cases, statutes, and legal opinions in seconds. Some tools even predict likely case outcomes based on previous decisions, which can support better litigation strategies (Surden, 2019).

DOI: 10.1201/9781003606604-17

Automation of legal tasks is also reshaping the daily work of lawyers. Activities such as contract review, due diligence, and compliance checks, traditionally performed by junior lawyers, are now being done by intelligent software. Tools like *Kira Systems* and *Luminance* use machine learning to scan and analyze thousands of documents quickly, identifying important clauses or risks with a high degree of accuracy. This not only improves efficiency but also raises questions about how law firms will train and retain junior staff in the future (McGinnis & Pearce, 2014).

Blockchain is another disruptive force, particularly in the form of smart contracts. These are self-executing contracts with terms directly written into code. Once conditions are met, the contract automatically carries out its obligations. This technology is being explored in areas like real estate, supply chains, and intellectual property. While smart contracts won't replace lawyers completely, they do reduce the need for certain types of legal oversight (Mik, 2017).

Another key development is the growth of virtual legal platforms. Online services like *LegalZoom*, *Rocket Lawyer*, and *DoNotPay* now offer basic legal services such as drafting wills, creating business contracts, or appealing fines directly to the public. These platforms are much cheaper than traditional law firms and are especially popular among individuals and small businesses who might otherwise go without legal help. Some services even use chatbots to give automated legal advice, which challenges the traditional model of the lawyer-client relationship (Remus & Levy, 2017). Examples of these digital technologies and their effects on legal practice are summarised in Table 13.1.

TABLE 13.1
Examples of Digital Technologies Disrupting the Legal Profession

Example Technology or digital product type	Example Applications in Legal Practice	Key Disruption Effects
Artificial Intelligence (AI)	Legal research, contract review, predictive analytics (e.g. Westlaw Edge, Harvey)	Reduces time and cost; challenges traditional junior roles
Legal Automation tools	Due diligence, compliance, document scanning (e.g. Kira, Luminance)	Automates routine tasks; redefines efficiency and resourcing
Blockchain & Smart Contracts	Transaction execution, self-enforcing legal agreements	Disintermediates traditional oversight roles in areas like IP or real estate
Virtual Legal Platforms	Self-service legal help (e.g. LegalZoom, DoNotPay)	Expands access to justice; disrupts one-to-one legal service models
Online Courts / ODR	Remote hearings, asynchronous resolution during/post-COVID	Improves accessibility; introduces digital literacy and fairness concerns
Cloud Computing	File sharing, collaboration, virtual client management	Enables mobility and global practice; raises data security risks

Source: Author, adapted from Surden (2019), McGinnis and Pearce (2014), Mik (2017), Remus and Levy (2017), and Susskind (2020, 2021).

The COVID-19 pandemic accelerated another form of disruption: online courts and digital hearings. In many jurisdictions, lockdowns forced courts to move proceedings online. While initially seen as a temporary measure, remote hearings and online dispute resolution (ODR) are now becoming more common and, in some places, even permanent. This shift has improved accessibility for some litigants, but also raises concerns around digital literacy and the digital divide (Susskind, 2023).

Cybersecurity and data privacy are also critical issues in this digital shift. Law firms handle sensitive client information, and as they adopt cloud-based systems and online platforms, they become attractive targets for cyberattacks. This has led to a growing market for legal technology focused on secure document storage, e-signatures, and compliance with privacy laws like the GDPR.

Finally, the legal market is becoming more global and connected. Digital tools make it easier for lawyers to collaborate across borders and for clients to access legal advice from anywhere. This is disrupting national regulations that traditionally controlled who could provide legal services in each country, pushing legal regulators to rethink professional boundaries.

In summary, digital disruption is reshaping many parts of the law profession from how legal services are delivered to how lawyers are trained and how justice is accessed. While this brings many opportunities for innovation and efficiency, it also creates new risks and challenges that the profession must actively address.

HOW DOES THE LAW PROFESSION NEED TO DIGITALLY TRANSFORM?

The law profession is increasingly expected to adapt to a rapidly changing digital environment. Transformation in this context is more than just adopting new tools, it involves rethinking legal processes, roles, education, and the overall mindset of the profession. To stay relevant and effective, the profession must embrace change at multiple levels: technology, workflow, education, and culture.

Integrating Advanced Technologies

One of the most immediate transformations needed is the integration of advanced digital technologies into everyday legal practice. Artificial intelligence (AI) is already playing a growing role in areas like document review, due diligence, and risk assessment. Tools such as *Harvey*, a generative AI built on OpenAI's technology, are being adopted by major law firms like Allen & Overy and A&L Goodbody to support tasks traditionally done by junior lawyers (Thompson, 2023). These AI tools can read, understand, and summarize large volumes of legal text, enabling lawyers to work more efficiently.

Blockchain also holds promise for automating and securing legal transactions through smart contracts, which self-execute once conditions are met. This is particularly useful in areas such as real estate and international trade (Mik, 2017). Meanwhile, cloud computing allows for secure remote access to case files, collaborative work on legal documents, and streamlined client communications, which have become standard practices since the pandemic (Susskind, 2023).

Rethinking Legal Processes and Service Delivery

Legal workflows must also be redesigned to take full advantage of these technologies. Many routine legal tasks such as legal research, contract drafting, and client onboarding can now be automated. This doesn't replace lawyers but instead allows them to focus on more complex, strategic work (McGinnis & Pearce, 2014). Law firms must move from traditional hierarchical models to more agile and client-responsive structures.

There is also a shift toward more data-driven legal practice, where data analytics inform litigation strategy, risk assessment, and client advice. For example, platforms now exist that can predict the likelihood of case outcomes based on previous judgments and judicial behaviors, which adds a predictive edge to legal counsel (Surden, 2019).

Modernizing Legal Education and Training

Another critical area for digital transformation is legal education. Law schools need to prepare students for a legal world that is increasingly shaped by technology. A growing number of institutions globally such as Stanford, Harvard, and Melbourne Law School, now offer subjects or streams in legal innovation and legal tech (Cimphony AI, 2024). These programs introduce students to AI, automation, blockchain, and even coding fundamentals.

Curricula must also evolve to include interdisciplinary learning, where law students work alongside peers from IT, data science, and business faculties. This collaboration mirrors real-world legal challenges that span legal and technical domains. In addition, ethics education must now include topics such as algorithmic bias, client data security, and the limits of AI decision-making (Remus & Levy, 2017).

Continuing professional development is equally important. Practicing lawyers must be offered opportunities to learn new digital tools and understand how these tools are regulated and ethically applied in practice (International Bar Association, 2024).

Fostering a Culture of Innovation and Adaptability

Technology alone won't transform the law profession. Cultural change is just as important. Leaders within law firms and legal departments need to champion innovation, not just tolerate it. This includes budgeting for new technologies, rewarding experimentation, and encouraging new service models that are more client-focused (Susskind, 2023).

Professional associations can also support this shift by updating practice standards and offering guidance on adopting legal technologies. Without strong leadership, digital transformation efforts often remain fragmented or superficial.

In summary, the legal profession must go beyond simply adopting tools. It must rethink how law is practiced, how lawyers are trained, and how innovation is supported. Doing so will not only help the profession keep up with change it will also allow it to lead it.

WHERE IS THE LAW PROFESSION AT IN ITS DIGITAL TRANSFORMATION JOURNEY?

The legal profession is at a pivotal point in its digital transformation journey. While there has been notable progress in adopting technologies such as artificial intelligence (AI), cloud computing, and automation, the extent of integration varies significantly across different regions, firm sizes, and practice areas.

ADOPTION OF EMERGING TECHNOLOGIES

Recent surveys indicate a growing awareness of generative AI (GenAI) among legal professionals. However, actual implementation remains limited. According to the 2024 Legal Industry Report, while 67% of larger firms (with six or more lawyers) are familiar with GenAI concepts, only 24% have adopted legal-specific GenAI tools in their practices. This suggests that, despite recognition of AI's potential, many firms are still in the early stages of integration, often hindered by ethical concerns and a lack of trust in AI-generated outcomes (Black, 2024; Link Legal, 2024).

The American Bar Association's 2024 Legal Technology Survey Report further highlights this cautious approach. While 73% of firms utilize cloud-based legal tools, and AI-driven discovery tools are gaining traction, there remains a significant portion of the profession that has yet to fully embrace these technologies. The report emphasizes that firms investing in strategic technology integration are more likely to maintain a competitive edge in an increasingly digital legal landscape (American Bar Association, 2024).

STRATEGIC PLANNING AND LEADERSHIP ENGAGEMENT

Despite the evident benefits of digital transformation, many law firms lack a comprehensive strategy to guide this transition. The 2024 Report on the State of the US Legal Market notes that only half of large law firms have an overarching digital transformation strategy at the c-suite level (Thomson Reuters, 2024a). This absence of strategic planning may impede the effective adoption of new technologies and hinder firms from realizing their full potential in a digital environment. Recent industry analysis also highlights that the legal sector is entering a fundamentally new phase of digital and operational transformation, requiring firms to rethink traditional service models (Thomson Reuters Institute, 2024).

EDUCATIONAL INITIATIVES AND SKILL DEVELOPMENT

Legal education institutions are beginning to recognize the importance of integrating technology into their curricula. Law schools such as Harvard, Stanford, and Melbourne Law School have introduced specialized programs focusing on legal technology and innovation. These initiatives aim to equip future legal professionals with the necessary skills to navigate a tech-driven legal landscape.

However, the pace of curricular reform varies, and many institutions are still in the process of developing comprehensive programs that address the intersection of law and technology (Cimphony AI, 2024). This lag in educational reform may contribute to a skills gap in the profession, where new graduates are not fully prepared to meet the demands of a digitally transformed legal environment.

In summary, the legal profession has made strides in adopting digital technologies, but the journey toward full digital transformation is ongoing. While awareness and initial integration of tools like AI and cloud computing are increasing, challenges such as strategic planning, ethical considerations, and educational preparedness remain. Addressing these issues is crucial for the profession to fully realize the benefits of digital transformation and to continue providing effective and efficient legal services in the modern era.

WHAT KEY ISSUES AND CHALLENGES IS THE LAW PROFESSION FACING IN ITS DIGITAL TRANSFORMATION JOURNEY?

The legal profession is making progress toward digital transformation, but several key challenges continue to slow its momentum. These challenges are multifaceted, involving ethical concerns, slow adoption of technology, skill gaps in the workforce, financial constraints, heightened client expectations, and growing cybersecurity threats.

Ethical and Regulatory Concerns

One of the most pressing issues is the ethical and regulatory implications of using digital tools particularly artificial intelligence (AI) in legal practice. Questions surrounding algorithmic bias, the preservation of client confidentiality, and the transparency of AI-driven legal decisions are central to current debates. The International Bar Association (2024) stresses the need for ethical frameworks and professional standards that can guide lawyers and law firms in responsibly adopting AI.

Resistance to Technological Adoption

Despite the availability of legal tech tools, many firms particularly small to mid-sized practices, remain hesitant to embrace these technologies. The reasons include a lack of familiarity, fear of making mistakes, and a general preference for traditional methods. According to the American Bar Association (2024), while a majority of firms have adopted cloud-based tools, far fewer have integrated AI-based platforms into their legal work, showing a cautious and incremental approach to transformation.

Workforce Development and Skill Gaps

A lack of digital skills among legal professionals is another barrier. As legal technology evolves, lawyers are expected to be proficient not only in traditional legal knowledge but also in using tools like contract automation platforms, legal analytics, and case management software. American Bar Association reveals that only 4% of law firms consider their lawyers to be "very proficient" with legal technology, while 67% rate their lawyers as average or below in tech proficiency. Additionally, over half of the firms identified a "lack of tech-savvy users" as a significant barrier to adopting legal technology (American Bar Association, 2024). Therefore ongoing training and professional development to ensure lawyers can effectively use new technologies is important.

Financial Constraints and Investment Challenges

Digital transformation also requires significant investment, and not all firms have the capacity to fund this shift. Technology acquisition, system upgrades, and employee training often come at a high cost, which can deter smaller firms from making substantial changes. As noted in the Thomson Reuters (2024a) State of the US Legal Market report, firms that invest in digital infrastructure tend to perform better over time, but financial barriers continue to affect widespread adoption.

Evolving Client Expectations

Clients today expect more transparent, efficient, and cost-effective services. The growing presence of online legal platforms and alternative legal service providers (ALSPs) has intensified competition, forcing traditional firms to rethink how they deliver value. The Law Society of England and Wales (2024) reports that clients increasingly seek legal services that are digitally accessible and more aligned with modern consumer experiences. Recent industry research also shows that clients increasingly prefer firms that use cloud-based tools and offer digitally streamlined services (Clio, 2024).

Cybersecurity Risks

As law firms digitize more of their operations, they also become more vulnerable to cyber threats. Protecting sensitive client information is now a top priority. Yet, many firms especially smaller ones lack comprehensive cybersecurity systems. According to the American Bar Association (2024), while more than half of US firms have formal cybersecurity policies, attacks such as phishing, ransomware, and data breaches are still common. A summary of these key challenges and their potential consequences is presented in Table 13.2.

While the legal profession is beginning to embrace digital tools and workflows, significant challenges remain. Ethical concerns, slow adoption, skills shortages, funding difficulties, evolving client demands, and cybersecurity risks all pose real barriers to transformation. Overcoming these challenges requires not only technical solutions but also leadership, investment, and a cultural shift within the profession.

TABLE 13.2
Example Challenges to Maximizing the Legal Profession's Digital Transformation

Example Challenges	Description	Consequences if left Unaddressed
Ethical and Regulatory Uncertainty	Concerns around AI transparency, algorithmic bias, client confidentiality	Erodes trust; slows adoption; invites malpractice risk
Resistance to Change	Cultural attachment to precedent and traditional workflows, especially in small to mid-size firms	Low tech uptake; missed innovation opportunities
Digital Skills Gap	Many lawyers lack proficiency with tech tools and platforms	Workflow inefficiencies; diminished service quality
Financial Constraints	High cost of legal tech adoption, training, and infrastructure	Exclusion of smaller firms; growing digital divide
Changing Client Expectations	Clients demand more affordable, tech-enabled, transparent services	Market share shifts to legal startups and ALSPs
Cybersecurity Risks	Rising exposure to phishing, ransomware, and data breaches	Legal liability; reputational damage; regulatory penalties

Source: Author, adapted from International Bar Association (2024), American Bar Association (2024), Thomson Reuters (2024a, 2024b), Law Society of England and Wales (2024).

ARE THE LAW PROFESSION'S STRATEGIC LEADERSHIP ENTITIES, CURRICULA, AND PROFESSIONALS PLAYING THE ROLES THEY SHOULD BE PLAYING IN DIGITAL TRANSFORMATION?

The digital transformation of the legal profession is a multifaceted endeavor that requires active participation from strategic leadership entities, legal education institutions, and individual professionals. Assessing their current roles reveals both progress and areas needing improvement.

Strategic Leadership Entities

Chief Legal Officers (CLOs) and other legal leaders are increasingly taking on broader roles beyond traditional legal advisory functions. According to Deloitte's 2024 Chief Legal Officer Strategy Survey, CLOs are leading or jointly leading multiple enterprise-wide transformation initiatives, including digital transformation and workforce/talent transformation (Deloitte, 2024). This shift indicates a growing recognition of the importance of integrating legal strategy with overall business objectives (Punt & Fancher, 2024). However, while CLOs are engaging in strategic initiatives, there is still a need for more comprehensive digital transformation strategies within legal departments. The same survey highlights that many legal functions are in the early stages of maturity concerning digital initiatives, suggesting room for growth in aligning legal operations with technological advancements (Deloitte, 2024).

Legal Education Curricula

Legal education institutions are beginning to adapt their curricula to better prepare students for a technology-driven legal landscape. Law schools in North America, Europe, and the Asia-Pacific region have introduced specialized courses and programs focusing on legal technology, data analytics, and innovation (Cimphony AI, 2024). For instance, Melbourne Law School offers courses on legal technology and design, providing students with practical experience in legal tech tools and methodologies.cimphony.ai

Despite these advancements, the integration of technology into legal education remains inconsistent. Many institutions face challenges such as limited resources, resistance to change among faculty, and the need for interdisciplinary collaboration (Cimphony AI, 2024). Addressing these issues is crucial to ensure that future legal professionals are equipped with the necessary skills to navigate the evolving legal environment.

Legal Professionals

Individual legal professionals are at the forefront of implementing digital transformation in practice. The adoption of technologies such as artificial intelligence, cloud computing, and automation tools has the potential to enhance efficiency and client service delivery (Punt & Fancher, 2024). However, the pace of adoption varies, with some professionals embracing these tools while others remain hesitant due to concerns about reliability, ethical implications, and the potential impact on traditional legal roles.

Continuous professional development and training are essential to bridge the skill gap and foster a culture of innovation within the legal profession. Encouragingly, there is a growing emphasis on upskilling and reskilling initiatives to support legal professionals in adapting to technological changes (Punt & Fancher, 2024).

While strategic leadership entities, legal education institutions, and individual professionals have made strides in embracing digital transformation, there is still significant work to be done. A coordinated effort is required to develop comprehensive strategies, integrate technology into legal education, and promote continuous learning among legal professionals. By addressing these areas, the legal profession can better position itself to meet the demands of a rapidly evolving digital landscape.

WHAT ARE THE IMPLICATIONS OF SHORTCOMINGS BY THE LAW PROFESSION'S STRATEGIC LEADERSHIP ENTITIES, CURRICULA, AND PROFESSIONALS?

The digital transformation of the legal profession is not merely a technological shift but a fundamental change in how legal services are delivered and experienced.

Shortcomings in strategic leadership, educational curricula, and professional adaptability can have profound implications on the profession's ability to meet contemporary demands.

Erosion of Competitive Advantage

Law firms that lag in adopting digital technologies risk losing their competitive edge. Clients increasingly expect efficient, technology-driven services, and firms that fail to meet these expectations may see a decline in client retention and acquisition. The 2024 Future of Professionals Report indicates that 79% of law firm respondents anticipate AI having a high or transformational impact on their work within the next five years, underscoring the urgency for firms to embrace technological advancements (Thomson Reuters, 2024b).

Workforce Displacement and Skill Gaps

The integration of AI and automation in legal processes threatens to displace roles traditionally held by junior lawyers and support staff. Tasks such as document review and legal research are increasingly being handled by AI, necessitating a shift in skill sets. Without proactive reskilling and upskilling initiatives, there is a risk of significant workforce disruption (Watkins Law, 2025).

watkinslawforthepeople.com

Educational Disconnect

Legal education institutions that fail to incorporate technology-focused curricula contribute to a growing disconnect between academic training and professional requirements. Graduates may find themselves ill-equipped to navigate the modern legal landscape, leading to decreased employability and effectiveness in practice. The lack of emphasis on interdisciplinary skills, such as data analytics and technological proficiency, hampers the profession's evolution (IE Law School, 2025).

Ethical and Regulatory Challenges

The adoption of AI in legal services raises ethical and regulatory concerns, including issues of bias, transparency, and accountability. Without clear guidelines and oversight, there is a risk of undermining public trust in the legal system. The International Bar Association emphasizes the need for ethical frameworks to govern the use of AI in legal contexts (International Bar Association, 2024).

The shortcomings in strategic leadership, educational curricula, and professional adaptability pose significant risks to the legal profession's future. Addressing these challenges requires a concerted effort to integrate technology into all facets of legal practice, from education to service delivery, ensuring that the profession remains relevant and effective in the digital age.

WHAT CAN THE LAW PROFESSION'S STRATEGIC LEADERSHIP ENTITIES, CURRICULA, AND PROFESSIONALS DO TO MAXIMIZE THEIR CONTRIBUTION TO THE PROFESSION'S DIGITAL TRANSFORMATION EFFORTS?

To effectively navigate the digital transformation, the legal profession must adopt a multifaceted approach involving strategic leadership, educational reform, and proactive professional development.

Strategic Leadership Entities: Driving Innovation and Integration

Strategic leadership within law firms and legal departments plays a pivotal role in steering digital transformation. Leaders must champion the adoption of technologies such as artificial intelligence (AI), cloud computing, and automation to enhance efficiency and client service. According to KPMG (2024a), legal departments are increasingly integrating legal technology into their operations, emphasizing the need for a central source of truth and interoperability to streamline processes. Moreover, leadership should foster a culture that embraces change and continuous improvement. This includes investing in training programs to upskill employees and encouraging collaboration between legal and IT teams to ensure seamless technology integration (KPMG, 2024b).

Curricula: Embedding Technology into Legal Education

Legal education institutions must revamp their curricula to prepare future lawyers for a technology-driven landscape. Incorporating courses on legal technology, data analytics, and cybersecurity is essential. Cimphony AI (2024) highlights that law schools prioritizing tech integration produce graduates ready for the digital landscape, emphasizing the importance of practical experience with legal tech tools. Additionally, fostering interdisciplinary collaboration by integrating legal studies with computer science and business courses can provide students with a holistic understanding of how technology intersects with law (Cimphony AI, 2024). This approach equips graduates with the skills necessary to innovate and adapt in a rapidly evolving legal environment.

Legal Professionals: Embracing Lifelong Learning and Adaptability

Individual legal professionals must commit to lifelong learning to stay abreast of technological advancements. Engaging in continuous professional development through workshops, certifications, and online courses can enhance their proficiency in emerging legal technologies. The International Bar Association (2024) underscores the importance of training and adoption, noting that the impact of AI on law firms necessitates substantial changes in structure, organization, and business models. Furthermore, professionals should actively participate in shaping the ethical and regulatory frameworks governing legal technology. By contributing to discussions on best practices and standards, they can help ensure that technological integration upholds the core values of the legal profession.

Maximizing the contributions of strategic leadership entities, educational institutions, and legal professionals is crucial for the successful digital transformation of the legal profession. By embracing innovation, reforming curricula, and committing to continuous learning, the profession can enhance its resilience and relevance in the digital age.

CONCLUSION

This chapter examines the digital transformation of the legal profession, highlighting how technological advancements such as artificial intelligence (AI), blockchain, cloud computing, and automation are disrupting traditional legal practice. It explores the ways in which these technologies are reshaping legal service delivery, professional roles, and client expectations.

The chapter begins by detailing how AI-powered tools, such as legal research platforms and contract automation software, are improving efficiency but also raising concerns about workforce displacement and ethical considerations. Blockchain is discussed as a key enabler of innovations like smart contracts, while online legal platforms and virtual courts are noted for improving access to justice and challenging traditional lawyer-client relationships.

It then considers how the profession must respond by integrating advanced technologies, rethinking workflows, and modernizing legal education. Curricular reforms and interdisciplinary collaboration are highlighted as essential to equip future lawyers with both technical and ethical competencies. The chapter identifies barriers such as resistance to change, financial constraints, skill gaps, and cybersecurity risks, which are slowing down the pace of transformation.

An assessment of the roles played by strategic leaders, educators, and professionals suggests that while progress is being made, a lack of coordinated strategy hampers transformation efforts. The implications of inaction are significant, including erosion of competitiveness, workforce disruption, educational disconnects, and reduced public trust in legal systems.

The chapter concludes by recommending proactive measures: leadership commitment to innovation, embedding technology in legal education, and lifelong learning for professionals. These steps are presented as vital for ensuring that the legal profession remains relevant, efficient, and resilient in a digitally evolving world.

DISCUSSION QUESTIONS

1. In what ways has digital disruption reshaped the traditional roles and processes of the legal profession?
2. What are the most significant barriers preventing widespread digital transformation across law firms of varying sizes?
3. How are legal education providers adapting to prepare students for technology-driven legal practice, and what gaps still exist?
4. What ethical and regulatory considerations arise from the use of AI and automation in legal practice? How should these be addressed?

5. Compare the roles played by strategic leadership entities, educational institutions, and legal professionals in the digital transformation journey. Which group holds the most influence and why?
6. What are the potential consequences for law firms and professionals who fail to engage with digital transformation?
7. What specific actions can legal professionals take to ensure they remain relevant and effective in a digitally evolving legal environment?

REFERENCES

American Bar Association. (2024). *Legal Technology Survey Report 2024.* https://www.americanbar.org/news/abanews/aba-news-archives/2025/03/aba-releases-survey-tech-trends/

Cimphony AI. (2024). *Legal Tech in Legal Education: Global Perspectives 2024.* https://www.cimphony.ai/insights/legal-tech-in-legal-education-global-perspectives-2024

Clio. (2024). *Legal Trends Report 2024.* https://www.clio.com/resources/legal-trends/2024-report/

Deloitte. (2024). *The 2024 Chief Legal Officer Strategy Survey.* https://www.deloitte.com/content/dam/assets-shared/docs/services/legal/2024/2024-clo-strategy-survey-report-final.pdf

IE Law School. (2025). *Innovation beyond technology: The crucial role of skills in driving change in the legal profession.* https://www.ie.edu/lawahead-center/wp-content/uploads/sites/610/2025/05/INFORME-LAWAHEAD-2025-1.pdf

International Bar Association. (2024). *The Future is Now: Artificial Intelligence and the Legal Profession.* https://www.ibanet.org/document?id=The-future-is+now-AI-and-the-legal-profession-report

KPMG. (2024a). *10 Predictions: The Legal Department of the Future.* https://kpmg.com/xx/en/our-insights/ai-and-technology/legal-department-of-the-future.html

KPMG. (2024b). *Where to Begin? Digital Transformation for Law.* https://assets.kpmg.com/content/dam/kpmgsites/uk/pdf/2024/07/digital-transformation-for-law.pdf

Law Society of England and Wales. (2024). *Five challenges facing the legal sector in 2024.* https://www.lawsociety.org.uk/topics/business-management/partner-content/five-challenges-facing-the-legal-sector-in-2024

Link Legal. (2024). *Legal Industry Report 2024: Digital Readiness in Law Firms.* https://linkforlegal.com/wp-content/uploads/2024/09/ALL-LegalIndustryReport-2024-Digital.pdf

McGinnis, J. O., & Pearce, R. G. (2014). The great disruption: How machine intelligence will transform the role of lawyers in the delivery of legal services. *Fordham Law Review, 82*(6), 3041–3066.

Mik, E. (2017). Smart contracts: Terminology, technical limitations and real world complexity. *Law, Innovation and Technology, 9*(2), 269–300.

Punt, R., & Fancher, D. (2024). *Doing more, on a wider stage: Chief legal officers and enterprise transformation.* Forbes. https://www.forbes.com/sites/deloitte/2024/11/04/doing-more-on-a-wider-stage-chief-legal-officers-and-enterprise-transformation/

Remus, D., & Levy, F. (2017). Can robots be lawyers? Computers, lawyers, and the practice of law. *Georgetown Journal of Legal Ethics, 30*(3), 501–558.

Surden, H. (2019). Artificial intelligence and law: An overview. *Georgia State University Law Review, 35*(4), 1305–1337.

Susskind, R. (2020). *Online courts and the future of justice.* Oxford University Press.

Susskind, R. (2021). *Tomorrow's lawyers: An introduction to your future* (3rd ed.). Oxford University Press.

Susskind, R. E. (2023). *Tomorrow's lawyers: An introduction to your future.* Oxford University Press.

Thompson, M. (2023). Generative AI in law: The rise of Harvey. *LegalTech News*, *5*(2), 45–48.

Thomson Reuters. (2024a). *2024 Report on the State of the U.S. Legal Market.* https://www.thomsonreuters.com/en/press-releases/2024/january/2024-report-on-the-state-of-the-us-legal-market

Thomson Reuters. (2024b). *The future of professionals: How AI is impacting the legal profession.* https://legal.thomsonreuters.com/blog/legal-future-of-professionals-executive-summary/

Thomson Reuters Institute. (2024). *The New World is Here for the Legal Industry: 2024 Report on the State of the U.S. Legal Market.* https://legal.thomsonreuters.com/blog/the-new-world-is-here-for-the-legal-industry/

Watkins Law. (2025). *The AI transformation of legal employment: Opportunities, risks, and strategic adaptation.* https://www.watkinslawforthepeople.com/the-ai-transformation-of-legal-employment-opportunities-risks-and-strategic-adaptation/

14 Case Study of the Digital Transformation of Engineering

INTRODUCTION

The engineering profession, long regarded as a foundation of technological advancement and societal development, is undergoing a significant transformation as a result of digital disruption and the broader push toward digital transformation (Skog et al., 2018). As industries and communities increasingly adopt digital technologies, engineers are confronted with both unprecedented challenges and emerging opportunities that compel a redefinition of their roles, competencies, and societal contributions (Legner et al., 2017). This chapter examines the multifaceted impact of digital disruption on the engineering profession, explores the strategic pathways required for successful digital transformation, and evaluates the profession's current progress, key challenges, and leadership responses. It also assesses the evolving roles of curricula and practitioners and considers the broader implications of inaction, concluding with actionable strategies to enhance the engineering profession's capacity to lead in the digital era.

HOW THE ENGINEERING PROFESSION BEING DIGITALLY DISRUPTED

The engineering profession is currently experiencing disruption driven by the rapid incorporation of advanced digital technologies that fundamentally reshape conventional methods, processes, and outputs (Legner et al., 2017). Technologies such as artificial intelligence (AI), the Internet of Things (IoT), big data analytics, cloud computing, and additive manufacturing are revolutionizing how engineers conceptualize, design, and maintain systems (Khanna & Kumar, 2020). For instance, AI and machine learning are enabling predictive maintenance and generative design, which enhance structural efficiency and operational precision (Leonard & Tyers, 2023). Similarly, IoT technologies support real-time infrastructure monitoring, significantly improving asset management in civil and mechanical engineering contexts (Bongomin et al., 2020). Digital twins, which is virtual replicas of physical systems are also transforming performance optimization across sectors including aerospace and energy (Adebiyi et al., 2024).

These innovations are not merely augmenting existing practices; they are disrupting them. They automate routine tasks, shift the engineer's role from manual execution to data-informed decision-making, and necessitate increased interdisciplinary

DOI: 10.1201/9781003606604-18

TABLE 14.1
Digital Disruption Technologies in Engineering

Technology	Application in Engineering
Artificial Intelligence (AI)	Predictive maintenance, generative design
Internet of Things (IoT)	Real-time infrastructure monitoring
Big Data Analytics	Performance optimization and decision-making
Cloud Computing	Remote collaboration and data storage
Additive Manufacturing	Rapid prototyping and production
Digital Twins	Virtual replicas for performance simulation
Building Information Modeling (BIM)	Collaborative design and planning

collaboration (Bi et al., 2023). For example, Building Information Modeling (BIM) has superseded traditional drafting in civil engineering, requiring mastery of collaborative, data-rich platforms (Kannegieter, 2015). Likewise, in software engineering, agile and DevOps methodologies demand rapid, iterative development, fundamentally altering project workflows (Tonesh & Vamsi, 2024). As a result, engineers are being pushed to transcend traditional technical boundaries and embrace a new digital paradigm characterized by agility, adaptability, and collaborative innovation (see Table 14.1).

NEED FOR THE ENGINEERING PROFESSION TO DIGITALLY TRANSFORM

Digital transformation in engineering entails a deliberate and comprehensive integration of digital technologies aimed at improving efficiency, fostering innovation, and delivering added value across the engineering lifecycle (Khanna & Kumar, 2020). Unlike disruption, which is often external and unanticipated, transformation is strategic and proactive, requiring institutions and individuals to reconfigure core practices and mindsets (Gumaelius et al., 2024). This includes embedding computational tools such as AI-driven optimization and data analytics into routine decision-making (Huang, 2023), as well as adapting manufacturing processes toward Industry 4.0 frameworks that incorporate robotics, IoT, and cyber-physical systems (Hernandez-de-Menendez et al., 2020).

However, digital transformation is not solely about adopting technology. It also involves a cultural shift. Engineers must engage in continuous professional development to remain conversant with emerging tools and platforms (Fajar, 2025). Soft skills such as collaboration, adaptability, and global communication are becoming increasingly vital as projects span disciplines and geographic boundaries (Whysall et al., 2019). Simultaneously, sustainability must be elevated as a core objective, with digital tools used to model and implement environmentally responsible solutions (Borkovich et al., 2015). Digital simulations, for example, can improve the performance of renewable energy systems, aligning the engineering profession with global sustainability imperatives (Jiao et al., 2021). Ultimately, digital transformation redefines engineering by shifting its value proposition toward responsiveness, creativity, and broader societal relevance.

WHERE THE ENGINEERING PROFESSION AT IN ITS DIGITAL TRANSFORMATION JOURNEY

The engineering profession currently occupies a transitional position in its digital transformation journey, marked by uneven progress across disciplines and geographic regions (Fajar, 2025). Sectors such as aerospace and automotive engineering have made significant strides, incorporating technologies like digital twins, automation, and AI into core functions (Hazrat et al., 2023). Leading firms such as Boeing and Tesla exemplify how digital technologies can be leveraged to streamline operations and reduce time-to-market. By contrast, disciplines like civil engineering show slower uptake, particularly in developing regions where financial and technical constraints limit the adoption of smart infrastructure tools like BIM (Kannegieter, 2015).

While large firms are actively investing in digital upskilling and process integration, small and medium-sized enterprises (SMEs) often lack the resources to do the same (Wagg et al., 2020). Academic institutions are beginning to adjust curricula to include digital competencies, but reform is inconsistent, and many programs continue to emphasize traditional models of engineering education (Roy & Roy, 2021). Moreover, professional societies such as IEEE and ASCE are promoting digital literacy and ethical standards, yet uptake of these initiatives remains limited in less resourced contexts (Choi et al., 2023). In sum, while the profession is progressing, its transformation remains fragmented and incomplete.

KEY ISSUES AND CHALLENGES THE ENGINEERING PROFESSION FACING IN ITS DIGITAL TRANSFORMATION JOURNEY

A number of persistent challenges are impeding the engineering profession's digital transformation. Chief among them is a significant skills gap. Many practicing engineers lack familiarity with key technologies such as AI, IoT, and big data analytics, largely because their education did not include these domains (Broo et al., 2022). While reskilling programs exist, they are often costly, time-consuming, and inaccessible to engineers in smaller firms or developing regions (Craps et al., 2021). In addition, the cost of implementing advanced digital infrastructure, including hardware, software, and cybersecurity, can be prohibitive (Didas et al., 2024).

Resistance to change also hinders progress, as engineers accustomed to traditional methods may be reluctant to adopt new tools or processes (Bongomin et al., 2020). Interoperability issues further complicate integration, especially when digital platforms are proprietary and incompatible across departments or organizations (Brunetti et al., 2020). Furthermore, cybersecurity risks are intensifying with the rise of interconnected systems, posing threats to data integrity and operational safety

TABLE 14.2
Challenges in Engineering Digital Transformation

Challenge	Description
Skills Gap	Lack of familiarity with emerging technologies
Cost Barriers	High cost of digital infrastructure
Resistance to Change	Reluctance to adopt new tools and processes
Interoperability Issues	Incompatibility across platforms and departments
Cybersecurity Risks	Threats to data integrity and safety
Ethical Concerns	Algorithmic bias and accountability in AI systems

(Susskind & Susskind, 2015). Ethical considerations, especially surrounding algorithmic bias and accountability in AI-driven systems, remain unresolved and pose further barriers (Legner et al., 2017). Together, these challenges create friction that slows the pace of transformation and highlights the need for a more coordinated and inclusive approach (see Table 14.2).

ARE THE ENGINEERING PROFESSION'S STRATEGIC LEADERSHIP ENTITIES, CURRICULA, AND PROFESSIONALS PLAYING THE ROLES THEY SHOULD BE PLAYING IN DIGITAL TRANSFORMATION?

Strategic leadership entities, including professional associations and industry organizations, play a pivotal role in the engineering profession's digital future, yet their contributions remain inconsistent. Bodies such as IEEE and ASCE have taken commendable steps by developing digital certification frameworks and best practice guidelines (Choi et al., 2023). However, these efforts often fall short in reaching smaller enterprises and under-resourced regions. A lack of standardization in digital protocols also impedes seamless collaboration, highlighting the need for stronger advocacy and coordination at the institutional level.

Curriculum reform is underway in many academic programs, with digital subjects such as AI, data analytics, and BIM being introduced (Smith et al., 2024). Nonetheless, the pace of change is uneven, and a significant portion of engineering education remains rooted in outdated models that do not reflect current industry needs (Hazrat et al., 2023). This disconnect exacerbates the skills gap and leaves graduates underprepared for the demands of digitally driven workplaces.

At the individual level, engineers exhibit varied responses to digital transformation. While some professionals actively engage in lifelong learning and adopt new tools, others resist change due to time constraints, limited access, or unfamiliarity (Adebiyi et al., 2024; Hernandez-de-Menendez et al., 2020). Collectively, these gaps indicate that while each stakeholder group is making progress, their efforts are not yet sufficiently aligned to drive transformation at scale.

IMPLICATIONS OF SHORTCOMINGS OF THE PROFESSION'S STRATEGIC LEADERSHIP ENTITIES, CURRICULA, AND PROFESSIONALS

The disjointed response by leadership bodies, educational institutions, and professionals has significant ramifications for the engineering profession. The persistence of a digital skills divide reduces the profession's competitiveness and limits its capacity to contribute to innovation-driven sectors (Smith et al., 2024). As firms increasingly prioritize digital capabilities, engineers lacking such skills risk obsolescence. For example, those unable to adopt BIM may lose out on projects to more digitally fluent competitors (Hazrat et al., 2023).

Outdated curricula deepen this gap, producing graduates whose competencies are misaligned with industry expectations (Gumaelius et al., 2024). Simultaneously, a lack of leadership in promoting universal standards and ethical digital practices constrains collaboration and innovation (Shelby et al., 2013). Cybersecurity vulnerabilities and ethical ambiguities in AI applications further threaten public trust (Nickel, 2020). Left unaddressed, these shortcomings could erode engineering's traditional status as a pillar of innovation and render it less influential in shaping the digital economy.

WHAT THE ENGINEERING PROFESSION'S STRATEGIC LEADERSHIP ENTITIES, CURRICULA, AND PROFESSIONALS CAN DO TO MAXIMIZE THEIR CONTRIBUTION TO THE PROFESSION'S DIGITAL TRANSFORMATION EFFORTS

To accelerate digital transformation, leadership organizations must adopt a more inclusive and forward-looking approach. They should design scalable, affordable training programs that utilize online platforms to reach a broad spectrum of professionals, including those in SMEs and developing regions (Huang, 2023). Establishing and advocating for global standards will improve interoperability and promote ethical best practices across engineering sectors (Chance et al., 2021). Partnerships between academia and industry can also support infrastructure investments and foster innovation ecosystems (Legner et al., 2017).

In parallel, engineering curricula must be reimagined to balance foundational knowledge with digital expertise (Smith et al., 2024). Academic programs should integrate applied courses in AI, IoT, and data analytics, while also promoting interdisciplinary education that bridges engineering, computer science, and sustainability (Brunetti et al., 2020). Lifelong learning models, including micro-credentials and modular certifications, should be widely accessible to support continuous professional development (Diogo et al., 2023).

Professionals themselves must take responsibility for adapting to change. Embracing digital tools, participating in peer learning networks, and seeking mentorship are crucial for keeping pace with evolving demands (Craps et al., 2021; Zhang et al., 2024). By fostering a culture of collaboration and adaptability, engineers can redefine their professional identity and take a leadership role in shaping the digital future of the discipline.

CONCLUSION

The engineering profession stands at a critical juncture in its digital evolution. While digital disruption has already begun to reshape traditional practices, full-scale digital transformation demands a coordinated, strategic, and inclusive effort by professionals, academic institutions, and leadership bodies. Embracing emerging technologies, updating curricula, overcoming resistance to change, and addressing ethical and interoperability challenges are essential steps toward sustaining the relevance and impact of engineering in the digital age. Without proactive alignment among stakeholders, the profession risks falling behind more agile, digitally adept fields. To lead in an increasingly data-driven and interconnected world, engineers must redefine their roles through continuous learning, cross-disciplinary collaboration, and a commitment to innovation and sustainability.

DISCUSSION QUESTIONS

1. How can engineering professional bodies balance the need for universal digital standards with the diverse needs of subdisciplines and regional contexts to ensure effective digital transformation across the profession?
2. What strategies can universities employ to accelerate curriculum reform, ensuring graduates are equipped with both traditional engineering skills and cutting-edge digital competencies?
3. How can small and medium-sized enterprises (SMEs) overcome resource constraints to adopt digital technologies, and what role should larger firms and professional societies play in supporting them?
4. What are the ethical implications of integrating AI and autonomous systems into engineering practices, and how can the profession develop frameworks to address issues like algorithmic bias and accountability?
5. How can engineers foster a culture of continuous learning and adaptability within their organizations to keep pace with rapid technological advancements and drive digital transformation?

REFERENCES

Adebiyi, T. A., Ajenifuja, N. A., & Zhang, R. (2024). Digital twins and civil engineering phases: Reorienting adoption strategies. *Journal of Computing and Information Science in Engineering*, *24*(10), 100801.

Bi, Z., Jin, Y., Maropoulos, P., Zhang, W. J., & Wang, L. (2023). Internet of things (IoT) and big data analytics (BDA) for digital manufacturing (DM). *International Journal of Production Research*, *61*(12), 4004–4021.

Bongomin, O., Gilibrays Ocen, G., Oyondi Nganyi, E., Musinguzi, A., & Omara, T. (2020). Exponential disruptive technologies and the required skills of industry 4.0. *Journal of Engineering*, *2020*(1), 1–17. 4280156.

Borkovich, D. J., Skovira, R. J., & Breese-Vitelli, J. (2015). New technology adoption: Embracing cultural influences. *Issues in Information Systems*, *16*(3), 138–147.

Broo, D. G., Kaynak, O., & Sait, S. M. (2022). Rethinking engineering education at the age of industry 5.0. *Journal of Industrial Information Integration*, *25*(1), 1–8. 100311.

Brunetti, F., Matt, D. T., Bonfanti, A., De Longhi, A., Pedrini, G., & Orzes, G. (2020). Digital transformation challenges: Strategies emerging from a multi-stakeholder approach. *The TQM Journal*, *32*(4), 697–724.

Chance, S., Lawlor, R., Direito, I., & Mitchell, J. (2021). Above and beyond: Ethics and responsibility in civil engineering. *Australasian Journal of Engineering Education*, *26*(1), 93–116.

Choi, Y., Pessoa, M. V. P., & Bonnema, G. M. (2023). Perspectives on modeling energy and mobility transitions for stakeholders: A Dutch case. *World Electric Vehicle Journal*, *14*(7), 178.

Craps, S., Pinxten, M., Knipprath, H., & Langie, G. (2021). Exploring professional roles for early career engineers: A systematic literature review. *European Journal of Engineering Education*, *46*(2), 266–286.

Didas, M., Chali, F. H., & Noe, E. (2024). Facets related to challenges and prospects of cloud computing adoption in resource-constrained settings: Systematic review analysis. *International Journal of Advanced Computer Research*, *14*(66), 18.

Diogo, R. A., dos Santos, N., & Loures, E. F. (2023). Digital transformation of engineering education for smart education: A systematic literature review. *Reliability Modeling in Industry 4.0*, 2023, 407–438. https://doi.org/10.1016/B978-0-323-99204-6.00002-9

Fajar, F. (2025). Technological innovations in engineering practices: A phenomenological study of Engineers' adoption of new technologies. *Journal of Multidisciplinary Research and Innovation*, *1*(1), 14–22.

Gumaelius, L., Skogh, I. B., Matthíasdóttir, Á, & Pantzos, P. (2024). Engineering education in change. A case study on the impact of digital transformation on content and teaching methods in different engineering disciplines. *European Journal of Engineering Education*, *49*(1), 70–93.

Hazrat, M. A., Hassan, N. M. S., Chowdhury, A. A., Rasul, M. G., & Taylor, B. A. (2023). Developing a skilled workforce for future industry demand: The potential of digital twin-based teaching and learning practices in engineering education. *Sustainability*, *15*(23), 16433.

Hernandez-de-Menendez, M., Escobar Díaz, C. A., & Morales-Menendez, R. (2020). Engineering education for smart 4.0 technology: A review. *International Journal on Interactive Design and Manufacturing (IJIDeM)*, *14*, 789–803.

Huang, J. (2023). Digital engineering transformation with trustworthy AI towards industry 4.0: Emerging paradigm shifts. *Journal of Integrated Design and Process Science*, *26*(3–4), 267–290.

Jiao, R., Commuri, S., Panchal, J., Milisavljevic-Syed, J., Allen, J. K., Mistree, F., & Schaefer, D. (2021). Design engineering in the age of industry 4.0. *Journal of Mechanical Design*, *143*(7), 070801.

Kannegieter, T. (2015). The future of engineering. *Engineers Australia: Civil Edition*, *87*(6), 42–53.

Khanna, P., & Kumar, S. (2020). Engineering 4.0: Future with disruptive technologies. In: Rosa Righi, R., Alberti, A., Singh, M. (eds) *Blockchain technology for industry 4.0: Secure, decentralized, distributed and trusted industry environment*, 131–147. Springer, Singapore. https://doi.org/10.1007/978-981-15-1137-0_7

Legner, C., Eymann, T., Hess, T., Matt, C., Böhmann, T., Drews, P., & Ahlemann, F. (2017). Digitalization: Opportunity and challenge for the business and information systems engineering community. *Business & Information Systems Engineering*, *59*, 301–308.

Leonard, P., & Tyers, R. (2023). Engineering the revolution? Imagining the role of new digital technologies in infrastructure work futures. *New Technology, Work and Employment*, *38*(2), 291–310.

Nickel, P. J. (2020). Trust in engineering. In: *The Routledge handbook of the philosophy of engineering* (pp. 494–505). Routledge.

Roy, M., & Roy, A. (2021). The rise of interdisciplinarity in engineering education in the era of industry 4.0: Implications for management practice. *IEEE Engineering Management Review*, *49*(3), 56–70.

Shelby, R., Ansari, F., Patten, E. L. I., Pruitt, L., Walker, G., & Wang, J. (2013). Implementation of leadership and service learning in a first-year engineering course enhances professional skills. *International Journal of Engineering Education*, *29*(1), 1–14.

Skog, D. A., Wimelius, H., & Sandberg, J. (2018). Digital disruption. *Business & Information Systems Engineering*, *60*, 431–437.

Smith, E., Pardo, A., Mills, J., & Birbeck, D. (2024). Curriculum renewal to enhance the acquisition of professional skills and engagement with professional practice across engineering programs. *Australasian Journal of Engineering Education*, *29*(2), 154–165.

Susskind, R., & Susskind, D. (2015). *The future of the professions: How technology will transform the work of human experts*. Oxford University Press.

Tonesh, K., & Vamsi, M. (2024). Transforming software delivery: A comprehensive exploration of DevOps principles, practices, and implications. *Journal of Data Acquisition and Processing*, *39*(1), 585–594.

Wagg, D. J., Worden, K., Barthorpe, R. J., & Gardner, P. (2020). Digital twins: State-of-the-art and future directions for modeling and simulation in engineering dynamics applications. *ASCE-ASME Journal of Risk and Uncertainty in Engineering Systems, Part B: Mechanical Engineering*, *6*(3), 030901.

Whysall, Z., Owtram, M., & Brittain, S. (2019). The new talent management challenges of industry 4.0. *Journal of Management Development*, *38*(2), 118–129.

Zhang, W., Wang, S., Sun, J., & Wang, C. (2024). Global evolutionary trends of the discipline of engineering education and their empirical implications. *Engineering Education Review*, *2*(4), 145–160.

15 Case Study of the Digital Transformation of Nursing

INTRODUCTION

The nursing profession, long a foundational pillar of healthcare delivery, is undergoing a significant transformation propelled by the rapid evolution of digital technologies (Knop et al., 2024). These innovations present unprecedented opportunities to improve patient care, streamline clinical workflows, and elevate health outcomes (Marques & Ferreira, 2020). However, alongside these benefits, digital disruption introduces complex challenges that reshape traditional roles and demand new competencies from nurses (Isidori et al., 2022). This chapter investigates the multifaceted impact of digital disruption on nursing, the transformative actions required to adapt, the current status of implementation, and the structural and professional challenges involved. It also examines the responsibilities of strategic leadership bodies, the role of nursing education, and the engagement of practitioners, ultimately offering strategies to strengthen the profession's position in an increasingly digital healthcare ecosystem.

HOW THE NURSING PROFESSION IS BEING DIGITALLY DISRUPTED

Digital disruption in nursing is driven by the integration of advanced technologies that are transforming long-standing clinical practices (Knop et al., 2024). The widespread adoption of Electronic Health Records (EHRs) has replaced paper-based documentation, enhanced data accessibility but requiring nurses to navigate complex digital systems (Herrmann et al., 2018). Telehealth and virtual care have expanded nursing practice beyond physical settings, enabling remote consultations and patient monitoring, yet necessitating proficiency in digital communication and interpretation of data (Fuller & Hansen, 2019).

Wearable devices and Internet of Things (IoT) technologies generate continuous patient data, prompting a shift toward data-informed, anticipatory care planning (El Khatib et al., 2022). Artificial intelligence and machine learning tools are now used for predictive analytics, such as identifying patients at risk of clinical deterioration, although they raise ethical and practical concerns around trust and responsibility (Stokes & Palmer, 2020). Robotics and automation are also increasingly integrated into routine functions like medication dispensing, which frees nurses for higher-level tasks but requires familiarity with these systems (Ergin et al., 2022). These technological advances are redefining nursing workflows and expectations,

DOI: 10.1201/9781003606604-19

TABLE 15.1
Digital Technologies Disrupting Nursing

Technology	Impact on Nursing
Electronic Health Records (EHRs)	Replaces paper documentation, improves data access
Telehealth	Enables remote consultations and monitoring
Wearable Devices & IoT	Provides continuous patient data for anticipatory care
Artificial Intelligence	Supports predictive analytics and risk identification
Robotics & Automation	Automates routine tasks, enhances efficiency

compelling professionals to adapt while preserving the interpersonal and empathetic core of their practice (see Table 15.1).

NEED FOR THE NURSING PROFESSION TO DIGITALLY TRANSFORM

In response to these disruptions, the nursing profession must undergo a deliberate and systemic digital transformation. Central to this process is the integration of technology into everyday practice to improve efficiency, accuracy, and patient engagement (Marques & Ferreira, 2020). This requires embedding digital literacy and technical competencies into both pre-service education and continuing professional development, ensuring that nurses are adept in the use of EHRs, telehealth systems, and AI-based tools (Weston, 2020).

Beyond technical proficiency, transformation also involves a cultural reorientation, one in which innovation is embraced, and technology is viewed as a tool for enhancement rather than an obstacle (Canfell et al., 2022). Seamless interoperability across digital systems is crucial for supporting coordinated care, which depends on the efficient exchange of clinical data (Booth et al., 2021). Furthermore, nurses must be able to interpret complex data from wearable technologies and predictive models to inform personalized care strategies (Kavanagh, 2021). The use of mobile health applications and other digital tools also empowers patients, positioning nurses as guides in the digital health landscape (Tiase & Henderson, 2022). For digital transformation to succeed, nursing must strike a careful balance between technological advancement and the profession's enduring commitment to compassionate, patient-centered care.

CURRENT STATE OF THE NURSING PROFESSION'S DIGITAL TRANSFORMATION JOURNEY

The nursing profession is currently situated in a transitional phase of its digital transformation, marked by measurable progress alongside significant inconsistencies in adoption. Electronic Health Records are now commonplace in high-income countries, with more than 90% of U.S. hospitals having adopted certified EHR systems by 2023 (Apathy et al., 2025). Telehealth saw widespread implementation during the COVID-19 pandemic, increasing the presence of nurses in virtual care environments.

However, more advanced technologies such as AI and IoT remain in their early stages of integration (Knop et al., 2024). For example, while AI tools for early detection of conditions like sepsis are being piloted, broad adoption is hindered by costs, training gaps, and ethical dilemmas (Yip et al., 2025). Educational institutions are gradually embedding digital content into nursing programs, including health informatics courses, but this development is uneven and lacks global standards (Longhini et al., 2022). In lower-resourced and rural areas, infrastructure and access limitations create stark digital divides (Konttila et al., 2019). Thus, while the profession is advancing toward digital maturity, disparities in readiness and resources highlight the need for more cohesive and inclusive strategies.

KEY ISSUES AND CHALLENGES THE NURSING PROFESSION IS FACING IN ITS DIGITAL TRANSFORMATION JOURNEY

Despite signs of progress, the nursing profession faces several pressing challenges that hinder digital transformation. A substantial digital skills gap persists, particularly among nurses who entered the profession before the digital era and have limited exposure to emerging technologies (Isidori et al., 2022). Resistance to technological change is also common, with some practitioners perceiving new systems as disruptive to their autonomy or as increasing their workload (Knop et al., 2024). Technical barriers such as interoperability limitations contribute to fragmented data systems and inefficiencies in care delivery (Canfell et al., 2022).

Ethical concerns, including data privacy and the potential erosion of human connection in care, further complicate the adoption of digital solutions (Nowrozy et al., 2024). Financial constraints, especially in low-resource settings, restrict access to advanced tools and infrastructure (El Khatib et al., 2022). Moreover, the speed at which technology evolves often outpaces curriculum reform and the provision of professional development, leading to uneven preparedness (Kavanagh, 2021). Persistent workforce shortages and rising burnout levels, intensified by the demands of mastering new systems, place additional strain on already overburdened professionals (Fuller & Hansen, 2019). These intersecting challenges call for targeted interventions to support sustainable and equitable transformation across the profession (see Table 15.2).

TABLE 15.2
Challenges in Nursing Digital Transformation

Challenge	Description
Digital Skills Gap	Limited exposure to emerging technologies among older nurses
Resistance to Change	Perception of technology as disruptive or burdensome
Interoperability Issues	Fragmented data systems hinder coordinated care
Ethical Concerns	Data privacy and loss of human connection
Financial Constraints	Limited access to advanced tools in low-resource settings

SUFFICIENCY OF THE PROFESSION'S STRATEGIC LEADERSHIP ENTITIES, CURRICULA, AND PROFESSIONALS'S ROLES IN THE PROFESSION'S DIGITAL TRANSFORMATION

Strategic leadership bodies, educational institutions, and individual professionals all have essential roles to play in advancing nursing's digital transformation, though their efforts have so far been inconsistent. National and international nursing organizations have developed guidelines and position statements on digital health, including telehealth and informatics, but these initiatives often react to developments rather than proactively shape them (Cummins et al., 2021).

In academia, nursing curricula are gradually incorporating digital competencies, yet progress is uneven, and many programs still emphasize traditional clinical skills over technological fluency (da Silva Tiago & Mitchell, 2024). On the ground, nurses vary in their engagement with digital tools. While some act as early adopters and champions of innovation, others remain skeptical due to insufficient training or concerns about clinical relevance (Tiase & Henderson, 2022). The lack of alignment among leadership, education, and practice hinders the profession's capacity to fully leverage technological opportunities and weakens its voice in the broader health technology discourse.

IMPLICATIONS OF SHORTCOMINGS OF THE PROFESSION'S STRATEGIC LEADERSHIP ENTITIES, CURRICULA, AND PROFESSIONALS

These shortcomings carry significant consequences for the nursing profession's ability to navigate and shape digital transformation. Without a cohesive leadership strategy, policy responses remain fragmented, failing to account for emerging technologies or systemic inequalities in access (Laukka et al., 2022). Curricular deficiencies result in a workforce that is ill-prepared for digital environments, which can compromise patient safety and lead to adverse outcomes. Inadequate training in EHR use, for example, has been linked to clinical errors in several studies (Nowrozy et al., 2024).

Professional disengagement, whether due to burnout or skepticism, slows implementation and prolongs the time needed to realize the benefits of technologies like telehealth (Conte et al., 2023). In underserved regions, these gaps exacerbate existing disparities, leaving vulnerable populations further behind in digital care access (Wang et al., 2024). Perhaps most critically, the profession risks ceding its leadership role in digital healthcare innovation to other disciplines unless it more fully embraces transformation (Konttila et al., 2019).

WHAT THE PROFESSION'S STRATEGIC LEADERSHIP ENTITIES, CURRICULA, AND PROFESSIONALS DO TO MAXIMIZE THEIR CONTRIBUTION TO THE PROFESSION'S DIGITAL TRANSFORMATION EFFORTS

To fully contribute to digital transformation, the nursing profession must adopt a collaborative and forward-looking approach. Leadership entities should establish proactive, evidence-informed policies that anticipate future technological developments and promote equity in digital access (Laukka et al., 2023). These strategies should include advocacy for increased investment in infrastructure, as well as the development of regulatory standards for the use of AI and IoT in clinical care (Tischendorf et al., 2024).

Nursing curricula need to be comprehensively updated to integrate digital health competencies, including data analytics, telehealth, and cybersecurity, as foundational components of professional training (da Silva Tiago & Mitchell, 2024). The use of simulation-based learning and digital laboratories can enhance readiness. Continuing education programs must also be expanded and tailored to meet the needs of diverse nursing populations, especially in under-resourced settings (Tischendorf et al., 2024).

At the individual level, nurses should adopt a growth mindset and commit to lifelong learning to keep pace with technological change (Navarro Martínez & Leyva-Moral, 2024). Importantly, stronger partnerships among professional associations, academic institutions, and technology developers can foster innovation and ensure that nurses are not passive adopters, but active co-creators of digital solutions. With alignment across these domains, the profession can shape the future of healthcare in ways that are both technologically advanced and ethically grounded.

CONCLUSION

The nursing profession stands at a decisive juncture as it contends with the complexities of digital disruption and transformation. Technologies such as EHRs, telehealth, and artificial intelligence present powerful opportunities to enhance care, but they also necessitate a reconfiguration of education, leadership, and day-to-day practice. While notable progress has been made, persistent challenges – including skills gaps, resistance to change, and systemic inequities – continue to impede progress. Strategic alignment among professional bodies, educators, and practitioners is vital to overcoming these obstacles. By adopting a proactive and inclusive approach, the nursing profession can not only adapt to the digital age but also lead its evolution, ensuring that technology strengthens rather than diminishes the humanistic values at the heart of nursing.

DISCUSSION QUESTIONS

1. How are specific digital technologies, such as Artificial Intelligence and telehealth, reshaping the core responsibilities of nurses, and what are the potential benefits and risks for patient care?
2. What barriers are most significant in preventing the nursing profession from fully embracing digital transformation, and how can these be addressed at the institutional and individual levels?
3. To what extent are current nursing curricula adequately preparing students for a digitally transformed healthcare environment, and what specific changes should be prioritized to close any gaps?

4. How can strategic leadership entities in nursing balance the need for rapid digital adoption with the ethical concerns surrounding data privacy and the human-centered nature of nursing practice?
5. What role should nurses play in the development and implementation of new digital tools, and how can collaborative partnerships with technology developers enhance this process?
6. Considering the digital divide in healthcare settings, particularly in rural or under-resourced areas, what strategies can ensure equitable access to digital transformation for all nurses and patients?
7. How can the nursing profession foster a culture of continuous learning and adaptability among professionals to keep pace with the rapid evolution of digital technologies?
8. What are the potential long-term consequences for the nursing profession if it fails to address shortcomings in leadership, curricula, and professional engagement in digital transformation efforts?

REFERENCES

Apathy, N. C., Holmgren, A. J., Nong, P., Adler-Milstein, J., & Everson, J. (2025). Trending in the right direction: Critical access hospitals increased adoption of advanced electronic health record functions from 2018 to 2023. *Journal of the American Medical Informatics Association*, *32*(1), 71–78.

Booth, R. G., Strudwick, G., McBride, S., O'Connor, S., & López, A. L. S. (2021). How the nursing profession should adapt for a digital future. *BMJ*, *373*, 1–5.

Canfell, O. J., Meshkat, Y., Kodiyattu, Z., Engstrom, T., Chan, W., Mifsud, J., & Sullivan, C. (2022). Understanding the digital disruption of health care: An ethnographic study of real-time multidisciplinary clinical behavior in a new digital Hospital. *Applied Clinical Informatics*, *13*(05), 1079–1091.

Conte, G., Arrigoni, C., Magon, A., Stievano, A., & Caruso, R. (2023). Embracing digital and technological solutions in nursing: A scoping review and conceptual framework. *International Journal of Medical Informatics*, *177*, 105148.

Cummins, M., Kennedy, R., McBride, S., & Carrington, J. (2021). Policy priorities in nursing informatics: The American academy of nursing informatics and technology expert panel in 2020. *CIN: Computers, Informatics, Nursing*, *39*(3), 120–122.

da Silva Tiago, R., & Mitchell, A. (2024). Integrating digital transformation in nursing education: Best Practices and challenges in curriculum development. In: *Digital transformation in higher education, part b* (pp. 57–101). Emerald Publishing Limited.

El Khatib, M., Hamidi, S., Al Ameeri, I., Al Zaabi, H., & Al Marqab, R. (2022). Digital disruption and big data in healthcare-opportunities and challenges. *ClinicoEconomics and Outcomes Research*, 563–574.

Ergin, E., Karaarslan, D., Şahan, S., & Çınar Yücel, Ş. (2022). Artificial intelligence and robot nurses: From nurse managers' perspective: A descriptive cross-sectional study. *Journal of Nursing Management*, *30*(8), 3853–3862.

Fuller, R., & Hansen, A. (2019). Disruption ahead: Navigating and leading the future of. Nursing. *Nursing Administration Quarterly*, *43*(3), 212–221.

Herrmann, M., Boehme, P., Mondritzki, T., Ehlers, J. P., Kavadias, S., & Truebel, H. (2018). Digital transformation and disruption of the health care sector: Internet-based observational study. *Journal of Medical Internet Research*, *20*(3), e104.

Isidori, V., Diamanti, F., Gios, L., Malfatti, G., Perini, F., Nicolini, A., & Gaudino, A. (2022). Digital technologies and the role of health care professionals: Scoping review exploring nurses' skills in the digital era and in the light of the COVID-19 pandemic. *JMIR Nursing*, *5*(1), e37631.

Kavanagh, J. M. (2021). Crisis in competency: A defining moment in nursing education. *Online Journal of Issues in Nursing*, *26*(1).

Knop, M., Mueller, M., Kaiser, S., & Rester, C. (2024). The impact of digital technology use on nurses' professional identity and relations of power: A literature review. *Journal of Advanced Nursing*, *80*(11), 4346–4360.

Konttila, J., Siira, H., Kyngäs, H., Lahtinen, M., Elo, S., Kääriäinen, M., & Mikkonen, K. (2019). Healthcare professionals' competence in digitalisation: A systematic review. *Journal of Clinical Nursing*, *28*(5–6), 745–761.

Laukka, E., Hammarén, M., Pölkki, T., & Kanste, O. (2023). Hospital Nurse leaders' experiences with digital technologies: A qualitative descriptive study. *Journal of Advanced Nursing*, *79*(1), 297–308.

Laukka, E., Pölkki, T., & Kanste, O. (2022). Leadership in the context of digital health services: A concept analysis. *Journal of Nursing Management*, *30*(7), 2763–2780.

Longhini, J., Rossettini, G., & Palese, A. (2022). Digital health competencies among health care professionals: Systematic review. *Journal of Medical Internet Research*, *24*(8), e36414.

Marques, I. C., & Ferreira, J. J. (2020). Digital transformation in the area of health: Systematic review of 45 years of evolution. *Health and Technology*, *10*(3), 575–586.

Navarro Martínez, O., & Leyva-Moral, J. M. (2024). Digital transformation led by nurses and nursing Managers' priorities: A qualitative study. *Journal of Nursing Management*, *2024*(1), 8873127.

Nowrozy, R., Ahmed, K., Kayes, A. S. M., Wang, H., & McIntosh, T. R. (2024). Privacy preservation of electronic health records in the modern era: A systematic survey. *ACM Computing Surveys*, *56*(8), 1–37.

Stokes, F., & Palmer, A. (2020). Artificial intelligence and robotics in nursing: Ethics of caring as a guide to dividing tasks between AI and humans. *Nursing Philosophy*, *21*(4), e12306.

Tiase, V. L., & Henderson, M. D. (2022). The future of nursing in a digital age:: Planning for rapid change. In *Nursing and informatics for the 21st century-embracing a digital world*, *3rd* Edition, *Book 4* (pp. 171–186). Productivity Press.

Tischendorf, T., Hasseler, M., Schaal, T., Ruppert, S. N., Marchwacka, M., Heitmann-Möller, A., & Schaffrin, S. (2024). Developing digital competencies of nursing professionals in continuing education and training–a scoping review. *Frontiers in Medicine*, *11*, 1358398.

Wang, B., Shi, X., Han, X., & Xiao, G. (2024). The digital transformation of nursing practice: An Analysis of advanced IoT technologies And smart nursing systems. *Frontiers in Medicine*, *11*, 1471527.

Weston, M. J. (2020). Nursing practice in the digital age. *Nurse Leader*, *18*(3), 286–289.

Yip, S. S. W., Ning, S., Wong, N. Y. K., Chan, J., Ng, K. S., Kwok, B. O. T., Anders R. L. & Lam, S. C. (2025). Leveraging machine learning in nursing: innovations, challenges, and ethical insights. Frontiers in Digital Health, 7, 1514133. https://doi.org/10.3389/fdgth.2025.1514133

16 Case Study of the Digital Transformation of HRM

INTRODUCTION

Human resource management (HRM) is undergoing a profound transformation as it navigates the twin forces of digital disruption and digital transformation (Qamar et al., 2021). Digital disruption, marked by rapid advancements in technologies such as artificial intelligence (AI), blockchain, cloud computing, and automation, is fundamentally reshaping organizational structures, altering employee expectations, and redefining the nature of work itself (Varma et al., 2023). In parallel, digital transformation demands a more strategic integration of these technologies across all organizational functions, including HRM, in order to remain agile, responsive, and competitive (Bhardwaj et al., 2025). Against this backdrop, this chapter explores how digital disruption is reshaping HRM practices, the strategic transformation required to meet these challenges, and the current state of HR's digital evolution. It also examines the roles of leadership, education, and professional development in enabling change, identifies barriers that hinder progress, and offers actionable strategies to enhance HRM's contribution to organizational digital maturity.

HOW THE HRM PROFESSION IS BEING DIGITALLY DISRUPTED

Digital disruption in HRM is evident through the adoption of advanced technologies that are transforming traditional practices (Huda & Hambali, 2025). Innovations such as AI-driven recruitment platforms, predictive analytics for workforce planning, and blockchain for secure employee data management are revolutionizing how HR professionals attract, develop, and retain talent (Kambur & Yildirim, 2023). For example, AI-powered chatbots streamline the candidate screening process and foster personalized communication, improving recruitment efficiency and employee engagement (Rabenu & Baruch, 2025). Similarly, big data analytics enable HR departments to forecast turnover, evaluate performance, and customize learning interventions with a degree of accuracy previously unattainable (Wiblen & Marler, 2021). Automation further enhances efficiency by taking over repetitive tasks such as payroll processing and compliance reporting, allowing HR professionals to refocus on strategic initiatives (Strohmeier, 2020).

However, these advancements are not without their challenges. The emergence of the gig economy, driven by platforms like Upwork and LinkedIn, has disrupted conventional employment models, compelling HR to manage increasingly diverse and fluid workforces (Amany, 2025). The rise of remote work, accelerated by cloud-based tools, introduces new complexities in maintaining employee engagement and assessing performance across distributed teams (Stone et al., 2025). These disruptions

DOI: 10.1201/9781003606604-20

TABLE 16.1
Technologies Disrupting HRM

Technology	Application in HRM
Artificial Intelligence (AI)	Automated recruitment, chatbots, predictive analytics
Blockchain	Secure employee data management
Cloud Computing	Remote access to HR systems, scalability
Big Data Analytics	Workforce planning, performance evaluation
Automation	Payroll processing, compliance reporting

necessitate a rethinking of traditional HR paradigms and call for a redefinition of the HR function in a technology-driven world. Thus, while digital disruption introduces significant opportunities for innovation, it also demands a recalibration of HR's role in navigating organizational change (see Table 16.1).

NEED FOR THE HRM PROFESSION TO DIGITALLY TRANSFORM

To remain strategically relevant, HRM must go beyond incremental innovation and fully embrace digital transformation. This entails the integration of technology not only into operational processes but also into strategic decision-making frameworks (Rabenu & Baruch, 2025). A digitally transformed HR function relies on data-driven approaches that use AI, machine learning, and analytics to enhance areas such as recruitment, learning, and organizational agility (Imperatori, 2018). For instance, predictive hiring models that analyze past performance and cultural fit can help identify candidates with high potential, improving both talent acquisition and retention (Kambur & Yildirim, 2023). Likewise, immersive technologies such as virtual and augmented reality are being used to deliver personalized, scalable, and effective training solutions (Khandelwal & Upadhyay, 2021).

Crucially, digital transformation also requires a cultural evolution within HR. Professionals must cultivate a digital mindset, one characterized by openness to innovation, agility, and a commitment to continuous learning. This shift involves redefining HR's identity from an administrative support function to a strategic partner capable of shaping organizational direction through people analytics and workforce insights (Sharma & Kohli, 2024). Moreover, placing the employee experience at the center of HR strategy is essential. By leveraging digital platforms, HR can create more seamless, engaging, and responsive interactions that meet the expectations of a digitally literate workforce (Amany, 2025). In sum, the digital transformation of HR is as much about mindset and purpose as it is about technological capability.

CURRENT STATE OF THE HRM PROFESSION'S DIGITAL TRANSFORMATION JOURNEY

The HR profession currently occupies a transitional space in its digital transformation journey, marked by uneven progress across sectors and geographies (Vardarlier, 2019).

Organizations in technology-intensive sectors, such as finance, IT, and telecommunications, have led the way by deploying AI-based talent management systems, cloud-based HR platforms, and mobile applications that enable real-time feedback and performance tracking (Huda & Hambali, 2025; Zhang & Chen, 2024). These organizations are actively using digital tools to anticipate workforce needs, enhance employee experiences, and align HR strategy with broader business objectives.

In contrast, many organizations in more traditional industries or within the small-to-medium enterprise (SME) segment continue to rely on legacy systems and manual HR processes (Ulatowska et al., 2023). This reliance hinders their capacity to derive insights from data or to respond effectively to digital disruption. The profession, therefore, is characterized by a fragmented landscape of digital maturity, where factors such as organizational size, industry sector, and access to resources shape the pace and depth of transformation (Nicolás-Agustín et al., 2022). While a growing number of HR professionals are adopting digital tools, many still face significant barriers, including limited digital literacy, budget constraints, and organizational resistance to change. These disparities highlight the urgent need for coordinated efforts to build digital capabilities across the profession and ensure that HR is fully equipped to meet the demands of a digital future.

KEY ISSUES AND CHALLENGES THE HRM PROFESSION IS FACING IN ITS DIGITAL TRANSFORMATION JOURNEY

The digital transformation of Human Resource Management (HRM) presents a range of persistent challenges that complicate its implementation. A foremost concern is the significant skills gap among HR professionals (Minbaeva, 2021). Many practitioners lack the technical competencies necessary to deploy and manage advanced tools such as artificial intelligence, data analytics, and blockchain (Sharma & Kohli, 2024). This shortfall is exacerbated by the limited availability of targeted training programs focused on building digital capabilities within HR functions (Imperatori, 2018). Compounding the problem is organizational resistance to change. Employees and leaders accustomed to conventional HR practices often view new technologies with skepticism, fearing automation will erode human interaction or lead to job displacement (Gilch & Sieweke, 2021).

Another critical issue lies in the realm of data ethics and privacy. The use of AI and predictive analytics raises legitimate concerns about the security of employee data and the risk of algorithmic bias, particularly in recruitment and performance evaluation processes (Du, 2024). Compliance with stringent data regulations, such as the General Data Protection Regulation (GDPR), further adds complexity to digital initiatives (Fenwick et al., 2024). Additionally, financial limitations restrict the ability of smaller organizations to invest in advanced HR technologies, creating a disparity in digital readiness across sectors (Dhanpat et al., 2020). Collectively, these challenges highlight a pressing need for strategic interventions to ensure HRM can fully leverage digital transformation opportunities (see Table 16.2).

TABLE 16.2
Challenges in HR Digital Transformation

Challenge	Description
Skills Gap	Lack of technical competencies among HR professionals
Resistance to Change	Skepticism and fear of job displacement
Data Ethics	Concerns about privacy and algorithmic bias
Financial Constraints	Limited resources in SMEs
Curricular Misalignment	Outdated HR education and training

SUFFICIENCY OF THE HRM PROFESSION'S STRATEGIC LEADERSHIP ENTITIES, CURRICULA, AND PROFESSIONALS'S ROLES IN THE PROFESSION'S DIGITAL TRANSFORMATION

Strategic leadership bodies such as the Society for Human Resource Management (SHRM) and the Chartered Institute of Personnel and Development (CIPD) are instrumental in guiding HRM's digital trajectory. These organizations have made strides in promoting digital literacy, offering certifications in areas like HR analytics and technology (Radel, 2019). However, their efforts remain fragmented, with a tendency to emphasize broad HR competencies rather than the specialized digital skill sets now essential to modern HR practice (Harrison et al., 2021). There is a growing need for these entities to articulate coherent industry standards and provide clear, actionable roadmaps for digital transformation.

The same limitations are evident in HR curricula, which often fail to reflect the technological demands of contemporary practice. While some academic and training programs have introduced modules on HR analytics or digital platforms, many still prioritize traditional topics such as recruitment, labor law, and employee relations (Parks-Leduc et al., 2018; van Beurden et al., 2024). This curricular misalignment leaves graduates ill-prepared to contribute meaningfully to technology-driven HR initiatives (Goulart et al., 2022). HR professionals themselves also demonstrate varied levels of engagement. Although some actively pursue upskilling opportunities, others remain tethered to conventional practices, resisting technological change (Radel, 2019). Without coordinated and proactive engagement from leadership bodies, educators, and practitioners, HR's transition into the digital era remains uneven and underwhelming.

IMPLICATIONS OF SHORTCOMINGS OF THE HRM PROFESSION'S STRATEGIC LEADERSHIP ENTITIES, CURRICULA, AND PROFESSIONALS

The consequences of these shortcomings are far-reaching. Inadequate leadership and the absence of standardized frameworks delay the widespread adoption of digital best practices, resulting in a fragmented transformation process (Mantzaris & Myloni, 2023). This lack of cohesion undermines HRM's capacity to act as a strategic partner in organizations increasingly reliant on digital intelligence. Outdated curricula contribute to a continuing talent deficit, as new entrants to the field are insufficiently prepared for roles that require fluency in technology and data interpretation (Harrison et al., 2021).

Moreover, the reluctance of some HR professionals to embrace change risks diminishing the profession's influence within the organizational hierarchy. As firms increasingly depend on real-time analytics and automated systems for strategic decisions, functions such as data science and IT may assume responsibilities traditionally held by HR (Dhanpat et al., 2020; Zhang & Chen, 2024). Should this trend persist, HRM risks becoming a reactive rather than proactive function, sidelined in key conversations about organizational growth and innovation. The implications, therefore, are not merely operational but existential, as the profession's relevance may be called into question.

WHAT THE HRM PROFESSION'S STRATEGIC LEADERSHIP ENTITIES, CURRICULA, AND PROFESSIONALS DO TO MAXIMIZE THEIR CONTRIBUTION TO THE PROFESSION'S DIGITAL TRANSFORMATION EFFORTS

To enhance their contribution to digital transformation, HR leadership entities, educators, and professionals must embrace a more integrated and forward-looking approach. Leading organizations such as SHRM and CIPD should take the initiative to develop comprehensive frameworks for digital transformation. These should include well-defined competencies in areas such as digital strategy, analytics, and change management (Harrison et al., 2021). Disseminating these frameworks through industry certifications, webinars, and collaborative platforms can ensure broader access and uptake (Mantzaris & Myloni, 2023). Partnering with technology firms could further expand opportunities for skill development and tool adoption.

Educational institutions and training providers must also recalibrate HR curricula to align with current and future industry demands. This includes embedding modules on artificial intelligence, cloud-based HR systems, and data visualization, supported by practical case studies and hands-on projects (van Beurden et al., 2024). Industry-academic partnerships can ensure that learning content remains relevant and responsive to technological advancements (Harrison et al., 2021). On an individual level, HR professionals must commit to continuous professional development by enrolling in courses, attending workshops, and engaging with digital learning platforms such as Coursera or LinkedIn Learning.

Just as importantly, HR professionals should act as change agents within their organizations. By advocating for digital innovation and leading efforts to secure employee engagement with new technologies, they can foster a supportive culture for transformation (Wiblen & Marler, 2021). When aligned with organizational goals and informed by up-to-date expertise, HR can reposition itself as a strategic driver of innovation and a vital contributor to digital success.

CONCLUSION

The HRM profession stands at a pivotal moment, shaped by the dual forces of digital disruption and transformation. While some progress has been made, particularly in digitally mature organizations, significant barriers persist, including skill deficits, institutional inertia, and ethical concerns surrounding data use. Strategic leadership bodies, educators, and HR professionals themselves have not yet fully met the demands of this new landscape. However, by establishing cohesive frameworks, reforming outdated curricula, and cultivating a mindset of lifelong learning and innovation, the profession can reclaim its strategic relevance. In doing so, HRM will be better positioned to drive organizational performance and resilience in the digital age.

DISCUSSION QUESTIONS

1. What are the most significant barriers preventing HR professionals from fully embracing digital transformation, and how might these be addressed through institutional or individual strategies?
2. In what ways do current HR curricula in universities and professional training programs fall short of preparing graduates for a digitally driven workplace, and what reforms would make these programs more relevant?
3. What ethical dilemmas arise from the use of technologies like artificial intelligence and analytics in HR practices, and how should HR professionals navigate these challenges while maintaining trust and compliance?
4. To what extent does the digital mindset, characterized by openness, adaptability, and innovation, contribute to successful HR digital transformation, and how can this mindset be fostered across different organizational cultures?
5. How might the failure of HR professionals to proactively engage with digital transformation impact the future relevance and strategic influence of the HR function within organizations?
6. Considering the varying levels of digital maturity across organizations, how can smaller firms with limited resources still participate meaningfully in HR digital transformation efforts?

REFERENCES

Amany, S. (2025). A review of digital human resource management: Transforming HR practices through technology. *Luminis Applied Science and Engineering*, *2*(1), 65–71.

Bhardwaj, S., Chopra, R., & Pandita, D. (2025). Navigating the digital evolution of HRM: an integrative review. *International Journal of Organizational Analysis*. ahead-of-print. https://doi.org/10.1108/IJOA-10-2024-4895

Dhanpat, N., Buthelezi, Z. P., Joe, M. R., Maphela, T. V., & Shongwe, N. (2020). Industry 4.0: The role of human resource professionals. *SA Journal of Human Resource Management*, *18*(1), 1–11.

Du, J. (2024). Exploring gender bias and algorithm transparency: Ethical considerations of AI in HRM. *Journal of Theory and Practice of Management Science*, *4*(03), 36–43.

Fenwick, A., Molnar, G., & Frangos, P. (2024). The critical role of HRM in AI-driven digital transformation: a paradigm shift to enable firms to move from AI implementation to human-centric adoption. *Discover Artificial Intelligence*, *4*(1), 34.

Gilch, P. M., & Sieweke, J. (2021). Recruiting digital talent: The strategic role of recruitment in organisations' digital transformation. *German Journal of Human Resource Management*, *35*(1), 53–82.

Goulart, V. G., Liboni, L. B., & Cezarino, L. O. (2022). Balancing skills in the digital transformation era: The future of jobs and the role of higher education. *Industry and Higher Education*, *36*(2), 118–127.

Harrison, P., Tosey, P., Anderson, V., & Elliott, C. (2021). HRD professional education provision in the UK: past, present and future. *Human Resource Development International*, *24*(2), 200–218.

Huda, N., & Hambali, R. (2025). Redesigning the Digital Organization: A Systematic Literature Review on the Role of HRM in Orchestrating Agile and Hybrid Transformations. *Taylorian Insights: Journal of Management Review*, *1*(1), 35–45.

Imperatori, R. B. B. (2018). HRM 4.0: The digital transformation of The HR department. In: *Human resource management and digitalization* (pp. 67–86). Routledge.

Kambur, E., & Yildirim, T. (2023). From traditional to smart human resources management. *International Journal of Manpower*, *44*(3), 422–452.

Khandelwal, K., & Upadhyay, A. K. (2021). Virtual reality interventions in developing and managing human resources. *Human Resource Development International*, *24*(2), 219–233.

Mantzaris, K., & Myloni, B. (2023). Human resources under technological transformation: what HR professionals believe in an international scale. *Employee Relations: The International Journal*, *45*(1), 172–189.

Minbaeva, D. (2021). Disrupted HR? *Human Resource Management Review*, *31*(4), 100820.

Nicolás-Agustín, Á, Jiménez-Jiménez, D., & Maeso-Fernandez, F. (2022). The role of human resource practices in the implementation of digital transformation. *International Journal of Manpower*, *43*(2), 395–410.

Parks-Leduc, L., Rutherford, M. A., Becker, K. L., & Shahzad, A. M. (2018). The professionalization of human resource management: Examining undergraduate curricula and the influence of professional organizations. *Journal of Management Education*, *42*(2), 211–238.

Qamar, Y., Agrawal, R. K., Samad, T. A., & Chiappetta Jabbour, C. J. (2021). When technology meets people: the interplay of artificial intelligence and human resource management. *Journal of Enterprise Information Management*, *34*(5), 1339–1370.

Rabenu, E., & Baruch, Y. (2025). Cyborging HRM theory: from evolution to revolution–the challenges and trajectories of AI for the future role of HRM. *Personnel Review*, *54*(1), 174–198.

Radel, J. (2019). Human resources management and human resources development. In *Handbook of vocational education and training* (pp. 765–787). Springer, Cham.

Sharma, R. C., & Kohli, D. (2024). Embracing digital transformation for sustainable development: The synergy between learning organizations, human resource management, and service quality. *Journal of Chinese Human Resources Management*, *14*(3), 3–17.

Stone, D. L., Dulebohn, J. H., Murray, B., & Lukaszewski, K. M. (2025). *The future of human resource management*. Emerald Group Publishing.

Strohmeier, S. (2020). Digital human resource management: A conceptual clarification. *German Journal of Human Resource Management*, *34*(3), 345–365.

Ulatowska, R., Wainio, E., & Pierzchała, M. (2023). Digital transformation in HRM of the modern business service sector in Finland and Poland. *Journal of Organizational Change Management, 36*(7), 1180–1192.

van Beurden, J., Borghouts, I., van den Groenendaal, S. M., & Freese, C. (2024). How Dutch higher HRM education prepares future HR professionals for the impact of technological developments. *The International Journal of Management Education, 22*(1), 100916.

Vardarlier, P. (2019). Digital transformation of human resource management: Digital applications and strategic tools in HRM. In *Digital business strategies in blockchain ecosystems: Transformational design and future of global business* (pp. 239–264). Cham: Springer International Publishing.

Varma, A., Dawkins, C., & Chaudhuri, K. (2023). Artificial intelligence and people management: A critical assessment through the ethical lens. *Human Resource Management Review, 33*(1), 100923.

Wiblen, S., & Marler, J. H. (2021). Digitalised talent management and automated talent decisions: the implications for HR professionals. *The International Journal of human resource management, 32*(12), 2592–2621.

Zhang, J., & Chen, Z. (2024). Exploring human resource management digital transformation in the digital age. *Journal of the Knowledge Economy, 15*(1), 1482–1498.

Index

Note: Page references in **bold** refer to tables and with "n" refer to endnotes.

For Product Safety Concerns and Information please contact our
EU representative GPSR@taylorandfrancis.com Taylor & Francis
Verlag GmbH, Kaufingerstraße 24, 80331 München, Germany